Capital, Interrupted

Capital, Interrupted

Agrarian Development and the Politics of Work in India

Vinay Gidwani

University of Minnesota Press
Minneapolis · London

Portions of chapter 3 were previously published in "The Unbearable Modernity of 'Development'? An Essay on Canal Irrigation and Development Planning in Western India," *Progress in Planning* 58, no. 1 (2002): 1–80. Portions of chapter 4 previously appeared in "The Cultural Logic of Work: Explaining Labor Deployment and Piece-Rate Contracts in Matar Taluka, Gujarat, Parts I and II," *Journal of Development Studies* 38, no. 2 (2002): 57–108. Portions of chapter 5 previously appeared in "Limits to Capital: Questions of Provenance and Politics," *Antipode* 36, no. 3 (2004): 527–42. Portions of the Afterword were previously published in "I Offer You This, Commodity," in *Politics and Practice in Economic Geography,* ed. Adam Tickell, Jamie Peck, Eric Sheppard, and Trevor Barnes (London: Sage Publications, 2007).

Photographs were taken by Vinay Gidwani.

Maps were created by Sula Sarkar.

Published by the University of Minnesota Press
111 Third Avenue South, Suite 290
Minneapolis, MN 55401-2520
http://www.upress.umn.edu

Library of Congress Cataloging-in-Publication Data

Gidwani, Vinay K., 1965–
    Capital, interrupted : agrarian development and the politics of work in India / Vinay Gidwani.
        p.   cm.
    Includes bibliographical references and index.
    ISBN 978-0-8166-4958-7 (hc : alk. paper) — ISBN 978-0-8166-4959-4 (pbk. : alk. paper)
        1. Agriculture — Economic aspects — India — Gujarat.   2. Capitalism — India — Gujarat — History.   3. Patidars — Social conditions.   4. Patidars — Economic conditions.   5. Capitalism — Philosophy.   I. Title.
    HD2075.G8G53   2008
    338.10954'75 — dc22   2008005822

Printed in the United States of America on acid-free paper

The University of Minnesota is an equal-opportunity educator and employer.

15 14 13 12 11 10 09 08   10 9 8 7 6 5 4 3 2 1

For Krishin and Sunanda, you were extraordinary.

Contents

INTRODUCTION

Sutures

In 1960, near the start of his academic career, Stuart Hall published an article with the intriguing title "The Supply of Demand." Extending the ideas of Richard Hoggart and Raymond Williams,[1] Hall presaged the concerns that he was to elaborate in a more famous 1989 article, "The Meaning of New Times," which many orthodox Marxists read as Hall's public defection from Marx to Foucault and for which he was severely upbraided in journals such as *Capital and Class, New Left Review, New Socialist, New Statesman,* and *Feminist Review.*[2] "The Meaning of New Times" was read as a disavowal of left politics. It was not. It candidly repeated, now in response to a modified historical conjuncture cemented ideologically by Thatcherism, an unremittingly *political* question: Did the Left possess the acuity to both recognize the transformations taking place under the "new capitalism"—particularly the positive appraisals of capitalist change by diverse working classes, combined with the gravitation of the English working class toward Thatcherite conservatism in the 1980s—and adapt its thinking to the political demands of the time? Hall's fear was that a doctrinaire Left, wedded to an expressive theory of history and ideology,[3] would simply watch from the sidelines as a politically retrograde articulation of economy with other elements of society eroded "the traditional cultural and political loyalties upon which the left based itself."[4] The departure of Margaret Thatcher and the defeat of John Major by Tony Blair's New Labor were in no manner a repudiation of Hall's diagnosis. If anything, the Right-leaning economic and social policies of New Labor in Britain and the so-called New Democrats in the United States under Bill Clinton provided troubling confirmation of Hall's thesis. It seems clear in retrospect that Hall was wrongly castigated for asking an inconvenient question that the Left everywhere should continue to ask: How do we organize in order to advance our political agenda at a time when the hegemony of a variously disfigured and regionally variegated Chicago School capitalism is globally ascendant?[5]

For anti-authoritarian Left projects committed to producing the conditions of *common life*—social justice, economic security, and well-being for *all*, not just a privileged few—the revival of market fundamentalism has been doubly challenging. It has meant, on one front, mustering effective strategies to counter the powerful and wide-ranging forces arrayed alongside neoliberalisms. The easy response—heap condemnation on economic liberalization and capitalist enterprise—suffers from lack of intellectual and political imagination. It fails to acknowledge that capital's power might lie in its solvent energies. Capitalist accumulation regularly widens inequalities. But capital's selective indifference to rank within diverse trajectories of growth can erode, even dislodge, sedimented orders. The challenge is how to annex and attach capital's solvent energies to equalitarian ends. On another front, the Left has faced the task of finding resources and ideas to contest bizarre and dangerous liaisons that have emerged in various parts of the world between a religious Right (often funded by affluent diasporic communities in the West), "intermediate classes" (comprising rich peasants, petty traders, owners of family businesses, and collusive factions of the bureaucracy that implement state regulations),[6] and disaffected segments of the working class (whose livelihoods have been displaced or put at risk by new regional and global flows of capital). In many ways, the second of these two fronts has posed the more daunting battle for the Left. Take India, for instance. Over the course of the past two decades, Hindu nationalism (or *Hindutva*, as it is popularly known) has become a hegemonizing force; its ideological glue has been able to combine disparate segments of society into a major political bloc. Within the geography of this powerful configuration, some regions have emerged as a vanguard. The western Indian state of Gujarat, the site of this book's empirical and theoretical engagements, has become the laboratory for a particularly virulent form of ethnonationalism that is violently intolerant of minorities.[7] The consolidation of Hindutva in Gujarat raises urgent questions: What are the stakes for Left theoretical practice, and how can it

Map 1. India, with Gujarat shaded. Courtesy of Sula Sarkar.

support positive actions that affirm life in common against exclusionary articulations of religious and petty capitalist authoritarianism? The resounding verdict for Chief Minister Narendra Modi's Bharatiya Janata Party in the December 2007 Gujarat State election has sharply upped the stakes. The opposition Congress Party's moral turpitude and lack of political imagination, combined with Modi's tactical shrewdness and oratorical ability to stitch together a populist "Gujarati pride" agenda that tapped into the Hindu majority's development desires, sectarian prejudices, security fears, and regional resentment, enabled the BJP to capture 117 out of 182 legislative assembly seats—far in excess of most expert predictions. Gujarat's brand of majoritarian development that strives to be inclusive of non-Muslim populations such as tribals and backward classes and castes may well become the template for a refurbished Hindutva; in short, the kernel of a populist, Hindu nationalist political and economic program that could have surprising electoral traction if adeptly marketed through regional allies.

In this respect and others, the theoretical and organizational challenge that looms in contemporary India is comparable in importance, though not in form, to the task that confronted Lenin at the turn of the twentieth century: how to build a revolutionary Bolshevik movement within the confines of an autocratic Tsarist state and against unrelenting opposition from the forces of international capital. While the historical forces at play then were different, the lesson for present times lies in learning from Lenin's ability to strategize within the political conjuncture. His strategic vision was framed boldly. He asked, in a now famous question: "What is to be done?" It was precisely this question that Stuart Hall repeated in 1960.

Now, it may seem odd to juxtapose a nonorthodox Marxist intellectual like Hall alongside a figure like Lenin, widely regarded as an icon of Marxist orthodoxy and authoritarian party politics. It is not my intention to dispute this rendering of Lenin, only to suggest that Hall and Lenin shared a common organizational concern: that a politically effective class alliance centered about working-class radicalism and unity cannot be taken for granted merely because a certain deterministic Marxist orthodoxy proclaims it. Neither the class alliance, nor working-class radicalism, nor working-class unity is preordained.[8] Like Lenin, Hall recognizes that it is the task of leftist intellectuals to elucidate the challenges and opportunities for political change and the task of political leadership to achieve the necessary unity—an alliance between different factions of the working classes and with other marginalized groups—through strategic actions. This, pure and simple, is hegemony.[9] Hall and Lenin obviously inflect the task of political leadership differently, but it is clear that in positing the (relative) autonomy of the political, both reject, on the one hand, the "scientism" of the Second International (Bebel, Kautsky, Plekhanov) and, on the other, the "spontaneism" of certain factions within the Russian and German Social-Democratic parties (Luxemburg, Liebknecht, Parvus) as well as the Narodniks (populists).[10] Furthermore, hegemony does not imply "voluntarism of the party." Neither Lenin nor Hall has grand illusions about the impact of theoretical mediation: "Such intellectual mediation is limited in its effects, for, according to the Spinozist formula, its sole freedom consists in being the consciousness of necessity. However, it does entail the emergence of an articulating nexus that cannot simply be referred to the chain of a monistically conceived necessity."[11] In short, political action must recognize and respond to the "conjuncture," that is, to "the balance of forces, and state of overdetermination of the contradictions at any given moment."[12]

There is, however, no guarantee that political practice—the attempted articulation of elements that produces a discourse (such as Thatcherism, Hindutva or Radical Social Democracy, for instance)—will result in determinate or permanent effects. A "historic bloc" may well emerge but, constitutively, the forces that compose it will continue to remain mobile, even unstable, and in constant need of repair. That does not imply, however, to not try at all; what else is there to do? Both Lenin and Hall believe that politics is the willingness to risk, to wager. What theoretical practice—a labor like any other—can elucidate is *where* to wager (although not necessarily when or how). In this respect, theoretical practice is prey to the same aleatory forces that buffet historical configurations.

This returns us to the question of hegemony. As noted, hegemony for Lenin means leadership of a class alliance. Gramsci's earliest use of the term, in "Some Aspects of the Southern Question" (1926), has the imprint of Lenin all over it—not in the least surprising given his interactions with theoreticians of the Comintern. It is only subsequently that Gramsci theorizes the content of the hegemonic link via a recuperated notion of ideology. Several studies have traced the emergence of the concept of hegemony,[13] but perhaps Laclau and Mouffe characterize its open political logic best:

> [T]he concept of hegemony fills a space left vacant by a crisis
> of what, according to Plekhanov's "stagist" conception, should
> have been a normal historical development. For that reason,
> hegemonization of a task or an ensemble of political forces belongs to
> the terrain of historical contingency. In European Social Democracy,
> the main problem had been the dispersion of working-class positions
> and the shattering of the unity postulated among these by Marxist
> theory. The very degree of maturity of bourgeois civilization reflected
> its structural order within the working class, subverting the latter's
> unity. By contrast, in the theory of hegemony as it was posed in the
> Russian context, the limits of an insufficiently developed bourgeois
> civilization forced the working class to come out of itself and to take
> on tasks that were not its own. The problem, then, was no longer to
> assure class unity, but to maximize the political efficacy of working-
> class struggle in a historical terrain where contingency arose from the
> structural weakness of the bourgeoisie to assume its own tasks.[14]

There are two points to note here about hegemony: it emerges to fill a gap in political praxis *as well as* theory. Without it, Marxist theory (of a certain deterministic variety) is left confronting an embarrassing lack of fit between infrastructural economic relations of production and the revolutionary proletarian consciousness that is supposed to arise from it by virtue of historical development. Hegemony, then, sutures two *wounds:* first, it foresees the emergence of a revolutionary class alliance sutured together under the leadership of certain factions of the proletariat who are able to forsake their economic-corporate inter-ests;[15] second, it sutures together frayed theory so it can be a coherent unity again. The term "suture," employed by Laclau and Mouffe in their exposition of socialist strategy, is *not* metaphorical. As Michèle Barrett points out in her incisive essay on Laclau and Mouffe:

> Conventionally, in English, meaning "stitch," the term suture is rendered by the Oxford English Dictionary as "the joining of the lips of a wound," and this original surgical meaning is given a neat modern gloss in Landry and Maclean's remark that "a 'suture' marks the absence of a former identity, as when cut flesh heals but leaves a scar marking difference." Laclau and Mouffe present us with a body politic whose skin is permanently split open, necessitating ceaseless duty in the emergency room for the surgeons of hegemony whose job it is to try and close, temporarily and with difficulty, the gaps. (This patient never makes it to the recovery ward). . . . Their application of the concept of suture to the field of politics carries with it an idea that Derrida's work on deconstruction has made influential: the traces of the old cannot be destroyed but remain as sedimentary deposits—even, and indeed especially, where the new is trying hardest to exclude the old.[16]

This is a compelling formulation because it affirms that the work of hegemony is always unstable, never seamless, and never able to erase the traces of its labors.

Perhaps I can be even more exact. Although hegemony is frequently thought to operate at the level of consciousness and consists in the excess of consent over coercion, a close reading of Gramsci reveals that the ethicopolitical terrain of hegemony is always a material and imma-nent one "characterized by the combination of force and consent vari-ously balancing one another, *without force exceeding consent too much.*"[17] More to the point, both force and consent enter into an achieved unity, a class alliance, *marked by the wounds* of that process. (Isn't "consent" simply another way of naming relations of force that have managed to secure certain willing conducts?) It is here, at an ontological level, where "being" exists as an interplay of forces, that we begin to find points of intersection between two theorists of power—Antonio Gramsci and Michel Foucault—who are often held separate or juxtaposed without adequate intellectual justification. (This is a prospective encounter that I recapitulate at greater length in chapter 3.)

This brings up the matter of the "agrarian question," which is a generative theme for this book. My central claims in this respect are simple. First of all, I claim that the problem (or problems) encapsulated by the agrarian question (first formulated as "the peasant question" by Engels, and later also known as the "rural problem" or the problem of agrarian transition) foreshadows the problem made visible by the term "hegemony"; namely, a *gap* between observed phenomena and the predictions (and embedded political desires) of theory, concerning the prospects of a capitalist transformation of agriculture. The agrarian question summarizes the dilemma of how to confront this breach and suture the open wound left by it.

In Independent India, the left-liberal solution (transmitted as Nehruvian technocratic socialism) is prefigured by the colonial problematic of development—although development's passage into the postcolony, as I show in chapter 2, is also lacerated by profound discontinuities. As a program of transformation, post-1947 development planning is imagined foremost as a suture to the rural problem—a formulation that effectively summarizes, given the sheer mass of the agrarian sphere, the task of modernizing a "backward" nation and bringing the flickering nation to presence. Development is therefore charged with the work of filling in and repairing that will bring fragments of nation that are out-of-joint with time into line with the normative agenda of capital accumulation and economic growth. How this causality is reversed starting with critiques of *dirigisme* in the 1980s, such that capital now becomes the presupposition for development, is a fascinating phenomenon. One productive approach is to examine—in the approximate manner of a Polanyian "double movement"—how capitalism sublates what is an external support for it, development, by recoding itself as the immanent cause of development.

If development was paraded as the liberal-socialist suture for postcolonial India's myriad wounds, it begs the question whether the left had a different solution to offer. Some sections of the left might have wished it, but as a loose and contentious ideological front in search of electoral constituencies among the poor and the discriminated, it was difficult for the organized left to disavow the promises of "development." Marxists among them criticized the Nehru-Mahalanobis model of centralized planning (see chapter 3), objecting that it failed to involve the working classes in the planning process, along the lines of the "people's democracies" of Eastern Europe.[18] They also argued that the second Five-Year Plan "should have mandated a thoroughgoing process of nationalization, whereby the state would not merely start new industries, but take under its wings the private firms already in operation."[19] Amid this discontent, the problematic of development emerged unscathed. And as the early decades of Independence unfolded, left intellectuals found themselves stranded between the historical differences of India and the universalizing summons of Marxist economism. The long and sometimes insular debates that consumed Indian academic Marxism from the late 1960s into the early 1980s were symptomatic of this predicament. Unable to interrupt either the lure of development or the pieties of left orthodoxy, Marxist intellectuals could only lament the failure of a properly capitalist transformation of agriculture to produce, via the process of de-peasantisation and polarization, the necessary surplus for industrialization, an initial home market for manufactured goods, and an agricultural proletariat that could participate in a communist revolution.

Karl Kautsky, literary executor of Marx and Engels, leader of the German Social Democratic Party, and leading spokesman of the Second International, was first to give the agrarian question public prominence through his remarkable 1899 two-volume study. There, he uncannily anticipated the anxieties of Indian academic Marxism:

> With the growth of our party [the German Social Democratic Party], and the crisis in agriculture, it has now become one of the most important practical questions with which Social Democracy currently has to deal. The intervening period has also seen Marxism emerge as the basis for the socialist movement everywhere: and Volume III of *Capital,* with its brilliant treatment of ground-rent, has also now been published. However, agricultural development has given rise to phenomena which do not appear to be reconcilable with Marxist theories. The agrarian question has also, therefore, become a central problem of theory.[20]

What is the problem of theory that the agrarian question was foregrounding? In the introduction to his study, Kautsky writes (and I quote at length because these are instructive passages):

> At first the peasantry did not cause Social Democracy too many headaches. . . . The first years of its existence were fully

taken up with organizing the urban proletariat. And it expected
that economic development would carry out exactly the same
preparatory work on its behalf in the country as had taken
place in the towns—with the struggle between small and large
establishments leading to the elimination of the former, leaving
the easy task of winning over the mass of the rural population as a
purely proletarian party. . . .

[But now] Social Democracy has grown so enormously that it
has outgrown the towns. Yet as soon as it takes to the countryside it
runs head on into the same mysterious force which had previously
prepared such surprises for earlier democratic-revolutionary
forces. Far from making a rapid exit from the rural scene, small
farms continue to exist. And the advance of large farms is a slow
one—sometimes even reversing entirely. *The whole economic edifice
on which Social Democracy has based itself, and on which it relies,
seems to go awry the moment it tries to apply it to agriculture. The
inapplicability of the theory would not only demand a complete
transformation of Social Democracy's tactics, however: it would require
a transformation of its most fundamental principles.*[21]

In these few words, Kautsky reveals how the agrarian question foreshadows the question of hegemony—the desperate desire for a solution,
a suture, which will rescue theory from its own shortcomings by compelling a delinquent reality to conform to the predictions and desires of
(until that moment, certain) knowledge.

What, then, is this book all about? In a sentence, it strives to
assemble a genealogy of agrarian capitalism and labor politics in central Gujarat, India. By "genealogy" I mean, after Michel Foucault, a
geography and history "without constants,"[22] where analysis proceeds
not from the certitudes of given categories but instead takes as its
philosophical task to ask how those categories acquired their givenness
and with what consequences. It requires no less than a "critical ontology of our selves."[23] Adopting this limit-attitude, I audit the various
elements that have combined in specific, though not always anticipated, ways to produce the agrarian present of a particular region. As
indicated, this is not an exercise in conventional spatial history. In *The
Arcades Project*, Walter Benjamin issues the demand for "a philosophy
of history that at all points has overcome the ideology of progress" and
proceeds to denounce "the 'establishment of a continuity' in history,
because the only evidence of that continuity is that of horror."[24] This
summons, always vigilant of the geographic and epistemic power of
"Europe" and, equally, the importance of interrupting it, succinctly

captures the method by which I try to proceed—although my success in remaining ceaselessly true to it remains to be seen. A narrative by itself recuperates certain continuity for the space-times of agrarian transformation, and it is not always possible to sustain the caution required to produce an interrupted account that is alert to its own conditions of possibility.

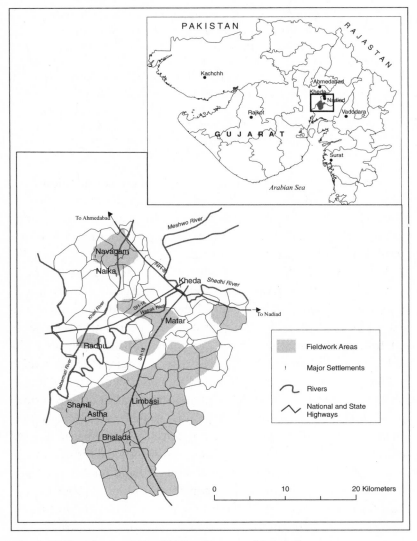

Map 2. Fieldwork areas, Matar Taluka. Courtesy of Sula Sarkar.

Empirically, the core question that anchors this enquiry is straight-forward: How did Lewa Patels become the dominant caste of agrarian capitalists in the central Gujarat region, and how should we account for their eroding rural dominance in recent decades despite an agroecological upheaval—the advent of canal irrigation—that putatively favors consoli-dation of the status quo? In attempting to answer this question, through a mix of archival, ethnographic, and survey research spanning most of 1994 and 1995 and several intermittent periods since, extending up to 2004, I very quickly discovered that one of the givens of my empirical investigation—the Patel "caste"—did not stratify into *that* concrete form until the late nineteenth century. This meant that in order to do justice to my central question, I would have to engage far more insistently with the dynamics of caste and class formation and the variegated conflicts surrounding these processes than I had initially anticipated or sought. The deeper I delved, the more dissatisfied I became with existing theories of capitalist accumulation and labor relations. These theories inevitably failed to register capital's "para-sitic" existence: how it draws its force by attempting to divert or attach itself to other kinds of energy or logic—cultural, political, nonhuman—whose contributions, like those of histo-ry's subalterns, are erased from conventional accounts.[25] It was apparent that the axiomatic medium of our social existence—"capitalism"—also begged a critical genealogy. This book, therefore, is also an investigation—but a provisional one—into how multiple elements combine to produce the complex whole we know as "capitalism." The subdistrict of Matar, the site of a landmark socioeconomic survey in 1929 by the Gandhian economist, J. C. Kumarappa, serves as a remarkable field laboratory for tackling these interlaced questions.

Capital, Interrupted is arranged into five chapters, as well as this introduction, where I have tried to lay out the overarching theoretical and empirical concerns of the book, and the afterword, a conclud-ing reflection on the political economy of knowledge. Although the Patels function as the locus and vehicle of my narrative, the book is not intended as a biography of that caste. Its primary aim, as I have men-tioned, is to generate a genealogical account of capitalism that traces how it was configured in its distinctive form across central Gujarat over the course of roughly two hundred years. What historical forces were instrumental to the fabrication of a capitalist space-economy?

This question compels an engagement with the nitty-gritty of colonial governance in Gujarat under the Bombay Presidency and the broader philosophical canvas of British liberalism, which ultimately furnished ideological grounds for colonial policies.

In Gujarat, as elsewhere, British administrators came to favor some colonized subjects over others: while the importance of political expediency to consolidate dominion cannot be dismissed lightly, nor can the importance of "development," liberalism's defining problematic. The fraught encounter with Empire exposed the inner contradictions of liberalism: its advocacy of "liberty" and the "natural rights of individuals" at home weighed against the stark realities of state authoritarianism and denial of civil liberties in the colonies. The idea of development—as a staged and orderly historical progress of civilizations, combining change with stability—arrived as a benefactor that rescued liberalism from its thorny predicament, supplying justification for colonial rule and a normative template for colonial policies, whether land settlements or projects of social reform. By conveniently foregrounding in the colonies the technical domains of *society* and *economy*, which had only just begun to crystalize in Europe, and circumscribing the arena of *politics*, colonial rule was legitimized as a program of civilizing. The righting and purging of various forms of "waste"—unruly conducts, things, and natures (in short, matter perceived as out of place)—was a central, if understated, aspect of this mission. (As I will demonstrate, the figure of "waste" has found unexpected and powerful afterlives in the postcolony.)

Thus, my principal argument in chapter 1 ("Waste") is that liberalism in India, organized around the problematic of development, attempted to assemble not merely the conditions for economic conduct that would multiply the production of wealth but that this objective was inseparable from—and hence concurrent with—attempts to transform moral conduct as well. Abstractly, this meant that the capitalist space-economy that took shape in Gujarat and other British dominions within India in the nineteenth and twentieth centuries was a process of *channeling* and *forming* in desired ways the errant matter of native subjects and their physical environments. Posed in these terms, colonial government through its political-economic knowledge and apparatuses of security can be viewed as a modality of power that seeks to achieve an optimal regulation—an equilibrium of *internment* and *circulation*—of nonhuman flows as well as human bodies with their dispositions and desires. Both are, I contend, crucial for the production of capitalist "value." Indeed, Michel Foucault's summary rendering of governmentality as the "conduct of conduct" can be reread in this framing as incitement to a *regime of value,* where value signifies both norms of conduct as well as the substantive foundation of economy and society (as evidenced in the labor theories of value that anchored the political-economic systems of Adam Smith and David Ricardo). Colonial rule in India was, in this respect, a crusade against various forms of waste*ful* conduct that threatened order and design. Not surprisingly, "virtue" *and* "progress," "character" *and* "industry," "conduct" *and* "economy," were the paired keywords of both liberalism and colonial government.

Lewa Patels, the dominant caste in central Gujarat, are also one of the most visible and affluent caste groups in India and boast a global diasporic presence.[26] But how did they emerge in this sociological form? Chapter 2 ("Birth") shows how their coagulation as a corporate entity was enabled by a historically and geographically contingent articulation of class, gender, and political relations under colonial rule. I begin by documenting how and why colonial land settlement policies came to favor certain colonized subjects over others, including groups that eventually organized themselves under the caste name "Patel." My argument further demonstrates the manner in which colonial forms of knowledge, including concerns over the problem of female infanticide, combined with hypergamous marriage practices and ongoing political and economic convulsions among Kanbi and Patidar class factions to produce a geographically ordered Patel caste with a regulative aesthetics that might be described as rural cosmopolitanism. But as I also underscore in chapter 2, the Patels constitute (and have long been) a "ruptural unity": an achieved hegemonic alliance always troubled by internal fissures.

Chapter 3 ("Machine") tracks the career of agrarian capitalism in Independent India, especially Gujarat, by surveying the political dynamics unleashed by the postcolonial development machine. In chapter 1, we see how liberalism, when confronted by Empire, sanctioned the curtailment of political liberty but commended itself for civilizing the habits and expanding the economic liberty of the colonized—supplying grit to the historian Ranajit Guha's provocative claim that colonial government in India was an instance of "dominance without hegemony."[27] Britain's government in India was never answerable to those it ruled;

instead, it was accountable to the British Parliament and, thereon, to enfranchised members of the British public. The democratic state that took birth after Indian Independence in 1947 embraced "development" as its raison d'être. Under Nehru, especially, development was anointed as the force that would bind together fractured geographies to produce a modern nation, "India."[28] However, there were two consequential differences from the colonial era in this embrace of development:

1. Nehru's anti-imperial sensibilities (informed by his readings of Lenin and Luxemburg and his attraction to Fabian Socialism) drained "development" of its moral baggage as a civilizing project and instead recast it as a project of sovereign socialism.
2. It was apparent from the outset that this new project of development, if it was to forge a nation, would have to be broadly acceptable to the nation's electorate, with all its geographic wrinkles and inequalities.

The first of these two considerations ensured that until the early 1980s the market remained handmaiden to the developmental state, which, through the Five-Year Plans, tried to render India as an abstracted problem-space on which development planning could operate. Through a detailed local analysis of the workings of development in central Gujarat, I show, however, that this centripetal desire was in perennial tension with the centrifugal forces that are always at play within hegemonic projects—a constitutional instability that electoral democracy within a heterogeneous society further provokes. Development's diagrammatic effects at once deepened and undermined capitalist production in rural Gujarat. As events in Gujarat since the late 1960s demonstrate, rural as well as urban power-holders correctly read the political and ecological vectors set in motion by postcolonial development policies as threats to the status quo. They reacted predictably by lending muscle and financial support to a series of violent agitations, first against *dalit* (Scheduled Caste) minorities and subsequently against religious minorities. In short, Gujarat's aggressive brand of ethnonationalism involves, among other factors, the dangerous re-activation of a Hindu normativity that is implicit in the milieu by elite anxieties about the secularist program of development.

Capital accumulation is shot through by supplementary energies that both enable and confound. This is starkly revealed in the peculiar self-fashioning of Patels. On the one hand, they style themselves as frugal and peerless capitalist farmers and entrepreneurs; on the other hand, they exhibit a history of wasteful conducts designed to secure rank and social status. These disparate imperatives, which have been at particular historical moments complementary (and crucial to their consolidation as a sociological collectivity), are at other moments contradictory. Chapter 4 ("Distinction") contends that the quest for social distinction by Patel farmers sits in continuous tension with the demands of capitalist production. I show how a logic of social calculation fused to a body politics of self-improvement, that is historically set in motion by the thickening of agrarian capitalism, ultimately leads to the prevalence of forms of labor contract—such as piecework arrangements—that appear to be inefficient from the standpoint of capital accumulation and rational choice theory. Through detailed analysis of labor deployment that draws upon primary and secondary research, I develop a critique of both Marxist and New Institutional economic approaches to the study of labor relations, instead demonstrating that a profit- or class-centered economic rationality is always contaminated by other (potentially interruptive) cultural logics. This foray into the micropolitics of work stages the theoretically more abstract concerns of chapter 5 ("Interruption"), where I stitch together readings of Karl Marx's *Grundrisse*, A. N. Whitehead's process philosophy, and postcolonial critiques of historicism to reveal capitalism as an incomplete totality constantly striving for self-adequacy. In place of understanding capitalism as a seamless totality à la Hegel, in which parts obediently mirror the interior logic of the whole, I instead dwell on the moment of negativity in capital's repeated and diverse spatiotemporal encounters with labor as a site of fear and desire. Here, the *Grundrisse* is indispensable as a theoretical and political tract because it shows us, on the one hand, capital's desire to capture "living labor" as use-value for itself and its permanent fear that labor could become otherwise; on the other hand, it underscores how labor's desire to be otherwise is counterbalanced by its fear that without capital it may not be able to remain actively employed (thereby jeopardizing its reproduction). Thus, *Grundrisse* is never naïve: it confronts head-on structural necessity and the repeating incarceration of labor through capture, but retains fidelity to possibilities for liberation within—or more forcefully, as a result of—capital's desire for accumulation and the geographies written into this.

In order to spur these insights, early in chapter 5 I confront an unlikely remark by Jacques Derrida, in which he claims to have never opposed the dialectic. He follows this up with a cryptic plea for "thinking a dialecticity of dialectics that is itself fundamentally not dialectical."[29] Using this as a foil to think through the disquiet that several quarters of the left experience with Marxist political economy, both in terms of its putative epistemology and the politics it seems to sanction, I ask whether the movement of the "dialectic" metonymically implies synthesis, sameness, unity, and identity as conventional wisdom has it; or whether it can be reclaimed for antitotalitarian projects as a force of nonidentity and difference.

More broadly, chapter 5 gathers up the arguments made in previous chapters to make the case that even a category as seemingly self-evident as "capitalism," in some profound sense, is open to question. If a profit-centered rationality anchored to a relentless logic of accumulation (the subordination of production to the "law of value" in classical Marxist theory) is upheld as the deus ex machina of capitalism, then it is not clear how to talk about a social formation where that motive is contaminated, consolidated, and continuously interrupted by other logics; where institutional arrangements must work overtime to ensure that circuits of capital accumulation do not come to a grinding halt.

The core of chapter 5 is a staged encounter between the radical geographer David Harvey and the historian Dipesh Chakrabarty. I combine this with a reading of Marx's *Grundrisse* and ethnographic instances to generate a distinction between a "politics of labor" and a "politics of work." I contend that even though capitalist production dominates the universe of human (and nonhuman) activity, these activities are not reducible to—*not mere expressions of*—capital. Instead, we are forced to confront a "complex whole" *where production activity oriented to profit-taking for accumulation interdigitates with other value-creating or normative practices.* Moreover, we encounter a dense circuitry of humans *and* nonhumans that capitalist value must traverse in the garb of product, commodity, and money in order to be affirmed. By rethinking the ontology of capital in this manner, I hope to leave no room for its renderings—within radical geography, liberal economics, or postcolonial studies—as an organic unity that unfolds in accordance with an underlying logic, such as an interior "law of value," a guiding "law of supply and demand," or the subliminal will to freedom of "Spirit." In short, I try to thwart overt and residual forms of historicism.

The afterword ("Aporia") confronts the political economy of knowledge production and the dilemmas that mark this book as a *commodity*, which desires to exist differently. Can it?

Ultimately, this book is *itself a wager*. And this wager, as I have been saying, has to do with how we conceptualize this becoming-being called "capitalism." My claim is that we cannot think or support counter-hegemonic political practice that affirms life in common unless we first engage in good theoretical practice. This book is about a theoretical practice that can be adequate to this politics.

CHAPTER ONE

Waste

Virtue

On May 14, 1861, Jadunathji Brijratanji Maharaj, a leader of the
Vaishnavite Vallabhacharya sect, filed a libel suit in the Bombay
Supreme Court against Karsandas Mulji, a Gujarati social reformer and
editor of *Satya Prakash* (a Gujarati-language weekly), and Nanabhai
Rustomji Ranina, the newspaper's printer. In his petition to the court,
the Maharaj charged the defendants Mulji and Ranina with defaming
him in an article published in their newspaper on October 21, 1860.[1]
The allegations that Mulji and Ranina had made against Jadunathji
Maharaj (and other Maharajas of the Vallabhacharya sect) were sensa-
tional. He was accused of "immoral practices," such as throwing "gulal
[red powder] and coloured water through a syringe on women's breasts
and touching them"—actions that Mulji, invoking the authority of the
Hindu Shastras, condemned as the equivalent of "adultery." During the
libel trial that ensued, witnesses provided even more lurid descriptions
of Jadunathji's misbehavior with women: throwing gulal and squeez-
ing the breasts of a Bhatia girl and later having intercourse with her,
pressing the hands of women with his toes to indicate sexual interest
in them, and kissing a young girl in his bedroom and later receding
into the inner chambers with her. Mathuradas Lowji, a witness for the
defense, noted that women devotees of the Vallabhacharya Maharajas
were encouraged to "sing *garbis* [songs] of an amorous character in the
presence of Maharajas; such as 'I was asleep and you woke me,' 'you will
ease my mind if you take me,' 'you are my husband.'" These indictments

gathered their moral weight from the stated precepts and practices of the Vallabhacharya sect, which, among other entailments, enjoined "the [male] devotee to offer his body, mind and property to the Maharaj ... [where] this is implied to mean wife, sons, daughters, self and all personal belongings."[2]

But it was not the unqualified proprietorship of men over women endorsed by the Vallabhacharya sect that bothered social reformers like Karsandas Mulji and two British judges, Sir Joseph Arnould and Sir Mathew Asusse, who presided over the libel trial. The right of men to control *their* women was never at stake. Rather it was precisely the opposite that was at issue, namely, the seeming inability of the Maharajas' male followers to regulate the desires and sexuality of their "impressionable" women. Karsandas Mulji was by all accounts a bold reformer. But his ideal woman resided within the secured space of tradition, her sublime qualities protected (because she was incapable of protecting herself) from the seductions of both degenerate Hinduism and European liberalism. Who was this ideal woman? In Mulji's words, she was one who "delights the heart of a man and who overpowers him by her pure love. Observe her traits, she walks gently. She speaks only sweet, melodious words. She is both mild and guileless. She neither sits idly nor wanders here and there. She neither eats nor drinks like a glutton. . . . She carries out all her work. She uses her God-given intelligence and tries to remain honest and virtuous in all her deeds."[3]

It is worth noting that in the entire trial proceedings of the Maharaja libel case, the views of women, whether followers of the Vallabhacharya sect or not, were never once solicited. They remained a silent presence, spoken for but never heard. They were rendered as a faceless terrain upon which men of different interests and persuasions sparred over the parameters of moral and religiously sanctioned conduct. What appeared to disturb Mulji and the British judges most in the entire Jadunathji Maharaj affair was the incitement to sexual "licentiousness" by women encouraged by the doctrines of the Vallabhacharya sect. The corrosion of virtue—evident in the apparent abandonment by women of their modesty and purity in pleasuring the Maharajas—was read by Mulji and the judges as a grave and imminent threat to the social order because it struck at the core of its stability, the patrilineal family. Reacting to evidence of the songs sung by women of the Vallabhacharya sect,

Sir Joseph Arnould, one of the two presiding judges at the trial, frothily proclaimed that they were

> passionate with all the passion of the East-erotic pantings for fruition of a lover who is also a God: as it said of the gopis in the *Vishnu Puran,* every instant without Krishna they count a myriad of years, and forbidden by fathers, husbands, brothers, they go forth at night to sport with Krishna, the object of their love. So these hymns, sung at this day, as the plaintiff [Jadunathji Maharaj] admitted, by the wives and daughters of the Vallabhacharyans to their Maharajas, express the most unbridled desire, the most impatient longing for the enjoyment of adulterine love.[4]

The second presiding judge, Sir Mathew Asusse, was open in his disapproval, declaring that "[a]ll songs connected with the God Krishna, which were brought before us were of an amorous character, and it appeared that songs of a corrupting and licentious tendency, both in idea and expression, are sung by young females to the Maharajas, upon festive occasions, in which they are identified with the God, in his most licentious aspect."[5] The trial concluded in favor of the defendant, Karsandas Mulji. Although the evidence presented at the trial was persuasive in demonstrating the self-aggrandizing and crudely exploitative actions of the Vallabhacharya Maharajas toward their women devotees, it also demonstrated the regulative and gendered workings of liberalism: on the one hand, of the filtered liberalism of indigenous social reformers like Mulji; on the other hand, the imperial liberalism of British judges like Arnould and Asusse. Their odd but not unlikely alliance was stitched together by firm conviction in liberalism's commitment to reason, liberty, and progress and by an equally steadfast conviction (reminiscent of Auguste Comte) that progress was "the development of order." In the Indian setting, this demanded both the education and training of women and the regulation of their virtue so that, ultimately, the integrity and purity of the home could be secured and, thus, the stability of society itself.[6] If the twin convictions of a post-Lockean commitment to the natural rights of individuals and liberty secured by the human powers of reason and an evangelical fixation with control of morality and conduct seem, in retrospect, incompatible on liberalism's own terms, they capture with unusual clarity the checkered life of its defining "problematic" *development.*[7]

Liberalism's Problematic

There now exists a large, critical literature on the apparatus of development that is indebted primarily to Foucault's analytics of power/knowledge. Awkwardly styled as "postdevelopment," the critics who populate this genre tell us that the power of development lies in its capacity to provoke within those who are interpellated as "underdeveloped" the desire for the proximate rewards of a better life and the eventual hope of coevalness with those already "developed." The incitement of this desire, in turn, sanctions a re-*placement* of authority in the hands of bureaucrats and technocrats with putatively expert knowledge to implement development.[8] The invocation of expertise and the framing of development as a problem of engineering also have the politically convenient effect, from the standpoint of the developmental state, of depoliticizing (it is claimed) a deeply fraught process of change. These insights are repeatedly documented in the new development literature, and I see no point in regurgitating them.[9]

Here I want to concentrate on showing how development becomes the defining *problematic* of liberalism and, by association, colonial government. Some preliminaries then, at the risk of reproducing common knowledge: the concept of the "problematic" as I employ it here comes from Althusser.[10] In Althusser's rendering, the problematic is that which brings out within a given ideological formation "*the objective internal reference system of its particular* themes, the system of *questions* commanding the *answers* given by the ideology."[11] Althusser does not claim that ideology is an organic unity or, more precisely, an expressive totality à la Hegel—a *Zeitgeist*.[12] Quite the obverse, the goal of theoretical practice, according to Althusser, is to show how every ideological formation is a *structured* unity that is constituted through a problematic. However, the problematic is neither a worldview *(weltanschaaung)* nor the underlying unity "of the thought of an individual or epoch which can be deduced from a body of texts by an empirical, generalizing reading."[13] Rather, it bears (more than incidental) resemblance to Foucault's *diagram*. Like it, the problematic is that which makes objects and problems available in certain forms to the subjects of an ideological (or in Foucault's oeuvre, discursive) formation. It is "*itself an answer* ... to *the objective problems posed* for ideology *by its time*."[14] It makes *visible* but, equally important, renders *invisible*—as "forbidden vision"—certain objects and problems: "[T]he invisible is not ... simply what is outside the visible (to return to the spatial metaphor), the outer darkness of exclusion—but the inner darkness of exclusion, inside the visible itself because defined by its structure."[15] It is important to note that although in the works for which he is best known, *For Marx* and *Reading Capital,* Althusser does not allude to class (and other) antagonisms that striate ideologies into "regions" (Althusser, the philosopher, is fond of geographic metaphors), in his later writings he concedes this oversight. However, this concession does not, apparently, alter his concept of the problematic, which, as the "absolute determination *of the forms in which all problems must be posed,* at any given moment," is able to allow for differences within an ideological formation.[16] The significance of this caveat will be evident as I analyze the colonial problematic of development.

But one final clarification before I return to that topic: Althusser's conception of ideology and his tendentious distinction between ideology and science have generated bitter, often tedious, controversy—the sources of sharpest contention being Althusser's avowed rejection of ideology as having to do with "ideas" and the imputation that he ends up rendering ideology as a surrogate for "error" and science as a surrogate for "truth."[17] My goal here is neither to recuperate Althusser nor to wish away the contradictions and oversights in his writings. By the same token, I would not be bothering with him if I did not think his writings have something valuable to contribute theoretically and politically. Spinoza's influence on Althusser's thought—both because of the magnitude of its imprint and how understated Althusser's debts are to Spinoza, particularly in the early writings—is of special interest. For example, one way to effect a distinction between ideology and science that evades the arid binary of falsity and truth is to think of science as a making visible of precisely those invisible blanks that an ideology's problematic legislates, of bringing to light (there *are* Deleuzian tints here) objects and problems that are necessarily invisible within a given ideology, because they are forbidden by it. The product of science is a newly constituted terrain of previously unseen objects and problems governed by a new problematic. It is science in that it renders unobvious the "obviousness" of ideology.[18] Where does this science come from? It neither originates from the "interior" of the sovereign thinking individual, *res cogitans,* who, possessed of Reason, inaugurates scientific knowledge; nor does it come from an "exterior," a nonideological region outside of ideology. Ideology itself is the substrate or "prehistory" of science that continues to exist alongside, and indeed *within,* science. In short, there are no pure—Althusser says "rationalist-speculative"— categories of ideology or science *in general:* more pointedly, both ideology and science exist as *process,* ideology as the process of "practicosocial" or "lived" practice and science as the process of "theoretical practice."[19] The rub here is that ideology is never abolished or, as Althusser enigmatically puts it, "ideology has no history."[20]

How, then, does science emerge? Althusser consistently maintains that science is the overdetermined product of theoretical labor, which one *must* strive after but whose birth, as an "epistemological break," is never guaranteed.[21] Here is Althusser's antihumanist, antihistoricist account of scientific "discovery":

> [Science] is not born out of nothing, but out of a process of labor by which it is hatched, a complex and multiple process, sometimes brightened by a flash of lightning, but which normally operates blindly, in the dark, because "it" never knows where it is headed, nor, if ever it arrives, where it is going to surface. It is born out of the unpredictable, incredibly complex and paradoxical—but, in its contingency, necessary—*conjunction* of ideological, political, scientific (related to other sciences), philosophical and other *"elements,"* which at some moment *"discover," but after the event, that they needed each other,* since they come together, without however recognizing one another, in the theoretical shape of a new-born science.[22]

Where is the stamp of Spinoza in this formulation? Warren Montag tells us that Spinoza's "revolution," which was so scandalous to philosophy and theology alike, was to examine Scripture not as a coherent whole exhibiting the perfection one would expect of the Word of God, but rather as a "material artifact composed of elements . . . [as] a composite, fabricated at a later age out of contradictory, incomplete and diverse materials." To take Scripture "as it is," as Spinoza proposed, is to take "its gaps, lacunae, inconsistencies and outright contradictions of doctrine and narrative, as irreducible."[23] There is no "essence" buried deep in the text, no justification for a hermeneutic that recreates the meanings of "parts" by assuming them to be expressions of a Divine, hence perfect, whole. Instead, interpretation must proceed by exposing the "unconscious" of the text, "the need to deny, to make invisible that which it makes visible by diverting our attention from it."[24] The possibility of science, to return to the issue at hand, lies precisely in a strategy of reading (or, more generally, thinking), which is also a theoretical labor, that analyzes "a text's defenses and conflicts"—in short, what Althusser calls a "symptomatic reading."

As for the question of ideology, Althusser, as I said, refuses to equate it with "ideas"; instead, in a famous turn of phrase he describes ideology as "the imaginary relationship of individuals to their real conditions of existence."[25] Elsewhere, he writes that "ideology is a matter of the *lived* relation between men and their world."[26] In what sense can "imaginary" be "lived," or is Althusser simply confused here? Montag, exposing Spinoza's impact on Althusser's thought, is once again instructive:

> The term "imaginary" . . . which many commentators have associated
> with the psychoanalyst Jacques Lacan, probably owes more to
> Spinoza's definition of the imaginary as the inversion of causes and
> effects in human life: we imagine we are the origins, causes and
> masters of our thought, speech and action when in fact we are simply
> unaware of the causes that have determined us to think, speak and
> act as we do.[27]

Thus, ideology exists in the obviousness—empirical immediacy—of our world and the actions we take, imagining ourselves to be the center of initiatives. Contrary to the impression that, say, an expeditious reading of Gramsci might produce, ideology for Althusser is not instrumental. It cannot be, since it exists as a virtual, unconscious structure that is realized only in practice. So rather than valorize ideology itself as the weapon par excellence of counterhegemonic politics (Gramsci's innovation), Althusser instead clears a modest space for philosophy as a theoretical practice that can and must attempt to be *partisan* in political struggle: hence, his reformulation of philosophy as "class struggle in theory."[28]

British Political Economy and the Government of Empire

On, then, to the matter of "development." I begin by observing the tremors of a shift in the political rationality of colonial rule in the second quarter of the nineteenth century, from a regime of sovereign power to a regime of governmental power. This is hardly a novel or even controversial axiom. Hints of this transformation, which was not a clean or uniform "rupture" but rather an untidy and geographically uneven one, are palpable in such classic works on colonial India as Eric Stokes's

The English Utilitarians and India (1959), Bernard Cohn's essays from the 1950s and 1960s, Ranajit Guha's *A Rule of Property for Bengal* (1963), Francis Hutchins's *The Illusion of Permanence: British Imperialism in India* (1967), and S. Ambirajan's *Classical Political Economy and British Policy in India* (1978).[29] I take cue from David Scott's perceptive commentary on colonial governmentality, where he examines how this form of modern power differs from older forms of political rationality both in its *point of application* and its *field of operation:*[30]

> [I]f modern power is concerned with disabling non-modern forms of life by dismantling their conditions, then its aim in putting in place new and different conditions is above all to produce governing-effects on conduct. Modern power seeks to arrange and rearrange these conditions (conditions at once discursive and nondiscursive) so as to oblige subjects to transform themselves in a certain, that is, *improving* direction.[31]

In short, governmental power operates by attempting to be coextensive with the ethical government of the self. It seeks to reinscribe the security of the State with the security of society and population.[32]

The cameralist "science of police," whose rudiments were first elaborated in Germany at the beginning of the seventeenth century, is a movement in this direction; but as Foucault notes, "it was thanks to the perception of the specific problems of the population, and thanks to the isolation of that area of reality that we call the economy, that the problem of government finally came to be thought, reflected and calculated outside of the juridical framework of sovereignty."[33] Regrettably, Foucault portrays governmentality as a Western and largely undifferentiated mode of power, thereby erasing its internal and imperial geographies. The career of colonial government in the British dominions instead suggests an emergent complex of power/knowledge that involved the aleatory suturing of three separate forces:

> First, the German cameralist "science of police" with its emphasis on the use of numbers-based information *(statistiks)* as a way to make "visible"—and, hence, operational—certain abstractions (society, commerce, economy, etc.) and thereby strengthen the fiscal and military security of centralized government.

> Second, British liberalism with its zealous exploration of the subjective dynamics of self-rule in the context of declining monarchical

power (to which we must add a deep Newtonian skepticism of the observed particular prior to the late eighteenth century).[34]

Third, a dour and secularized British evangelicalism that was—like the doctrine of Utilitarianism that came to saturate British liberal thought in the nineteenth century—highly moralistic in its standards of human conduct and interventionist in preaching the principles of individual probity and hard work (which it considered of universal applicability).[35]

The hugely influential writings of John Locke (1632–1704) had cleared space for the combining of these disparate elements. But it was left to Adam Smith's discourse of political economy, systematized in *The Theory of Moral Sentiments* (1759) and the companion *Wealth of Nations* (1776), to effect (as *unwitting conduit* rather than *witting creator*) the articulation of these three forces and give credence to a mode of power whose principal objective was to become the governance of conduct. Smith's description of "political economy" in Book IV of *Wealth of Nations* is especially telling in this regard:

> Political economy, considered as a branch of science of statesman or legislator, proposes two distinct objects: first, to provide a plentiful revenue or subsistence for the people, or more properly to enable them to provide such a revenue or subsistence for themselves; and secondly, to supply the state or commonwealth with a revenue sufficient for public services. It proposes to enrich both the people and the sovereign.[36]

Moreover, unlike David Hume, who was "content to construct theories from a combination of abstraction, introspection, and experience, Smith ... wanted to base political economic knowledge on numbers"[37]—despite his serious reservations about the reliability of existing numerical records. Smith's affinity to numbers can be explained in part by his desire to make abstractions like "the market" that loomed large in his theory legible to legislators who would ultimately craft policy by providing them (in the form of properly presented numerical information) an interpretive tool to grasp the normative truth of his theoretical system. Thus, what *Wealth of Nations* and its system of political economy managed to achieve—incidentally rather than purposively—was a retrospective assimilation of the key elements of German cameralist science and British liberal philosophy.[38] The practical consequences of this transformation were first felt in the colonies, particularly in India, well before its backwash reached the shores of the metropole.[39]

Smith's governmental doctrine was transmitted to the Indian scene by his acolytes, most notably the Reverend Thomas Robert Malthus and Richard Jones, who successively held the Chair in Political Economy at Haileybury College, the institution established by the Court of Directors of the East India Company in 1805 to train future civil servants destined for administrative posts in India.[40] Also closely associated with the Company were Jeremy Bentham, the philosopher-jurist who codified the doctrine of Utilitarianism; David Ricardo, who sat on its Court of Directors; and James Mill—Bentham's erstwhile secretary and lifelong disciple and a close confidánte of Ricardo— whose weighty, six-volume *The History of British India* (1818), a savage critique of Indian civilization and a programmatic call for British intervention to transform India's "despotic" traditional institutions,[41] secured him employment as Assistant Examiner at the Company. But throughout, it was Smith and *Wealth of Nations* that remained the guiding ideological influence on India-bound civil servants. As Ambirajan notes:

> [T]he lectures at Haileybury were mainly based on Adam Smith, the students being given an elementary course on the production, distribution and exchange of wealth. They were also introduced to "the different systems of taxation which have prevailed or do prevail, in the World; to the connection of these with of occupying the soil; to reaction of these systems on the wealth and mechanism of nations, especially Asiatic nations" and, finally, to barter, exchange, money and credit.[42]

Of course, neither Smith nor the line of eighteenth- and nineteenth-century thinkers who were influenced by his treatise on political economy ever codified "development" as liberalism's defining instance. Rather they trucked in a cognate term, "progress." The Christian eschatological roots of this idea are well known, but its continuities with Christianity should not be exaggerated. Although liberalism and its antecedents were theistic in proclamation insofar as nature and human existence were thought to derive meaning within an overarching divine plan, the epistemic ruptures of the seventeenth and eighteenth centuries had displaced God into "God," a philosophical entity whose existence was henceforth inferred from "evident instances of design in the world" rather than a being whose existence was taken as axiomatic to all else.[43]

Thus, to make a claim for secularization was to understand God as subsequent to human powers of reason rather than prior to or constitutive of it. It was to render God and, by extension, time and space, immanent.[44] When Hans Blumenberg writes in his panoramic book, *The Legitimacy of the Modern Age,* that "the idea of progress extrapolates from a structure present in every moment to a future that is immanent in history" or when he characterizes progress as "the continuous self-justification of the present, by means of the future that it gives itself, before the past, with which it compares itself,"[45] it is the subordination of history to human will—or, better yet, history as a record of *progressive* betterment in life brought about by human actions guided by reason—that Blumenberg is describing.

What about "development"? From popular usage we know it as a term that is equated with progress. But, while cognate, it is not identical to the idea of progress. Indeed, my contention is that "development" becomes the name for liberalism's problematic—what liberalism *can no longer think without*—when the fraught confrontation with Empire, especially in the late eighteenth and nineteenth centuries, fully exposes the inner contradictions of liberalism. Its advocacy of "liberty" and the "natural rights of individuals" at home weighed against the stark realities of state authoritarianism and denial of civil liberties in the colonies. The problematic of development (as the horizon of liberal thought) sutures the secular time and telos of progress to both a secular conception of space and a moral onus of trusteeship (whose paternalism takes its most vivid form in "the white man's burden"). By this procedure development repairs the damaged integuments of liberal logic, providing, at once, justification for colonial rule and a normative template for colonial policies, whether land settlements or projects of social reform. Furthermore, the vision enabled by development foregrounds the programmatic domains of "society" and "economy"—and imparts pungency to corollary fields of knowledge such as "culture"—while evacuating the "political" of its primacy and potency.[46] A symptomatic reading of Empire and development discloses the illiberal "supplement" of liberalism. Offered up as a doctrine of freedom and inclusion, liberalism's certitudes are constantly secured by the violence of exclusions. Glimpses of this unseemly scaffolding were already visible in Locke's defense of English colonialism in America (although the modern doctrine of development is yet to congeal).

Locke makes an ingenious move when he is confronted with the objection that English settlers in the New World are dispossessing Native Americans of lands that are rightfully theirs. He invokes "evidence," what any reasonable person can affirm, to show this is not the case. What are these "matters of fact" that Locke invokes to demonstrate that Indians can't be considered owners of property? The Indians roam freely over the land, without enclosing it. When they do enclose it (as coastal Indians, whose lands white settlers coveted, did) their practice of letting it lie fallow every three years "demonstrated that they did not make rational use of it." More so, even when they cultivate land, it was never to its "best possible use." And the clinching evidence? Since the Indians had apparently few needs, "they lacked the desire to accumulate wealth," which meant, of course, that they would never have "interest in exploiting the earth's potential to the fullest." To add to this, the Indians did not have a unified, centralized, and codified system of authority. Nor did they, evidently, have a shared language. How, then, could they be said to constitute a society? These were matters of fact, for any reasonable observer to see. Thus, lacking what Locke regarded as the basic prerequisites of political society, the Indians "were not entitled to have their territorial integrity respected by others."[47]

This line of reasoning provides a preview of debates that were to occur more than a century later around land settlement policies in India, particularly the issue of ownership. By then, although "progress" was still liberalism's reigning watchword, it had begun to accumulate layers of meaning that would soon render it in its modern form, "development," with its plural connotations of an orderly and staged spatiotemporal process of change; of deepening rationality and individual choice, with "culture" as achieved distance from "nature" as a core indicator of reason and progress; and most significantly, where "utility" joined to the "laws of political economy"—in short, society organized by capitalist relations—has become the reigning moral metric for all actions, public and private.

It is under the lengthening shadow of development, a problematic yet to be codified but already operative, that liberalism oversees the birth of a new modality of power in the colonies, "government." The concern with government is, of course, not new. But it is primarily viewed, for instance in the seventeenth-century political theories of Grotius, Pufendorf, Hobbes, and Locke, as a problem of order. Hence, starting from very different premises about human nature and the conditions that obtain in the state of nature, Hobbes and Locke arrive at disparate justifications for the existence of a sovereign entity (the Leviathan, or the State) and its rightful powers. It is true that Locke, by his emphasis on education in bringing conscience, desire, and reason into "mature harmony," his rejection of morality as a human construct that is relative to different times and places, the importance he places on labor and wealth accumulation, his delineation of the individual and voluntaristic origins of civil society, and his demarcation of the State's primary role as protector of private property, supplies the foundations of Whig political ideology and many of the philosophical raw materials from which both development and the art of government will be eventually fashioned. Rousseau's *The Social Contract* for instance, which Foucault identifies as a pivotal influence in the genealogy of governmental power, owes a singular debt to Locke's *Second Treatise of Government.*[48] Nevertheless, the diagram of power that organizes Locke's political writings is that of "sovereignty." He anticipates a new modality of power, which is evident from the severe circumscriptions he places on sovereign power, but is not yet in a position to break from the older diagram.

In a well-known aphorism, Foucault describes governmental power as "the conduct of conduct." Unlike sovereign or tributary power which was "directed principally at the points of extraction of wealth ... because tributary power was largely concerned to ensure that bodies knew their place, that they obeyed when commanded,"[49] the substance upon which governmental power seeks to work is human "conduct." But conduct itself is seen as the attribute of individuals who make up a population and a society. These are, of course, categories that are intimately familiar—indeed, commonsensical—today. But the imagination they summon of aggregated, causally bound, and patterned entities was still congealing in the eighteenth century,[50] as was the doctrine that the political and financial security of the State lay ultimately in providing conditions for the welfare or self-betterment of the population—that is to say, in the State's ability to motivate "responsibilized" freedom and rational conduct on part of subjects. Hence Foucault's adumbration that

> [W]hat government has to do with is not territory but rather a sort of complex composed of men and things. The things with which in this sense government is to be concerned are in fact men, but men in their relations, their links, their imbrication with those other things which are wealth, resources, means of subsistence, the territory with its specific

qualities, climate, irrigation, fertility, etc.; men in their relation to that
other kind of things, customs, habits, ways of acting and thinking, etc.;
lastly, men in their relation to that other kind of things, accidents and
misfortunes such as famine, epidemics, death, etc.[51]

This figuring of state power, which I find compelling, presages what in
modern textbooks has been called the "developmental State." It indicates, for instance, that with governmentality, rational conduct comes
to be equated with an "economic" disposition, in the combined sense of
orientation and action; that this form of conduct by individuals can be
promoted by intervening tactically on "nature," both human and nonhuman, to make it conducive for economic conduct; and that this is the
preeminent charge of government. This is a characteristically bold and
provocative exposition by Foucault. And, again characteristically, it has
inexplicable blind spots. There is, for instance, no acknowledgment anywhere in Foucault's essay on governmentality on the role of colonialism in
the emergence and consolidation of this new mode of power (and, therefore, no explicit comment on liberalism or its transformation by Empire).
More significantly, although Foucault likens this new form of power to
an "economic pastorate" and identifies political economy as its principal
form of knowledge, there is no recognition of the fact that the discourse
of economy that solidifies in the eighteenth and early nineteenth centuries through the writings of Hume, Turgot, Quesnay, Ferguson, Bentham,
Smith, and Ricardo is also always a moral-ethological discourse.

Thus, my principal argument in this chapter is that liberalism in
India—held together by the problematic of "development"—attempts
to assemble not merely the conditions for economic conduct that will
multiply the production of wealth but that this objective is inseparable
from (and hence concurrent with) attempts to transform wasteful forms
of moral conduct as well. This meant that the capitalist space-economy
that took shape in Gujarat and other British dominions within India in
the nineteenth and twentieth centuries was a process of *channeling* and
forming in desired ways the errant matter of native subjects and their
physical environments. Thus rendered, colonial government through its
political-economic knowledge and apparatuses of security can be viewed
as a modality of power that strives for an optimal balance between the
internment and *circulation* of nonhuman flows as well as human bodies
with their dispositions and desires.[52] Both are, I suggest, crucial for the
production of "value" under capitalism. Indeed, Foucault's summary

rendering of governmentality as the conduct of conduct can be now read as incitement to a regime of "value," where value signifies both norms of conduct as well as the elusive foundation of classical political economy (particularly the theories of Smith and Ricardo).[53] Virtue and progress, character and industry, conduct and economy—these were, after all, the affine keywords of liberalism and colonial government.

Drainage

It is 1862 in Matar Taluka:

> I have already mentioned that a considerable tract of black soil, now waste, especially between Limbashee and Chanor, might be converted into valuable rice land. This tract is now next to valueless, owing to the presence in the soil of what the natives called "Khar," which is, I believe, sesqui-carbonate of soda, and covers the ground with a white efflorescence. This "Khar," the natives say, is near Limbashee, annually increasing, and encroaching upon the cultivated lands, which it soon completely ruins. Where it comes from I cannot determine, but two facts about it are pretty clear: first, that it is very apt to appear where the rain water of the monsoon is permitted to stagnate, and dry up on the land, as is the case in the tract above mentioned; next, that if lands subject to it are drained, manured, and cultivated with care for a few years it generally entirely disappears. I think, therefore, that in all probability, at a trifling cost, the water which now makes this tract of country valueless, might be drained from off it, and stored up in tanks for irrigation, and that in a few years we might see that which is now a barren plain standing thick with rice crops, as valuable as those of Jeytalpoor Kharree villages, and paying a heavy revenue.[54]

The writer is Captain C. J. Prescott, Superintendent of Revenue Survey and Assessment for the province of Goozerat (hereafter, Gujarat). Following the prescribed bureaucratic channel, his settlement report (Report No. 542 of 1862, dated December 31, Camp Bhullada) with recommendations for tax levies reaches J. W. Hadow, Collector of Kaira. Hadow's response, roughly three weeks later (Report No. 77 of 1863, dated January 23, Mehmoodabad) is meticulous. He disagrees with Prescott on several fronts, including Prescott's diagnosis of the Limbashee-Chanor tract. He writes in the distanced, authorizing third person:

> As regards the tract of land noticed in this paragraph as at present a barren waste, the Collector, who has been over nearly the whole of

it, much doubts whether any benefit would result from any attempt
made to reclaim or improve it. It forms, the Collector believes, a
portion of an extensive salt marsh, now nearly dried up in the fair
season, but during the rains a dismal swamp which was originally
covered by the sea or under sea water during the high spring
tides. . . . The soil of this tract appears to be thoroughly impregnated
with a kind of salt termed by the natives "Khar," which, as soon
as the ground dries, finds its way to the surface, and covers it in
patches—what Captain Prescott describes—a "white efflorescence,"
presenting an appearance, in parts, of ground covered with the
hoariest sprinkling of snow. There can be no doubt of the tendency
of the "Khar" to encroach on the adjoining lands, and it might prove
advantageous to adopt measures to present *this* at least, if it be not
considered advisable to try the experiment of reclaiming a portion.[55]

Let's make the land productive by draining excess water and channeling it to
irrigation tanks, where it can be confined and discharged in a more controlled
manner, suggests Prescott. No, says Hadow, the land can't be redeemed, but
the movement of salt poses a threat to adjoining agricultural lands, so let's
focus on confining the salt. Hadow concedes, however, that the more general
problem of poor drainage in the subdistrict—identified by Prescott as one
of the chief causes of rainwater stagnation and the "excessively unhealthy"
state of Matar—is an issue of urgent concern. With Prescott, he applauds
the efforts of the late Mr. Jordan, who, as Deputy Collector of Ahmedabad,
planned out and implemented a system of drains in Matar between the
years 1831 and 1840, "with great skill, and at a very low cost." He endorses
Prescott's conclusion that the "immediate effect of this measure was, not
only . . . that the district became much healthier, but that the revenue rose
considerably, remissions greatly decreased, and the cultivators began rapidly
to accumulate wealth."[56] *Channeling is an economy of government.* But now,
thirty years later, the drains are filling up and are in need of "thorough repair"
under the oversight of a "competent Engineer." *Expertise, the channeling of
information, is an economy of knowledge.*

Hadow's report makes its way to B. H. Ellis, Revenue Commissioner
for the Northern Districts of Gujarat, who responds, again with great
alacrity. Within a fortnight, he writes back to Hadow:

The important subject of drainage, discussed in Captain Prescott's
12th and following paragraphs, demands early attention. A copy of
his remarks, and of the portion of your memorandum relating to
them, will be forwarded to Colonel Bell, with a request that he will

direct the Executive Engineer to survey the country next season, and ascertain what works are required to secure the stability of the revenue and the healthiness of the districts. I hope that an officer will shortly be appointed to the exclusive charge of the Kaira districts, and the drainage of this district should be one of the first objects to engage his attention.[57]

Why did I choose to follow this particular thread of the exchange, on drainage, from the original settlement report for Matar Taluka? Perhaps it is because the Limbashee-Chanor tract that is the object of concern for Prescott, Hadow, and more distantly, Ellis, is an intimately familiar landscape, one that I have trudged across several times. Time is "folded, wadded up," says Michel Serres, "it develops more like the flight of Verlaine's wasp than along a line, continuous and regularly broken by dialectical war," such that when a person "comes to rest on a spot, he sometimes finds himself far off but also sometimes very close to foreignness."[58] And so it occasionally feels, when I walk the area on visits to Matar, as if in the company of Prescott and Hadow, as if the vector of history never was. The tract still exudes a whitish hue from the patches of salt that encrust the soil. Some patches are so thick that they have congealed into a hard pan where agriculture of any sort is impossible. (The construction of a huge pond for the storage of drinking water in the village of Pariyej, on the southwestern corner of the Limbashee-Chanor tract, has raised the area's groundwater level and further aggravated the problem of salinization. I discuss this further in chapter 3).

But the salt layer is uneven; and here and there, where it is lighter, a good initial monsoon can wash away the surface salt, allowing farmers to plant this shallow bowl-like terrain with rice. So Prescott was right in one sense: the tract in question will support rice cultivation. But his optimism was misplaced. When rice does grow it is rarely so well that the "barren plain" is transformed into one "standing thick with rice crops, as valuable as those of Jeytalpoor Kharree villages," as predicted in his report of December 31, 1862.[59]

The concerns of revenue officers like Prescott, Hadow, and Ellis regarding drainage, or of the two judges—Arnould and Asusse— regarding the licentious behavior of the Vallabhacharya Maharajas are, as I want to show, interwoven and overdetermined instances of the discourse of "waste" that foreshadows the problematic of development.

Figure 1. Salinized tract between Limbasi and Chanor, 2004.

Waste and Value

My reading of governmentality is motivated in part by an early and peculiar obsession of empire, and one that percolated into its later phases, albeit with diminished moral fervor: namely, the problem of waste.[60] A short biography of this idea provides an anatomical peek into colonial rule: its imperative to generate revenue and spur commerce and capitalist production, its fixation on character and conduct, and its relentless manufacture of knowledge—erecting what John Stuart Mill was to call a "government of record," as if the strangeness of India could be domesticated by sheer volume of empirical data.[61]

But let's begin in the present, with a dictionary. The *Oxford English Dictionary* furnishes the following catalog of negatives for the noun "waste": unusable or unwanted material; a large area of barren, typically uninhabited land; land that is desolate, empty, cheerless, monotonous, useless, uncultivated, or unproductive. The verb "to waste" fares little better: to waste is to use carelessly, extravagantly, or to no purpose; fail to make full or good use of; to damage, destroy, squander, discard, dissipate, fritter away, or let lapse. A wastrel is a wasteful or worthless person and, in informal usage, a "waster" is a person who does little or nothing of value. Waste is, of course, the specter that haunts value, the latter to be understood, as I have mentioned, as both the elusive linchpin of classical political economy leading up to Marx and in its normative sense as template for moral conduct. In fact, it takes little to surmise that the colonial discourse around "waste" was substantially a theory of value whose effects were to cast in sharp relief the physical infirmity and cultural inferiority of Indians, thereby clearing ground for a permanent colonial presence and, equally vital, for development as the answer to liberalism's imperial contradictions.

Standard economic histories of British rule in India have tended either to pass over the question of waste altogether or treat it as a relatively innocuous sideshow in land settlement debates. There is no doubt that land revenue generation was a constant imperative for the British and an especially urgent one in the initial phase of self-financing Company rule. So it is not surprising that this has induced a temptation to understand waste as merely a revenue category designating tracts of land that were not generating taxes for the exchequer, or were doing so poorly. But this narrow rendering of "waste" is a serious mistake in my estimation. As a concept, "waste" tersely condenses an entire early history of liberalism, most significantly the articulation of seventeenth-century "natural rights" liberalism (of John Locke and his followers) with the eighteenth- and nineteenth-century political economy liberalism (of Adam Smith and his interlocutors)—a joining of such force that its effects continue to set the parameters for policy debates today.[62]

On what basis can such a strong claim be sustained? The answer requires a return to 1812, the year when the East India Company's Court of Directors in London issued its *Fifth Report on East India Affairs*.[63] One of the most significant policy documents in the history of Company Raj, the *Fifth Report* marked a decisive shift away from Cornwallis's Bengal system of *zamindari* settlement and an endorsement of Thomas Munro's alternative Madras system of *ryotwari* settlement. The principal difference between the two lay in the nature of the settlement. Under *zamindari*, a superordinate category of landlords and tax farmers, lumped together as zamindars, were recognized as final proprietors at the expense of multiple layers of subordinate rights holders, including direct producers (who were granted the nominal legal protection of a rent ceiling—a limit on how much zamindars could extract from them; a gesture that was meaningless in the absence of formal records of subordinates' rights and of means to enforce them). In ideology and institutional form, the Permanent Settlement in Bengal was "a frank attempt to apply the English Whig philosophy of government," whose ultimate footing lay in the political philosophy of Locke and his identification of landed property as the kernel of political society. Locke, of course, held this out as a universal principle and, as we have seen, had no compunctions in justifying colonial settlements and seizures of native lands in America on the basis of his moral-political doctrine.

"[G]overnment has no other end but the preservation of property"[64]— this touchstone of Whig ideology, in practical terms, meant reducing the function of government to the bare necessary task of ensuring the security of person and property through an overarching system of laws (homegrown in Britain but displaced as universally true). This principle of minimal intervention took on a curious form in India; on the one hand, it meant a hands-off policy toward local customs, traditions, and systems of justice; on the other hand, it sought to graft an imported and abstract legal apparatus on top of these. It was, in effect, a system of double government. As to the issue of "permanence," this lay in the intent expressed in the Bengal Code of Regulations of 1793 to fix the *jumma* (revenue assessment) for the duration of a zamindar's lifetime,[65] on the grounds that this expectation of stability was crucial in inducing the landowner to make "improvements in agriculture which are essential to their own welfare as to the prosperity of the state."[66]

In contrast to the Bengal system, Munro's Madras system *(ryotwari)* challenged the legitimacy to ownership of superordinate classes and instead proposed a direct settlement with the land's cultivators *(ryots)*. Whereas Cornwallis, an aristocrat, drew his administrative ideas from Whig doctrine, Munro grew up in bourgeois circumstances and his ascent to fame within colonial administration was accidental rather than destined. Munro's views on the form of settlement that ought to be implemented in Madras Province were most heavily influenced, it seems, by his experiences as a military campaigner and administrator in South India and less so by doctrines such as Utilitarianism. Eric Stokes is probably correct, however, in suggesting that Munro's proclivity for Romantic ideals led him to be sympathetic to the "noble peasant" and to rule by "a paternal and simple government" of a kind that would have been inconceivable to Cornwallis.[67]

The administrative differences between the zamindari and ryotwari settlements were undoubtedly large (the latter, for instance, demanded a laborious land survey and investigation into the ownership rights of individual plots as a prerequisite to implementation); and so, too, it might seem, were their philosophical divisions. The extent to which the Bengal system favored large landowners over small cultivators was clearly more contiguous with prevailing Whig doctrine of society in England. On the other hand, there was room for argument that the Madras system favoring ryots or direct producers was more strictly consistent with the original property rights doctrine of Locke, with its emphasis on the mixing of labor with nature as the rudimentary act that establishes property. Moreover, there was a plasticity to Utilitarianism that made it compatible with both forms of settlement: Cornwallis and his supporters of the zamindari settlement could plausibly argue that their emphasis on minimal government and rule of law was a faithful rendition of Utilitarian principles (inaugurated in Locke, elaborated by Beccaria, and systematized through Bentham) to achieve the greatest happiness or welfare for the greatest number. Contrarily, those in favor of Munro's ryotwari scheme could assert that by ignoring the rights of immediate cultivators and leaving tenants and other subclaimants unprotected the zamindari settlement in fact endorsed the privileges of a few at the expense of the many in a manner quite antithetical to the spirit of Utilitarianism.[68]

Whatever the administrative and partisan differences between the two systems, on one key issue they were alike: each perceived the problem of waste in the colonized territories of India with grave concern. Writing in 1894, just a little over hundred years after the Permanent Settlement in Bengal, the British historian W. W. Hunter underscored the critical but nebulous influence of waste in that policy in these words: "Even in regard to the all-important question of Waste Lands, whose vast extent and difficulties of reclamation determined both Cornwallis and the Court of Directors [of the East India Company] to declare the Settlement permanent, the area was absolutely unknown in any District."[69] The oddness of this statement is obvious: on the one hand it is able to claim with apparent conviction that the extent of waste lands in Bengal was enormous, on the other it nonchalantly states that the actual area was unknown. Is this simply an instance of sloppy logic? If so, how is one to account for Cornwallis's claim from 1789 that one-third of the Company's territories lay "waste"?[70] After all, the information in existing land registers, inherited from prior rulers of Bengal, was considered unreliable, and Cornwallis did not have access to the results of a new land survey. These impressionistic remarks were able to carry their degree of conviction, I suggest, precisely because they were generated by a network of premises that had already rendered "India" as an object in imagination. The summoning of magnitudes was a rhetorical sleight-of-hand; shorthand, as it were, for what was already known—the immeasurable cultural difference separating the British from the Bengalis.[71] In short, colonial empiricism exemplified Kant's critique of Hume, in that sense data—and statements that claim their basis in "brute facts"—are never free of presuppositions.[72]

When and where did the concept of waste emerge? The *Oxford English Dictionary* traces the word's origin to the Latin *vastus* meaning "unoccupied, uncultivated," and its entry into Middle English via Old Northern French. Its enrollment as a political-juridical concept, as best as I can gauge, dates to the late thirteenth century, when it was invoked, according to C. Reinhold Noyes, as a curb on the usufruct rights of tenants. Noyes writes:

> At first the tenant had the "right to use and abuse the land, to cultivate it or leave it uncultivated, to keep all others off it. . . ." In fact he had an almost absolute Austinian right of user—"a general, indefinite right of using it as he pleases." Nevertheless, actions for waste, while probably new, were brought. In the course of time, "just as the law gave specific relief if the lord ejected his tenant, so the same relief was granted if the tenant used his land in a manner inconsistent with the nature of the interest granted." . . . By the end of the 13th century it was settled that the tenant for years must keep the premises in repair.[73]

Thus, the juridical doctrine of waste rolls back the customary protections of tenants, granting manorial lords more of a say in their tenants' uses of time and space. Noyes notes, furthermore, that under this new doctrine those who have interests in an object are enjoined to keep its "aggregate value" intact. In this manner, waste is witness to its political birth as a disciplinary technology. It persists in this form through the political and philosophical turbulence of the intervening centuries until the seventeenth century, when it is reactivated as a moral category in the enormously influential writings of John Locke. Locke, as we have seen, articulated a moral-political ideology that defended the virtues of individual labor, the sanctity of property acquired by mixing labor with objects, and the natural rights of individuals; he relegated the state to the limited role of regulation and securing of men's property.[74] These stipulations, which were to become the founding premises of Whig and Utilitarian liberalism in the following century, not only established the inseparability (and patriarchy) of freedom and property but also sanctioned how that property was to be used.

> [W]hatsoever he tilled and reaped, laid up and made use of before it spoiled, that was his peculiar right; whatsoever he enclosed and could feed and make use of, the cattle and product was also his. But if either the grass of his enclosure rotted on the ground, or the fruit of his planting perished without gathering and laying up, this part of the earth, notwithstanding his enclosure, was still to be looked on as waste and might be the possession of any other.[75]

We observe in Locke's words a continuation of the thirteenth-century doctrine of waste. He recodes this claim as a moral injunction with a suppleness of logic that is audacious:

> God commanded, and his [man's] wants forced, him to labor. That was his property which could not be taken from him wherever he had fixed it. And hence subduing or cultivating the earth and having dominion, we see, are joined together. The one gave title to the other. So that God, by commanding to subdue, gave authority so far to appropriate; and the condition of human life which requires labor and material to work on necessarily introduces private possessions.[76]

And from here, Locke, despite being trapped within an older grid of sovereignty, is nevertheless able to transport us to the doorsteps of the yet-to-be-inaugurated diagram of governmentality.

> [N]umbers of men are to be preferred to largeness of dominions; and . . . the increase of lands and the right employing of them is the great art of government; and that prince who shall be so wise and godlike as by established laws of liberty to secure protection and encouragement to the honest industry of mankind, against the oppression of power and narrowness of party, will quickly be too hard for his neighbors; but this by the bye.[77]

What Locke develops in the slender *Second Treatise* is nothing less than the essence of both good government and what it means to be "human"; namely, to labor, to exert industry, and to improve nature lying "waste."

Anything less is to abdicate on the wishes of God and to put in question the rights that individuals are entitled to within political society.[78] In this stunning formulation, to be recognized as a political human is to labor, to exert industry, and to improve—add value to—nature lying idle or waste.

But if personal labor is, in fact, the fount of property, how does Locke justify the property rights of manorial lords and other categories of superior holders? Here, the unthought of Locke's thought—the conditions of its emergence—stands exposed. At one point in the *Second Treatise,* he writes that "different degrees of industry were apt to give men possessions in different proportions, so [the] invention of money gave the opportunity to continue and enlarge them."[79] One possible inference here is that Locke is offering a justification for inequalities in the distribution of wealth and the status quo on the grounds that it is a natural outcome of commerce, which is driven by a sense of industry, facilitated by money, and enabled by original labor. This is a tepid defense of bourgeois wealth,[80] let alone aristocratic privilege. More telling is this assertion:

> We see in commons, which remain so by compact, that it is the taking any part of what is common and removing it out of the state of nature leaves it in which begins the property, without which the common is of no use [it is "waste"]. And the taking of this or that part does not depend on the express consent of all the commoners. Thus the grass my horse has bit, the turfs *my servant has cut,* and the ore I have digged in any place where I have a right to them in common with others, become my property without assignation or consent of anybody. The *labor was mine,* removing them out of that common state they were in, has fixed my property in them.[81]

Here, what should rightfully be the servant's—if Locke is to be consistent in his argument that the basis of property lies in one's own labor—is elided by rendering the servant as a *mere placeholder* for the master: the servant's labor doesn't count! In this slip lies revealed the ideological edifice of Locke's philosophy and why liberalism, the political ideology he foreshadowed, dovetails so well with capitalism. Locke is the protocapitalist thinker par excellence.

I previously said in this chapter that it was Adam Smith who, unknowingly, became the chain of mediation between diverse social forces and made possible the transition to governmental power in Britain.[82] Smith's economic theories, along with those of Thomas Malthus (at the time, Chair in Political Economy at the East India Company's Haileybury College), were the principal influences on David Ricardo's 1817 *On the Principles of Political Economy and Taxation*. In addition to the curriculum at Haileybury, we have the direct line of descent to land taxation policies in India through James Mill, who, in 1819, came to occupy the highly influential position of Assistant Examiner for the India Correspondence at East India House, and was an ardent proponent of Ricardo's ideas concerning rent. According to William Barber, Mill foresaw a surgical intervention by government that would remove the "immense barriers to the natural interplay of market forces" that had been erected by traditional society: "Through the implementation of the scientific tax, the market would be perfected. Simultaneously, the state would be assured of the revenues required to ensure security to person and property and to guarantee incorruptibility in the administrative and judicial systems. The resulting structure, in turn, would activate unused potential in the private sector."[83]

The presence of Smith and Ricardo is obvious in this line of reasoning. But also palpable are the specters of François Quesnay and Jeremy Bentham. Whereas Smith's writings provided the suture between governmental power and the fetal problematic of "development,"[84] and Ricardo's were decisive in supplanting a theory of value grounded in exchange with one grounded in the producing activity of labor,[85] the theories of the French physiocrats Mirabeau and Quesnay linked a notion of "surplus product" to the accumulation of wealth in society.[86] Philip Francis, author of the Plan of 1776, which was the (ultimately, under-acknowledged) precursor to the 1793 Permanent Settlement in Bengal, was, like Adam Smith, an admirer of physiocratic views.

> Land, according to the physiocrats, is the source of all wealth. Their theory of value is based on an analysis of agricultural production in which, much more than in industry, the difference between the value of labor power and value created by its use appears in its most tangible form. It is this difference, the *produit net*, which is the surplus appropriated by the owner of land as rent. The physiocrats claimed to have invented the mechanism which in their ideal society would ensure the reproduction of this surplus and its correct distribution. The

social philosophy upon which this doctrine implicitly rested "consisted in placing above everything else private property, especially property in land."[87]

In this formulation "waste" lurks silently as the abject of "value." Whereas Locke had advanced a labor theory of property (*not* value), the physiocrats formulated the prototype for a labor theory of surplus value (which Ricardo was to appropriate) in defense of an agrarian capitalist order.[88] With agriculture theoretically established as the bulwark of society and progress, Mirabeau, in his *La Philosophie Rurale*, was to proclaim: "Agriculture is a manufacture of divine institution in which the manufacturer has as his partner the Author nature [and co-author, labor], the Producer of all goods and all wealth."[89] And so the semiotic equation of "waste land" with the "irrational" is quietly but irrefutably cemented. How can a rational society allow land to lie underutilized or idle?

Finally, there remains the issue of Bentham's contribution to the congealing discourse of waste that was to exert such a tall shadow on colonial policies in India. His influence was indirect, but arguably the one that has extended the longest into India's postcolonial era. Writing around the same time as Quesnay and Smith, Bentham rendered visible the image of a state that would commit itself to the positive tasks of "police"—indeed, where its sole raison d'être would be police guided by the Greatest Happiness Principle.[90] This is clearly articulated in *A Fragment on Government,* where he writes:

> Now, then, with respect to actions in general, there is no property in them that is so calculated so readily to engage, and so firmly to fix the attention of the observer, as the *tendency* they have *to,* or divergency (if one may say so) *from,* that which may be styled the common end of all of them. The end I mean is *Happiness:* and this *tendency* in any act is what we style its *utility:* as this *divergency* is that to which we give the name of *mischievousness.* . . .
>
> From *utility* then we may denominate a *principle,* that may serve to preside over and govern, as it were, such arrangement as shall be made of several institutions or combinations of institutions that compose the matter of this science: and it is this principle, that by putting its stamp upon the several names given to those combinations, can alone render *satisfactory* and *clear* any arrangement that can be made of them.[91]

It is well known that Bentham's own political views—that is to say, his deployment of the principle of "greatest good for the greatest number"—went from a defense of Whig paternalism in his heydays to an advocacy of radical democracy by the 1820s (he died in 1832). The codifications of his ideology by his self-professed disciples is, however, an entirely different matter.[92] I showed above that as an "-ism" the principle of utility maximization was innately plastic: it lent itself equally well to supporters of the Bengal zamindari system as well as its detractors who put their weight behind the Madras ryotwari system. Although the latter was to win out after 1812, this was mostly a matter of indifference with regard to the question of waste because both systems ultimately occupied the same discourse, one that was comfortable taking an impressionistic spatial image (to which it blithely attached magnitudes) and turning it into a general conclusion about "native" character. Alexander Dow, who wrote the three-volume *The History of Hindostan* in 1770, was able to sum up the nature of India's inhabitants in one word: "indolent."[93] Robert Orme, who was employed as a historiographer with the East India Company, asserted in his 1782 treatise *Of the Government and People of Indostan:* "Confirmed in his contempt of a pusillanimity and an incapacity for resistance, suggested to him by their physiognomy and form, it is well if he [the European] recollects that the poor Indian is still a man."[94] Possibly influenced by these astute observations, James Grant, one of the indirect architects of the Permanent Settlement, offered this lament about the state of finances in Bengal:

> Taking all the ground in tillage [in Bengal] in the course of the year, to be 35 million of the small ryotty begas [bighas: a unit of land], of which perhaps, *from the constitutional indolence of the inhabitants, only one-third is in actual cultivation during each of the three seasons,* khereef [monsoon], rubbi [winter], and bhadovy [summer], we may reckon for every 25 begas of the whole, one laboring farmer or ploughman, who with a family of five persons, male and female of all ages, will make the aggregate of peasantry, including manufacturers to be eight million four hundred thousand, in a total population of 10 million souls allowed to the soubah [province] entire. The gross product of the land, with the labor performed in different degrees *by such a body of people . . . cannot reasonably* be estimated . . . at a greater rate than 6 rupees per bega, amounting in all to 21 krore of rupees.[95]

In Grant's remarks, we can observe the operation of discourse as a network of linked statements: one precept—"constitutional indolence" that breeds "waste"—standing in, metonymically, for another that goes unnamed—"lack of ability" or "deficiency of reason." On numerous occasions, John Shore, who was closely involved in the deliberations that led up to the Bengal settlement as a member of the Governor General's Supreme Council in Calcutta, dredged up the trope of Oriental despotism that had entered European discourses by 1746 with the publication of Baron de Montequieu's opus, *L'Esprit des lois (The Spirit of Laws)*.[96] Commenting on Bengal's zamindars, a class he clearly mistrusted but eventually agreed to support in the 1793 settlement as the putative vanguard of an agrarian capitalist transformation, Shore declared:

> If a review of the zemindars in Bengal were made, it would be found that very few are duly qualified for the management of their hereditary lands; and that, in general, they are ill-educated for this task; ignorant of the common forms of business . . . ; inattentive of the conduct of it. . . . [T]hey have been decried as an useless, idle, oppressive race, practicing every species of extortion, or countenancing it by their inactivity and ignorance.[97]

In that same minute, he went on to assert that "[a] property in soil, must not be understood to convey the same rights in India, as in England; the difference is as great as between constitution and arbitrary power. Nor are we to expect under a despotic government fixed principles or clear definitions of the rights of the subject."[98] This line of reasoning was carried one step further by James Grant and John Shore in their reviews of land settlements implemented in Bengal subsequent to the reign of the Mughal emperor, Akbar. They noted that the original assessment *(assul)* of Toori Mal, dating back to 1582, had multiplied several times in the intervening two hundred years due to, they argued, layers of arbitrary taxes *(abwab)* imposed by the avaricious rulers who followed. And this, it was reasoned, simply compounded the disincentives to cultivation and agricultural investment generated in the first place by the absence of well-defined and secure property rights. How else, after all, was one to explain the large numbers of temporary *(paikasht)* tenants in Bengal? This population of temporary cultivators, in their telling, was mobile rather than sedentary because, given the despotic features of rule in

Bengal, it made sense for them to travel from one zamindari to another in search of low rents. But lacking long-term interest in a fixed plot of land, they failed to apply themselves in cultivation and left in their wake a trail of waste.

Like all discourses, there were discontinuities and fissures within the colonial discourse of waste. Hence, while Shore was decrying the zamindars of Bengal, his superior Lord Cornwallis, in a minute recorded three months to the day after Shore's derisory minute, could assert it was "for the interest of the State, that the landed property should fall into the hands of the most frugal and thrifty class of people, who will improve their lands . . . and thereby promote the general prosperity of the country." Cornwallis was referring to the zamindars. How were they to be made "frugal and thrifty"? Cornwallis had the answer. In that same minute (once again contradicting Shore), he opined that the wasteful "habit which the zamindars have fallen into . . . has originated not in any constitutional imperfection in the people themselves, but in the fluctuating measures of government."[99] The implication was straightforward: Eliminate inconstancies in government and the bad habits will disappear. This chain of thought, that proper human behavior was principally a matter of "good administration," echoed the core beliefs of both Whig philosophy and Benthamite Utilitarianism. Thus, the trope of waste came to dramatize the difference/distance that separated Europe from India. We feel its trace in James Mill's colorful denunciation of Hindu civilization in his massive *The History of British India:*

> The Hindu is a sort of a sensitive plant. His imagination and passions are easily inflamed; and he has a sharpness and quickness of intellect which seems strongly connected with the sensibility of his outward frame. Another remarkable circumstance in the character of the Hindus; in part, too, no doubt, the effect of corporeal weakness, though an effect in some sort opposite to that excitability which we have immediately remarked, is the inertness of disposition, with which all men have been so forcibly struck in observing the conduct of this peculiar race. The love of repose reigns in India with more powerful sway, than in any other region probably of the globe. "It is more happy to be seated than to walk; it is more happy to sleep than to awake; but the happiest of all is death." Such is one of the favourite sayings, most frequently in the mouths of this listless tribe, and most descriptive of their habitual propensities. Phlegmatic indolence pervades the nation.[100]

Postscript

Time can fold back on itself. The specter of waste continues to haunt capitalist desire. In 2001, the fear of "phlegmatic indolence" made a return. To commemorate the "liberation" of "the present-day Indian reader ... by recent economic reforms" that were enabling this reader "to pursue free enterprise and be self-driven to ensure a better quality of life for the individual in particular and society in general" the New Delhi–based Liberty Institute published an abridged version of Samuel Smiles's 1859 best-seller, *Self-Help: With Illustrations of Conduct and Perseverance.*[101] The imagination does not have to struggle too hard to surmise who its present-day Indian reader might be. Writing the foreword to the abridged edition, Gurcharan Das (ex-CEO of Proctor & Gamble, India, and himself the best-selling author of *India Unbound*), celebrates the rags-to-riches story of Narayana Murthy, founder and CEO of the software firm Infosys, which has become an icon of India's post-reform transformation. "Every nation must have its heroes," says Das—and who better than Murthy, who epitomizes Samuel Smiles' s injunction of self-help?[102]

Smiles's book, a Victorian manual of right conduct—the art of self-government—was an assemblage of homilies that echo the tropes of colonial liberalism. In chapter 1 ("Self-Help—National and Individual"), we read:

> National progress is the sum of individual industry, energy, and uprightness, as national decay is of individual idleness, selfishness, and vice. What we are accustomed to decry as great social evils, will, for the most part, be found to be only the outgrowth of our own perverted life; and though we may endeavor to cut them down and extirpate them by means of law, they will only spring up again with fresh luxuriance in some other form, unless the conditions of human life and character are radically improved. If this view be correct, then it follows that the highest patriotism and philanthropy consist, not so much in altering laws and modifying institutions, as in helping and stimulating men to elevate and improve themselves by their own free and independent action.
>
> This spirit of self-help, as exhibited in the energetic action of individuals, has in all times been a marked feature in the English character, and furnishes the true measure of our power as a nation.

Chapter 3 ("Application and Perseverance") follows with this:

> To wait patiently [for progress], however, men must work cheerfully. Cheerfulness is an excellent working quality, imparting great elasticity

to the character. As a bishop has said, "Temper is nine tenths of Christianity;" so are cheerfulness and diligence nine tenths of practical wisdom. They are the life and soul of success, as well as of happiness; perhaps the very highest pleasure in life consisting in clear, brisk, conscious working; energy, confidence, and every other good quality mainly depending upon it.

And, then, in chapter 7 ("Energy and Courage"):

A man's character is seen in small matters; and from even so slight a test as the mode in which a man wields a hammer, his energy may in some measure be inferred. Thus an eminent Frenchman hit off in a single phrase the characteristic quality of the inhabitants of a particular district, in which a friend of his proposed to settle and buy land. "Beware," said he, "of making a purchase there; I know the men of that department; the pupils who come from it to our veterinary school at Paris, *do not strike hard upon the anvil;* they want energy; and you will not get a satisfactory return on any capital you may invest there." A fine and just appreciation of character, indicating the accurate and thoughtful observer; and strikingly illustrative of the fact that it is the energy of the individual men that gives strength to a state, and confers a value even upon the very soil which they cultivate. As the French proverb has it: *"Tant vaut l'homme, tant vaut sa terre."*

Twenty-first-century India is not the only destination to which Samuel Smiles has traveled. In 1886, with the help of translators, he could be found in Egypt at the Self-Help Society, providing Egyptians helpful advice on how best to overcome their character defects.[103] He was also in Bombay in 1867. Remember Karsandas Mulji, the fearless social reformer we met at the start of this chapter? Samuel Smiles was his favorite author.

CHAPTER TWO

Birth

Original Sin

I had finally convinced Haribhai Bansibhai Patel to give me a tour of the Patel *khadkis*[1] in the sprawling village of Ambodi.[2] This took some convincing because Haribhai now lives with his three brothers and their joint family on the outskirts of Ambodi, in an imposing two-story cement house. They had moved to the house in 1987, he said, to get away from the congestion and filth *(gandgi)* of the main village. Haribhai gestured around him as we walked through the dank, narrow lanes of the khadki, packed tightly with two-hundred-year-old stone-and-brick houses and the ripe smell of open sewage, as if to make me appreciate why it had been so necessary for him and his brothers to relocate. I reminded myself that Veblen's ghost was alive and well in Kheda, that the desire to make a public statement about achieved status, an important consideration among well-to-do rural families—but especially, it seems, the Patels—was probably the more compelling reason for the move. After all, the shit-clogged toilets and open drains of Haribhai's new home were hardly models of hygiene. But I kept silent as Haribhai continued the tour. He pointed out their old house in the khadki—a solid, darkly lit, two-room place—now rented to a distant relative's son. I was told that these days several houses in the khadki were either rented or lying empty, their owners living in Ahmedabad, Baroda, Nadiad, or Bombay, or, in many instances, the United Kingdom and the United States of America. Families within a khadki are regarded as descendants from a common ancestor and are forbidden from intermarrying. But Haribhai could not

Figure 2. Patel *agevans* (notables) at the Narsanda home of Professor Ambalal S. Patel (center), author of *Badlaatu Gaam (Changing Village)*, a biography of Narsanda.

resist telling me about a recent scandal where a Patel boy and girl from the khadki had eloped in contravention of caste strictures. (Unlike parts of rural north India where such an act would have almost certainly invited violent retaliation against the couple, the Patels of Ambodi boycotted the couple for a time and then simply accepted their union. Haribhai mentioned this casually, but clearly with the intention of underscoring how civil Patels are in their conduct. A few days earlier I had repeatedly asked him about allegations by Baraiya friends in a nearby village that Patels in Ambodi were a rough bunch, with a reputation of retaliating aggressively against perceived intra- and intercaste infractions. I read Haribhai's remark as an oblique rebuttal of my suspicions.)

Our next scheduled stop was the clothing store in the main market area of Ambodi that is owned by Haribhai's brother, Maganbhai. But I asked if we could first take a quick tour of Ambodi so as to get a sense of its layout. Haribhai was happy to oblige. As we passed from the *vas* (living quarters) of the Patel to that of the Baraiya, cement houses, paved streets, and roadside drainage yielded to a freer mix of mud and cement houses, dirt lanes with pooled water and piles of trash, and drains that sometimes amounted to little more than furrows in the ground. There were considerably more women and children out on the streets. In sharp contrast to the Patel vas, the topography here seemed more fluid, less restrained. The Rohit (chamar) and Harijan (bhangi) vas lie at the back of the village, the former on undulating land that is crisscrossed by narrow paths that are prone to waterlogging and almost impassable in the monsoons. We were told this by an old man who wanted to know who I was. When informed that I was a visitor from America, he pointed at a waterlogged stretch of his lane (this was in early November, well after the end of monsoons) and said to Haribhai: "How many times have we pleaded, the roads are in disrepair, children are constantly bitten by mosquitoes, but does the panchayat do anything? No." The old man's comment was intended as an indirect jab at Patels, who have controlled Ambodi's panchayat since 1954, having held the sarpanch's seat eight of the ten times there have been village elections (the two exceptions were cyclical appointments, mandatory under panchayati raj law, of a woman and a Scheduled Caste sarpanch).

From the Rohit vas we descended into a gulch that served as a connecting path to an old, unpaved village road that once was the main artery between Ambodi and outlying villages to the north, along and beyond the Sabarmati River, in Dholka Taluka. Haribhai told me to step carefully and I saw why: the path was covered with dung and human excrement almost the entire distance—a walk of a half kilometer or so—from the Rohit vas to the Harijan vas. Several young children were squatting by the edge of the path, in a swarm of flies, defecating. Unlike the Rohit vas, there are several single-story cement homes in the Harijan vas. They were built under the Indira Awaas Yojna, a government scheme that is meant to provide suitable housing for the poor. The funds originate in the central government, are supplemented by state contributions, channeled to the jilla (district) panchayat, and flow thereon to the various village panchayats. Seepage losses along the entire administrative route are common and steep (by some estimates, totaling anywhere from 50 to 60 percent of allocated funds). The houses in the Harijan vas were small, densely packed, and poorly ventilated. In many cases, their cement façades were crumbling. They stood in line opposite a putrid nullah, a clogged channel that is supposed to ferry liquid waste out of the village. Haribhai, who was once active in local politics and seemed to be well acquainted with everyone in Ambodi, called out to a Harijan woman washing clothes in her tiny frontyard: "Hoy, sister, this nullah is so dirty, does it carry the water out or not?" She made no reply, merely thrust her face out toward the nullah—as if dismissing the obviousness of the question—and went back to pounding her bundle of clothes. Surveying the squalor around me, I was reminded of a conversation with Haribhai's brother Mrinalbhai in 1997. I had inquired about the economic condition of *dalits* in Ambodi. Mrinalbhai, an ex-schoolteacher, had responded that of all the *asprushya* (unclean) castes in Ambodi, the *bhangis* (Harijans) were the best off because, in his words, even though they now had other sources of income—prostitution among them, he remarked!—they continued to claim their traditional right to receive charity from the higher-caste residents of Ambodi. When I had pressed why upper-caste elites, such as Patels, felt compelled to give alms to Harijans if they now found it so disagreeable, he replied that to not do so would risk being seen as *kanjoos* (miserly) and would invite *sharam* (shame). According to Mrinalbhai, whereas higher-caste groups remained mindful of their obligations to the lower castes, the bhangis, because of their *khoti danat* (wrong or opportunistic disposition), had no qualms about exploiting the upper castes.[3]

Eventually, Haribhai and I arrived at Maganbhai Bansibhai's cloth store. Maganbhai is the youngest of the four brothers in the joint family and the most entrepreneurial. I was keen to know what he thought about the relative affluence of Patels versus the relative poverty of the Thakurs/Baraiyas in Ambodi. I posed this question to him fully aware of a history of past confrontations between the Baraiyas and the Patels, and of the accusations of numerous Baraiyas in Ambodi and elsewhere that Patels (Maganbhai among them) had managed to capture possession of their lands through usurious lending practices and subterfuge.

> Magankaka: You see yourself, Vinaybhai, how backward the Thakurs
> are in their social affairs. The earlier generations of thakurs
> squandered their time and money on alcohol and opium.
> The thakur community condoned the use of opium by
> saying it was a social custom rather than a vice *[vesan]*.
> They also waste a lot of money on customs like *mameru*
> [where the sister's brother is expected to give presents and
> sometimes contribute large sums of money to underwrite
> his niece's wedding]. Moreover, the *sasravada* [girl's
> family] feel obligated to present a new set of clothes to the
> *varpaksh* [boy's family] everytime they come for a visit. . . .

[With a laugh] Of course it's good for our business! Look, Vinaybhai, it would take the Thakurs ten thousand years to reach our [the Patels'] level of advancement.

Vinay: Why do you say that?

Magankaka: Do you know Jersey cows? It's like breeding a Jersey calf *[bacchdo]* from a non-Jersey parent. It takes three generations to produce the Jersey calf, but for thakurs to become like us it will take countless generations! Their traditionalism is in their blood *[roodichust'ta thakuron ni lohi ma chhe]*. Their lands have come to us because of their wasteful social expenditures.

Interestingly, Maganbhai had no qualms acknowledging that Patels have been able to dispossess Ambodi's Baraiyas of their lands.[4] But he laid the blame squarely at the feet of the Thakurs. He said nothing, for instance, about how his moneylending business or practices of store credit in return for usufruct rights to land had allowed his family to accumulate property. He implied that the Baraiyas' tendency to squander money on social rituals was the material expression of an innate debility. He paraded a Social Darwinist argument in support of his claims. His allusion to Jersey cows and evolution exploded any facile anthropological claim about the "native" or boundedly "cultural" character of his discourse. We should expect no less because, as I will recount in chapter 4, many Patels explicitly describe themselves as a "modern" caste and reveal, in their self-description and practices, an entanglement with terms that we would commonly associate with Western epistemes. A number of Patels I have talked to over the years are quick to note the economic and social achievements of their caste, which, in turn, they attribute to the fact that Patels are "progressive," "hardworking," able to manage their affairs "rationally" and "intelligently," and quick to adapt to changing circumstances.[5] They commonly cite their mobility across occupations and borders as evidence of this entrepreneurial drive *(saahas)*. Mobility and, more broadly, the willingness to depart from the customary is the contrast that lurks in the Gujarati word *roodichust'ta* that Maganbhai used to characterize the Baraiyas. *Roodichust'ta* literally means adherence to tradition or custom. But it can be read as backwardness (someone who is *rood* is someone who is stuck to outdated modes of behavior, who does not move with the time) or rootedness (implying lack of extralocal mobility). In Maganbhai's comments, roodischust'ta thus comes to signify the localness of work and habitation—circumscribed mobility—that is the mark of inferiority. Slowness in time and limitations of mobility are combined to relay limitations of nature. Maganbhai's story underscored that dispossession *and* the work of political amnesia that forgets this history are the universal marks of class. Karl Marx captured this double move with savage brio in *Capital:*

> [P]rimitive accumulation plays approximately the same role in political economy as original sin does in theology. Adam bit the apple, and thereupon sin fell on the human race. Its origin is supposed to be explained when it is told as an anecdote about the past. Long, long ago there were two sorts of people; one, the diligent, intelligent and above all frugal elite; the other, lazy rascals, spending their substance, and more, in riotous living. The legend of theological sin tells us certainly how man came to be condemned to eat his bread in the sweat of his brow; but the history of economic original sin reveals to us that there are people to whom this is by no means essential. Never mind! Thus it came to pass that the former sort accumulated wealth, and the latter sort finally had nothing to sell except their own skins. And from this original sin dates the poverty of the great majority, who, despite all their labor, have up to now nothing to sell but themselves, and the wealth of the few that increases constantly, although they have long ceased to work. Such insipid childishness is every day preached to us in the defence of property.[6]

The Lewa Patels of central Gujarat—particularly from the region known as the Charotar[7]—are a global diaspora and one of the most visible and affluent caste groups in India. A recent history of the Lewa Patels commissioned by the Charotar Patidar Kutumb in London is suggestive of how an influential segment of the Patel community views itself:

> The *Leva Patidars of Charotar* have been closely associated with agriculture from ancient times right up to the 20th century. . . . According to the *Varna* model, the *Leva Patidars of Charotar* belong to the *vaishya* section of society as their ancestors farmed land and belonged to the cultivator caste *Kanbi* (or *Kurmi*) meaning "one who cultivates land." The word "*Kanbi*" is thought to be derived from the word *Kutumbin* (meaning family). The word *Kutumbin* is still used to describe extended family relationships. In the past, the *Leva Patidar* community has claimed both *Kshatriya* and *Vaishya* status in society based on the services performed against unreasonable land

revenue demands during both the Muslim (1307–1757 A.D.) and Maratha (1758–1818 A.D.) periods in Gujarat. The basis of continued allegiance to the *Vaishya Varna* came from owning agricultural land and cultivating cash crops for trade during the late Maratha and British (1818–1947 A.D.) periods in Gujarat. In modern times, the main occupation of the *Leva Patidar* community is in small businesses, the professions or employment in "white collar" jobs so the allegiance remains with the *Vaishya Varna.*[8]

How did the Lewa Patels emerge in this putatively sociological form, and to what extent does sociology translate into what Antonio Gramsci calls "corporatism" (a collective consciousness that is *for-itself*)? In contrast to conventional approaches to caste in India— namely, caste as structural expression of a ritual hierarchy of purity (Louis Dumont's thesis); caste as a cognate of race (G. S. Ghurye's thesis); caste as the cultural expression of class (the Marxist thesis, associated with scholars like Gerald Berreman); or caste as crystallized product of colonial representation (Nicholas Dirk's argument)—my argument here is that the Patel caste is an overdetermined entity, enabled by historically and geographically contingent articulations of class, gender, political, and religious elements. I show the manner in which nature, colonial land settlement policies, and political and economic transformations among Kanbi and Patidar class fractions intersected with hypergamous marriage practices to produce a geographically ordered Patel caste with a distinct regulative aesthetics (that I discuss in chapter 4). I draw on both secondary and archival sources to show that Patels constitute (and have long been) a "ruptural unity": an achieved hegemonic alliance always multiple and always troubled by internal fissures.

But while the Patels are different-in-themselves, they have acquired a reputation of acting in their corporate interests—often retaliating violently against other, especially lower-caste, groups. This point becomes salient in understanding how perceived erosion of corporate power in the wake of development interventions and agrarian transformations in the post-Independence period has prompted upper-caste groups such as Brahmins, Thakkar and Jain Vanias, and Patels to participate in antireservation and communal mobilizations and to endorse the Hindu normativity of right political parties such as the Janata Party in 1970s and now its ideological descendant, the Bharatiya Janata Party.

Two Deaths for a Territory

If historiography is history fused to "writing that conquers," then it is an operation that has been often activated by death.[9] Take, for example, the year 1800, which was an exceptionally good one for the British East India Company. Two unexpected deaths enabled the Company to extend its control across much of Gujarat. First, the Nawab of Surat died without leaving any heirs, allowing the British to assume exclusive control of Surat and its territories. The rest of Gujarat at the time was divided between two suzerainties, Sindhia and Gaikwad, both in subsidiary alliances to the Maratha Peshwa in Poona. The death of Govindrao Gaikwad, the Maratha chief Baroda that same year created the second window of opportunity for the British. Govindrao's brother Anandrao took the *gadi* (throne) at Baroda but was challenged by his cousin, Malharrao, who was based in Kadi near Ahmedabad. Both factions sent emissaries to Bombay to seek assistance from officials of the Company, and Jonathan Duncan, who was then governor of Bombay, decided to intervene. He chose to support Anandrao of Baroda, who was, in many respects, the weaker side in the dispute but held the key to Gujarat by virtue of his control of Baroda, a city of great commercial, financial, and strategic importance. Baroda's hinterland included the highly productive agricultural tracts of Kheda—a vital consideration for Duncan and his council, who wished to increase the revenues of Bombay Presidency and "extend the trade of individual Company servants who coveted greater influence in the cotton-growing regions of Gujarat."[10] Equally important, though, were the strategic and military considerations. Parts of central Gujarat were under the control of Sindhia, whose "army was commanded in part by able French officers."[11] The French presence in Gujarat, set against the intense military and mercantile rivalry between the Britain and France, must have weighed heavily on Duncan's mind. A third death in 1800, this time of one the last able ministers of the Peshwa Baji Rao, added to the sense of urgency. With the minister's death, struggles between various factions to control the weak Peshwa multiplied within the Maratha Confederacy.

Duncan took action, dispatching a military contingent headed by Major Alexander Walker to Baroda in January 1802, with instructions to give "weight to the British arbitration" and to assume, at the earliest possible opportunity, the civilian role of British Resident at Baroda. In Anandrao, Walker found a ruler who was not only incapable of confronting Malharrao but whose principality was deeply in debt and under the de facto control of moneylenders and powerful bankers known as *potedars*. Mindful of his orders to act expeditiously, Walker led an expedition against Malharrao within weeks. The war began in February and ended in May, with Malharrao's official surrender. On July 11, 1802, Walker reentered Baroda as its first British Resident, marking a new chapter in Gujarat's polity. The Company meantime advanced Anandrao a loan secured against a lien upon the revenues of several *parganas* (subdistricts) in order to pay out the moneylenders and potedars and check their influence over Baroda's affairs.[12]

While these events were unfolding in Baroda, a much larger drama was unfurling in Poona. In 1801, the Peshwa, Baji Rao, had rashly provoked one of his powerful subordinates, Jaswant Rao Holkar, by "having his brother trampled to death beneath an elephant."[13] Intent on revenge, Holkar invaded the Peshwa's territories and in October 1802 captured Poona. Baji Rao fled to Bassein and sought help from the British, who readily obliged—but after concluding a specially designed subsidiary alliance that was formalized as the Treaty of Bassein. The provisions of the treaty—that a force of more than six thousand men commanded by British officers be stationed within the Peshwa's territory in perpetuity, paid for by ceded territories yielding revenues of twenty-six lacs of rupees—reduced the Peshwa from the head of a once-formidable Maratha Confederacy to a client power of an even larger imperial system. The Gaikwad of Baroda was implicated in the treaty as a subsidiary of the Peshwa, and in order fulfill the obligation to underwrite British troops had to cede the parganas of Mahudha, Nadiad, and Matar, along with the town and fort of Kaira (hereafter, Kheda). In 1805, these were administratively assimilated into a new district (*zilla*), Kheda, with H. W. Diggle—previously Walker's Assistant Resident in Baroda—as its first Collector and Magistrate. In 1817, when Montstuart Elphinstone inflicted a final defeat on the Marathas and negotiated the Treaty of Poona, the Gaikwad was compelled to cede additional territory to the British—including the parganas of Mehmedabad and Thasra, half of Petlad (an extremely wealthy pargana), as well as the areas of Alindra and Antroli. All of these were brought under Kheda zilla. The subsequent acquisition of Kapadvanj and Bhalej in exchange for Bijapur in north Gujarat completed the expansion of the Kheda Collectorate.

The Messy Task of Ruling

After formal political control, came the formidable challenge of administration, particularly land revenue administration. Company officials encountered a complex geography of land rights and revenue obligations, neither written down nor based around any systematic principle of assessment. Although several subsequent historians have characterized the revenue administration implemented within Bombay Presidency as a *ryotwari* system[14]—a direct settlement, bypassing intermediaries, between government and individual producer *(ryot)* with rights in a given plot of land—this description belies the untidy and politically expedient nature of revenue administration that took form in Kheda and other parts of the Presidency. Although the Gaikwad—and before him, the Maratha Peshwa and the Mughals—had been able to establish control over portions of Kheda, several villages and tiny self-styled principalities had remained sovereign and defiant. Correspondence between officials in the early years of British rule paints a picture of turbulence. To the south, in the ravinous tract along the Mahi River, numerous villages remained subject to exactions by "Koli" and "Thakur" chieftains, who frequently also raided and robbed travellers attempting to ford the Mahi River. To the north and the west, bordering Ahmedabad, "Rajput," "Koli," and "Garasia" chiefs were said to resist subjugation to superior authority, rule by fear over their subjects, and impose arbitrary cesses upon them. An 1804 report by Henry Diggle to his superior Lieutenant Colonel Walker, the Resident at Baroda, was typical in its appraisal of the prevailing situation:

> [E]very Gracia village is in itself a fortification . . . and every village is surrounded by a mud wall, many of these having in the centre a high stone tower. . . . This is to guard against the attack of their neighbour. Amongst the Gracias it is melancholy to relate the frequency of murders. . . . It is with indifference that the life of a fellow creature is taken as that of any beast of the field. It is a point of honour amongst Gracias to give protection of the perpetrators of the most vile deed, who has deserted his village.[15]

Colonel Walker, on his part, informed the Secretary to the Government of Bombay that as a result of prevailing anarchy in the troubled *(mehwasi)* areas, "the bonds of society [have] been broken" and lands once cultivated had reverted to waste ("a wide and pathless jungle [holds] undisturbed possession of the country"). Elsewhere, he described the "Koolee," "Bheel" and "Garasias"—terms that he used interchangeably and without further specificity—as people who are "thieves by profession, and embrace every opportunity of plundering either public or private property."[16] Lieutenant Colonel P. M. Melville, writing in 1825, noted disparagingly that the rule of the Koli chiefs had "been only that of tyranny and oppression." As discussed in chapter 1, such opinions became increasingly common among colonial administrators in India as the influence of early Orientalists like Robert Clive, Warren Hastings, and William Jones waned within Britain and belief in the superiority of Whig values and institutions took hold. Increasingly, local rulers and inhabitants came to be represented as uncivilized, indolent, arbitrary in their dealings, and not worthy of trust, in polar contrast to the civilized, industrious, and professional conduct of the colonizers. The problem of "waste lands," which so preoccupied Cornwallis and Munro in their settlement operations, was correlated within emergent colonial discourse to the native inhabitants' "lack of character." In those settings where cultivation and revenues appeared to be languishing or performing below expectation—and, with few exceptions, this was almost always the official diagnosis—certain segments of the population such as "coolies," or else their "despotic" rulers, were held culpable for the prevailing state of stagnation. Thus, a politically instituted *relation* of difference was promulgated within colonial knowledge as a sign of Absolute Difference, with consequential effects for agrarian structure and change.

The problematic of development was critical in the production of striated thought and its corresponding geographies. As discussed previously, development valiantly rescued liberalism from its internal contradictions: enabling it to sanction an imperial program of ordered change that would pull the colonized up the ladder of progress, but never so completely that colonized subjects would become self-identical with their rulers and thereby deserving of the same political rights. This prospect of erasure of racial and cultural distance, far too threatening, was asserted out of existence within colonial discourse (especially when confronted with evidence of miscegenation). The category "nature" and its cognates performed double duty in this respect. On the one hand, nature discharged a self-descriptive function for European colonizers as presupposition for their "culture" (hence, nature as the *before* of culture that was nevertheless the necessary premise *after* which and a result of which Europe's modernity could fashion itself). Obversely, nature operated as a disqualifier against the colonized by standing in for those alternatively strange, hostile, errant, and innocent elements, which were not beyond the reach of time (and hence culture) per se, but resistant to the liaison that would produce the "ordered front" of entities that grants development its coherence and power as a continuous upward vector of time.[17]

Like several of his contemporaries, as well as officers who were to participate in Kheda's administration subsequently, Alexander Walker failed to see that the coolies he so disdained might not be a homogenous people at all, but rather an array of differentiated groups with disparate histories and geographies of movement, settlement, and state interactions. Officials at mid-century, who were more finely attuned to social difference (possibly because of the growing practical importance of ethnology in imperial administration), noted signifi-cant differences between Talabda, Baraiya, Chumvalia, and Patanwadia Kolis, particularly the often "expert" agricultural skills of the first two in contrast to the latter. The Superintendent of Revenue Survey and Assessment, Gujarat, Captain C. J. Prescott, who was charged with conducting new revenue survey settlements in the various Talukas of Kheda Collectorate, observed in an 1862 memo pertaining to Matar Taluka that its population "is entirely agricultural, and is principally composed of coolies, although there are great number of koonbies, patidars and Rajpoots, and a good many cultivating Mussulmans. Many of the coolies are nearly as skilful and industrious as koonbies, possess good houses and a great deal of agricultural stock."[18] Later, in another report that was part of the same correspondence, he favorably com-pared the Talabda coolies of Matar to the "thriftless" and "improvident" Chumvalia coolies of Kapadvanj. These distinctions were, of course, self-serving—ethnology as instrument of colonial governmentality. But they do expose the homogenizing impulse of early British admin-istration in Gujarat (exemplified in the persons of Diggle, Morison, Steadman, Walker, and others) where knowledge struggled to stabilize a kinetic landscape of forces.[19]

Indeed, Neil Rabitoy points out that very few of the servants of the Bombay Civil Service appointed to official positions in Gujarat had prior experience of judicial or land revenue administration and "[a]n even smaller number were conversant in Marathi or Gujarati."[20] Most came to depend heavily upon one or more Indians, usually elites from the Maratha bureaucracy, as a source of information. For example, the previously mentioned Henry Diggle "relied heavily upon the services of a locally prominent Indian named Esswant Rao Bappuji, at least until 1809."[21] Similarly, Alexander Walker's conclusions about the *mehwasi* coolies were almost certainly shaped by the native bureaucrats who assisted him in his early administrative initiatives.[22] Not innocuously, they were mostly Brahmins who dominated the Gaikwad administration and who are likely to have been resentful and exasperated at their failure to contain and assimilate the Thakur/Garasia chiefs to Baroda rule.

Even so, as administrators of an ultimately conservative bent, neither Walker nor Jonathan Duncan (the first Governor of Bombay) attempted to confront garasia counterclaims to the Company's power. To the contrary, Walker expressed sympathy for the garasias' attempts to resist subordination by outside powers and even declaimed that they had "special rights." All this was to change in 1812, one of those eventful moments that produces the "past" immanently within the historiographic operation and lends narrative its temporality. That year, Sir Evan Nepean took over as Governor of Bombay from Duncan. Meanwhile, Byrom Rowles had followed Diggles as Collector of Kheda in 1810. Both Nepean and Rowles were committed to a system of direct *(amani)* management by Europeans that would, in the words of Nepean and his Council, remove "a useless and unprofitable race of native officers" and improve the state of the districts. A key ruling by the Board of Control of the East India Company in London in 1812, which officially rejected Corwallis's system of permanent settlements with zamindars and extended support to Thomas Munro's Madras ryotwari system (see chapter 1), was critical in catalyzing the policy of intervention that gripped Bombay Presidency from 1812 to 1819, under Nepean.[23]

Those Wily Patels

The district administrative structure that preceded British rule in Gujarat started with the *Komavisdar*, an imperial appointee of the Maratha confederacy who was entrusted with overall revenue and executive powers. Below him came the *Desais* and the lesser *Amins*, whose jobs were to ensure that state revenues were collected in a timely and orderly manner—either by revenue farmers, called *ijardars*, who annually bid for collection contracts, or by the village-level *Patels*.

The Patels were responsible for both the maintenance of law and order in villages and revenue payments. The Desais and Amins were assisted in their duties by the *Muzmudar,* the head revenue official, whose job was to oversee the performance of *Talatis* (village-level accountants) and to maintain records of land rights and revenues. According to Choksey, "[T]he office of the Patel was hereditary and he was often termed as a *zamindar....* [H]e wielded great influence with the *ryots* and was the trustee of the interest of both the villagers and the Government.... Yet, with all [his] powers, he was not the proprietor of the village *as he posed to be on the advent of the British.*"[24]

From 1803 to 1812, the British persisted with the inherited system of revenue collection, which consisted primarily of extortionary revenue farming by ijardars, with Desais often doubling up as ijardars. This changed with Nepean's arrival. The post of Komavisdar was eliminated and a direct system of revenue collection from village Patels was initiated. The implementation of this new system revealed that the Desais and Amins had been misappropriating large sums of money from the revenue exchequer.[25] Determined to end their influence, the Bombay government appointed its own set of village talatis in 1814, paid for the government and answerable to the District Collector. In addition, Governor Nepean, at the urging of Byrom Rowles, also demanded "the compulsory registration of all alienated or rent-free land."[26]

To understand why the Desais, Amins, and Patels quite correctly viewed these policies as attacks on "the very basis of their wealth . . . and their control over cultivators" some background on the process of land alienation is necessary. There were several ways by which land could be alienated, some a mark of state patronage or fealty, others a reflection of the limits of state power, and still others a byproduct of administrative subversion. In the first category fell various gradations of *inam* lands, including those provided to state officials like Desais and Amins in the form of *dasturis* for ongoing services (rarely, inam grants could encompass an entire village or set of villages). In the second category came *vanta* lands, comprising both the mehwasi villages that lay outside formal state control as well as tracts of land *within* government villages that were claimed as *garas* by the kinfolk of a locally powerful Koli *thakur* or *raja.* Depending on the ability of the state to enforce superior rights, some *vanta* lands paid tribute *(salami)* while others did not. However, unlike the government *(khalsa* or *talpad)* lands, the assessment on vanta lands was a fixed amount rather than a share of the agricultural output.[27] In the case of talpad lands, part of the revenue was payable in kind as crop and part was owed in Baroda coin, requiring that cultivators sell surpluses. As such, what the British encountered in central Gujarat was a system of agricultural production that was not per se profit oriented but *was* monetized *and* integrated into vibrant regional circuits of commerce, credit, and manufacturing.[28] The third category of rent-free land included the so-called *gherania* (mortgaged) and *vechania* (sold) lands. These were plots that had been alienated, illegally, either from the *talpad* or from the village common land (called *muzmoon*) that was set aside for pasture and firewood.

Who was it that managed to alienate these plots, and how? And why would they want to do this in a milieu where opportunities for cultivation-driven profit were uncertain, if not entirely unfamiliar? Those who appear to have gained most from this practice were Desais, Amins, Patels, and their cronies—primarily the *Matadars* and *Patidars,* who were superior and inferior coparcenaries, respectively, in sharehold *(narwadari)* villages.[29] Let's recall that at the district level Desais and Amins discharged the function of revenue collection and enforcement, and the village-level revenue collection and payment was the responsibility of the Patel. The Patel could be an appointed official, with hereditary rights; or, in sharehold villages, simply the eldest Matadars on the village council. When a cultivator's revenue fell in arrears or when, in a sharehold village, a Matadar or Patidar was unable to meet his share of the revenue obligation for a village, the Desais, Amins, or Patels would extend a line of credit to him or simply pay the defaulter's share in lieu of land. The creditor then either sold the land outright (vechania land) or else mortgaged it (in which case the usufruct rights on this gherania land reverted to the lender). In most situations, the vechania and gherania plots were khalsa lands that belonged to the government, but with the connivance of the village, Talati were erased from the talpad and assigned to the lender. As clerk to the Patel, who received an annual grain allowance from villagers for his services, the Talati was rarely in a position to object to this irregular practice.[30] The lenders were, meanwhile, typically Desais, Amins, and Patels because, by virtue of their positions and revenue responsibilities, they had managed to cultivate regional networks of credit with traders *(vanias),* moneylenders *(sahukars)* and urban financiers *(potedars)* that were simply not available to ordinary cultivators. In short, credit was (and continues to be) an immensely powerful instrument of control for the local elite in Kheda—so much so that credit and social prestige have become semiotically entangled in everyday language. Hence, the Gujarati word *abroo,* which Patels and others frequently invoke as a way of describing reputation, honor, or family prestige, also means "creditworthiness."[31]

Control of land provided further leverage. In a densely populated district like Kheda, land was crucial for reproduction, which translated into opportunities to rack-rent subholders and tenants and to deepen their political subjugation. Practically, an expansion in alienated landholdings meant a subtraction from the state's revenue entitlement; it also meant more renter-surplus for the landowners. Little wonder then that Desais, Amins, and Patels reacted with consternation to Collector Rowles's call for the registration of all alienated lands and to the Regulation of 1814 issued by the Bombay Council, which ordered the establishment of a regular paid staff of village accountants.

On September 16, 1815, the Desais of Nadiad and an Amin of Mahudha—all of the Lewa Kanbi subcaste—summoned a meeting of village leaders, most of whom were Patidars (co-sharers in narwadari).[32] They resolved that they would pay land revenue only at the annual rates determined by local custom and would not enter into revenue contracts with the British so long as the new Talati system operated. They pledged to outcaste anyone who broke this resolution. Colonial officials declared these actions a "conspiracy" and "a crime against the state."[33] The Assistant Collector, Robert Barnewell, promptly arrested the Desai and Amin ringleaders and locked them in a house in Kheda. Barnewell then toured the district with a troop of soldiers appointing Talatis, who were largely Brahmins. The attempted revolt appears to have received little support from ordinary Kanbi cultivators who, as subholders or tenants of the Patidars, evidently welcomed the controls sought by the new bureaucratic order. The Nadiad Desais were jailed for four years and, in addition to the payment of a large fine, were deprived of a good deal of the land which they had grabbed during the eighteenth century.[34]

Ultimately, though, the worst fears of the agrarian elite were not confirmed. This is somewhat surprising given the ambitious mandate of the survey and settlement operations—initiated in Broach (hereafter referred to as Bharuch) in 1812 and extended to the rest of British Gujarat after the 1812 advisory from London—to map, measure, and classify in minute detail the existing agrarian landscape.[35] The appointment of well-paid Talatis, directly answerable to the Collector, probably diminished the capacity of Patels to alienate new government lands to themselves and their supporters.[36] But the impact of this policy was felt much more keenly, and with adverse effect, by Rajput *girasias* (also known as *talukdars*) and the various categories of Koli *mehwasdars* (independent chiefs), whose powers to exact taxes from their tenants in *mehwasi* villages were commuted—under threat of military action—to 20 percent of revenues, now directly gathered from cultivators by the government Talati. Over the years, this practice reduced many wealthy and previously autonomous chiefs to mere leaseholders of the British government, "or, if left in charge of their estates, the enhancement of the government share of the revenue, subdivision and their own improvidence left them weakened and impoverished."[37]

What about the Patels? By 1818, two of the three ringleaders of the 1815 protest action had been freed on pardon after a successful petition to the Court of Superior Tribunal (the third, who had escaped from prison in 1817, was pardoned soon thereafter upon claiming temporary lapse of reason). One of the principal organizers, Ajoobhai Prabhudas, was even allowed to resume the office of *desai* in 1826. In restoring Ajoobhai to his post, colonial officials noted he was a member of the "first Kanbi family of Gujarat" and that his return to the position of desai would be "hailed by the community with great satisfaction."[38] Ultimately, even the new method of settling the revenues of Kheda villages that took shape between 1816 and 1825 did not drastically undercut the power of Patels and their allies.

Nominally a ryotwari settlement that was painstakingly conducted, village by village, in practice it relied heavily on "[c]ommittees of local hereditary revenue officers and village headmen . . . to fix government demands upon the landholders of their villages."[39] Patels "now had to submit to arbitration of a committee of their peers" and settlements were fixed for a period of five to seven years, whereas earlier Patels alone would determine annual rates of assessment. This placed formal limits on the power of landowners, such as Patels and their supporters, to extort subholders and tenants. But enforcement of policy was thin, direct cultivators had neither the knowledge nor the will to seek legal remedy in case of rack renting, and the settlement provided no legal protections to tenants' rights. Furthermore, with revenue payable in three cash-and-grain installments (later commuted to cash entirely) in November, December, and March, Patels retained leverage as primary lenders to cultivators—both, landholders and tenants—facing shortfalls. Most perniciously, Patels were able to exert considerable influence in the identification of landholders *(khatadars)* during the village survey and settlement process. Substantially, then, the agrarian elite of Kheda continued to remain powerful despite Nepean's stated intention to thwart them. Their cause was immeasurably boosted when Elphinstone, who succeeded Nepean as Governor of Bombay in 1819, displayed considerably more sympathy toward preserving local hierarchies and expressed open reservations about policies that undermined the Patels.[40] In 1821, for instance, he confirmed the powers of matadars in narwa villages to form a ruling oligarchy responsible for police and administrative matters, effectively deepening their control over the agrarian masses.

Relying on revision survey correspondence from the 1860s, David Hardiman writes that of "the 571 villages of Kheda, 90 were recognized as narva" and almost all (80 out of 90) in the Charotar tract.[41] Yet, Alexander Rogers, writing in 1892, noted on the basis of an 1826 official report that of government villages settled in Kheda "[t]here were only 97 *senja* (directly-managed) to 437 Narwadari villages."[42] This sharp discrepancy presents intriguing possibilities on the uneasy coupling of colonial power/knowledge. One possibility is that Rogers misstates his figures. Another, more plausible interpretation is that Rogers, like the Bombay Civil Service officers who preceded him, did not always distinguish clearly between narwa tenure with a few well-defined co-parcenaries *(matadars)* and the homologous khatabandhi tenure with several smaller coparcenaries or shareholders *(patidars,* also registered on the books as khatadars).[43] Hence, in an 1863 memo drafted in conjunction with the revision settlement of Matar Taluka, Captain C. J. Prescott, Superintendent of Revenue Survey and Assessment for Gujarat, made this telling remark: "[V]ery great eagerness was shown by all classes of cultivators to get their names entered as Survey occupants of land . . . and, especially *in the case of lands held on the 'Khatabundy' (Nurwadari) tenure it was often difficult to decide whose name ought to be entered."*[44] The question begs to be asked: Since the 1820–26 survey and settlement operations in Kheda did not issue formal landownership deeds, *was a clear separation ever effected between sharehold rights and ownership rights, or were the two implicitly conflated in a revenue-collection system which assigned that task to village Patels?*

And, given the prevailing ambiguity in property claims as late as the 1860s, were associates of Patels preferentially granted ownership *(khatedari)* rights? Finally, a third possibility is that Robertson's source from 1826, in arriving at a figure of 437, classified as narwadari villages both those with shareholder responsibility for revenue as well as ryotwari villages whose tax collection had been awarded to Patels and other "substantial cultivators" on what were known as raiyatwar leases.[45]

Despite at first inviting the ire of the British, it is evident that Desais and other members of the traditional elite soon established a relationship of active collaboration with the new rulers. The practice of revenue farming, initially endorsed by Alexander Walker during his tenure at Baroda, continued in revised forms (including the raiyatwar lease).[46] All this suggests that the appointment of government-paid Talatis caused an initial disruption to the agrarian order, but having once impressed their authority, the British were content to let the practical imperative of revenue collection override any abstract principle of political economy such as the Ricardian theory of rent, that James Mill from his perch at East India House, had begun to push on the Company's India servants.

This does not mean that the theory of rent was ignored: it continued to emit a force field that was first realized in the attempted standardization of *bighoti* (per vigha[47]) money rates in Kheda by several junior officials, and later in the Bombay Survey and Settlement System of 1837 developed by George Wingate and H. E. Goldsmid, in which they attempted to give empirical and administrative content to Ricardo's theory of rent. Indeed, the Wingate-Goldsmid system, a taxonomic scheme with detailed instructions for classifying and assessing individual plots of land, was to have immense consequences for agrarian relations via the revision surveys undertaken in Bombay Presidency from the 1840s onward (and in Kheda in the 1860s).

What is clear is that unlike the Koli and Rajput elite—the mehwasdars and talukdars—who were decisively reduced to the status of leaseholders paid an annual allowance at the sufferance of the Bombay government, the Lewa Kanbi powerholders of Kheda *did not* suffer a similar decline in status.[48] The British very quickly came to regard them as the backbone of Gujarat agriculture—the substrate that would provide capitalist entrepreneurship—and took care to ensure that they were not undermined. Colonial documents brim with praise for the agricultural skill and industry of Lewa Kanbis, even though those same documents contain ample evidence that certain denominations of Koli cultivators were often as good, or even better, than their Kanbi counterparts. The crystallization of stereotypes is vividly illustrated in the vacillating remarks of E. C. Ozanne, the Survey Commissioner and Director of Land Records in the 1890s for the Northern Division, Bombay Presidency. In one report, he grudgingly conceded that "many of the Kolis of Matar are nearly as skilful and industrious cultivators as Kunbis,"[49] yet in another report filed that same year he declared that "the Koli Dharalas [of Matar Taluka] are notoriously lazy, unthrifty and unskilful!"[50]

Eric Stokes alleges that "[t]he British administrative mind had always reverted in its consideration of the agrarian problem to the mental shorthand expressed in the notion of fixed ethnic types. Agricultural performance, it believed quite simply, could be directly predicated on the 'tribe' or caste of the agriculturist."[51] His claim, while monolithic in conjuring a guiding intellect, clearly echoes a recurring theme in colonial land policies. Thus, the consolidation of sentiments in favor of one type of landed elite (the Patels) but not another (the Koli mehwasdars) is consistent with policies elsewhere in India—for instance, Benares and Bengal, where the British intervened politically to affirm the land rights of *zamindars* (feudal intermediaries) but divest those of petty rajas.[52] These policies, as I have indicated here and in chapter 1, were a temporally disjointed blend of moral philosophy, economic imperatives, and political expediency.

The State of Capture

"One of the fundamental tasks of the State is to striate the space over which it reigns, or to utilize smooth spaces as means of communication in the service of striated space."[53] Every state formation, in other words, desires and depends upon apparatuses of capture that can police flows or capacities in ways that optimize its security. Where security is equated, as under liberalism, with capitalist social relations, three instruments—rent, profit, and taxation—become the apparatuses par excellence for capturing the potential *(puissance)* of land, labor, and money, respectively.[54] But capture is never preordained and history written as necessity—and, by implication, continuity (whether immanent, as in certain Marxist undertakings; or transcendent, as in certain versions of eschatology or Hegelianism)—only produces the pieties of order. Necessity *does* exist. But it comes to exist, by aleatory means, "as the becoming necessary of the encounter of contingencies."[55]

Contingencies and nonhuman elements, such as weather and the locusts that decimated crops across the province of Gujarat in 1813, assisted immeasurably in the process of colonial state capture. Depressed grain prices between 1819 and 1824, a modest recovery followed by low grain prices for almost three decades after 1826, the sharp increase in money-rate assessments in the early 1820s, severe droughts in 1824–25, 1833–35, and 1838–89, an ill-timed system of revenue installments, and a credit squeeze exacerbated by a dual currency system, all combined to weaken itinerant and petty cultivators in the early decades of British rule. None of these elements had the power of historical necessity, but they combined to generate a process of immiserization that was ultimately critical in securing the prospects of agrarian capitalism in central Gujarat after roughly 1850. Koli commoners, who were economically and politically the most vulnerable to begin with, were to emerge the hardest hit in this process.[56]

In Matar Taluka, where the population of Kolis (primarily of the Baraiya and Tadbda denominations) has always been high in comparison to the heart of the Charotar tract, cultivated area had expanded 31 percent between 1806–7 and 1818–19[57] as a result of rising prices (abetted by the famine in north Gujarat and Kathiawad in 1812–13 and 1813–14) and a period of political quiet under early British suzerainty. But by the late 1840s, the concatenation of factors that I have just listed had driven cultivation down and enervated the masses. Between 1820 and 1850, the inhabitants of Kheda experienced widespread and severe scarcity in 1819–20, 1824–25, 1833–35, and 1838–39. The progression of the 1824–25 drought set against the rigidities introduced by colonial land revenue policies illustrates how unequal access to credit and ability to cope with agricultural fluctuations can prove vital in differentiating a peasantry.

The proximate cause for the 1824–25 scarcity was a failure of the monsoon during the primary *kharif* agricultural season, but this "was preceded in some villages of the district by two years of deficient agricultural production, due first to heavy and excessive rains in 1822, and subsequently, to deficient rains in 1823."[58] In a rain-fed economy cultivators would customarily plow fields in May and early June in anticipation of the monsoon. But given the value of seed capital to the farming enterprise, they would not sow their kharif seed *until* sufficient rain had fallen to ensure its germination. Heavy rains between June 4 and 7, and light showers on June 13 and 14, 1824, prompted cultivators to seed their fields with kharif crops—bajri, jowar, and, where possible, rice—which are harvested in October and November. But no rain fell again until August 21, stunting or severely damaging these crops. Then, once more, there were a series of showers suitable for sowing a late kharif crop. Cultivators sowed bajri, pulses like *chana, muth, mug, tur,* and *udid,* and *kussumbi* (safflower grown for its dye). Those who could afford to sowed tobacco. But September was again extremely hot and dry, damaging the growth of the late kharif crops as well. Since the viability of *rabi* (winter, dry season) crops like wheat depends heavily on sequestered soil moisture, the poor monsoon of 1824 is likely to have affected rabi cultivation—productivity as well as area cultivated—adversely: "Households without large stores from previous harvest(s), without alternative sources of income, or without stocks of alienable assets would have suffered, not only during the scarcity year, but at least until the kharif harvest of 1825/6."[59] In short, a failed monsoon meant that poorer households had to find ways of surviving for eighteen months or more without an assured source of income, as well as scrape together seed capital for the next round of kharif and rabi crops. Moreover they had to try to preserve their livestock, particularly draught animals. How did they survive?

Since stalks of bajri and jowar *(kadbi),* the staple fodder, were no longer available they would have had to rely heavily on grass and leaf forage from fallow and *muzmoon* lands (village commons) to feed animals. A variety of wild foods from trees and shrubs would have supplemented the household's food needs.[60] But the primary means of survival were to draw down accumulated food stocks and to then employ habituated strategies: shrink household consumption; borrow grain and money, usually at usurious rates of interest; pledge labor services, often becoming attached servants; or emigrate. With the exception of the first strategy, all the rest involved even deeper imbrication in relations dependence vis-à-vis Kheda's elite—whether Patels and Patidars, Thakkar traders, or urban Jain and *vania* moneylenders. A particularly troubling aspect of these crises, given prevailing gender inequities, was the neglect and consequent mortality of female children. It is reasonable to surmise that the process of immiserization triggered by the 1824–25 drought was repeated during the droughts of 1833–35—which was even more severe—and of 1838–39.

British policies aggravated the vulnerability of lesser cultivators. The timing and spacing of actions is as crucial to relations of power, as the intensity of actions. Colonial officials wanted control; they produced misery. Following Mughal and Maratha custom, taxes were collected in three installments—November, December, and March. But whereas previous authorities had collected their share of produce in grain or money *after* harvest, the British insisted on collecting the November installment *while* the kharif crop was still standing in the field, in order to avoid understatement of outputs by village Patels. Moreover, a money-acre rate was now more widespread than it had been under previous administrations. Remissions were less readily granted, even in poor agricultural years. This combination of demands meant that lesser ryots had to rely on moneylenders or affluent village persona, who charged a hefty premium, in order to meet the tax levy.

The dual currency system that was in operation added to the cultivators' woes. In the early 1820s, the British had introduced Company coin in their Gujarat territories, hoping to replace the Baroda rupee. Although, officially, cultivators could pay their revenue in Company or Baroda rupee it had come to be "widely believed . . . that the government taxes were payable only in the former currency." Village officers—Patels and Talatis—stoked this belief, both in order to avoid the trouble of examining the authenticity of Baroda coin and avoid "personal liability if such rupees were rejected by the Treasury."[61] For a number of reasons, including heavy expenditures on war in Burma between 1824–26, British coin was in short supply.[62] These factors, again, drove peasants into the hands of the moneyed classes. In order to pay their revenues cultivators would first sell their produce for Baroda rupees, which they would subsequently change with vanias for Company rupees. Although in principle the exchange rate between Company and Baroda coin was fixed by the British, vanias imposed arbitrary exchange rates to their advantage and the disadvantage of peasants.

No Bhats

Meanwhile, the Koli and Rajput chieftains who ruled in semi-autonomy over the so-called *mehwasi* areas of Kheda District were indirectly undermined on another front by the hard line adopted under the reformist administration of Governor Evan Nepean against the sacerdotal caste of Bhats. Concentrated in Matar Taluka, the Bhats (also known as Vahivanca Barots) were a bardic community of genealogists and mythographers who, during the Mughal and Maratha administration of Gujarat, had come to perform a critical political function: furnishing surety for a range of transactions and activities, including realization of government revenue, recovery of private debts, security in mercantile dealings, recovery of stolen property, protection from robbers during travel, and apprehension of criminals. [63]

> The efficacy of bhat security rested on the willingness of the bhats
> to resort to *traga,* or self-suffering, in order to force compliance
> to an agreement. In cases where a client would refuse to honor a
> contract the bhat who had signed as security would attempt to force
> compliance by means of *traga.* This usually involved self-inflicted
> wounds on the arms or, occasionally, fasting *(dharna)* on the step
> of the offending party. . . . The responsibility for the shedding of
> sacred blood or for the pain incurred by the bhat as a result of fasting
> would fall on the delinquent client. If these techniques failed to bring
> compliance, the bhats were prepared to employ more drastic measures,
> including the murder of a relative or, as a last resort, suicide.[64]

The administration of Governor Nepean came to regard the influence of the Bhats—"all the power of Government" as Byrom Rowles, Collector of Kheda at the time put it—as an affront to British authority and moral values, and antithetical to the system of direct and efficient government that it sought to install. Through a series of military and judicial confrontations, the Bhats were stripped of their securitization functions, thereby depriving the Koli and Rajput rulers who had employed the services of Bhats in negotiating revenue payments with Mughal and Maratha administrations of their primary source of collateral. Meantime, the persistent threat of military action by the British in pursuit of their revenue demands meant that the mehwasi chieftains were increasingly compelled to turn to moneylenders and bankers, who frequently charged usurious rates of interest, in order make good on their taxes at the appointed times. This further eroded their power.

Subsumption to Capital

As my story suggests, by the 1830s and 1840s the economic circumstances and political influence of Kolis and Rajputs (commoners as well as aristocrats) was in steep decline across central Gujarat. This was, by contrast, precisely the period when Lewa Kanbi peasants and Patidar estate-holders began to condense into an articulated form—a social identity as it were—that entailed both a more aggressive self-regulation of economic and ritual practices as well as a more ferocious defense of perceived corporate interests. This meant that they were able to handle the political opportunities and challenges of the times as a collective, despite their sharp internal class divisions and frequent outbreaks of factional strife. They petitioned colonial officers and protested colonial policies as a group. They employed group suasion and, sometimes, strong-arm tactics to subdue local rivals, particularly Kolis.[65] Most important, when it came to cultivation they aided each other financially. Kanbi peasants, unlike their Koli counterparts, were able to tap into spatial networks of credit whose linchpins were Jain and Thakkar traders and affluent Patidar families from the fertile heart of Kheda District. Ready access to credit allowed Kanbis to defend their assets during economic crises, invest in land improvements, weather agronomic risks, and practice a better form of agriculture than other groups. It also opened up possibilities for capital accumulation by movement of surpluses within a space economy with uneven patterns of development and asynchronous growth cycles,[66] when conditions for this became more conducive.

By the 1850s, Britain had begun to feel disappointment with India as a supplier of raw materials. This, combined with the disquiet generated by the Revolt of 1857 (which unleashed fears over the future of British rule in India), spurred investment in various forms of infrastructure that would permit freer movement of bulk commodities, labor, troops, military equipment, information, and natural resources. The task of development took on renewed urgency, although within its doubled regime of "value"—economic and ethological (see chapter 1)—the economic began to predominate.[67] It should be pointed out that the land revenue system that had been put in place in Kheda in the 1820s was regressive from a taxation standpoint. Rates, on the whole, were scaled such that the marginal tax was flat; that is, if one *vigha* of land was assessed at x rupees, then the rate on another vigha of the same quality belonging to that same khatedar was also assessed at x rupees (rather than, say, $2x$ rupees, as the case would have been under a progressive tax scheme). This meant that between households of similar size with roughly comparable consumption needs and per-vigha productivity, the less-landed household had to submit a greater proportion of its product (income) as tax. In 1840, the Government of Bombay made this revenue system more rigid by declaring that, henceforth, tax remissions would only be granted "in years of absolute or almost total failure of the crops"[68] over an entire subdistrict (Taluka) and *not* in cases of partial crop failure or failures affecting individual cultivators. This sanctioned insensitivity to differences in the revenue payment capacities of cultivators left poorer peasants in precarious positions during low rainfall seasons (more so during successive bad years) and faced with the prospect of repaying loans and clinging on to assets during a good year, while richer peasants expanded their wealth.

One of the less noted but more consequential policy decisions of the British administration was the Summary Settlement Act of 1863. Passed in the shadow of the 1857 rebellion in northern India, it was intended as a preemptive measure against political instability in other parts of the country. Under its provisions,

> all alienated lands were subjected to a fixed annual payment
> calculated at the rate of two annas for each Rupee of the assessment
> it *[sic]* would bear if they were not alienated. . . . [The] quit-rents thus
> imposed were fixed in perpetuity and were not liable to increase or
> decrease on any new assessment. The settlement of the alienations
> proceeded along with the Bombay Survey and Settlement [the
> revision survey implemented in Kheda District in the early 1860s].
> Whenever alienated lands were discovered, notices were issued
> against their owners containing the stipulations of the summary
> settlement, and these were mostly accepted. This implied a significant
> reduction of the taxes to be paid by the owners of the lands under
> the privileged tenures [*narwardari,* khatabundy, etc.], which made up
> some 50 percent of the total cultivated area of the district.[69]

The figure of "history," like the finite lives of humans and nonhumans it anticipates and orders within the flow of time, is textual—an effected coherence, always supplemented by the real. But not all effects register equally in the fabrication and representation of history, as we now know from a rich seam of subaltern historiographies. Some effects have more force in terms of securing desired conducts—and securing the narratives of history that subsequently re-present those actions—than others. And so it was at mid-century, when a potentially mortal blow to the estate-owning Patidars was thwarted by the singular efforts of W. G. Pedder,

Survey Settlement Officer for Gujarat. Pedder persuaded his superiors that the powerful narwadari tenures of Kheda ought to be read not as variants on the zamindari tenure of landlords and tenants (which had fallen in disfavor after the 1812 *Fifth Report* and, subsequently, James Mill's ascent to power at East India House), but as an altogether different form—of village coparcenaries that were not antithetical to the principles of ryotwari settlement. The timing and content of Pedder's intervention was critical. It preserved the principal instruments of class domination that were at the disposal of Kheda's Patidars: their estates, their access to networks of credit, and, above all, their ancestral claims to *kulin* (original lineage) status that brought them vast dowries for their sons from *akulia* Patidars and Lewa Kanbi peasants looking to embellish their families' reputations and economic prospects by marital association with *kulia* families.

The economic transformations of the 1860s and 1870s that were to catapult the Lewa Kanbi–Patidar coalition to its position of unequalled domination over central Gujarat—a regional preeminence that has weakened over the decades leading up to the present but is far away from crumbling—unfolded against this political backdrop. But, once again, it was contingency that was catalytic in stratifying necessity. The 1857 financial panic in the United States (sparked by the failure of the New York branch of the Ohio Life Insurance and Trust Company on August 24 of that year) had prompted British investors to withdraw capital from U.S. banks. The combination of unemployed capital in search of a spatial fix and the subsequent American Civil War from 1861 to 1865 had a galvanizing effect on the economy of India, including Gujarat. The antebellum South had been the principal supplier of cotton to Britain and the world; but as the North began blocking the South's cotton exports, leading to an acute shortage in international markets, the price of cotton in India and elsewhere soared. Kheda's agrarian economy, which had been embedded within multiple circuits of capital—moneylending, merchant and trading, banking, and proto-industrial—for several centuries prior to British rule without exhibiting, however, a formal subsumption of labor to capital, was now jolted in precisely that direction.

The arrival of a Central India Railway line in the town of Mehmedabad, near Kheda, in 1863 was an electric moment; equally significant was the construction of a dense network of metalled roads across the district.[70] Sensing new opportunities for profit, urban merchants and moneylenders began to advance money to ryots to cultivate cotton and other cash crops like tobacco. Despite the occasional note of developmentalism that punctuates Marx's analysis, his observations on the effects of various forms of capital conjure up a vivid image of the transformations that must have been underway in Kheda in the 1860s. For example, on the operations of merchant capital, he writes: "The development of trade and commercial capital always gives production a growing orientation towards exchange-value, expands its scope, diversifies it and renders it cosmopolitan, developing money into world money. Trade always has, to a greater or lesser degree, a solvent effect on the pre-existing organizations of production, which in all their various forms are principally oriented to use-value."[71]

The 1857–58 period witnessed two seismic events with global aftershocks—the Revolt of 1857 that began with the sepoy uprising in Meerut on May 10, 1857, and lasted thirteen months, and the aforementioned financial crisis in the United States. Amid this tumult, large amounts of surplus capital—primarily from Great Britain—searching for places to go, had begun flowing into India from the early 1850s to fund the construction of railways and other infrastructure. The resulting increase in the supply of treasure in circulation led to unprecedented inflation, which registered in markets as a dramatic increase in price levels. The arrival of railways combined with rising crop prices had two salutary effects on Kheda's agrarian economy. First, as already mentioned, it led to an expansion in lending activity. Second, it sparked an expansion in cultivation, especially of commodity crops. In Matar Taluka, for instance, the cultivation of government and alienated lands increased by some 15 percent between the early 1840s and 1863, when a new survey was implemented.

This survey was to become a critical third element in the thickening of capitalist social relations in central Gujarat. The production of space through tactics of government—coercion, law, fiscal initiatives, systems of classification, and so on—has deep implications for the conduct of the governed: this was the singular lesson imparted by the new survey. On the one hand, its imminent implementation generated apprehension among cultivators over the security of their property rights—who therefore rushed to till tracts of land that had been lying uncultivated. The substantial increase in crop prices also prompted a so far absent form of speculation in land, with the same net effect—an expansion in cultivation as a way of staking and securing property rights. The figure of "waste"—always lurking at the margins of colonial discourse—made a cameo appearance. One historian describes the hubbub in Matar Taluka this way:

> The Superintendent of the Kheda Survey, Cyrill Jackson Prescott, had never seen anything like the eagerness of the people in the greater part of Matar to obtain possession of government waste lands. Nearly all the waste lands had been used for the pasturage of the village cattle, and the people were "excessively unwilling" to permit them to be taken up for cultivation.[72]

On another front, the anxiety to extend cultivation was sharpened by a consequential provision in the new Survey: a change in the tax code requiring cultivators to pay full assessment on lands previously used for grazing. Although the economic boom catalyzed by the American Civil War subsided after 1865, scarcity across north India in 1868–69 and then again in 1870–71 kept crop prices in Kheda District high by historical standards.

Marrying Up and Moving Up

Lewa Kanbis cultivators were the principal beneficiaries of this pivotal economic conjuncture. I suggest that initial class differentiation within the Lewa Kanbis and between Kanbis and estate-holding Patidars was indispensable to the construction of an endogamous caste identity and that an emergent caste identity was, in turn, instrumental, at least until the end of the nineteenth century, for class accumulation.

Buoyed by colonial policies favoring them and the post-1850 agricultural boom, Patidars and ordinary Kanbis associated strategically, but unequally, in the unforeseen making of the Patel caste. It became the goal of every Lewa Kanbi to ascend to the level of Patidari status, both by accumulating land and through the tradition of hypergamy—that is, the marriage of daughters to grooms from higher-ranked (*kulin*) families. For these kulin Patidar families (especially those from the most prestigious villages in the fertile heart of Kheda known as Charotar), hypergamous marriage alliances became a channel for enormous wealth accumulation. By contrast, for ordinary Lewa Kanbis, their goal of wealth accumulation was found to be frequently at odds with the desire for status, because dowries or groomprice payments that were required to effect marital alliances with higher-ranked families were steep, and a severe drain on accumulated surpluses. There is frequent mention in historical accounts of Lewa Patels driven to financial ruin by extraordinary dowries, and of bitter complaints about the exploitative practices (soshan) of the Kheda Patidars.[73] By the mid-1870s the entire region of central Gujarat was re-coded as a hierarchical "space of distinction": with the Charotar tract, where the Patidar gentry resided—the most desirable site for marital alliances—designated as its nucleus.

One of the most disturbing aspects of the practice of hypergamy was the rise in the incidence of female infanticide among the high-ranking Patidar families, who, for obvious economic reasons, preferred to get women from lower-ranking Kanbis; the daughters of landed Patidars, as a result, faced a scarcity of grooms of their rank, and marrying down was not a permitted option.[74] The practice of female infanticide appears to have snaked down the class ladder. Colonial officials like H. R. Cooke implicated the huge dowries that ordinary Lewa Kanbis felt obligated to offer for girls (they could amount to eighteen hundred rupees or, in some instances, even three thousand rupees—in those days, astronomical sums) as the leading cause for the high incidence of female infanticide in the community.[75] In fact, the issue of female infanticide had regularly consumed colonial officials in Bombay Presidency in the years leading up to the Maharaja libel case (see chapter 1). In 1847, the Collector of Ahmedabad district, Mr. Fawcett, had opened an investigation into female infanticide among the Lewa Kanbis; his initiative was soon followed by a similar inquiry by Mr. Webb, Collector of adjoining Kheda District.[76] Threats of sanction followed. But hampered by lack of solid evidence and community secrecy, and probably apprehensive about alienating a group that they had come to regard as the backbone of Gujarat's agrarian economy, colonial officials eventually allowed pragmatism to trump principle. A zealous administrator or social reformer here and there ensured that the specter of infanticide was never fully put to rest. But after the turmoil of the 1857 mutiny and the passage of India from Company territory to the British crown, a policy of intervention quietly yielded to a policy of compromise and tacit agreement with Lewa Kanbi agevan (leaders) that they would self-monitor and punish acts of female infanticide within their community. Enforcement was thus delegated to the accused.

The practice of hypergamy—the proximate cause for female infanticide—was founded at least partly on the premise that daughters married into wealthier households would neither have to sell their labor power nor work in the fields; in short, their work in *public* would be minimized. There was no guarantee, however, that their household work would diminish as well, but this really was not a decisive element for distinction. Ironically, then, the de-objectification of women's work (her dual withdrawal from commoditized work and public work) went hand-in-hand with women's objectification as status goods within the Lewa Kanbi community. Indeed, women's value as status goods seems to have become directly linked to her degree of withdrawal from the orbit of public work. It was as if public display of her body, most profane when her labor power was sold to an employer, would compromise her femininity and sexual purity.

Lewa Kanbis managed to prosper economically despite the drain of hypergamous alliances. We have noted already how the tax system came to be biased in the favor of landed households. W. G. Pedder, who was the Revenue Commissioner for Gujarat in the 1860s, acknowledged that "at [the new low revenue] pitch the profits of superior husbandry are of course [bound to be] much larger than the bare remuneration of unskilled cultivation, but that this should be the case, is one of the great objects of the Survey system."[77] And although legally tenants were now protected against arbitrary rents (which were to be fixed by the District Collector), in practice rack renting not only continued but also was tolerated by colonial officials. Tenants who were most affected by rack renting were primarily Koli lessees—and to a small degree, the poor Kanbi lessees—of Patidar landlords. Moreover, despite the official strictures against rack renting, there was no attempt to enforce the tenurial security of tenants and sharecroppers. Landlords could reclaim their lands at will.

T. R. Fernandez, Deputy Superintendent of the Gujarat Revenue Survey, writing in connection with the 1893 Revision Settlement for Matar Taluka, once again reveals the degree of colonial prejudice in favor of Patels:

> There are three principal castes which contribute the largest quota
> towards making up the agricultural population, viz., Kolis, Kunbis and
> Rajputs. The Kunbis are chiefly found in the villages north of an east-
> and-west line drawn through Traj, and in the border villages in the
> south; while the intervening area is mainly in the possession of Kolis
> and Rajputs. The Kunbis, as usual, are thriving and, generally speaking,
> well-to-do, even those found in the tract occupied by the other castes; as

witness Khandhli, Traj and Limbasi. The Kolis and Rajputs are, I regret
to say, very poor. The Patel [headman] of Heranj, a Rajput, personally
handed to me a long petition describing the extreme poverty of his
village people. I visited the village, and then not only inspected the
lands, but at the request of the Patel also went into some of the houses.
The lands I found to be very good, and the cultivation very fair, but
the condition of the houses was wretchedly poor. Trying to understand
why such opposite circumstances existed side by side, *I discovered that
the [Koli/Baraiya] cultivators habitually sold nearly all their stock of
manure to the Kunbis of the neighbouring village of Khandhli,* where in
consequence high garden cultivation was everywhere visible! To prove
further that the cause of their poverty was solely due to their own
indolence and thriftlessness, when I went to the adjoining village of
Alindra, which is a thriving Kunbi village, I learnt that the clearance
of the large village tank, for which a large sum had been sanctioned
last year, was almost at a standstill, owing to the scarcity of laborers;
and the work, which should be finished in one year, was going to take
three years. Later on I learnt that the village officials had applied to the
Collector to have the work taken over by the Executive Engineer. *If the
Kolis and Rajputs are extremely poor, which no doubt they are, it seems to
me they have only themselves to blame,* for no government in the world
could make their circumstances any better than they are.[78]

Fernandez implies that the abject economic condition of Kolis is linked
to their tenuous control over means of production; in this case, manure.
Like Pedder, he is quick to conflate the issue of access with the issue of
personal enterprise. Just as Pedder in an earlier report failed to say why
Baraiyas and Kolis had inferior access to credit, Fernandez fails to examine why the Kolis of Heranj "habitually" sell their stock of manure to the
Kanbis of Khandhli. In an amazing twist of logic, Fernandez proceeds to
blame the failure to excavate the reservoir in Alindra, "a thriving Kunbi
village," on Kolis—whose reticence to work becomes the root cause for
the "scarcity of laborers"!

Just as colonial administrators chose to neglect the tenurial security
of various Koli and poor Kanbi tenants and gave the blind eye to rack
renting, in the same manner they elected to ignore the passage of land
by mortgage and usury into the hands of Patidar farmers. Here double
standards are again apparent. On the one hand, the British professed
an almost pathological dislike for *sahukars* (professional moneylenders), whose usurious activity they identified as directly responsible for
agricultural backwardness and the dispossession of peasants from their

land.[79] Hence, consecutive Settlement Officers in Kheda District (and Matar Taluka) expressed concern when the Record-of-Rights revealed that land was moving into the hands of moneylending nonagriculturists *(sahukars)*, and relief when an opposite trend was observed. But similar concerns were not voiced when evidence indicated concentration of land in the hands of moneylending Patidar cultivators. Thus, this blatant pronouncement of one Settlement Officer:

> Where there are villages of bad cultivators in close conjunction with villages of good cultivators, and there is any possibility of . . . their land passing into the hands of skilful husbandmen it is necessary to be very cautious about lowering the pitch of assessment. . . . It is indisputable that a very large number of Dharala [Koli] landowners will be economically happier and more prosperous if they work not independently, but under an energetic and experienced landlord [Patidar] agriculturist. And it is not in the interests of the public at large to encourage by too low rates—indolence, thriftlessness and indifference.[80]

The situation I have described for Kheda District is apt to have been slightly different in Matar Taluka, merely because in contrast to central Kheda the proportion of homogenously Koli/Baraiya villages was larger in this western enclave of Kheda.

Overall, however, Matar Taluka bore the stamp of Patel domination like the rest of the district. Since ownership patterns rarely corresponded to the revenue boundaries of villages, it was very often the case that a large Patel farmer from one village commanded substantial holdings in adjacent villages, which is to say that the sphere of influence of the Patel community frequently extended well beyond the village frontier. Ownership was not the only means by which Patels controlled means of production like land and labor. One British official noted that "a good many patidars who cultivate land also lend money."[81] Typically, loans were given on security of land. This meant that the borrower had to leave a portion of his land in the lender's safekeeping. During the loan period, usufruct rights to the land reverted to the lender, who had the option of self-cultivating or retaining the borrower as a sharecropper *(bhagidar)*. If the loan was not repaid within a certain number of years, de facto control (and, often, de jure ownership if the land in question was an "alienated holding") shifted to the lender. Thus, the mortgage transaction was a clever way for Patels to accumulate land.

Few periods in Matar's modern history can compare to the years 1899 to 1917, which rank as one of the bleakest in the annals of western India. In 1899, Matar received only 6.72 inches of rainfall between June and October. July and August, when moisture is absolutely critical for the survival of the young crop, passed without a drop of rain. In September, by which time crop failure was almost complete, a scant—and, by then, meaningless—two inches of rain fell.

The year 1900 was better in terms of total rainfall, but worse in terms of its distribution. There was absolutely no rain in June to wet the soil, and only 3.75 inches in July, when most cultivators sow their monsoon (kharif) crop. August was better, with 16 inches of rain, but September had little rain and October none. In 1901, the famine returned, with little to no rain in June and September, and feeble precipitation in July and August. Once more, crops failed. The year 1903 witnessed a partial failure of crops; and 1904 was again disastrous, with only 9.72 inches of rainfall over the entire monsoon. Partial rainfall failures re-occurred in 1911, 1915, and 1917. The last of these rainfall failures sparked the famous Kheda Satyagraha of 1918, when a large number of cultivators—the majority of them Lewa Kanbis—refused to pay land revenue to the British colonial authorities.[82]

To summarize, average rainfall between 1898 and 1917 was only 24.27 inches, as opposed to 35.15 inches between 1877 and 1892.[83] The cataclysmic famine of 1899, etched in folklore as the chhapanio dukal, was, by far, the most ravaging. The population of the subdistrict plunged from seventy-nine thousand in 1891 to sixty-one thousand in 1901, with most of the mortality occurring between 1899 and 1901.[84] The cattle population also declined precipitously from a total of 42,826 animals in 1892 to 26,509 animals by the time of the next livestock census in 1906. The severest decline was in the population of adult milch cattle and young stock. There was also a 135 percent increase in the population of goats, which are well known to be more resilient than cattle to fodder shortages because of their less particular diet (rising goat populations are often taken as a sign of environmental degradation). Finally, there is documentary evidence that some cultivators moved out of agriculture altogether. Not only did the recorded agricultural population of Matar subdistrict (consisting of cultivators and farm laborers) drop from approximately fifty-one thousand in 1891 to forty-five thousand by the time of the 1911 census;[85] but the number of small ploughs in the sub-district also fell by 40 percent between 1892 and 1906.[86]

By far the most telling evidence of the devastation wreaked by successive years of rainfall failure—on the physical productivity of land and on cultivator confidence—was the explosion in "grass or fallow" (occupied but uncultivated) land from 8.21 percent of net cropped area in 1893 to 21.46 percent in 1916. The sharp fluctuation in the area of cultivable waste between 1891 and 1916 also reveals the vulnerability of cultivators in this desperate period. The tenor of colonial narratives did not change during these years. When the famines of 1899–1901 decimated the population of Kheda—with the district collector of Kheda reporting in May 1900 that "the large majority of persons, who now swell the death-roll, are Dharalas, a caste of Kolis"[87]—colonial officials most loudly lamented the decline in the Lewa Kanbi population. L. V. M. Robertson, the Assistant Settlement Officer for Kheda, worried that

> The famine gave a tremendous setback to agricultural prosperity and the poor seasons which have been so frequent since have retarded recovery. The serious decrease in the Kunbi population has affected the taluka adversely. . . . The reason usually given is that Kunbis are deterred by consideration of expense from marrying and having large families.[88]

Food and relief camps in the district, where individuals could receive a daily wage in exchange for work, were inundated by hunger-stricken families during the famine years, even though working and living conditions in these camps were abysmal.[89] Patidars were among them. But because of their superior resources, they were ultimately able to cope with and recover from these two calamitous decades less traumatically than members of other caste groups, whose control over production means and whose access to urban social networks were far more tenuous. It was, in fact, in these two decades that the first wave of Lewa Kanbis migrated to East Africa and struck the roots of a diaspora that was to later become extraordinarily powerful. Part of the wealth accumulated abroad, first in salaried and pensioned colonial jobs, later in trade and commerce, was repatriated by Lewa Kanbis to their places of origin in Kheda, where it served to further concentrate assets in the hands of their community. In short, through the spatial—indeed, global—diversification of economic activity, the Lewa Kanbis were not only able to ride out a sequence of natural calamities but emerge even stronger at the end of it. Able to straddle different worlds, and adroitly transfer information, resources and sensibilities across them, they congealed as a pan-scalar community of "rural cosmopolitans."

In these years, the appellative "Patel," which originally applied to the village official in charge of tax collection and law and order, now came to be adopted wholesale as a surname by Lewa Kanbis as a mark of their corporatism (a hegemonic alliance with the estate-owning Patidars) and their rising status across Gujarat. The Patidar Yuvak Mandal, established in 1908 as a caste association that would promote education among Lewa Kanbi youth and organize grassroots political support for the nationalist movement, consolidated their power. Patels never ceased to be a ruptural unity. But formally they became one. The official declaration of caste amalgamation came with the 1931 census conducted by the British, when Lewa Patels, patrician and plebeian, unanimously reported their caste as "Patidar." A caste was formally born.

CHAPTER THREE

Machine

Extremely private and urgent:

Date: 2/2/96

Respectfully for,
District Collector *Saheb*
District Collector's Office
Kheda

Subject: Investigation of irregularities in the building of shelters for farm laborers

Honorable Sir,

This is to humbly apprise you that approximately sixty houses have been built on both ends of Limbasi village. In this work, requisite materials have not been used. Subsequently, even the wood used has been of an inferior variety and work on the interior is subpar. Initially, in the first phase of construction extremely raw bricks were used in the foundation. Even the associated materials [gravel, cement, etc.] that were applied on top of the bricks were inadequate. When this work was going on I had petitioned the district and Taluka *panchayats* to probe the matter but nothing was done and so I request you confront those concerned, who passed [issued certificates of clearance to] this sort of deliberate "time-pass" [an Indian idiom connoting casual or cavalier] work, as well as the contractor and the panchayat officials who were involved in this.

Yours truly,

This letter, which I have translated from Gujarati, was written by an unusual man who befriended me early during my stay in Matar Taluka. A self-described follower of Gandhi and Sri Aurobindo, he has been deeply involved in village and Taluka politics. He is not without his faults or blind spots, some of which are stark. But along with an unparalleled understanding of political developments in Kheda, he can claim the legacy of a mostly lone five-decade crusade against corruption in the Taluka that has made him deeply unpopular with local power brokers. The man I allude to will go unnamed. His continuing "experiments with truth" *(satya na prayog),* as he calls them (after Gandhi), revolve around an evolving philosophy of praxis that draws on the thought of both Gandhi and Aurobindo Ghosh and are continually tempered against lived experience. His life as a peasant intellectual merits a longer and separate story, not a subordinate treatment here. But his imprint on what follows will be self-evident. So too, I hope, will be my use of his letter as the opening gambit. On the face of it, the letter simply documents a tired story of petty corruption: the misuse of development funds by a village panchayat. It also repeats a familiar historical gesture: the nonelite's appeal to higher authority to right the wrongs being committed in the sovereign's name, unbeknownst to him, by errant local officials. There is a painful naiveté to this act; the man I speak of has written tens of such letters, almost always without receiving a response. Because he *believes* in development and its possible justice, he is undeterred. Letters such as the one I have translated mark the machinic power of development and its nonidentical effects. Its centrality is continuously reinscribed through public rituals: televised ribbon-cutting ceremonies, periodic gestures of state munificence, and raucous stump speeches by India's vast army of professional politicians. But it is in the everyday—in the desire for development that circulates within uncountable routine acts of anger, disappointment, frustration, and hope—that its effects are most densely realized and its power most reliably nourished. This is the truth of a letter destined to elicit nothing.

Machine Is Not Metaphor

The literature on development (as well as development and India) is so large that to claim to say something different on the subject is both tiresome and pretentious. My claim is therefore less a stake to novelty than an argument about the uncanny workings and persistent power of development. How did development come to matter in such ubiquitous ways? Through what tactics and apparatuses does it plot life-improving associations? How does it rely on connections between human and nonhuman bodies? What are its modes of power and surprise? I work through these questions in order to track the itinerary of development in postcolonial India and to think how agrarian transformations might have contributed to the seismic changes that have wracked Gujarat since the late 1960s. As a slew of scholars have demonstrated, the development machine is one of the most powerful anthropological machines of the past two centuries.[1] It is a peculiar machine, unusually adaptive, that has worked in conjunction with a range of other powerful machines or diagrams: pastoral, sovereign, liberal, disciplinary, communist, governmental, communitarian, and capitalist. Its appeal undoubtedly lies in its distinctive modality: *improvement* (a modality that includes, as we saw in chapter 1, a permanently renewed war against waste). This is an ordering design that is compatible with multiple historical diagrams, secular and nonsecular.

In what sense is development a machine? *It is an abstract machine that reorganizes the conditions—or ecology—of human life for its betterment.* "The diagrammatic or abstract machine," Gilles Deleuze and Félix Guattari write, "does not function to represent, even something real, but rather constructs a real that is yet to come, a new type of reality."[2] Development constructs *by* connecting. More exactly, a machine *is its connections and effects.* This is true of concrete machines like a bicycle, or a slightly more abstract machine like a hand connected to a tool that gives the handtool a functionality that neither hand nor tool alone possesses, or a diagrammatic machine like development that enables a new cartography of forms and functions. Machines bring into relation—join—previously separate parts. These connections are not static; they are flows that transform the parts that are put into relation together (think of the wear and tear of a bicycle's parts after repeated use). Since relations *are* flows, it means that the parts in a machine can never be self-adequate, that is to say, identities in a Platonic sense.

I was powerfully reminded of the machinic power of development on a stay in the village of Pinglaj several years ago. Pinglaj, in the northeast fringe of Matar Taluka, is one of the poorest villages in the region (I narrate its odd tale in chapter 5). During this particular visit, I chanced into a conversation with an old Nayak woman and her middle-aged son.

Nayaks are an "out-of-caste" group and numerically small in central Gujarat.[3] Locals call them *bajavala*—they play musical instruments, often as part of bands that perform popular music at weddings. Nayaks also participate in street theater, such as ritual enactments of *Ram Lila*. Perhaps because of their small numbers (and thus low impact in the numbers game of electoral democracy), they have not been targeted by state affirmative actions with the same zeal as other, larger, out-of-caste groups in the area. The particular Nayak household in question was one of the poorest in Pinglaj. This was not immediately obvious. Their *jhuggi* (hut), at one corner of the village, stood in an immaculately clean compound bounded by a live cactus fence. As we began talking, I noticed that the jhuggi was badly in need of repair. Its thatched roof was frayed and the mud façade was crumbling in several places. The old woman *(dosi)* spoke in a cracked and barely discernible voice.[4] I had to strain to hear what she was saying. She said that her son, Kanu, was unmarried. No greeting, just that.

As first words these struck me as odd, and it took me few minutes to fathom the timing and significance of her statement. I was an outsider, and seeing dosi's middle-aged son but no spouse I must have wondered at the wife's absence—or that at least *ought* to have been my chain of thought within dosi's emplacing logic. What went unsaid but was too obvious to ignore was the reason why: Kanu could not afford to marry. It was a confession to the sort of poverty that prevents participation in even the most rudimentary of social trappings. Kanubhai, it turned out, didn't have a steady job. He was a peddler of bangles and other assorted women's wares. He got these on credit from large traders in the towns of Kheda or Bareja and tooled around villages on his rusty bicycle trying to sell them at a small mark-up. The uncertainty of his existence clearly weighed on Kanu. I asked him whether he or his mother had ever availed of government schemes directed at the uplift of the rural poor. His answer was oblique. He told me how Nayaks were once Brahmins in Mehsana District, which lies a hundred miles north of Matar Taluka in the state of Gujarat. They were shunted out of caste society because an ancestor once sheltered a beautiful Patel girl from a Mughal prince, who wanted to forcibly marry her. In desperation, the girl's father sent her to the house of a Nayak for refuge. The Nayak pretended that the girl was his wife. The Mughal prince refused to believe this and threatened to kill him. He rightly suspected that the Nayak was a Brahmin. As proof of the girl's relation to the Nayak, the prince asked the Nayak to eat food prepared by her. He did so, thereby proving to the prince that he was not—could not be—a Brahmin, having eaten food prepared by a lower caste girl. In the act of saving the Patel girl, the Nayak and his entire community were ostracized by Brahmins. To this date, Kanu said, Nayaks live under the expectation of charity from Patels, as acknowledgment of their ancestor's noble deed. As historical fact, Kanu's story did not square.

As I have shown in chapter 2, Patels congealed as a "hard" caste identity only in the late nineteenth century. But this was hardly the point. I instead marveled how in Kanu's retelling, myth as memory was annexed to a political present where Patels dominate society. Kanu's story, which was not moored in a specific time or place, exposed his sedimented grievance: a history of repeated wrongs—sovereign injustice—against Nayaks. His identity was etched in betrayals by various rulers, including the present generation of Patels, who shun their historical obligation to Nayaks. But Kanu refused sympathy. He told his story stoically. This was his lot, the historical lot of his kinsfolk, and he would live with it. When I asked whether Kanu and his mother kept a milk animal for dairy income (I was introduced to Kanu and his mother by the then-secretary of Pinglaj's village dairy) he gave me an incredulous look and gestured with a turn of his shoulders to the almost empty compound in which we sat. Again, unsaid but unmistakable: *how can we afford to keep a buffalo or cow?* Kanu said he didn't expect handouts from *sarkar* (the State). But his relentless dignity was, once more, unable to mask the sense of wrong for the insistent neglect by the State. At this point, dosi, Kanu's mother, interjected:

Dosi: "After Indira*ma* [mother Indira], no one has helped us."

Vinay: "How do you mean?"

Dosi: "Only Indira's program was for the poor. Has anyone noticed us since?"
[I didn't immediately register that she meant the twenty-point program announced four days after the imposition of the Emergency in 1975].

Vinay: "Which program are you talking about, grandma?"

Dosi: "Don't you remember? Her program? What was it called? That one ... twenty-point ... ?"

Vinay: "Oh. . . ."

Dosi's remarks, now over a decade old, have lingered.

On June 12, 1975, Justice Jag Mohan Lal Sinha of the Allahabad High Court declared Prime Minister Indira Gandhi's election to the Lok Sabha void.[5] Exactly two weeks later, on June 26, Indira Gandhi declared a State of Emergency under the provisions of Article 352, Part XVIII of the Indian Constitution. Fundamental rights and civil liberties were suspended; political opponents, particularly journalists, were imprisoned (and in some instances "disappeared," presumed killed); workers were denied the right to strike, while industrialists were given a free hand to dismiss employees (roughly 500,000 workers were laid off within six months of the declaration of Emergency); trade and student unions were severely disciplined; strict censorship was imposed; and the draconian Maintenance of Internal Security Act (MISA) was put in place to deter public protest.

None of these, evidently, left an imprint on dosi's memory. It is true that events did not reverberate in Gujarat with the same intensity as in north India, where forced sterilization and slum demolition drives became the terrifying face of the Emergency for common people. But it is equally true that Gujarat was one of the early epicenters of mass protest against Indira's Congress in the 1970s, notably the *Navnirman andolan* (agitation) of 1974 that unseated Indira Gandhi's ally, Chimanbhai Patel, on charges of corruption and failure to stem rising prices of essential commodities. It is, of course, possible that dosi—illiterate and cut off from mainly urban political events—simply did not register that there was something called "the Emergency" (Gujarat-based political scientist Pravin Sheth mentions an all-India poll conducted in the aftermath of the Emergency where 29.75 percent of those surveyed "did not know about it, or . . . had no opinion about this traumatic experience"[6]). It is also possible that there was another reason: *the power of development.* Dosi remembered the period of the Emergency not as the low point of Indian democracy (*loksatta*) but as its high point, perhaps the only interruption in her life of continuous struggle and disappointment.

Four days after declaration of the Emergency, Mrs. Gandhi announced a twenty-point program aimed at the poor. She promised, among other things, to implement land reforms, abolish the practice of bonded labor, fix minimum wages for agricultural laborers, provide house sites to the rural landless, supply clothes to the poor, and expand employment opportunities for educated young people. Her speeches painted a Manichean struggle, asserting that it was to be able to implement this pro-poor program and defeat the rich who opposed it that she had been compelled to impose the Emergency. The actual achievements of the twenty-point program were painfully modest—with the exception, it would appear, of the scheme to allot housing sites to the rural landless. Aided by central financial assistance to cover the cost of acquiring and developing house sites, the states succeeded in distributing over three million sites in the first year after the Emergency, the great bulk of them in Uttar Pradesh and Gujarat, the two states where Mrs. Gandhi was most embattled.

Dosi, it turns out, was one of the beneficiaries. The unexpectedly large compound with its meager hut suddenly made sense. Very likely, the period of the Emergency was the only time that the State cared about her lot in life—when the development machine left its indelible trace, *connecting her to possibilities never before contemplated or since requited.* In his self-described "philosophy of organism" (as opposed to conventional philosophies of the subject of consciousness) A. N. Whitehead writes that "consciousness presupposes experience, and not experience consciousness . . . [t]hus an actual entity may, or may not, be conscious of some part of its experience."[7] This observation, it seems to me, captures dosi's and Kanu's memory-work and their autobiographies of mostly unrelieved injustice. For dosi, the period of the Emergency is the highlight of her life, the one moment when she was connected in ways that rendered the prospect of a better life a visible possibility, not merely a fleeting abstraction.

Development, in short, is no ordinary machine; it does its work as a "desiring machine." Desire is not a proper noun; it is a common noun. It traverses individuals (such as Kanu and dosi) but consists of supra-individual energies that are assembled and activated within particular concatenations of human and more-than-human bodies.[8] Development effects rely on such heterogeneous associations of humans and nonhumans, which, *in combination,* produce life functionings that would be impossible in the absence of connection. But *the emergence of novelty by combination* is also the source of surprise.[9] The interactions of previously unconnected materials, living and nonliving, have unanticipated effects: some foster life, others impede it. And lurking in a desiring machine like development is the omnipresent danger that the molecular desires it incites may metabolize into forces that are antiproductive (destructive of life) rather than productive (conducive to it). They may, in short, be annexed to a policy of "a macropolitics of society by and for a micropolitics of insecurity."[10] More on this later.

State Assemblages and Development Effects

To say that abstract machines map a reality to come is a truism. The challenge is to show how a diagram like development plugs into state or capitalist formations, thereby fabricating new machinic assemblages. In chapter 1, I argued that, whereas development was the defining problematic of colonial government, the tactics summoned for its execution were frequently illiberal—less concerned with the liberty of colonial subjects in India than with putting in place what a long line of officials from the 1820s to the 1890s thought were the proper apparatuses for conduct that would be conducive to the accumulation of capital as well as the health and security of the colonial state. The departure from laissez-faire liberalism had many sources, evangelicalism among them, but, as Eric Stokes has so brilliantly documented, it was undoubtedly Utilitarianism that left the deepest mark on colonial government.

As is well known, Utilitarianism was a philosophy of jurisprudence that came to be joined to liberal political economy via the theory of rent through the powerful influence of Jeremy Bentham's acolytes, Thomas Malthus, Richard Jones, James Mill, David Ricardo; and, subsequently, their followers, R. K. Pringle, Holt Mackenzie, George Keating, and Alexander Ross, to name but a few. Each of these individuals was deeply entangled with colonial administration in India. Their stentorian uptake of Utilitarianism left an indelible imprint on the conduct of government.[11] The overt breach with the putative universalism of liberal principles was justified most forcefully by James Mill, on the grounds that India was the exception that verified the rule. It was a country that was enervated by the overextraction of land rents from cultivators by despotic rulers. India was portrayed in his writings as the paradigmatic site of "bad" and "wasteful" government. Correspondingly, liberalism as the antidote was distilled into a Utilitarian philosophy of "good" and "efficient" government. Stokes has summarized the deductive reasoning of Mill's programmatic *Essay on Government:*

> Government originated in order to provide security for the motive to labor and accumulation; it existed to supply that "basis of expectation" which was property. Law created property by defining

rights and securing them under the threat of punishment. Since, therefore, law always operated at the expense of liberty and by the infliction of pain, it was important that it should be precisely adjusted so that the pain inflicted was outweighed by the pain prevented.[12]

In Mill's hands the "Indian question" was thus reduced to three issues: the form of government, the nature of the laws, and the form of taxation. In his influential position as Assistant Examiner (and later, Examiner) at the East India Company, where he was responsible for processing all Company correspondence pertaining to Indian affairs, Mill was unabashed in advocating that the Government of India ought to operate as a super-landlord, with the aid of a streamlined administrative hierarchy modeled after a military chain of command. As for liberty, he noted that "native subjects" were unfit for self-governance (a theme reiterated by his son, John Stuart Mill, in justifying the deviation from representative rule in India); and that in any case the Government of India was answerable to an elected British Parliament.

What was more important by way of abiding by liberal principles was for the colonial landlord government to implement an efficient and fair system of land assessments based on the (Ricardian) principle of rent. By so doing, government would neither subtract from the normal profits of cultivators nor, therefore, distort market prices by adversely affecting agricultural production. In fact, in guaranteeing political stability and negotiating a "permanent" (thirty-year) settlement directly with cultivators (bypassing tax-collecting superordinates and intermediaries), government would give impetus to individual initiative and capital accumulation. Thus endorsing a principle of authority *within* a principle of liberty—reducing political liberty to self-congratulatory statements of expanded economic liberty for the colonized—James Mill and his Utilitarian allies provided heft to Ranajit Guha's disputed axiom that colonial government in India was an instance of "dominance without hegemony."[13] British administration in this view neither produced nor critically depended upon hegemonic acquiescence to its rule. Despite fictions of self-governance (exemplified by the Provincial Legislative Councils) the Government of India was never answerable to those it ruled. Rather it was accountable to the metropole, to the British Parliament and, thereon, to enfranchised members of the British public.

The same cannot be said, of course, for the republic with its political system of electoral democracy that took birth in 1947. *It* could not dispense with the exercise of hegemony, which, as Antonio Gramsci famously noted in relation to the parliamentary regime, "is character-ized by the combination of force and consent variously balancing one another, without force exceeding consent too much."[14] Coextensive with colonial government, the defining problematic of the postcolonial pol-ity remained "development." But this was now to be, in a substantive sense (at least until the end of the Third Five-Year Plan), a process of "socialist" and, by implication, autonomous development, rather than development as a civilizing project dictated to a colonized periphery by its colonizing metropole. Moreover, it had to be a process of develop-ment that would be broadly acceptable to a national electorate with all its geographic wrinkles and inequalities. Quite simply then, postcolonial government with *its* diagram of development cannot be analyzed in the same manner as colonial government with *its* diagram of develop-ment. The former was and remains a state form that is answerable to a people,[15] albeit undercut and comprised by a number of vested interest groups; the latter, meanwhile, was accountable primarily to a representa-tive government (and by default, a people) elsewhere. This is not to deny contiguities between the two modes of State power—both sought the improvement of populations, and marshaled an array of tactics to this biopolitical end. Development is, after all, an ethical social project par excellence that wants to foster the conditions of life and curtail waste. But to characterize the colonial and postcolonial state as governmental does not imply they were identical. They could not be.

Indeed, the *social forces* set in motion by their respective tactics of government were substantially different. British rule was a "government of record," as John Shore and, later, John Stuart Mill put it.[16] And this prompted, among other forms of enumeration, the copious collection of statistics about economic conditions. One effect of these practices was to make it possible to imagine "India" as an *economy* with distinct subpopulations.[17] The other, in combination with programs of social transformation outlined in chapter 1, was an attempt to wean colonized subjects away from wasteful conducts and to embrace the imperative of "progress." The reactivation of protonationalist sentiments as economic nationalism of some times strident variety was an unexpected outcome of colonial empiricism. Dadabhai Naoroji, R. C. Dutt, and Mahadev Ranade are a few of the better-known economic nationalists who, in a series of polemical tracts and lectures, blamed British rule for India's poverty. They attributed India's lack of progress to exploitative colonial revenue policies and the decimation of domestic manufacturing, particularly artisanal production, by foreign (and primarily British) imports. The "draining" of India's wealth, an image popularized by Naoroji in the 1890s, was to become a powerful mobilizing theme for Indian nationalism in the first half of the twentieth century; and its effects continued to linger after 1947 as Nehruvian planning sought to shield newly independent India from the clutches of metropolitan capital. Ranade's portrayal of the economy in the late nineteenth century as the indispensable supplement to "nation" was eerily prescient of the ethos of post-Independence Indian planning. According to Ranade:

> The agitation for political rights may bind the various nationalities of India together for a time. The community of interests may cease when these rights are achieved. But the commercial union of the various Indian nationalities, once established, will never cease to exist. Commercial and industrial activity is, therefore, a bond of very strong union and is, therefore, a mighty factor in the formation of a great Indian nation.[18]

To sum, in a phrase, the tactics of colonial government were at once *integrative and distancing:* land revenue and settlement policies, the enumeration of communities, curbs on "immoral" conduct, the cultivation of character via education and laws, attempts to deepen markets and instill a market ethic, and the construction of arterial infrastructure (roads, bridges, railway lines, telegraph lines, irrigation canals, etc.) that would boost both the volume and velocity of matter-flows, particularly commerce and, more precisely, give form to a generalized commodity economy.[19] But within the state assemblage of colonialism the diagram of development was realized in union with the diagram of, first, "civilization" and later, "race." As I showed in chapter 1, the figure of waste—with its connotations of ill use, inefficiency, inertness, and ineptitude—came to dramatize the telos of this thought, indexing the biocultural distance/difference separating Britain from India.

Ideologies of difference lingered in the postcolony, as evidenced by state paternalism towards tribal and out-of-caste groups in Nehruvian India. Even so, these practices were offset by a radical sense of horizontal solidarity. The critique of nationalist historiography (and hagiography) by subaltern studies scholarship notwithstanding, it is clear that within the imaginary of the nation's political elite, tribals may have been "child-like" and "backward," *but they were "one of us"* (unlike colonial difference, which was premised on the principle of "not us and never quite us"). The electoral democracy that took root in the postcolony was deeply flawed. It failed to deliver effective citizenship rights to all, but in principle at least it *entitled* everyone to them. It wanted to initiate a process of social change that would be equalizing. It did not selectively consign some to the "waiting room of History" while their powers of reason gestated and inched toward political maturity. This was a profound rupture with British rule. The emphasis on (often heavy-handed) planning and order by design by deeply centralized agencies was, on the other hand, a profound continuity with British rule. Like their colonial predecessors, India's new rulers implemented a range of economic policies to boost the production of use-values but also, ultimately, the circulation and consumption of exchange-values. Thus, given the ambivalent break with colonial rule, it is perhaps apt to capture postcolonial government by the phrase *integrative and incorporative*.

I have insisted that development is a diagram. Since this claim is a cornerstone of my analysis, it is important to foreclose misunderstandings. I want to be clear that a diagram is *not* an inner essence, kernel, or "deep structure" that gives expression to a (phenomenal) social totality. Nor is it ideology, if by that one means a set of false ideas that obscure one's "true interests." Development, of course, operates as ideology within social formations, but when it does, it is in the resolutely material form of common sense that regulates people's lived relations of existence—their dispositions and practices with respect to each other and to governing apparatuses. No easy claim of untruth is implied. To wit, diagrams are structural, *present only in their determinate absence, and repeated and realized only in their differential effects.* Diagrams, moreover, are not immune to mutation from the dense weave of (often banal, everyday) practices and micropolitics of concrete assemblages that actualize them. And all diagrammatic effects are spatial: they map out *territories* (which various constitutional logics—states, capitalisms, nationalisms, castes, social movements, and so on—then claim as their terrain of operation).

Plugged into a nation-state assemblage, development is operationalized as a technical apparatus for improving the Nation's well-being.

It sediments into the raison d'être of state and summons practices aimed at qualifying "bare life" *(zoe)* as "proper life" *(bios)*—education, public health, municipal services, nutrition, pre- and postnatal care, vaccination drives, occupational safety, transportation, agricultural credit, small business loans, property laws, antipollution ordinances, recreational facilities, life and health insurance policies, unemployment assistance, gender-equalization programs, antidowry laws, and antipoverty schemes (such as the Jawahar Rozgar Yojna or the Indira Awaas Yojna in India) are some common instances of practices that seek to improve the general "life" of a nation's population. Equally, the health of a population means that certain subpopulations are considered expendable—in pathological instances, imperative to exterminate—for the security and well-being of the majority. Often this majority is not a *numeric* majority, but rather the dominant fraction—the people—that claims to be the nation's *ethnos*.

This means that the State—which, as Giorgio Agamben notes, always exists as "the state of exception"—reserves the right to unleash intrusive, punitive, displacing, and violent practices in the name of a greater good. In postcolonial India, for instance, the refrains of "national interest" and "the nation's development" have been unfurled as ready-made justification for industrial and large river-valley projects that dispossess marginalized populations of ancestral lands and resources, or else disrupt local ecosystems so severely that customary livelihoods become unviable. Moreover, an army of antidemocratic provisions—the Maintenance of Internal Security Act (MISA),[20] the Official Secrets Act (OSA), Section 144, and so on—has been ready at hand to quell antidevelopment agitations, demonstrating that law repeatedly operates by suspending itself. Witness the heavy-handed suppression of the Narmada Bachao Andolan by the Government of Gujarat, or of peasants in Singur and Nandigram by the Government of West Bengal.[21] Indeed, violence is implicit in the utilitarian calculus (Bentham's ghost!) that guides postcolonial development, even if its declared object is now the health of the nation rather than the preservation of Empire.

McKenzie Wark remarks that "[a]t the empty heart of the state, its camera obscura, is the primary act of violence by which it establishes the separation of objects from subjects, and its own prerogative in policing the plane upon which they may meet."[22] Recognition that violence is an *ontological* condition of biopolitical power and state logic corrects a tendency in governmentality studies to mistake its formative place. It is common to run across arguments contending that governmental rationality is unable to give proper account of violence, hence must be supplemented by other rationalities. Thus, in an otherwise superb recent book on development and the cultural politics of territory in Zimbabwe, Donald Moore finds it necessary to "draw from Antonio Gramsci's reflections on hegemony as a crucial complement to governmentality . . . [in order to] understand legacies of violence in relation to projects of rule."[23] Similarly, take David Scott's instructive monograph on colonial governmentality in Sri Lanka and Jamaica where he characterizes the modern political rationality of government as follows:

> [I]f with sovereignty, the relation between ruler and ruled is such that power reaches out like an extension of the arm of the prince himself, announcing itself periodically with unambiguous ceremony, with government, governor and governed are thrown into a new and different relation, one that is not merely the product of the expanded capacity of the state apparatus but of the emergence of a new field for producing effects of power—the new, self-regulating field of the social.[24]

While Scott's observation is characteristically acute, violence or its specter as tactic of government (to oblige subjects to act, as they ought) takes a backseat in his account. He is correct to remind us that governmental reason exceeds a sovereign problematic of state. But is the governmentalized state a diminished or necessarily less violent entity than its sovereign predecessor? Isn't it, in fact, the case that, far from disappearing, the logic of sovereignty is instead reinvented: repeated with difference within the new art of government? Doesn't the state itself, transformed by the diagram of government, emerge as a more flexible and spatially dispersed entity, with an expanded arsenal of managerial tactics—many of them violent in newly innovative ways?[25] Michel Foucault appears to have implied no less when he wrote, "[W]ith government it is not a question of imposing law on men, but of disposing things: that is to say, of employing tactics rather than laws, and even of using laws themselves as tactics—to arrange things in such a way that, through a certain number of means, such and such ends may be achieved."[26] In short, the power to curtail or take a life and the power to invest life itself (the usual distinction drawn between sovereign and governmental power) are not antithetical or mutually exclusive political rationalities. They are, rather, assorted and contiguous modes of power.[27]

Nation as Problem-Space

The story of postcolonial development planning in India has been competently told several times and from various ideological angles, so it is hardly necessary to narrate it once again.[28] It will do to highlight some of the key early aspects that expose how "India" was assembled in planning debates as an object of development.[29] Sukhamoy Chakravarty, who was intimately involved with the planning process, writes that Indian planners perceived six underlying causes for the country's "structural backwardness":

> First, the basic constraint on development was seen as being an acute deficiency of material capital, which prevented the introduction of more productive technologies. Secondly, the limitation on the speed of capital accumulation was seen to lie in the low capacity to save. Thirdly, it was assumed that even if the domestic capacity to save could be raised by means of suitable fiscal and monetary policies, there were structural limitations preventing conversion of savings into productive investment. Fourthly, it was assumed that whereas agriculture was subject to secular diminishing returns, industrialization would allow surplus labor currently underemployed in agriculture to be more productively employed in industries which operated according to increasing returns to scale. A fifth assumption was that if the market mechanism were accorded primacy, this would result in excessive consumption by upper-income groups, along with relative under-investment in sectors essential to the accelerated development of the economy. Sixth, while unequal distribution of income was considered to be a "bad thing," a precipitate transformation of the ownership of productive assets was held to be detrimental to the maximization of production and savings.[30]

Retrospective critiques always risk being churlish and obvious, but it is important to note that the program of national development, while sovereign in *intent,* was never so in practice. As early as 1946, in *The Discovery of India,* Jawaharlal Nehru had displayed an acute awareness of the constraints imposed by India's location within a capitalist world order brokered by the United States. Taking a realist geopolitical line, he observed: "The United States want open markets for their exports and do not look with favour on attempts by other powers to limit or control them. They want rapid industrialization of Asia's millions and higher standards everywhere, not for sentimental reasons but to dispose of their surplus goods."[31] This hard-headed analysis was softened, if slightly, by a hope that expansionism by the world's dominant powers would not precipitate conflict:

> Although the interests and activities of States overflow their
> boundaries and are world-wide, no nation can isolate itself or
> be indifferent to the political or economic fate of other nations.
> If there is no cooperation there is bound to be friction with its
> inevitable results. Co-operation can only be on a basis of equality
> and mutual welfare, on a pulling up of backward nations and peoples
> to a common level of well-being and cultural advancement, on an
> elimination of racialism and domination.[32]

Nehru's views here are doubly significant because they signal both the break from and the continued affinity with colonial development doctrine. He firmly rejects the ideology of race, but takes for granted that the nation and people of India are economically and culturally "backward." The coterie of brilliant technocrats Nehru gathered around him post-1947 shared his conviction and viewed themselves as the intellectual vanguard that would pull a backward nation into the historical present no longer out-of-joint with time. The telos of this thought was the Time of History—and more precisely, capitalist development—inhabited by the West. This pull was evident in the plan of development that was implemented. While a self-confessedly "socialist" project, committed to social equality[33]—with its chosen modus operandi the Five-Year Plan in the Soviet mode—its central thrust was always capital formation and its modeling biases, supply-side and production-oriented. Nehru's administration oscillated in its attitude toward domestic industrialists and foreign investments, but its public hostility to them was offset by its private actions.[34]

The statistician P. C. Mahalanobis, who was the principal figure behind the Second Five-Year Plan (1955–60) and responsible for prosecuting "the primacy of the capital goods sector thesis," summarized the Indian planning approach as follows in an article first published in 1959 in the Soviet journal *Soveremennyi Vostok:* "The economic theory of the highly developed countries appears to be basically static in character and they are concerned, above all, with the most efficient distribution of the stock of capital and of other resources and not with the problems of economic development through an increase in capital accumulation."[35]

What were these problems of economic development? Mahalanobis confronted this question directly in an interview with All-India Radio that same year. "The object of economic development," he told his listeners, "is the improvement of the level of living of forty crores of our countrymen. This means having a bigger and bigger supply of food, clothes, housing, and such other things, and greater facilities for medical care, housing, education and cultural amenities. That is, having more and more of what economists call consumer goods and services."[36]

None of this is, of course, antithetical to socialism; and there is ample evidence that Mahalanobis was committed to socialist economics (thus, the Russian economist Grigorii Alexandrovich Feldman, from the 1920s, was a formative figure in Mahalanobis' thinking). Pitambar Pant, another key figure in the planning process, was similarly inclined and of the firm opinion that poverty alleviation ought to be the primary end of Indian planning. Nehru himself, as the driving force behind the Five-Year Plans, was deeply influenced by Fabian socialism and Lenin's critique of imperialism from the 1930s onward.[37] But the fissures are evident: by associating economic development with an expansion in "consumer goods and services" in his All-India Radio interview—How will this happen? What will it entail if not the deepening of capitalism?—Mahalanobis reveals the contradictory predilections of Nehruvian thought. We should not be surprised, then, that the regime of accumulation that emerged by 1964 was a State capitalist one with socialist elements (public sector enterprises, cooperatives, and community development initiatives aimed at poverty reduction). History reveals that this regime, euphemistically labeled a "mixed economy" model, consolidated the power of domestic monopoly capitalists and failed to confront the entrenched rural power structure. Is this a logical conundrum, given that the Indian planning model has often been characterized as a variant of the Soviet model?

Chakravarty, whose assessment of the planning process is acute, remarks that "[t]he Indian development model of the mid-fifties is probably better viewed as a variant of the [Arthur] Lewis model.... In the original Lewis model, the principal actors were capitalists in the 'modern' sector, but in the Indian case a development bureaucracy was also assigned a major role."[38] To state the obvious, Indian planning although resistant to imperialism was never antithetical to capitalism; it accepted the telos of modernization inscribed in capital-centric, dual-economy models like those of Arthur Lewis.[39] And like the Lewis model, the initial Five-Year Plans treated agriculture as subordinate to industry. This emerges most clearly in the views of Dr. S. R. Sen, who was adviser on agricultural problems to the Planning Commission during the 1950s. In a December 1959 speech at the All-India Agricultural Economics Conference in Baroda, Sen explicitly termed agriculture a "bargain sector," arguing that it could be harnessed as a reservoir of "large unexploited potential which can provide the requisite surplus [for industrialization] with relatively low investment and in a comparatively short time after, of course, a certain minimum infrastructure has been developed."[40]

Two further observations underscore the compromised socialism of India's development planning. First, even though a Gandhian Plan (authored by S. N. Agarwal) was presented in the 1944 debates that led up to the post-Independence planning process, it was "never seriously discussed by either mainstream economists or its left-wing critics."[41] Instead, it was sidelined as an anachronism unfit for the economic demands of a young nation that had to modernize, and quickly.[42] Louis Althusser has described ideology as "the very element and atmosphere indispensable to . . . historical respiration and life."[43] Closely linked to his notion of a "problematic" (which I discussed in chapter 1), ideology as the operation and lived, imaginary relations of that problematic not only enables certain questions to be asked and for suitable answers to be culled from the range of available solutions, it also ensures that certain questions and answers can never be considered *even* if they are, in principle, available.[44] This was, as it were, the fate of the Gandhian approach: in full sight but largely invisible, never conceived as a *viable* economic option for an underdeveloped country (the experiments with cooperatives, cottage industries, community development, and khadi notwithstanding). Nehru, for example, despite his closeness to Gandhi recorded sharp disagreements—even bewilderment—with his mentor's position on questions of modernization and development as early as 1935.[45] In a 1939 letter to Krishna Kripalani, Nehru vigorously defended the development of large-scale industry—he evocatively called it "the big machine"—against an economic program built around the khadi movement and cottage industries. Nehru wrote:

> It is true, I think, that there are certain inherent dangers in big
> industry and the big machine. There is a tendency to concentrate
> power and I am not quite sure that this can be wholly eliminated. But

> I cannot conceive of the world or any progressive country doing away
> with the big machine. Even if this were possible, this would result in
> lowering production tremendously and in thus reducing standards
> of life greatly. For a country to do away with industrialization would
> lead to that country falling prey, economically and otherwise, to
> other more industrialized countries, which would exploit it. For
> the development of cottage industries on a widespread scale, it is
> obvious that political and economic power is necessary. It is unlikely
> that a country entirely devoted to cottage industries will ever get this
> political or economic power.[46]

Here, Nehru presents industrialization as the indispensable *prior* of
cottage economics, hinting that those who would seek to build a nation
on that exclusive principle are out of touch with geopolitical realities.
Such views spilled over into Nehru's circle of experts.[47] Thus, explaining on All-India Radio how the production of consumer goods could
be increased "continually" (a notion antithetical to Gandhi and khadi
advocates) Mahalanobis averred:

> How can this be done? To some extent by using traditional methods
> of production such as weaving and handicrafts and by employing
> idle hands to the fullest extent. This would give employment to
> millions of our countrymen who are sitting idle for the whole or a
> good part of the day for lack of gainful work. *But this can go only
> part of the way. To increase production in a really big way we must use
> machinery.* . . .
>
> I have been speaking so far at a somewhat abstract level. Let
> us consider the historical evidence. The level of living in Europe
> was probably the same as in India two or three hundred years ago.
> There is some evidence to suggest that, for the vast masses of our
> countrymen, the level of living has not changed very much since the
> time of Akbar. There has been, however, a revolutionary progress
> in Europe and America. This was possible only through the use of
> machinery driven by steam or electricity instead of by human or
> animal labor, that is, *through the progress of science and technology.*[48]

There is perhaps no clearer evidence of the historicism and tense affinity
to the West that characterized, both, the right *and* the left in post-
Independence India.

A second observation to note is the failure of Indian policymakers
to carry out a program of radical land reform, even though the Second
Five-Year Plan endorsed a program of land redistribution that would

form the basis for a progressive agrarian structure.[49] At the time, the economic argument for sustained land reform, an inverse relationship between land productivity and landholding size, had strong theoretical and empirical justification and support from economists in India and abroad. But in face of the political imperative of keeping rural power-holders quiescent land reform measures were confined to abolition of intermediary tenures and the half-hearted enforcement of land ceilings. Several factors influenced this course of action, which Partha Chatterjee and Sudipta Kaviraj among others have described, following Gramsci, as a "passive revolution":[50] First, the forceful presence of rural elites in the ruling Congress Party; second, an assessment that rural elites, if directly challenged, could severely jeopardize law and order; third, the absence of *evident* signs of mass unrest among peasant classes; and, finally, the assumption that the rural masses, who comprised a raw electorate, might be more effectively enrolled to the hegemonic project of nation-making through the mediation of rural power-holders, who could mobilize large vote banks.[51]

India's development planners wished to operate on the nation as a statistician might on a model—Mahalanobis, for example, was very fond of input/output analysis—but found their Comtean desire to reduce development to a technical problem constantly thwarted by the state assemblage of which they were part. Every diagram needs a machinery to realize itself. Indian planners inherited some of this machinery, whether infrastructure or bureaucracy. The rest, such as a Ministry of Community Development and Cooperation, development blocks, *panchayati raj* institutions, and various arteries of economic circulation, had to be created. Development required the state to distribute itself territorially in order to reach its target populations. But dispersion and proliferation of the state apparatus had an electric political effect, producing disagreements and conflicts wherever it came into contact with society. The battles that erupted, particularly at the district and subdistrict levels, were frequently about where to draw the lines between state and civil society. Local elites seeking to preserve or extend their influence and subaltern groups intent on escaping or weakening this influence fought to control newly formed conduits of development and development resources:

> The state constitutes the plane upon which classes come to
> represent their interests as class interests, but also where classes

seek to turn local and particular conflicts not of a class nature to their advantage. . . . Thus, the state, besides constituting the plane of abstraction for class conflict, adds to it dimensions of possible conflict and alliance by providing resources and recognition for other interests and desires. Whatever desire exceeds or falls short of commodification seeks a home in the state.[52]

To wit, on the one hand, development enabled the postcolonial state to spatialize and clot power in unprecedented ways. On the other hand, as it distributed itself (thereby growing its surface area) it multiplied points of social conflict and "rent-seeking." In a nutshell, the Indian development experience threw into stark relief an old contradiction in liberal political theory, namely, where does the state end and civil society begin? Antonio Gramsci, who gave an acute diagnosis of this problem, had contended that the boundaries were inherently fuzzy and, as a con-sequence, society only existed *as* "political society."[53]

Nehru's technocrats were no doubt mindful of these intensifying contradictions. But they plunged ahead anyway with their Five-Year Plans. They were summoned to a higher calling: to build a modern nation. This entailed, among other tasks, a familiar crusade against waste. Nehru captured these sentiments in a remarkable 1954 speech. Speaking to a meeting of the Coordination Board of Ministers for River Valley Projects in New Delhi, he admonished that "the 360 million peo-ple" of India wanted not "words, even though words may signify much"; rather "they want food . . . they want clothing . . . they want shelter . . . they want health." Having warned his audience that "[w]ords are tricky things always" and that they "are thrown at each other as a bomb might be thrown at a person" he launched a ferocious verbal assault, clearly intended to rouse:

We have to utilize the experience we have gained, pool our resources and prevent wastage. . . . We cannot allow the nation's resources to be wasted. Democracy has many virtues, but one of its concomitants is wastage of time and energy. Nevertheless, for many reasons, we prefer democracy to other methods of government. That does not mean that we cannot avoid waste. We cannot afford waste, because the basic thing is that we should go ahead. The devil is at our heels, or as they say, "*Shaitan peechhe ata hai, to bhagte hain.*" I should like you to have this kind of feeling. To hell with the man who cannot walk fast. It serves him right if he gets out of the ranks and falls out. We want no sluggards. . . . I want work and work and work. I want achievement. I want men who work as crusaders.[54]

We could pick at Nehru's words endlessly, not the least for the specter of waste that haunts them. But I want to dwell on their strong undertow of authoritarianism, which the enterprise of planning also embodies.

Planning is the epitome of what Gilles Deleuze and Félix Guattari term a "state-form of knowledge," in that it aims to sedentarize in order to then act upon the materials it has fixed. "Form" itself takes on two meanings; thus, development planning, on the one hand, "forms or orga-nizes matter" and, on the other hand, "it forms or finalizes functions and gives them aims."[55] Correspondingly, "knowledge" is understood as that which formalizes and integrates (stratifies, stabilizes) the "visible" and the "articulable," or, simply, that which is able to be "seen" and "said." In Indian development planning, this formalization—a spatialisation of vision—was achieved through a variety of inscription devices,[56] which included surveys, maps, input–output models, statistical tabulations, flow-charts, budgets, reports, strategic plans, institutional diagrams, fiscal and monetary policies, and pricing mechanisms. There were other pressing concerns of nation-making (particularly frayed regional unity, linguistic divisions, casteism, and religious discord) but they were rendered subordinate—perhaps in an act of willed ignorance—to problems of the economy. Doggedly modernist and socialist in its self-conception, Indian planning, like European liberalism and Stalinism before it, sought to evacuate the political from the stage.[57] The elevation of the economy to the dominant instance (and on this point the left and right parties were agreed[58]) meant that that the nation-state effectively became an abstracted "problem-space" on which development planning could write itself. Abstraction, the sine qua non of planning, is after all nothing more and nothing less than a way of producing and organizing space in the exercise of power.[59]

From the vantage point of India's development planners, the long 1950s in India were witness to two sharply different performances: on the one hand, the agrarian scene where in the perception of planners "instinct" flailed against the guiding force of "reason,"[60] generating a cycle of conflict and accommodation that turned land reform into a tepid spectacle; on the other hand, the industrial sector where the imprint of "economy" could be firmly asserted and where, as a result, the crackling drama of industrialization could unfold. The development plans underscore these beliefs. Compare, for example, the pattern of allocation of funds of the first three Five-Year Plans (Table 1).

The numbers reveal that by the time of the Second Five-Year Plan, industry had been anointed as the leading sector of the economy, commanding 21.1 percent of the planned outlay, as compared to 7.9 percent in the First Five-Year Plan and in stark contrast to agriculture's share of 11.3 percent in the Second Plan. But it would be myopic to merely flag industry's ascendance. The plan outlays speak vividly to the operations of postcolonial power. In the projection of nation as economy, frayed geographies are gathered into orderly categories for development. The theodicy of salvation, which insistently lurked within the secular edifice of colonial government, is replaced by the immanent commonplaces of health, literacy, social security, and wellbeing (which includes the expansion of wealth as well as the emergent metric of living standards).[61]

Development becomes coterminous with the expansion of goods and services—material "freedoms"—and the State itself, in the imagination of governors and the governed, takes on the function of an "economic pastorate." The consistently high outlays for transport and communications and the rising outlays for power[62] within the Five-Year Plans bespeaks the concern of planners to reinforce and multiply the channels which connect and combine human and nonhuman bodies into an economy. David Harvey has felicitously characterized capital as "value in motion": in other words, growth and accumulation require that money, raw materials, consumer goods, and various types of productive capital—including, especially, labor as variable capital—be able to circulate in order to match up with end users rapidly *and* widely (thereby sustaining a process of "expanded reproduction" rather than "simple reproduction").[63] In combination with the prominent outlays for social and community services, the patterns of allocation also testify to the new pastoral function of government as "the conduct of conduct,"[64] as well as the demands of hegemony. The governed in an electoral democracy, howsoever constricted in their range of conducts by existing structures of domination and the uncertain prospects of citizenship, nevertheless have some capacity to ask why those who govern should be in *that* relation to them, if only because, like planning, democracy is also a rule of numbers.[65] Only by destabilizing the self-evidences of that relation can

Table 1. Planned Public-Sector Outlays in the First Four Five-Year Plans, 1951–74 (Rs. Crores)

	Agriculture and allied sectors	Irrigation and flood control	Power	Industry and minerals	Transport and communications	Social and community services	Total
First Plan, 1951/52 to 1955/56							
Planned outlay	354 (14.9)	469 (19.7)	179 (7.5)	188 (7.9)	570 (24.0)	618 (26.0)	2378 (100.0)
Actual expenditure	290 (14.8)	432 (22.0)	151 (7.7)	97 (4.9)	518 (26.4)	472 (24.1)	960 (100.0)
Second Plan, 1956/57 to 1960/61							
Planned outlay	510 (11.3)	436 (9.7)	321 (7.1)	950 (21.1)	1340 (29.8)	943 (21.0)	4500 (100.0)
Actual expenditure	549 (11.8)	436 (9.3)	446 (9.5)	1125 (24.1)	1261 (27.0)	855 (18.3)	4672 (100.0)
Third Plan, 1961/62 to 1965/66							
Planned outlay	1068 (14.2)	650 (8.7)	1012 (13.5)	1784 (23.8)	1486 (19.8)	1500 (20.0)	7500 (100.0)
Actual expenditure	1089 (12.7)	665 (7.8)	1252 (14.6)	1967 (22.9)	2112 (24.6)	1492 (17.4)	8577 (100.0)
Fourth Plan, 1969/70 to 1973/74							
Planned outlay	2728 (17.2)	1087 (6.8)	2448 (15.4)	3631 (22.8)	3237 (20.4)	2771 (17.4)	15902 (100.0)
Actual expenditure	2320 (14.7)	1354 (8.6)	2932 (18.6)	3107 (19.7)	3080 (19.5)	2986 (18.9)	15779 (100.0)

Note: One crore equals 10 million.
Source: Adapted from Sukhamoy Chakravarty, *Development Planning: The Indian Experience* (Oxford: Clarendon Press, 1987), 108–9.

we properly understand how development comes to be the raison d'être of the postcolonial nation-state—irreducibly part of its ontology, such that it ultimately becomes impossible to speak of belonging to India without also gesturing to its development (or lack thereof).[66]

Although their socialist leanings initially committed Indian planners to a strategy of autonomous development—what Third World Marxists like Samir Amin would call "disarticulated development"—by the beginning of the Third Plan, in 1962, India had already entered "into an agreement with the United States on the large-scale import of food grains under PL480 (which enabled food grains to be imported, largely against payment in rupees and partly as a gift)."[67] The importance of maintaining, in the words of S. R. Sen, "a cheap food regime" for capital accumulation and growth trumped the concern for autonomy.[68] It took two severe and successive droughts, in 1965–66 and 1966–67, which led to catastrophic declines in food production, for planners to revisit the "industry-first" strategy of development. By then, the utopias of development planning had begun to crumble. The Fourth Five-Year Plan, drafted in 1965–66 but abandoned, was finally adopted in 1969 in revised form. Among its provisions was a new strategy of agricultural development. This was reflected in the considerably expanded plan outlay for "agriculture and allied sectors," which rose from 11.3 percent in the Second Plan to 17.2 percent by the Fourth Plan.

The theoretical justification for the agricultural development approach was furnished most forcefully in the work of the agricultural economist John Mellor and his followers. Writing in the mid-1960s, Mellor concerned himself with the problem of "agricultural modernization," which meant augmenting the stock of capital within "traditional agriculture."[69] This was a departure from classical dual-economy models, which subordinated agriculture to industry in the service of capital formation as per the Mahalanobis doctrine. Mellor, by contrast, maintained that capital stocks in a primarily agrarian economy like India were low to begin with because traditional cultivators did not have the proper attitude or spirit of entrepreneurship toward savings, investment, and consumption—a condition that could be partly attributed to poor production technologies, which in turn meant low marginal returns to capital. Like Dale Jorgensen, who was the first to propose a neoclassical dual-economy model in 1961,[70] Mellor stressed the importance of technological change or innovation in agriculture for capital accumulation;

unlike Jorgensen, he viewed such overall economic growth as a function of productivity advances within agriculture that required the introduction of both improved physical *and* institutional "inputs." Hence, material inputs like high-yielding or improved seed varieties, fertilizers, pesticides, irrigation, and better breeds of livestock had to be complemented by institutional inputs such as tenurial security, credit facilities, marketing networks, and research and extension in order for the effective deployment of the former.

Mellor's program claimed to offer a concrete answer to the question "How does agricultural modernization occur?" which dual-economy theorists for the most part had simply bypassed. Although Mellor pinpointed the specific factors that would catalyze the transition from traditional to modern (that is, capitalist) agriculture, his stages-of-development model—morphologically similar to Walt Rostow's stages-of-growth framework or Talcott Parsons' stages-of-society scheme—carried the burden of being historicist without being *historical*.[71]

How did the development policies set in motion by the initial five-year plans and subsequently by Mellor's new agricultural strategy reverberate in Gujarat, particularly in a hitherto rainfed agricultural tract like Matar Taluka? Did it produce the sort of modernization and capitalist transformation of agriculture desired by Indian planners? Did it erode existing social hierarchies detrimental to capital and promote an agrarian regime geared toward its accumulation? Did it manage to bracket the political and assert the primacy of the economic? Did the connections forged between human and nonhuman entities in order to foster improvements have unexpected effects—surprises from "novelty by combination"? If so, how did these play out? These are the empirical questions that I intend to confront in the following pages.

Hydropolitics

Gilles Deleuze and Félix Guattari think of the State not as a complex center from which power radiates but rather as a compositional logic, which wants to link disparate elements into a "molar" set capable of functioning in particular ways. They identify three forms of molar *identities* that States try to produce: Organisms, Signs, and Subjects. "The State," they write, "is a phenomenon of *intraconsistency*. It makes points resonate together . . . very diverse points of order, [that span] geographic, ethnic, linguistic, moral, economic, technological particularities."[72] Alain Badiou, after them (but also differently), elaborates on the question "What is the State"? He claims, as I will, that it is fundamentally *a unifying logic, which operates in geographically diverse sites through historically particular institutional materialities.* Thus, when I invoke the state I am thinking not just of arboreal knots of power such as ministries, departments, agencies, councils, commissions, courts, legislative assemblies, and the like, but more generically about *any apparatus of regulation that (a) orders diverse entities through a principle of composition; and (b) claims force of (formal or customary) law on its side—and frequently, sovereign exception in law—in order to accomplish this.* In Alain Badiou's reckoning, the state—he uses the term in its ontological and political senses—is an operation of "one-ificiation":

> The state is . . . a kind of primordial response to anarchy. The violent imposition order . . . is itself an intrinsic feature of [its] being as such. The state maintains order among the subsets, that is, it groups elements in the various ways required to keep them ultimately, in their proper, established places in the situation. The state does not present things, nor does it merely copy their presentation, but instead, "through an entirely new counting operation, re-presents them," and re-presents them in a way that groups them in relatively fixed, clearly identifiable, categories.[73]

Giorgio Agamben contends in a matching assessment that "In the final analysis the state can recognize any claim for identity. . . . But what the state cannot tolerate in any way is that singularities form a community without claiming an identity, that human beings co-belong without a representable condition of belonging."[74] In short, state logic is always technological, calculative, representational, and exclusionary. It seeks to connect—or, following the figure of the "camp,"[75] cordon—disparate elements (a multiplicity) into a set of some *thing: to make them one.* Why? So that the assembled order, inclusive or outcaste, is rendered functional in new ways. The developmental state deploys planning to fabricate *a nation-set that will perform development.* Similarly, the vectoral logic of late capitalism attempts, via its power centers, to modulate—exchange, convert, oscillate—various flows in order to make the world perform market-led accumulation.

The telos of improvement that is development requires nimble governance: statecraft as *management* of matter-flows that delicately balances movement and constraint, flow and formation. "One of the fundamental tasks of the State," Deleuze and Guattari remark, "is to striate the space over which it reigns, or to utilize smooth spaces as means of communication in the service of striated space."[76] Paul Veyne is more vivid. In his essay "Foucault Revolutionizes History," he likens the modern state to "an agent of the conservation department, who controls and channels [the natural tendencies of water systems and plant life] in such a way that natural processes can continue and plant life will not die out." "The agent-manager," he continues, "does not leave nature to its own devices: he meddles with it, but only in order to leave nature in better shape than before. He might be compared with a traffic cop who 'channels' the spontaneous movement of traffic so it will flow smoothly: that is his job." Veyne adds: "As a result drivers proceed in safety; this is called the welfare state, and it is the one we live in."[77] One is unlikely to find a better description or rationale for the gigantic river valley development projects and canal irrigation schemes that were undertaken during Nehru's reign.[78]

The state of Gujarat, unlike other parts of India, has lacked a history of large irrigation works. Even the Khari River system, which brings water to several villages in the northern portion of Matar Taluka[79]—and which, during British rule, was hailed as the most expansive surface irrigation system in Gujarat—was but a shadow of the massive irrigation projects implemented in Punjab, Sindh, Uttar Pradesh, and South India in the late nineteenth and early twentieth centuries. In fact, at "the beginning of the Five Year Plan period (i.e., before 1951) . . . Gujarat had no major or medium irrigation projects."[80] The Nehru-Mahalanobis model of development set in motion, as we have seen, a series of Five-Year Plans that allocated progressively larger sums of money for the construction of major, medium, and minor irrigation projects in India, including the state of Gujarat.[81] By the end of the Seventh Plan in 1992, Gujarat had an irrigation potential of 3.05 million acres through major and medium surface irrigation projects (primarily canals and tanks) from a projected total—surface plus groundwater—irrigation potential of 16.23 million acres.[82]

Large-scale canal irrigation as a technology of government is combinatorial: it attempts to direct the forces of nature, but with the explicit aim of altering the physical facts that regulate people's relations with each other and the things with which they interact. The Nehruvian state promoted hydraulic development as a biopolitical logic of composition that would make various energies resonate in a bodily order conducive to economic production and national unity.[83] The Mahi Right Bank Canal (MRBC) project was one of the earliest major surface-irrigation schemes commissioned in postcolonial Gujarat. By 2002, the MRBC was operational in 485 villages over seven subdistricts of Kheda. It had a culturable command area (CCA) of 525,567 acres, serviced by a main canal with six branches and thirty-eight distributaries. The climate of the MRBC command area is semi-arid with an average annual rainfall of 32.43 inches (823 mm).[84] The first stage of the project was completed in 1958 with the construction of the Wanakbori division weir in Balasinor Taluka of Kheda District. The primary purpose of the Wanakbori weir was to divert water from the river Mahi into the canal system. Since it had almost no storage capacity, the Wanakbori weir could at most provide supplemental irrigation for the *kharif* (monsoon) crop. The second stage of the MRBC project was completed in 1978 with the construction of the Kadana dam and reservoir in Santrampur Taluka of Panchmahal District. Although the reservoir was designed to supply perennial irrigation to the MRBC command area, in practice it has only tended to provide assured irrigation to the kharif crop and conjunctive, partial, and generally unreliable irrigation to the *rabi* (winter) crop. Even in 1992–93, one of its best performance years, the MRBC project managed to irrigate only 0.24 million acres in the kharif season and 0.18 million acres in the *rabi* season: in other words, well short of its designated irrigation potential in both crop seasons.[85]

Table 2. Pattern of Irrigation in Matar Taluka, 1893–1985 (in acres)

Year	Government canals	Tanks	Wells	Other	Total
1893					8,230
1915					6,201
1930					5,208
1966	21,068	565	4,133	3,930	29,696
1975	33,762	2,145	11,732	400	48,039
1985	47,300	4,455	57,762	625	110,142

Sources: Data for 1893, 1915, 1930, and 1966 from Table 5.1 in Vimal Shah and C. H. Shah, *Re-Survey of Matar Taluka* (Bombay: Vora and Co., 1974), 74. Data for 1975 from Table 2.9 in Vimal Shah, C. H. Shah, and Sudershan Iyengar, *Agricultural Growth with Equity* (Delhi: Concept Publications, 1990), 36. Data for 1985 from Table 4 in Kheda Jilla Panchayat, "District Agricultural Profile of Kheda District," mimeograph (Nadiad: Statistical Division, n.d.), 5.

I showed in chapter 2 how the American Civil War and almost concurrent arrival of the railway to Kheda District in 1863 dramatically accelerated the tempo of capitalism and give rise to new social orderings. And so it has been with the MRBC project. State knowledge, with its apparatuses of capture in waiting, has engraved itself on the agrarian landscape. As the canal's arboreal architecture—with a main trunk, major branches, and minor and subminor offshoots—has sliced through the landscape, it has produced in its path eddies of "dislocation,"[86] defining new terrains of power and resistance, and making possible the joining of old and new ensembles of surplus extraction. As an example, gross cropped area in the MRBC command area increased from 186,560 acres in 1975–76 to 517,922 acres in 1995–96. These dramatic effects have been achieved despite the canal project's truant performance—which includes conspicuous inequities in water flow between the main and branch canals on the one hand, and the distributaries on the other; overirrigation by cultivators (resulting in rising water tables and soil salinity) in segments of the canal where flows are generally adequate; and significant head-to-tail difference in supply across the MRBC system.[87] In Matar Taluka, the extension of two feeder branches from the MRBC project into the rainfed Limbasi tract in 1962 (thanks to well-pitched political lobbying, I was told) have transformed production in its fifty-seven-odd villages.[88] Initially only a handful of villages and, within them, a handful of plots gained from the canal. However, by 1975 fully 63 percent of the net sown area in the Limbasi villages had come under irrigation.[89] And by 1992–93, the area watered by the Matar and Limbasi branches of the MRBC, which feed the tract, had grown 300 percent from 16,475 acres in 1979–80 to 45,222 acres.[90]

Discussing bourgeois systems (of philosophy, governance, and economy) Theodor Adorno observes that they claim the mantle of science, and "scientific objectification . . . tends to eliminate qualities and transform them into measurable definitions. Increasingly, rationality itself is equated *more mathematico* with the faculty of quantification."[91] Adorno's words can stand in as a telegraphic manifesto of development planning and its stern technological aesthetic, which first stages a world as "standing reserve." Its logic of measure, which operates in practice as a flexible alliance between deductive reason and empiricist knowledge, is an extraordinarily powerful one, able to achieve unprecedented transformations of people and spaces as it pursues "the task of distributing

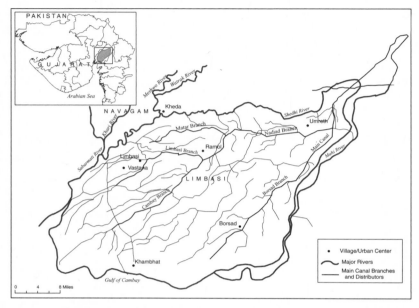

Map 3. Mahi Irrigation Circle, Nadiad. Index plan shows the canal and drains. Courtesy of Sula Sarkar.

the living in the domain of value and utility."[92] How successful is this distribution of "the living"? How effectively is the aleatory innoculated? How able is the State to ward off sources of surprise—the indeterminacies of novelty by combination that might thwart its desired composition of nature-society? Consider how irrigation has transformed the agrarian scene in Matar Taluka.

The mid-1960s were troubled years for Indian planning: expenditures related to the unforeseen war with China in 1962; anxieties over persistent food deficits; Nehru's death in 1964; the first Indo-Pakistan war in 1965. All conspired to put the planning process out of kilter and its certitudes on hold. The Fourth Five-Year Plan was postponed while planners reassessed their tactics. It was in the midst of this tumult, in 1965, that the Planning Commission of India funded a re-survey of Matar Taluka. Why Matar? Because, as we have seen, a large portion of the subdistrict had been recently folded into the MRBC command area and a baseline profile of Matar Taluka already existed thanks to the Gandhian economist J. C. Kumarappa's 1929–30 survey. A methodical assemblage of tables, charts and correlations, the re-survey brought to life a transposable image of an agrarian economy, ready to be programmed as input into the planning process. It confirmed the positive income and employment effects of canal irrigation and its role in narrowing interregional economic disparity between the Limbasi and historically well-irrigated Navagam Divisions of Matar.[93] A second, more sloppy, re-survey of the subdistrict conducted in 1974–75 (but only published in 1990) indicated that with the continued spread of canal and well irrigation in the Limbasi area there was a leveling of economic differences, both regionally and across occupational groups.[94] Both surveys recorded a resounding change in cropping pattern, from dry wheat or cotton single cropping, or cotton and pigeon pea intercropping, to predominantly paddy and dry wheat or paddy and irrigated wheat double-crop rotations. Earlier, when agriculture depended on the whims of the monsoon, double cropping was possible only in certain black-soil tracts that sequester water and then too only in good rainfall years. In the post-MRBC era, it became possible virtually every year and in almost all black-soil areas (and as the groundwater table of the area rose with seepage from canals, even on *goradu* lands with borewells).[95]

How does one squeeze into concepts and categories the fluid dynamics of water and the heterogeneous, frequently contentious relationships in which it is implicated? By abstracting from variety and flows, arresting the unruly *kinesis* of becomings in the instantaneous image of being. Essence, we know from the Greeks, is not merely the sense of beauty: *it is the sense of beauty that is the sense of order.* Take, for instance, a probability distribution with its graceful order of mean, median, standard deviation and so on. Its very possibility is testament to the taming of chance; or at the very least, to the possibility of that conceit. What will the benefit-to-cost ratio of an irrigation project be over its lifespan? How is water delivery likely to fluctuate from year to year and month to month? If x cubic feet per second of water are released at the head of a channel, what portion will reach the tail? How large are conveyance—evapotranspiration and seepage—losses likely to be? What proportion of cultivators in the command area of the irrigation network is likely to receive water on a regular basis? How effectively will cultivators be able to utilize irrigation capacity? How likely is it to boost agricultural production, and by how much? These are the sorts of probabilistic questions—lacerated by "ifs" and "buts"—that irrigation management confronts and must answer in order to provide a rationale for itself.[96] As a state intervention *more mathematico,* an irrigation scheme diagrams a particular kind of statistical transformation, which can be represented by a two-step process: assuming a positive correlation between water availability and (some vector of) farm-level output, irrigation, first of all, produces a narrower but mean-preserving distribution of aggregate output or use-values. More certain supply of water means less year-to-year fluctuations in production (in certain instances it may also mean less variance in output for a cross-section of beneficiary farms). The second step is to imagine a narrower distribution that is pushed over to the right on a horizontal axis that measures aggregate output, in short, a mean-enhancing distribution. More certain supply of water not only diminishes intertemporal variability in output, it actually boosts mean aggregate output. Cultivators, on average, are able to produce more than they used to before irrigation. None of these results is a technological given; more assured irrigation does not translate into higher average output without human mediation. Planners infer the transformed distribution from a behavioral model populated by rational cultivators, some risk-averse and others risk-neutral.[97] In short, *homo economicus* is an analytical prior in development planning. *He is also its desired effect.* How?

Power flows with water, literally, as cultivators now gain the capacity (or freedom) to conduct agriculture in ways previously not possible—or so goes the planning story. In fact, power circulates unevenly and wrestles to stratify forces that continuously evade its grasp (but more on this later). There is, however, one effect that cannot be ignored: how irrigation and other connective projects of development *intensify* a certain species of reason: *namely, an instrumental reason that is disposed to exchange-value production.* I want to be clear: the claim is not that development enables instrumental reason per se (such a claim would be absurd, even Eurocentric[98]). Rather, my claim is that development puts in place an infrastructure—a networked collective of humans and nonhumans—within which certain kinds of *economic* conducts now become intelligible, and compelling. I am referring to conducts that are staged within a calculative rationality, which weighs alternative courses of action through the abstracted calculus of money and marginal gain or loss. Such market rationality or, more exactly, conducts that are normatively oriented to capitalist "value" production, is always contaminated and in danger of being interrupted by other rationalities (see chapters 4 and 5). Market calculativeness is not a metaphysical *property* of humans; nor, for that matter, of the sovereign individual who inhabits mainstream rational choice theories. It is, instead, a place- and time-specific effect of a *dispositif* (that is, of a social-technical assemblage built up of humans and nonhumans).[99]

In an unexpected way, this is also one possible (and provocative) reading of the new economics of imperfect information—namely, that when *extra*human conditions for certain types of flows (information, commodities, labor, various other forms of capital) are absent, economic conduct oriented to market production may not only fail to occur, it may fail to occur because it is *not intelligible* to human agents given an existing network of associations. It goes without saying that neoclassical and new institutional economics are normative. They are forms of knowledge that are in concordance with capitalism and its desired forms of subjectivity (Karl Marx, famously, offered a comparable diagnosis of political economy in his *Economic and Philosophic Manuscripts of 1844*). But this is precisely why we should be attentive to the stories economists tell: they are not fabrications in a trivial sense; instead, they seek to fabricate a reality in which those tales will become intelligible narratives of life itself. The abstract concept of marginal value, in short, works on the same ontological plane as life and because of powerful institutional sanctions carries the viral potential to envelop—and become the explanatory index for—virtually all realms of human life.[100] If this disciplinary imperialism is a concern, deriding economics and its purveyors will not get us far. The task, a formidable one, is to produce countertales that can be affective of thought and conduct in different normative ways. As positive practice, hegemony (or counterhegemony) is not only about staking out oppositions but also about producing alternative possibilities for living and becoming. One could also add that hegemony, so conceived, is not about ideologies as ideas that can suture a historic bloc. It is not even about consciousness (in the voluntarist sense). It is, rather, about the laborious production of an assemblage—of words *and* objects—within which certain associations, hence certain *common* projects and conditions of life, become visible and sayable.

What is the evidence that canal irrigation and its retinue of development interventions has affected cultivators' conducts in intended ways? Although the absence of panel household data on production precludes analysis of trends in mean output, available information from

Table 3. Yields of Principal Crops in Matar Taluka, 1929–95 (kilograms per acre)

Crop	1929–30	1965–66	1974–75	1982	1995
Paddy	267	767	958	1235–1291	1392–2088
Bajra	89	212	396	918–1047	870–1218
Wheat	120	219	519	489–720	696–1218

Note: Figures represent range from lowest to highest per-acre production. Productivity figures are not adjusted for varietal substitution.
Sources: Data for 1929–30 and 1965–66 are from Table 16.7 in Shah and Shah, Re-Survey of Matar Taluka, 249. Data from 1974–75 are from Table 5.3 in Shah, Shah, and Iyengar, Agricultural Growth with Equity, 98. Data from 1982 are from Table 3 in GIAP, 24–26; figures are for irrigated paddy, kharif irrigated bajra, and irrigated wheat. Data from 1995 are from representative sample of cultivators, author's field survey, 1994–95.

Matar Taluka suggests notable average productivity gains in the postirrigation phase.[101] The lack of panel data also makes it difficult to contrast changes in the *variability* of output between the pre- and postirrigation phases (Table 3). But even if the desired data were available, the shift in cropping pattern and the continuous substitution of crop varieties by farmers would render a "before" and "after" comparison turbid. Hearsay evidence from numerous interviews with cultivators, laborers, and traders in several villages in the MRBC command area does suggest, however, that canal irrigation has dramatically reduced the likelihood of crop failures. Some interviewees responded that the probability of a "bad" (zero marketable surplus) year had declined from one in every two to one in every five or six. Moreover, the coefficient of variation[102] in annual rainfall—another measure of distribution—between 1982 and 1993, when contrasted with the coefficient of variation in the supply of irrigation water in the kharif season for the same period in the two main distributories serving the Limbasi area, appears to confirm a reduction in agronomic risk, at least at the aggregated subdistrict level if not necessarily at the level of individual plots (see Table 4).

   While the information in these tables permits the conjecture that production risk for cultivators in the irrigated Limbasi tract has in fact declined, what about the income risk of households who depend primarily upon agricultural wage labor for their livelihoods? Again, the available evidence on labor absorption in agriculture post-1966 suggests a diminution in income risk.[103] This finding is in line with a variety of economic studies over the past two decades which have shown

Table 4. Coefficient of Variation for Rainfall and Irrigation *(kharif)*,
Limbasi Division, Matar

Period	Rainfall	Traj Distributory	Limbasi Distributory
1982–93	0.40	0.26	0.35
1966–86	0.50	n/a	n/a
1876–1993	0.44	n/a	n/a

Sources: Coefficient of variations computed on the basis of rainfall figures from 1876
to 1993 obtained from MRBC Authority, Nadiad. Traj Distributory computed using
Traj and Limbasi Distributory figures obtained from MRBC Authority, Nadiad.
Irrigation performance figures were available only for the period 1979–93. For the
1981–82 agricultural year, the measuring station at Matar recorded an annual rainfall
of 1495 mm—twice the 1876–1993 normal of 750 mm. Hence, no irrigation water was
supplied to Limbasi Division in *kharif* 1981. Inclusion of zero supply in 1981 skews the
coefficient of variation for irrigation water unjustifiably, so I have limited the calculation
to the period 1982–93.

that a technological package of irrigation and modern (hybridized or
genetically modified) crop varieties normally results in increased labor
absorption per unit of land and that this trend is more pronounced and
permanent in the case of rice cultivation as opposed to wheat.

Hence, a well-regarded study by Chinnappa and Silva on the income
and employment effects of HYV paddy cultivation in North Arcot
District of Tamil Nadu showed that HYV paddy cultivation demands
16 percent more labor (in person-days per acre) for operations than
traditional varieties cultivated under rainfed conditions.[104] A roughly
concurrent investigation by the International Rice Research Institute,
also in North Arcot District, revealed that cultivation of high-yielding
as opposed to traditional rice varieties increased labor demand by
33 percent (from 175 days to 232 days).[105] The difference in estimates
between the IRRI and the Chinnappa-Silva studies indicates the sharp
regional variations in labor utilization that are characteristic of paddy
cultivation. But these studies and others collectively testify to the greater
employment opportunities generated by the cultivation of improved
and high-yielding varieties of rice.[106]

By 1974–75, 47 percent of all cultivators in Matar Taluka reported
use of improved or high-yielding varieties of paddy, and 49 percent
reported use of modern wheat varieties. There was no marked difference in the *incidence* of adoption across land-size classes, although data
on proportionate area planted under modern varieties—which would
indicate the *level of adoption* by size classes—is not available. By 1982,

the rate of adoption of modern varieties had risen to 98 percent, and once more it was broadly equal across size classes.[107] In 1994–95, my formal surveys in the villages of Shamli and Astha,[108] and informal surveys elsewhere, revealed that virtually all cultivators planted modern varieties of rice and wheat. In the case of rice, these included Gujarat-17, *masoori*, and *jirasar* (all of which are *sudhareli jaat*, that is, "improved varieties"). In the case of wheat, the varieties were GDD-496 (a high-yielding variety), HD-2189, and Gujarat-1 (both improved varieties, although Gujarat-1, which is locally also known as Arnej-3/13, requires fewer waterings than HD). Again, there was *no* marked variation by size class in the incidence of adoption of modern varieties.[109]

A back-of-the-envelope calculation suggests that the phenomenal expansion in paddy acreage alone in Matar Taluka, between 1965 and 1984 (see Table 5), must have generated approximately 5,248 additional person-years in farm employment,[110] with no need for downward compensation as a result of the roughly 5,000-acre reduction in acreage under pearl millet *(bajra),* whose cropping season competes directly with that of paddy.[111] The available data suggests that the introduction of canal irrigation has vastly augmented farm employment opportunities for wage labor in Limbasi Division and, through an increase in cropping intensity, diminished the seasonality (therefore, variability) of agricultural employment.

Meanwhile, a comparison of crop acreage statistics for 1965 and 1974 shows that early gains in labor absorption were from an increase in cropping intensity[112] as well as the possibility of cultivating irrigated varieties of the principal crops (Table 5). The former (rise in cropping intensity) increases the attractiveness of agriculture as investment opportunity for idle or underutilized capital elsewhere; the latter (cultivation of irrigated crops) increases labor utilization. The combined result is an expansion in surplus value extraction. Rise in cereal production was initially counterbalanced by a decline in the production of local pulses such as *tuver* (pigeon pea) and *chana* (chickpea), which are important components of rainfed agriculture. But this decline should be attributed less to a substitution of pulses by cereals (since they are typically planted in different soil types)[113] and more to a diversion of family and hired labor away from pulses to the more lucrative wheat crop, whose cropping season overlaps with that of tuver and chana. The large observed decline in net sown area under pulses between 1965 and 1974 supports this interpretation. Farmers in aggregate were calculating for profit, as their economic governors intended.

Table 5. Area under Principal Crops, Matar Taluka, 1965–85 (in acres)

Crop	1965–66	1974–75	1984–85	Change in acreage, 1965–84	Percent change, 1965–84
Paddy	32602	33087	73635	41023	125.83
Wheat	17287	23072	23152	5865	33.93
Bajra	20382	27635	15460	−4922	−24.15
Tuver	1650	302	3472	−1822	110.42
All cereals	80605	89540	116657	36052	44.73
All pulses	6430	1825	6980	550	8.55
Net sown area	113847	106810	137902	24055	21.33

Sources: Data for 1965–66 and 1974–75 from Table 2.15 in Shah, Shah, and Iyengar, *Agricultural Growth with Equity*, 42. Data for 1984–85 from Tables 4.5 and 4.8 in Panchayat, "District Agricultural Profile of Kheda District," 41–45, 56.

As minors and subminors were extended in the Limbasi area from the main branch canals and actual irrigated area expanded, there was a dramatic switch away from *bajra* (millet) and other so-called inferior cereals to quasi-cash crops like paddy—a trend that crop acreage statistics loudly register. Meanwhile pulses, which service the livestock economy, rebounded. To summarize, while initial gains in labor absorption were primarily due to an increase in cropping intensity, with the continuing diffusion of surface irrigation these gains increasingly started to derive from a shift in crop-mix heavily in favor of wet-rice cultivation[114]— although spread of multiple-cropping continued to be an important subsidiary factor. Indeed, area sown more than once in Matar Taluka (not shown in preceding table) increased almost 300 percent—from 9,180 acres in 1965–66 to 35,490 acres by 1984–85.[115]

Novelty by Combination

So, at least on the face of it, development interventions in Matar Taluka appear to have deepened the grip of capitalism and substantially altered the relation of the governed to their things, linking them even more tightly to "the domain of value and utility." But is irrigation the unqualified success it appears to be?

Agriculture is a variable ecology, an evolving and spatially heterogeneous collective of human and nonhuman interactions, not a sector in a planning model. Take rice farming. Soils and their molecular constituents (both organic and inorganic) have to be nurtured, some more than others. The cation exchange capacity (CEC) of soils, which determines how effectively they absorb plant nutrients in the form of ions, has to be enrolled or modified. Organic manures have to be applied at certain points, but not in such doses that they cause concentrations of iron and manganese to reach toxic levels in the soil-water solution. Certain plants (desired crops) have to be coaxed to grow, others (undesirable grasses and "weeds") have to be discouraged. The movements of animals (goats, cows, snakes, beetles, bees, grasshoppers, caterpillars, mealybugs, stem borers, brown planthoppers, whorl maggots, cutworms, rice panicle mites, and various bacteria, viruses, nematodes, blights, and fungi) have to be regulated. Water has to be induced to flow along particular vectors into the field—and out, as and when required. In the case of paddy, water also has to be sequestered in place to allow circulation of nutrients and to advantage rice saplings over rival flora competing for finite growing space and resources. During crucial bands of time, the sun has to (be beseeched to) shine, sending a shower of photons to activate photosynthesis and heat to enable a series of complementary chemical reactions. Above all, human activities have to be monitored and orchestrated in desirable forms and directions.[116]

On innumerable occasions, when I made the mistake of starting a conversation with the thickheaded question, "How is the farming?" I was told, "Vinaybhai, agriculture is a game of dice." They were right: experienced at close quarters, agriculture is a nerve-wracking gamble. But you might never guess sitting in the Block Development Officer's (BDO's) office or, further up the institutional chart, with the Minister of Agriculture in the state capital. The inscription devices that planners rely on—mathematical models, flow-charts, tabulations, maps, surveys, even agricultural field manuals—abstract (necessarily) from the humdrum and microgeographic uncertainties of cultivation in order to produce managerial guidelines. Farmers know this. As a result, they approach state agronomic knowledge with skepticism bordering on distrust. Many cultivators in Matar Taluka, for instance, regard with contempt the advice of the *gram sevak* (the village-level extension worker who is charged with disseminating state-sponsored agricultural programs—program information, agronomic techniques, new crop technologies, and so on—to cultivators).

The demarcation of "nature" and "society" is not peculiar to the West or its modernity. What is remarkable is Western modernity's obsession with the border separating the two and the constant attempts to rearrange what gets put on the side of nature and what on the side of society. Farmers in central Gujarat aptly describe the agronomic practices associated with the Green Revolution as *rasaaynik kheti* ("chemical agriculture"; but note that *rasaaynik* is also an alibi for "unnatural" or "foreign"). Enabled by canal irrigation, it tries to subdue the mobile surprises that nature springs by moving as many elements as possible to the side of society. Rainwater is substituted (and occasionally replaced) by engineered canal systems, ponds, tubewells, drip irrigation systems, or hydroponics. Seeds are crossbred or genetically modified against known disease and debilities (for instance, stalks that are too narrow and long—hence prone to breaking—are shortened). Cowdung, castor cake, and other forms of organic matter—so-called *desi khatar* ("domestic" or "traditional" fertilizer)—are substituted by industrially manufactured fertilizers such as ammonium sulphate, urea, single- and triple-superphosphate, and di-ammonium phosphate (DAP). Agricultural laborers, who are prone to disruptive impulses and ailments, are replaced (where possible) by mechanical contrivances. But control remains elusive despite such reorderings. The remarks of physicist-turned-economist Nicholas Georgescu-Roegen, penned over thirty years ago, return to haunt:

> [T]he strongest limitation to our power to predict comes from the entropic indeterminateness and, especially, from the emergence of novelty by combination. These are the most important reasons why our prehensions of nature cannot be reduced to the efficient cause as we know it from Aristotle. In the case of novelty by combination (of contemporaneous or consecutive elements), things simply happen, without either a *causa efficiens* or a *causa finalis*. . . . Nevertheless, some social scientists simply refuse to reconcile themselves to this verdict and, apparently in despair, have come out with a curious proposal: to devise means which will compel people to behave the way "we" want, so that "our" predictions will always come true. The project, in which we recognize the continual striving for a "rational" society beginning with Plato's, cannot succeed . . . simply because of its blatant *petitio principii:* the first prerequisite for any plan is that the behavior of the material involved should be completely predictable, at least for some appreciable period.[117]

The impulse to order, as we have witnessed previously, is a hallmark of modernity. Within this "culture of Reason," nature functions in deeply ambivalent ways. Nature is that which must be obeyed (in the form of "natural laws" that supply the foundation or model for human society).

But it is also that which is the source of the unexpected (natural events and calamities, which thwart human design). Nature is that which must be "mastered" and put in the service of human beings (as exhorted by Baconian science); but also, that which is a source of danger and menace (the "barbaric," "savage," "primitive," "irrational," and "feminine," which constantly threaten our *patri*mony).[118] It is, therefore, not a surprise to find modern irrigation characterized by environmentalists as a deal with the devil, with nature enlisted to that role. Thus, in *Pillar of Sand: Can the Irrigation Miracle Last?* Sandra Postel writes that modern hydraulic societies may have struck a Faustian bargain with nature:

> In return for transforming deserts into fertile fields and redirecting rivers to suit human needs, nature is exacting a price in myriad forms. Among the most threatening is the scourge of salt—the creeping, insidious menace that undermined the stability of several ancient irrigation societies, and that now places ours in jeopardy as well. . . . When farmers irrigate their crops, salts in the irrigation water get deposited in the soil. Even good quality irrigation water has salt concentrations of 200–500 parts per million (ppm) . . . [and] unless these salts are flushed out, enormous quantities can build up over the course of years.[119]

Postel, despite casting nature as the nemesis of human ambition, is clearly onto something. Surface irrigation, for instance, is hardly the only source of salinity.

> Salts can enter the root zone from below, as well. As irrigation water seeps through the soil from farm fields and unlined irrigation canals, the underground water table rises. Over time, if this water is not drained away, the root zone becomes waterlogged, starving plants of oxygen. In drier climates, when the groundwater gets to within a meter or two of the surface, plant roots pull it up through the upper layers of soil. The water then evaporates, leaving the salts behind. . . . Gradually, the salt buildup reduces the land's productivity, causing crop yields to decline.[120]

This description could be applied to large parts of Matar Taluka—although, in giving play to the high entropy effects of irrigation, my intention is to underscore how unplanned effects persistently exceed the conceit and desire of development planning. This ontology of process and surprise is vividly evoked in the philosopher A. N. Whitehead's notion of "concrescence." The concept, a cosmological one, is an extraordinarily generative one for thinking past various species of positivism and categorical thought (such as those reliant on divisions between nature and society). In Whitehead's philosophy, every entity that is one is also many—a togetherness of various components. Indeed, "one" and "many" are the mutual presupposition of actual entities that exist in a continuous process of reassembly that Whitehead calls "actual occasions." The world of permanent entities is replaced by a world of actual occasions, that is, vectors of singularities as "novel combinations." Whitehead writes: "Thus the 'production of novel togetherness' is the ultimate notion embodied in the term 'concrescence.' These ultimate notions of 'production of novelty' and of 'concrete togetherness' are inexplicable either in terms of higher universals [such as *nature* or *society*] or in terms of the components participating in the concrescence."[121] It is important to underscore that a concrescence is *not* an arbitrary combination of elements. Whitehead never implies that elements have the capacity to enter into relation with every other. Instead, every actual entity or occasion is a concrescence of "prehensions"—concrete facts of relatedness—that result in "a *conditioned* indetermination,"[122] or what Whitehead terms a "*real* potentiality." Salinization fits this description. It is a changing, geographically diverse, but conditioned process, catalyzed by novel combinations of (among other elements): soil properties and organic matter content; saline ingress from large salt-water bodies; pathways of surface water flows; topological features such as dips, elevations and undulations; drainage characteristics of an area; weather patterns (excessive heat or rainfall); and human interactions with a landscape via forms of cultivation, water use, fertilizer application, animal husbandry, and built environments (roads, canals, ponds, and so on).

Take Matar Taluka. In 1983, an estimate based on remote sensing data indicated problems of salinity in 17.3 percent of the subdistrict's land area and forty-nine of its eighty-two villages.[123] The soils in large portions of Matar are saline-sodic clay loams with a pH between 8.6 and 8.76, a high proportion of sodium cations, and a low proportion of calcium cations.[124] Anions and cations[125] exist in an adsorbed state on soil particles, particularly the clay fractions. Sodium (Na) tends to displace other cations as its concentration in the soil increases. Under waterlogged conditions, calcium (Ca) and magnesium (Mg) ions are displaced through a cationic exchange process:

$$\text{Ca-clay} + 2\text{Na} \leftrightarrow \text{Na}_2\text{-clay} + \text{Ca}^{++}$$
$$\text{Mg-clay} + 2\text{Na} \leftrightarrow \text{Na}_2\text{-clay} + \text{Mg}^{++}$$

Figure 3. Salt-affected agricultural land in an irrigated tract near the village of Limbasi, 2004.

Over time, a precipitate of calcium and magnesium salts accumulates in certain soil horizons. This precipitate—a mutating concrescence—is pulled into the top horizon of the soil profile by capillary action when hot weather causes rapid surface evaporation. Once deposited, a salt precipitate diminishes the ability of roots to draw water and nutrients from the top horizon, with adverse effects on rates of seed germination, the size of plants, and their grain yields.[126]

In Limbasi Division of Matar, an annual cycle of irrigated paddy and irrigated wheat cultivation, coupled with overzealous application of water to poorly drained fields, has compounded waterlogging, salinization, and pest outbreak problems. The fact that water is conveyed from one plot to another through the rudimentary and highly inefficient method of field-to-field gravity flow (rather than via lined field channels, on a rotational harvest system) has greatly exacerbated the problem of waterlogging. Indeed, the most direct ecological consequence of canal irrigation has been a steady rise in the level of the groundwater table. In low-lying portions of the MRBC command area, which includes Limbasi Division, the water table rose by between 0.34 meters (1.12 feet) and 6.12 meters (20.2 feet) over the thirty-four-year period from pre-irrigation 1957–58 to pre-monsoon 1992.[127] It was rising by almost a third of a foot every year in certain tracts. In 1975—a scarce decade after the canals had arrived—it was estimated that about 5,000 acres in Matar Taluka were waterlogged. In one of the worst affected villages, Pariyej, an estimated one-fourth of the village's 4,500 acres had been rendered uncultivable by 1995 as a result of salinization induced by periodic waterlogging. The proximate cause there is a large reservoir fed by the Khambhat Branch of the Mahi Right Bank Canal. The storage capacity of this reservoir, which supplies drinking water and conjunctive irrigation to villages in dry tracts west of Pariyej, was augmented in 1978 by raising its embankments twelve feet—with disastrous consequences for arable land that lies within a one to two mile radius of the reservoir. Some fields are now permanently under water; others carry a thick, fluffy encrustation of salts, making cultivation all but impossible. Agricultural production and on-farm employment have declined. Affected plot owners, many now forced to rely on erratic wage labor for livelihood, said that rice yields in their fields fell from twenty-four quintals (5,280 pounds) per acre in 1965 to four quintals in 1980; by 1990, yields were close to zero in most salinity-affected plots. Millet and wheat cultivation had to be discontinued, because these crops have poor tolerance for salinity. A Forest Department official complained to me that villagers from Pariyej and adjoining Bhalada, with prompting from local timber merchants, had taken to illegal, overnight felling of restricted species of trees in fields and on roadsides. He understood their economic predicament, he said, but could not condone an activity that had now become epidemic.

Whitehead reserves the term "society" for that nexus of actual entities that are ordered among themselves, such that the arrangement "is self sustaining; in other words, that it is its own reason." Specifically:

> The members of the society are alike because, by reason of their common character, they impose on other members of the society the conditions which lead to that likeness. . . . Thus a set of entities is a society (i) by virtue of a 'defining characteristic' shared by its members, and (ii) in virtue of that presence of the defining characteristic being due to the environment provided by the society itself.[128]

A State is a logic of "one-ification," but also, in Whitehead's sense, a society. An ordered nexus of actual entities, its heterogeneous components approximate a conjunctive unity. But they frequently operate in ways that are disjunctive—without foregoing their genetic likeness as a consequence. The management of canal irrigation is paradigmatic of the State's existence as an effected one that is (a conflicted) many. Canals smooth the flow of water across space but obstruct other sorts of flows. Thus, the latticework of channels that crease landscapes below dams frequently block natural drainage channels and contribute to waterlogging and salinization, *unless* there are well-maintained systems of artificial drainage. Even if alternative drainage channels are constructed, responsibility for upkeep and maintenance typically sits with a drainage authority that is frequently separate from, and poorly coordinated with, the canal authority.[129]

The MRBC system in Matar exhibits exactly this version of bureaucratic irrationality: in many years, drains remain uncleaned or in a state of disrepair while canals are up and running. This leads to sluggish drainage and backlogs of water that compound the waterlogging problem generated by cultivators' overzealous application of water to their fields. Big dams and the canal networks they enable also concentrate decision-making authority in the hands of large, authoritarian, and corrupt bureaucracies,[130] which, by their very nature, erupt the liberal fiction of state and civil society as separate operative domains. The management of the MRBC project reveals a state ripe for cannibalizing by society. In conversations, officials at the Mahi Irrigation Circle office in Nadiad confided that up to 70 percent of the annual working budget for the system was eaten up by staff in the canal bureaucracy.[131] Corruption also operates in multifarious ways at local levels. Ratilal Patel of Limbasi village purchased eighty *vighas* (46.4 acres) of land adjacent to the Nagrama *talav* (pond) for Rs. 7 lacs (US$15,500). After the purchase he discovered that the land was low-lying and prone to flooding when the nearby irrigation subminors were full, ferrying water to tailenders. The previous owner, Arvindbhai, used to bribe Irrigation Department field staff to temporarily shut down one of the subminors. Then, with a diesel pump he would drain water from planted fields, thereby ensuring that his rice crop—instead of staying submerged in water—dried out early enough in its gestational cycle. Ratilal does not believe in paying irrigation staff, he believes in getting things by *dum* ("force"). But

Table 6. Salinity-Affected Areas in Ten Villages of Limbasi Division, Matar, 1983

Village	Village Area	Low	Moderate	Severe	Total Affected Area	Percent Affected
Baroda	800	32	14	20	66	8.3
Bamangam	1136	193	33	244	470	41.3
Kharenti	930	0	63	37	100	10.8
Limbasi	2147	143	447	0	590	27.4
Macchiel	509	29	0	13	42	8.3
Matar	1566	0	59	22	81	5.2
Palla	349	17	16	10	43	12.3
Pariyej	1807	0	171	290	461	25.5
Radhvanaj	562	152	105	0	257	45.8
Sandhana	1122	176	74	0	250	22.3

Source: Adapted from K. A. Bhagwat, "Monitoring of Crop Production in Saline and Sodic Soils of Gujarat with the help of Remote Sensing," mimeo (Ahmedabad: ISRO-RESPOND Project, 1989), Table 4, p. 7.

dum works once or twice, after which the field staff stop cooperating. Ratilal spent Rs. 2 lacs ($4,500) on *matikaam* ("soil augmentation") of his eighty vighas. But his waterlogged rice crop failed. He put the land for sale at an asking price of Rs. 10 lacs, but could not find a buyer. Ratilal's case is not exceptional; corruption in irrigation management exacts a steep toll.

But it is a fraction of the productivity losses inflicted by waterlogging and salinity. In a field study of crop production in salinity-affected tracts in Matar Taluka, an ISRO study[132] found that yields of the popular Masuri rice variety were 60 to 80 percent lower in experimental plots with moderate to severe salinity than in fields with normal salinity (production was 16.4 quintals per acre in normal plots, 9.9 quintals in fields with moderate salinity, and 1.3 quintals in plots with severe salinity). (See Table 6.) To add to the toll, an increasingly hydric environment, salinity-weakened plants, and the emergence of pesticide-resistant strains of crop-dwelling insects and fungi, had led to a rising incidence of crop diseases in Matar's rice–wheat agricultural regime.

War Machine

The "novelty by combination" that the development machine pilots for the improvement of life—a betterment that becomes yoked to capital's *"general axiomatic of decoded flows"*[133] (that is to say, *deterritorialization by abstraction* of territory as property/rent, surplus labor as commodity/ profit, and exchange as money/value)[134]—has yielded an array of other surprises in Gujarat. Combined with the crisis of salinity, they have forced the upper-caste elite of the region (a number of them from agrarian origins, with deep investments in the countryside) to radically question accepted certitudes of rank and wealth. They had expected development in the postcolony to work *for* them. Instead it has confounded their expectations on multiple fronts. Working through and beyond *dirigiste* development, the tendrils of capitalism have unleashed "a universal cosmopolitan energy that overflows every restriction and bond"[135]—capital as *war machine*,[136] which threatens to "melt all that is solid into air." Against this backdrop, it is conceivable that elite embrace of a politics of communalism is both an expression of "molecular insecurity"[137] that is open to violent displacement against minorities, as well an orchestrated effort to recapture the state for their benefit. I want to be clear: I am not seeking to explain the deepening of Hindu sectarianism in Gujarat or the anti-Muslim pogrom of 2002 in all its complexity (those tasks have been take up by other scholars with far greater acumen in these matters[138]); rather, I want to suggest how a close examination of agrarian questions in the postcolonial period might illuminate some of the conditions of possibility of the *communal war machine*.

Let's continue, but with a short historical detour. We saw in chapter 2 how a loose and somewhat amorphous set of state functionaries-cum-estate-holders (Desais, Amins, Patel *patidars*) in central and south Gujarat congealed in an uneasy suture with Lewa Kanbi peasants over the course of the nineteenth century, giving rise to a new endogamous social group. This group crystallized into a harder caste identity in interaction with colonial policies (particularly those pertaining to land settlement and the census) as well as the nationalist agitation. "Patel"—a surname *(atak)* that gestured to their power on the rural scene—became the generic caste identifier (landed Patels frequently prefer the appellation "Patidar," which is a more exact description of their source of influence). The Patels were able to turn a series of drought and famine years in the early part of the twentieth century into economic opportunity by migrating in large numbers to East Africa, repatriating hard-earned surplus capital from wage labor and trade to consolidate their control over land in Gujarat. By the time of Independence, with caste heroes such as Sardar Vallabhbhai Patel at the helm of Congress Party politics (indeed, a serious contender to Jawaharlal Nehru for the post of Prime Minister), Patels had become a national force and the undisputed power-holders in Gujarat. This narrative of ascent has to be qualified by recurrent, sometimes entrenched, intracaste factionalism around marriage (particularly the perceived elitism of certain Patel villages in the Charotar), business opportunities, political gamesmanship, and so on. While Patels have the coherence of form that A. N. Whitehead (and after him, David Harvey) calls "permanence," substantively they have always been a "ruptural unity." Land reforms in Gujarat were initiated in this turbulent milieu.

The first attempt was in 1939, with the introduction of the Bombay Tenancy Act (at the time Gujarat was part of Bombay State). The principal objective of this Act was to secure permanent occupancy for tenants who had cultivated a plot of land for six years or more prior to January 1938. The Act also abolished the concept of a "tenant-at-will." But the Congress Party, which had sponsored the legislation, lost power in the Legislative Assembly soon thereafter and the implementation of the Act across Bombay State was postponed until 1946, when the party returned to power. In 1948, a more comprehensive legislation, the Bombay Tenancy and Agricultural Lands Act, was passed. It sought to regulate the relationship between landlords and tenants by fixing the latter's entitlements with respect to tenure, trees, rent, and house sites; by commuting crop-shares into cash (on the grounds ostensibly that this would make the rental contract more transparent); and by making illegal various cesses that were often added onto rents. In addition to these protections, tenants were given the option of purchasing the land they cultivated at a reasonable price (no more than six times the rent). In 1960, after Gujarat separated from Bombay State, a Land Ceiling Act was introduced that imposed limits on existing holdings as well as future acquisitions. To counter charges that the 1948 Act had provoked displacement of various categories of tenants by landlords, the legislation was amended in 1972 to prevent illegal terminations of tenancy and give dispossessed tenants another opportunity to stake ownership rights. The 1972 amendment came on the heels of the Congress Party split (in 1969) and Indira Gandhi's astonishing sweep to power in the 1971 general election—her Congress (R) faction captured 47 percent of the total vote and 350 of the 548 seats in the lower house of Parliament, the Lok Sabha, for an absolute majority—on the strength of a simple slogan that galvanized the imagination of the electorate.[139] It went:

> Kuchh log kehte hain, Indira hatao
> Mein kehti hoon, garibi hatao!

> (Some people say, get rid of Indira
> I say, get rid of poverty!)

In summary, the land reform legislations enacted in Gujarat and elsewhere were not gestures empty of redistributive intent. But the troubles in implementation they encountered spoke of their tenuous existence. Ghanshyam Oza, the reform-minded Chief Minister of Gujarat under whose watch the 1972 amendment was passed, encountered quick opposition from Bhailalbhai Patel, leader of the landowners' lobby, the Khedut Sangh. Bhaikaka (as he was widely known) argued that the Act would produce class conflict where none previously existed. Drawing on the motifs of village harmony and trusteeship—the village as family—that Mahatma Gandhi had popularized,[140] he ingeniously observed: "[T]he simple truth that the interests of all people working on land such as artisans, tenants, laborers are one and the same like a welded whole is not known; these interests do not conflict; they should be maintained in the integrated manner which can done by considering the family."[141] Although lower-class factions among the Patidars supported land reforms, the Khedut Sangh—which stood for the interests of the kulak faction within the caste—did not, likening it to the advent of communism.[142] By contrast, the Gujarat Kshatriya Sabha, whose rank-and-file membership consisted of various lower-caste groups that self-identified as Kshatriya and who were mainly tenants and petty cultivators, hailed the Act but did not follow up with a campaign for its implementation because the Sabha's leaders—principally, landed Rajput talukdars from Saurashtra and North Gujarat who stood to be adversely affected by the Act—chose not to. The Act also encountered friction from Patidar, Bania and Brahmin politicians who at the time dominated the Congress Party leadership and who were in many instances large landowners themselves.

The results of tenancy reforms, then, were decidedly mixed. What about central Gujarat specifically? The Dutch scholar, Mario Rutten, who did an ethnographic study of Patel entrepreneurship in Anand Taluka, offers a bleak appraisal, claiming that the "land-to-the-tiller" *(khedut huq)* program incited Patel landlords to evict large numbers of Kshatriya (Baraiya Koli) tenants from operated holdings into the ranks of the rural proletariat.[143] In nearby Matar Taluka, the short-term outcome was somewhat different. A comparison of results from J. C. Kumarappa's 1929–30 survey of Matar Taluka and the Planning Commission of India re-survey in 1965–66 that tried to be faithful to Kumarappa's sample of households indicates that Baraiya and Tadbda Koli cultivators not only came to dominate the small- and medium-size land categories as owner cultivators but also made inroads into the large fifteen- to twenty-five- and above twenty-five-acre size categories over the survey periods (Table 7). In short, tenancy legislation moved them into the middle peasantry; and although this upgrade was to be ephemeral, their prospects in the 1960s seemed infinitely better than those of tenants from Scheduled Caste *(dalit)* groups who, by and large, were displaced from their operated holdings by upper-caste landlords.[144] (Muslim households, notably, fared better than dalits in this shuffle.)

On balance, then, the upper-caste elite of rural Gujarat (and certainly of Matar Taluka) were able to thwart the leveling thrust of land reforms. The same cannot be said of subsequent, aleatory, events. The rapid ascent to wealth of certain Bharwad households in Matar is illustrative of the anxiety Patel, Brahmin, and Thakkar farmers have to come nurture about their previously undisputed control of the countryside. Ontologically, nature is a multiplicity of forces—never a closed set—ordered by knowledge under that particular name. What shall we call canal irrigation then—a society-nature hybrid or perhaps techno-nature? Whatever it is, it has sparked a dramatic shift in the cropping pattern in favor of paddy. Since paddy straw, which is a byproduct of cultivation, is a nutritive source of dry fodder, the areal extension of paddy in Matar subdistrict by roughly forty thousand acres since 1965 has greatly expanded the supply of dry fodder. Meanwhile, the explosion of grass along the irrigation minors and subminors that snake through the landscape has created new grazing areas for open-grazed livestock and a steadier supply of green fodder for stall-fed milch animals like buffalos and hybrid cows. With progressive improvement in the duration of water supplied in canals, particularly after 1978, grass now sprouts for at least seven to eight months of the year. In the remaining months, those who can afford it purchase green jowar *(Andropogau sorghum)* on the

Table 7. Distribution of Households by Occupation & Caste, Matar Taluka, 1929–30 and 1965–66 (figures are in percent)

Caste	Year	Cultivators in the size-group (in acres)					Agric. Labor	Artisans	Traders	Salaried	Misc.
		0 to 5	5 to 10	10 to 15	15 to 25	Above 25					
Patel	1929–30	2.80	1.00	1.20	41.20	43.40	8.70	5.90	0.00	0.00	7.10
	1965–66	8.40	20.80	34.30	39.40	29.40	2.10	0.00	4.90	16.00	6.30
Baraiya/ Koli Patel	1929–30	6.60	9.20	7.30	29.70	20.20	69.70	0.00	33.30	7.70	0.00
	1965–66	52.50	40.30	32.90	30.30	20.60	27.00	2.90	4.90	18.60	4.80
Rajput	1929–30	0.50	0.60	0.40	11.50	19.20	4.30	0.00	0.00	0.00	7.10
	1965–66	4.90	6.50	10.10	4.70	20.60	2.50	0.00	4.90	8.70	3.20
Brahmin	1929–30	4.70	1.30	1.60	2.40	1.90	0.00	0.00	0.00	23.10	21.50
	1965–66	0.90	2.60	0.00	4.70	2.90	1.60	0.00	7.30	12.30	17.50
Muslim	1929–30	7.50	7.30	7.30	8.50	9.60	4.30	0.00	0.00	7.70	7.10
	1965–66	16.90	14.30	15.20	9.30	8.80	9.80	0.00	17.10	11.10	11.20
Bharwad	1929–30	19.80	21.90	29.20	1.80	1.90	0.00	5.90	0.00	0.00	35.70
	1965–66	1.30	1.90	2.50	0.00	11.80	1.60	0.00	7.30	1.20	28.50
SCs	1929–30	53.40	52.80	44.10	0.00	0.00	4.30	0.00	0.00	0.00	0.00
	1965–66	6.20	3.90	0.00	4.70	0.00	16.40	2.90	0.00	6.20	1.60
Misc.	1929–30	7.40	5.90	8.90	4.90	3.80	8.70	88.20	66.70	61.50	21.50
	1965–66	8.90	9.70	5.00	6.90	5.90	38.90	94.20	53.60	25.90	26.90
Total	1929–30	100	100	100	100	100	100	100	100	100	100
	1965–66	100	100	100	100	100	100	100	100	100	100

Source: Vimal Shah and C. H. Shah, *Re-Survey of Matar Taluka* (Bombay: Vora and Co., 1974), p. 229.

market. The production of grass on the perimeters of cultivated plots and field channels has also risen. And the area under lucerne *(rachko)*, a protein-rich green fodder crop, has also grown steadily.

Bharwads and Rabaris, relatively lowly castes of pastoralists, have taken spectacular advantage of this. As recently as thirty years ago, they occupied the fringes of the village economy. They made a living by tending the cattle of large Patel landowners, for which they were paid twenty kilograms of wheat annually by each patron *(jajman)*. Today, with income earned from milk sales to village dairies that were established all across Kheda by the Anand Milk-Producers Union Limited (AMUL), a quasi-state cooperative body, Bharwad and Rabari households have achieved economic parity with their patrons in several villages of Matar; and in some places have supplanted them.[145] The development machine has connected them to previously unimagined possibilities. The contrast between the economic performance of Patels and Bharwads since the arrival of canal irrigation to Matar is underscored by an examination of land purchase and sale records maintained at the Subdistrict Registrar's Office in Matar town. It is worth clarifying that Patels as a norm attempt to keep land sales endogamous; Patel households who want to sell holdings face strong peer pressure to sell to fellow caste members. Although ordinarily fractious in their dealings, Patels I interacted with told me they were acutely aware of the need for solidarity in matters of caste dominance *(qum satta)* and therefore the importance of retaining control over land in a primarily agrarian economy.[146] Yet, the Subdistrict Registrar's records show that in 1994 four Patel households in the village of Shamli—which I surveyed—sold 58.3 acres to Bharwad families and a paltry 3.6 acres to a fellow Patel.[147] This pattern of transactions reveals the buying power of Bharwads, who, in this case, paid up to Rs. 60,000 (roughly $1,400) an acre for the land they acquired. Although solvent Patel households in Shamli contemptuously referred to the Patel families who sold land to Bharwads as *toot-ta ghar* ("declining families," in the process of breaking down), it was apparent that they could neither match the purchasing power of Bharwads nor effectively deploy the threat of moral condemnation as a way of internalizing land sales.

Field Notes: April 11, 1995

The highpoint of the day was the chance meeting with Navinbhai Naranbhai Bharwad, of Nadhanpur. There are twenty-five Bharwad families on the revenue register of Nadhanpur, but they live in a hamlet *(para)* midway between Nadhanpur and Limbasi. Such segregated existence is typical of Bharwads, who use space in a way that, on the one hand, ensures privacy from outsiders (including fellow villagers) but, on the other, dissolves any possibility of privacy within the community. Houses are typically arranged in rectangular fashion, facing into a common courtyard where cattle are jointly penned. This structure of habitation may have made eminent sense in the past when it was necessary to protect livestock from predators and thieves. Today it seems dysfunctional, an artifact of tradition, until we realize its important everyday role in reaffirming a sense of solidarity among Bharwads, particularly those of the younger generation who are increasingly choosing semi-urban and urban careers.

Navinbhai's family owns 120 vighas (seventy acres) of land in Nadhanpur and its vicinity, making them the largest landowners in the area. Kantibhai Patel, one of my hosts in Matar, had once told me that barely four decades ago the Bharwads of Nadhanpur were desperately poor—and had led a frugal, animal-like lifestyle. Navinbhai confirmed the abject poverty of Bharwads in the past. I inquired how his family had managed to accumulate 120 vighas. Navinbhai said dairying had provided the initial cash surplus. He candidly divulged that his family had invested this surplus in moneylending. "Much of the land which currently belongs to us was given as collateral *(giro)* and never reclaimed, or else sold to us by borrowers." His family continues to lend money.

When my conversation with Navinbhai meandered into the subject of how a field laborer, with little to offer as collateral, musters loans, Naranbhai replied that he must either plan in advance and save, borrow here and there from various relatives, or become a *mahinadar* (servant). "Does your family keep *mahinadars?*," I asked. I was told they maintain four *mahinadars*. "Do you lend them money?" "If we do, it's relatively small amounts—Rs. 1,000 to 2,000," answered Navinbhai. "It depends on the mahinadar's reliability, and how hard-working he is. We might charge him four to five percent interest, instead of two-and-a-half to three."

I was curious whether Bharwads, when in need of money, turn primarily to fellow members of the caste or whether they turn to outside sources. Navinbhai disclaimed any set pattern. "We sometimes borrow from other Bharwads, but we can just as easily procure funds from the Urban Cooperative Bank in Limbasi, or from large Limbasi-based rice traders like Ambalal Jethabhai Patel." "When Bhikubhai 'Banker' [Patel] was the manager of the cooperative bank we had an open credit line at the bank." The bottom line: lenders in the area know that the Bharwads of Nadhanpur have a steady agricultural and dairying income, hence are in a position to repay debts. Moreover, as Navinbhai clarified, moneylending is such a lucrative activity (at the normal 36 percent per annum rate of simple interest) that it is rare for individuals with cash surpluses to invest the money in National Savings Certificates, Kisan Vikas Patras, or similar government bonds. Bank-fixed deposits are unpopular (distrust of banks is widespread) and, in any case, yield a meager return; and only an educated few know enough about the stock market and share application procedures to purchase stocks. Moneylending, in short, has oiled the path to economic success for many—but certainly not all—Bharwads. It can be definitively said, however, that Bharwads possess more ready access to credit than members of other similarly placed caste groups.

A study of mortgage transactions in the villages of Shamli and Astha, where I did census surveys and ethnographic research, lends additional support to this emerging picture (see Table 8). The practice of mortgaging land, known locally as *giro pratha,* has a long—and sometimes sordid—history in Kheda District (chapter 2). In return for a loan, the landowner (or mortgagor) temporarily cedes control of his land to the lender (mortgagee). The length of mortgage agreements varies from one year to seven years, with explicit provision for contingent renewal on an annual basis in the case of some one-year contracts. There seems to be wide acceptance of a principle that if a loan is not repaid by the end of seven years it is legitimate for the lender to ask the borrower for a transfer of title. Thus, a mortgage transaction can either resemble a straightforward fixed-rate tenancy contract or, more commonly, an interlocked exchange involving credit for land. Although the motivations of landowners for out-mortgaging land vary, the transaction itself has increasingly come to symbolize erosion in a household's financial solvency, primarily because temporary transfers of use-rights to land in return for a loan (the yield from the mortgaged land representing interest on the loan) have *increasingly dissolved into permanent transfers.* In short, the mortgage transaction has become an indicator of household mobility rooted in local cultural understandings of economic well-being. It is also an ongoing source of "accumulation by dispossession."[148]

The story of mortgages in Astha and Shamli, summarized in Table 8, is instructive. The pattern of mortgage transactions establishes the strong economic position of Bharwads relative to other caste groups. Only one Bharwad household in Shamli appears as a mortgagor, indicating their lack of compulsion to obtain credit by offering land as collateral. By contrast, a few Patels *do* appear as mortgagors: 9 percent of households in Astha and 29 percent in Shamli. Overall, the evidence appears to confirm the story of a society in flux where previously marginalized groups like Bharwads—and even some Vaghris— are beginning to contest the economic primacy of Patels and other upper-caste groups. Consider, then, the Vaghris.

The Vaghris occupy a liminal position within Gujarat's social hierarchy, fitting uneasily within the caste/tribe divide[149]—although, in terms of their derisive treatment by the upper castes and their long history of being marginalized, they are socially on par with the

Table 8. Pattern of Land Mortgaging in Two Villages, Matar Taluka, by Caste Group, 1995

ASTHA Caste group	Total reporting households	No. who have kept land on mortgage	Percent mortgagees	No. who have given land on mortgage	Percent mortgagors
Brahmin	6	0	0.0	0	0.0
Patel	22	9	40.9	2	9.1
Panchal	26	5	19.2	4	15.4
Baraiya/Koli	62	10	16.1	27	43.5
Bharwad	10	2	20.0	0	0.0
Muslim	0	0	Na	0	0.0
Raval	0	0	Na	0	0.0
Vankar	0	0	Na	0	0.0
Rohit	18	2	11.1	6	33.3
Vaghri	1	0	0.0	0	0.0
Harijan	18	0	0.0	4	22.2
TOTAL	163	28	17.2	43	26.4

SHAMLI Caste group	Total reporting households	No. who have kept land on mortgage	Percent mortgagees	No. who have given land on mortgage	Percent mortgagors
Brahmin	7	2	28.6	1	14.3
Patel	17	7	41.2	5	29.4
Panchal	2	2	100.0	1	50.0
Baraiya/Koli	105	12	11.4	38	36.2
Bharwad	55	10	18.2	1	1.8
Muslim	13	0	0.0	4	30.8
Raval	11	0	0.0	1	9.1
Vankar	23	1	4.4	2	8.7
Rohit	53	0	0.0	11	20.7
Vaghri	21	3	14.3	0	0.0
Harijan	14	0	0.0	6	42.9
TOTAL	321	37	11.5	70	21.8

Note: Caste groups are arranged in descending order of ritual rank. Only major caste groups are shown in the table.
Source: Fieldwork data, 1995.

so-called Untouchable or dalit castes.[150] The term Vaghri appears to be etymologically linked to the Sanskrit word *wagura,* meaning "net"; hence, Vaghri is often translated as a "tribe of netters." The Vaghris have traditionally made a living as fowlers, hunters, sellers of toothbrushes *(datans),* and as petty cultivators. They are also reputed to be expert distillers of (illicit) liquor and master thieves—so much so that in 1911 colonial officials in Gujarat applied the Criminal

Castes and Tribes Act to the entire community, an onerous provision that for several years thereafter, until 1952, required every member of the Vaghri caste over the age of six to attend a daily roll call in front of the village *Patel* (headman).[151] In addition, they were required to provide corvée labor *(veth)* for the entourages of travelling colonial officials. The low standing of the Vaghri became embalmed in language, particularly in the everyday usage of upper castes.[14] On numerous occasions, I heard Patels admonishing children and adults behaving in unruly fashion by saying: *"Kem vaghran jevo vyavhar kare chhe?"* ("Why are you behaving like a Vaghri woman?"). Vaghris are described by the upper castes as unreliable, dirty, and foul-mouthed. And yet, when I was doing fieldwork in Matar I was told by several upper-caste informants, "Here, today, Vaghris rule"—an admission that Vaghris have prospered so much in recent years that their economic prominence can be no longer denied.

Sabarbhai Tadbda from the revenue village of Shamli is emblematic of the Vaghris' ascent. Until 1985, he owned barely half a vigha of land. He now owns seven vighas dispersed across three villages, has acquired usufruct rights to another seven, and plies a Tata 407 minitruck, which he purchased in 1994—in cash—for 315,000 rupees (approximately US$7,000). He uses the truck to convey his tomato harvest to various urban markets, wherever prices are best. In addition, he lends money on interest, and according to several villagers, has up to 100,000 rupees ($2,300) in circulation.[152]

Sabarbhai's case also reveals that the Vaghris have often relied on family and kin labor to engineer their economic ascent. They have begun to lease lands for tomato and melon cultivation, often paying stupendous rents.[153] The melon crop is short lived, whereas tomato extends for a month or two. Both are cash crops that require heavy inputs of fertilizers, pesticides, and purchased tubewell water. Melons are particularly laborious to grow. A good harvest *(fasal)* demands repeated weeding. Vaghris defray the enormous risk that accompanies their cultivation of these cash crops by minimizing their use of hired labor. They depend almost entirely on family labor and exchange labor from members of their community; in short, risk management via mobilization of labor surpluses across space. In one instance, the wife's parents had traveled from the village of Vaso (a considerable distance away) to assist with cultivation.[154] The connectivities of development have opened up new interstices for capital to enter. The case of the Vaghris illustrates how the "super-exploitation" of family or kin labor can oil the wheels of accumulation.

Capital has also permeated village economics through state-led dairy development initiatives. In conjunction with the Integrated Rural Development Programme (IRDP), which provides subsidized loans for acquisition of productive assets (including livestock) to marginal farmers and landless workers, it has opened up an alternative source of income for laboring households. Most of these households are from lower-caste groups that have historically had to be subservient to the landed middle castes, particularly the Patels. With income from milk sales now a possibility, several laboring households—particularly those from the Baraiya and Tadbda Koli subcastes—have opted to "withdraw," at least partially, from the labor market (see chapter 4 for an extended discussion). Patel farmers bitterly complain that "their laborers" *("aapda majoor")* have become more impertinent and unreliable after the advent of the dairy and will go to pains to demonstrate that milch cattle are a losing economic proposition.

Take, for instance, the case of N. M. Patel, who contends that the advent of the AMUL cooperative dairy has had a deleterious effect on agriculture. It has directly exacerbated the labor shortage because laboring households from Astha and its adjoining *paras* (hamlets) now prefer to maintain a buffalo or two and to live off that income rather than from wage income. He termed livestock income *aalas ni aavak* (idle income) and proclaimed that it had robbed laborers of their desire to work. N. M. Patel also announced that anyone who bothered to keep an account and feed cattle their required diet would realize that animal husbandry was a losing proposition. He quickly calculated an annual net loss of US$4.50 per buffalo, taking into account estimated costs of dry and green fodder, oilseeds, and medical insurance, and balancing that against revenue, primarily from sale of milk at an average rate of $0.18 per liter (adjusting for the fact that buffaloes lactate for roughly eight months in the year). This simple fact, N. M. said, escapes lower-caste households because they do not possess the "capacity" *(shramta)* to maintain accounts. This imputed lack of computational capacity in lower-caste individuals is naturalized in the rhetoric of Patel farmers by their portrayal of it as a genetic debility. For me it was a sign that irrigation combined with the dairy program has unleashed forces that are recoding previously undisputed social relations—and producing disquiet among the rural elite.

Vankars are a widespread dalit community in Gujarat. Traditionally weavers by occupation,[155] they came to be valued as paddy workers by employers from the Patel and Rajput castes—reputedly because they had nimble fingers that allowed them to transplant rice saplings and weed fields faster and more expertly than workers from other laboring groups. But there is another reason that quickly surfaces in conversations with Patel and Rajput employers: that unlike other dalit groups Vankars always "knew their place" in society ("*pota ni jigya jaanta hata*"). The implication is clear: Vankars were docile and rarely rancorous in their behavior with upper castes, unlike their fellow dalits (the Rohits, Vaghris and Bhangis). As ably documented by Marxist scholars, compliance or obedience is an attribute that employers value in workers.

But today's Vankars—empowered by constitutionally mandated social justice provisions that were woven into postcolonial development—are different. I interviewed twenty-three Vankar families in my survey of 353 households in the village of Shamli. Whereas older-generation Vankars still display deference toward upper-caste groups, younger-generation Vankars openly defy the prevalent caste hierarchy. Their attire and demeanor reflect their hostility to caste norms: many are better dressed than their upper-caste counterparts; they refuse to tolerate the use of the term *dhed,* an abusive term that upper castes frequently employed in conversations (and continue to in private) to describe Vankars; and they place a premium on education as a mark of their difference. It came as no surprise to learn that the majority of younger-generation Vankars are schooled outside the village.[156] Almost half of the twenty-three Vankar households have family members engaged in nonfarm employment: six work as clerks or chaperones in the subdistrict headquarter, two work in the diamond polishing industry in the city of Surat in south Gujarat, one works as a civil engineer in the Public Works Department in a provincial north Gujarat city, and one is a career politician (whose rise to prominence in local politics is signaled by the enormous house he has built in Shamli's Vankar quarter).

None of the Vankars holding nonfarm jobs is a woman. The proximate reason for this imbalance appears to be that even the more educated among the younger-generation Vankar women are unable to pursue jobs once married due to patriarchal norms that prioritize household duties as the primary obligation of married women. Notwithstanding persistent gender inequities in employment and intrahousehold relations, migration has clearly transformed the political consciousness of young Vankars (although more visibly among Vankar men, who are able to operate in the "public" sphere, than Vankar women, whose participation in the public domain remains tightly circumscribed). Ketanbhai Shamabhai Parmar, son of a Vankar *agevan* (caste elder), told me of the various indignities his father had to suffer in Shamli as late as 1975—among them unpaid work *(veth)* for prominent Patel families and restrictions forbidding him from walking in the village without headgear or within ten feet of a member of the upper castes, lest these actions "pollute" village hierarchs. Pointing to a portrait of B. R. Ambedkar (the charismatic founder of organized twentieth-century dalit politics in India), Ketanbhai vowed that Vankars and other dalits would one day displace upper-caste rule in Gujarat. In his view, education leading to off-farm employment (preferably in a secure government job) was key to this aspiration. With this goal in mind, and at considerable personal expense, he has recently dispatched his eleven-year-old daughter to a boarding school in the city of Ahmedabad. He foresees a future where his children will be no longer in thrall of sedimented hierarchies.

As a final example of the aleatory forces that are causing the inherited order to tremble, take the humble *Prosopis juliflora,* a perennial deciduous thorny shrub or small tree that can grow up to 10 meters tall, with a trunk up to 1.2 meters in diameter.[157] In raised areas with sandy loam soils *(goradu jamin),* which are conducive to tree growth, the rise in the groundwater level as a result of seepage from irrigation canals has promoted lush growth of *Azadrichta indica (limbdo),* whose leaves and bark are used medicinally and whose sturdy trunk supplies the skeleton for most *kaccha* dwellings in Matar. Other tree species have also flourished in the more hydric environment. They include *Soymida febrifuga (rayan), Syzygium cumini (jambu), Zizyphus mummularis (bordi), Punica granatum (dadham),* which are fruit trees; *Madhuca indica (mahudo),* whose bark and pods are concocted into a local liquor called *mahua,* which is very popular with Adivasi migrant laborers from the Panchmahals; *Ficus religiosa (peepul),* a shade tree, whose adventitious roots are often used as kindling; *Euphorbia neriifolia (thor),* a native cactus that has become increasingly popular for live-fencing of plots; *Spondias mangifera (amla),* whose fruit is used in a variety of herbal concoctions (especially hair oil). In the low-lying clay-loam tracts *(kali jamin),* where saline-brackish groundwater combined with the soil's modest cation exchange capacity (CEC) inhibit tree growth, the arrival of canal irrigation has nevertheless increased the areal density of certain preexisting species like *Salvadora persica (pilu), Bombax ceiba (samdo),* and *Capparis decidus (kerdo)* on field embankments. These species are lopped for firewood and provide shade in an otherwise bleak expanse, but are not otherwise useful.

But according to inhabitants, the most striking vegetational shift in the subdistrict in recent memory has been the proliferation of *Prosopis juliflora (gando bavar)* and the diminution in the density of *Acacia arabica (desi bavar).* The local name, *gando bavar,* literally means the "mad bavar"—and its hurried colonization of Matar Taluka is an unexpected tale of nonhuman intervention. *Prosopis* is fast growing, salt-tolerant, and drought-tolerant. Left unmanaged even for a short time it can colonize eroded or salinity-afflicted lands, forming dense impenetrable thickets. In Matar, thickets of *Prosopis* have become established in grazing lands, croplands, and along canal distributaries. Patel farmers, apt to own large tracts of land, complain about its presence incessantly—likening it to an enemy that lays their fields to waste and one they are unable to defeat. They recall that it was nonexistent in the Taluka three decades ago. Its seeds seem to have been first introduced via the droppings of migrating sheep and goatherds from arid Saurashtra, where gando bavar has a longer history. The vast improvement in grazing and cropping possibilities that resulted initially from canal irrigation not only accelerated the demand by cultivators for organic manure (sheep manure especially is regarded as highly nutritive for soils) but, independently of this demand, made Matar Taluka an increasingly attractive destination for nomadic pastoralists (Bharwads and Rabaris) from Dholka, Dhandulka, and Dhoraji Talukas of western Gujarat, where recurrent drought years and overgrazing has decimated grazing lands. These pastoralists migrate in small groups all the way from Saurashtra to Surat (in southern Gujarat) between November and June, usually residing in an area for four to six months— perhaps even owning a second home there and some cultivable land, but earning mostly through sale of milk and milk products to village dairies in the vicinities of their temporary areas of residence. The return migration to their home villages in Saurashtra begins with the first monsoon showers in June, along well-mapped routes. The herders try to ensure that the areas they travel through are reasonably well supplied with water and fodder for their migrant herds (of sheep, goat, cows, and/or camels). Night halts are usually in the fields of agriculturists with whom the leader of the band is acquainted. Depending on the time of year and the demand for organic manure, agriculturists either pay the pastoralists to fold their herds on their fields or else might exact a promise of future services for letting them pitch camp in their fields. Few charge.

Cultivators in Matar Taluka allege that gando bavar first took root in their subdistrict from seeds dispersed through the droppings of such migrant livestock. Cows avoid adult gando bavar shrubs as well as gando bavar seedlings because of its thorny texture. *Desi bavar (Acacia arabica)* seedlings, by contrast, are not thorny and can be grazed (although the mature plant itself is thorny). As a result, gando bavar develops relatively undisturbed. Its precocious ability to multiply and spread—it coppices exceedingly well—has allowed it to virtually colonize the subdistrict. Like some other robust species, *Prosopis juliflora* is able to flourish in a variety of growing spaces, from semiarid tracts and salinized patches to waterlogged areas as well as well-drained soils. Larger cultivators in Matar regard *Prosopis* as a menace because of its capacity to rapidly encroach on fields, and resent the recurring expenditure they incur in order to temporarily eradicate it. By contrast, gando bavar has been an unmitigated boon for landless households and those with marginal holdings. It has almost entirely erased the firewood crisis, providing them an assured and unhindered supply of fuel. In the past these households would rely on the beneficence of the landed elite to meet their daily fuel requirements, needing permission to lop small branches from trees growing in a landowner's fields or to gather cattle droppings and crop waste from fields for cooking. For some poor families, the sale of dried gando bavar twigs to tea-stall and restaurant owners in Kheda and Matar town in the employment-wise lean summer months has become an important seasonal component of their income portfolios. The returns are meager, but it is money in the pocket. Since children and older adults are the ones who usually undertake this activity, the opportunity costs are low.

I have so far described how development diagrams a complex transformation of "things" (especially, the things called "nature") and

Figure 4. Dried *gando bavar (Prosopis juliflora)* twigs for firewood, with a thicket of *Prosopis* shrubs in the background.

"people arranged in relation to things." This transformation enacts connections and encounters between forces. Gilles Deleuze writes that "[t]he power to be affected is like a *matter* of force, and the power to affect is like a *function* of force."[158] Thus, working through concrete assemblages—sign-matter regimes—development releases a multiplicity of forces to reassemble matter in space and summon particular sorts of "conducts" from human and nonhuman actors. *This,* pure and simple, is the power of development. What is the substantive connection between a problematic of development and development knowledges (coded most *forcefully* in the discipline of economics and its cognate fields)? Again, here is Deleuze: "Knowledge concerns formed matters (substances) and formalized functions, divided up segment by segment according to the two great formal conditions of seeing and speaking, light and language: it is therefore stratified, archivized, and endowed with a relatively rigid segmentarity." Note as well the entirely unsurprising resonances in Deleuze's use of "power" with Foucault's notion of the "diagram" and Althusser's concept of the "problematic": "Power [in contrast to knowledge] . . . is diagrammatic: it mobilizes non-stratified matter and functions, and unfolds with a very flexible segmentarity. It passes not so much through forms as through particular *points* which on each occasion mark the application of a force, the action or reaction of a force in relation to others, that is to say an affect like 'a state of power' that is always local and unstable."[159]

In these dense formulations, Deleuze anticipates how the "microphysics" of power simultaneously interrupt and re-inscribe the territorializations of space, time, and personhood desired by development knowledge. Foucault, it is well known, first deployed the term "microphysics"[160] to describe the capillary workings of power—constituting, as it were, *"an anatomo-politics of the human body"* that, under governmentality, is conjoined to *"a bio-politics of the population."*[161] One reading of "micro," then, is in terms of scale—the below-state scales at which power operates to secure the desired ends of government. From this perspective, government is not merely about state apparatuses conventionally rendered (the Planning Commission, the Reserve Bank of India, the Ministry of Agriculture, the Indian Farmers' Fertilizer Cooperative [IFFCO], the Government of Gujarat, the Gujarat Department of Irrigation, the Mahi Right Bank Canal Authority, the District Collector's Office, etc.). Rather, it is about the relentless upward and downward continuity of government: extending through self, family, community, and caste, as well as across parastatal forms like panchayats, educational institutions, religious organizations, and so forth. Government, thus, disassembles into multiple institutions—each with its own, albeit interconnected, mode of knowledge. The State too resolves itself into merely one, albeit extremely potent, codification of knowledge and power. In this antijuridical approach (as it has been sometimes termed) the State's unyielding *givenness*—its commonsense encrustation as brute fact of existence—is transformed. It is no longer an object that's *there*. So dispersed are its surface area and effects that it seems to extend *everywhere*, a strange materiality that is captured by an equally odd term, *state-effect*.[162]

Given all this, it is clear why the term "microphysics" is associated primarily with the scalability of power relations and why it is important to investigate the molar *and* molecular operations of government (see, for instance, chapter 4).[163] However, the Spinoza in Deleuze, always attentive to the kinetic play of forces and their infinite complexity, offers another—and, in some respects, more provocative—reading of "microphysics." Deleuze writes:

> It is true that, in Foucault, everything is practical; but the practice of power remains irreducible to any practice of knowledge *[savoir]*. To mark this difference in nature, Foucault will say that power refers back to a "microphysics." *But we must not take "micro" to mean a simple miniaturization of visible and articulable forms; instead it signifies another domain, a new type of relations, a dimension of thought that is irreducible to knowledge. "Micro" therefore means mobile and non-localizable connections.*[164]

Given how Deleuze has previously sketched the difference between "knowledge" and "power," it is clear that the figure of "thought" in the preceding passage harks at the constitutive instability of power, its "flexible segmentarity," as he puts it, as contrasted to the "relatively rigid segmentarity" of knowledge. *Thought as power, development as diagram, diagram as mobilizing force, development as thought* . . . this transitive chain of analysis carries us, I suggest, to at least two limits. First, an understanding of "development"—quite unlike postdevelopment scholars[165]—as a mobilizing force that *has* the capacity to expand "freedoms"[166] but that is also, by nature, unstable. And second, to the surprising prospect that a certain Gramsci can be brought into an embrace with a certain Foucault and a certain Deleuze to think about the operations of resistance within power.

What is the connection, then, between this certain Gramsci and his unlikely allies?[167] *If* hegemony—the concept most closely associated with Gramsci—is understood as a ruling ideology that functions by effecting a suture between different classes and class fractions, by producing a historic bloc, as it were; and furthermore, *if* this assemblage of ruling ideas is regarded as constitutively unstable—precisely because it bears the scars of suture, scars that can erupt once again into bleeding wounds unless continuously repaired by the work of hegemonizing—*then,* we are almost there. This rendering of hegemony, which I think is both tenable and faithful to Gramsci, has more than physiognomic similarity to Deleuze qua Foucault's analytics of power/knowledge. The set of ideas that name hegemony attempt to territorialize or capture disparate forces into a molar form (the historic bloc)—to this end, hegemonic projects deploy strategies of both consent and coercion. But capture is neither foreordained nor eternal. It is always contingent, always unstable.

"Hegemony," in this sense, approximates "knowledge" or "discourse." It is, after all, knowledge—the "visible" and the "sayable" percolating through more-than-human assemblages—that strives to persuade and elicit conducts *for* defined ends. And, like discourse, it is constantly shot through and unsettled by the mobility and reversibility of power.[168] "Counter-hegemony" or, alternatively, the reemergence of discontinuities within a historical bloc is an always open possibility. Finally, like "discourse" there is a tenable way to read "hegemony"—Gramsci *through* Althusser, for instance—as a collection of *lived* practices; "ideas" as relations of force that operate in molecular and unconscious ways upon conduct, and which only achieve legibility in doings and not on a Cartesian slate of consciousness.

These unlikely theoretical alliances enable us to think of the challenges issued by persons from historically subordinated groups—Bharwads, Vaghris, Vankars, and Kolis—to corporate domination by upper caste elites in rural Gujarat not in the standard model of "resistance," which presupposes planned human intent; but, instead, in terms of dislocating effects that traverse the microphysics of development. The mobile trajectories of power that work through human and nonhuman actors can produce surprises. Some of these surprises, as we have seen, feed the machine of capital. They are not, in that sense, precursors of radical politics. But they may nevertheless force open a breach for oppositional subaltern politics. I vividly remember a meeting with an ex-*sarpanch*, a Rajput *durbar*, in the village of Govindpura.[169] Let's call him Sohanbhai. Govindpura has a large irrigation tank, but its erratic reserve means that cultivators may or may not expect to water fields from it. When I asked Sohanbhai about the current economic situation of the village, he tiredly replied that fifty boys from the village were out that very moment illegally felling *desi bavar* trees, which they expected to sell to unauthorized wood dealers in the town of Kheda. "What can they do?" he asked. "They have to manage somehow." I noticed a man who had joined our conversation, uninvited. He was dressed in a spotless white *dhoti* and *kurta*. Unhesitatingly, he contradicted Sohanbhai: "There has been lot of improvement in the past twenty to thirty years." I looked at him in surprise. He explained that because of hardships, people in the village had become hard working and their vices (*vesan*) had declined. "Isn't this progress?" he asked. He left us then, explaining that his sister's son—a CBI man[170]—had come visiting. Sohanbhai clarified after his departure that the man was from one of the four Vankar households in Govindpura. He added that of the four tractors in the village, three belonged to Vankars. And only they have a private tubewell to irrigate their lands, he said, because they received government subsidies that others can't get. A previously silent onlooker spoke up. He told me not to believe anything the Vankar man had just said. They have relatives in government service and get all sorts of assistance from *sarkar* (the State), so it's easy for *dheds* to suggest that the conditions have improved. They haven't. The village is the same. "They have a sweet tongue, but their disposition is black"—in short, Vankars can't be trusted, the man implied. Sohanbhai nodded in assent. This deep resentment of *dalit* economic mobility and displacement of customary hierarchies is widespread among upper-caste elite and mid-level castes such as Baraiyas and Koli Patels, who do not qualify for affirmative action under Mandal or Baxi Commission guidelines.

In fact, decades-old fear of such a breach in status goes some way in explaining why Patels and other upper-caste elites began to migrate unevenly, from the mid-1950s, toward political parties that stood in opposition to the ruling Congress. While some Patel leaders, such as Chimanbhai Patel, stuck doggedly with the Congress even when its political fortunes waned, others, such as Bhailalbhai Patel and Babubhai Patel, broke away early from the Congress to join more or less right-leaning parties like Lok Paksh (People's Party) and Janata Front.[171] These formations, in combination with the Rashtriya Swayamsevak Sangh (RSS), became the antecedents of the Bharatiya Janata Party (BJP), which swept to power in Gujarat in March 1995 on a Hindu nationalist agenda—an agenda that has become ferociously communal in the years since, culminating in state-sanctioned killings of several hundred Muslims in February 2002 on the watch of Chief Minister Narendra Modi. That said, it is important to avoid the facile conclusion that Patels and other Gujarati upper-caste elites uniformly support Hindu sectarianism and violence. Indeed, I can anecdoctally think of many such individuals—friends and not, secular and devout—who are troubled by the Hindutva agenda. Several of them consider a mercantile temperament with its attendant cosmopolitanism to be the distinguishing hallmark of Gujaratis. But this worldview is offset by strong reluctance on the part of several, *even* those who claim Gandhi or the *sarvodaya* movement as political inspiration—in the case of close Patel acquaintances in rural

Kheda, the latter aspect hit me particularly hard—to criticize BJP rule
and to underplay the 2002 pogrom when asked. "Nothing happened to
Muslims in our village" was a common retort, when the issue came up;
another was to explain it away as a spontaneous act of retaliation by a
few aggrieved hotheads (*chhokrao*—"boys") in Amdavad. Still others
excused it as an aberration in an otherwise commendable record of
efficient administration and development achievements by Narendra
Modi's government.

Hindu normativity runs deep in Gujarat. Witness nineteenth- and
twentieth-century Gujarati literature (particularly revered figures like
K. M. Munshi, author of *Jaya Somnath*), the strongly sectarian sentiments
of Gujarati heroes such as Sardar Vallabhbhai Patel,[172] the popularity
of the Maha Gujarat agitation of the 1950s, the sway of Arya Samaji
movements in the late nineteenth and early twentieth centuries and of
the Swaminarayan sect today,[173] the celebration of contemporary social
reformers and saints like Sachchidanand, Pandurang Athavale, or Morari
Bapu, even Gandhi and *Gandhivaad*. Despite the progressive impulses
that cut through many of these mobilizations, there is undeniably a
powerful undercurrent of Hindu normativity in each. The belief that
Muslims are aggressive and predatory circulates as common sense—
reliably nourished by reminders (in political pamphlets, stump speeches,
news organs, and school textbooks) that the pillage of the temple in
Somnath by Mahmud Ghazni in 1026 was the initial step in Muslim
colonization of India.

E. P. Thompson once memorably wrote: "People are born into a
society whose forms and relations seem as fixed and immutable as the
overarching sky. The 'commonsense' of the time is saturated with the
deafening propaganda of the *status quo;* but the strongest element in
this propaganda is simply the fact that what exists exists." The fused
sense that Hindus are the historically persecuted majority and that the
cultural heritage *(sanskriti)* that gives Gujarat its distinctive character is
Hindu sits like immutable fact in much of Gujarat. This is the heritage
that Narendra Modi has extolled in his summons to *Garvi Gujarat*—a
phrase that reactivates the sentiments of "Jai jai garvi Gujarat," a poem
by the celebrated nineteenth-century poet-literateur, Narmad, which
some regard as the iconic expression of *Gujaratni asmita* (Gujarati identity).[174] To say, therefore, that Hindu normativity is the principal reason
Patels and other upper castes have come to support sectarianism and

Hindu nationalist parties like BJP amounts to explaining very little. The uncertainties and unfulfilled aspirations of urban life under deindustrialization conjoined to crony and authoritarian capitalism; the lurking violence of hyper-masculine society, most fully evidenced in Gujarat's shocking sex ratio of 883 female children to 1,000 male children in the 0–6 age category (the comparable all-India average in the 2001 Census of India, also low, was 927 girls for every 1,000 boys); declining agrarian dominance—thanks to political and ecological setbacks associated with development interventions, including affirmative action policies; and the deep anxiety and fury generated by this, particularly among youth, is a more promising line of inquiry. It also suggests how widespread upper- and middle-caste support for antireservation agitations in Gujarat in the 1970s and 1980s might have been displaced, through supple diffusion of ideology via varied spatial devices and apparatuses, into anti-Muslim rage.[175] The unexpected enrollment of dalit and tribal groups to the cause of Hindu nationalism—resulting in a bizarre and incendiary neopopulist historic bloc—is further testament to the psychological and political acumen of Sangh Parivar strategists in Gujarat. "What makes fascism dangerous," observe Deleuze and Guattari, "is its molecular and micropolitical power, for it is a mass movement."[176] In words that eerily echo events in Gujarat, they write:

> The masses certainly do not passively submit to power; nor do they 'want' to be repressed, in a kind of masochistic hysteria; nor are they tricked by an ideological lure. Desire is never separable from complex assemblages that necessarily tie into molecular levels, from microformations already shaping postures, attitudes, perceptions, expectations, semiotic systems, etc. Desire is never an undifferentiated instinctual energy, but itself results from a highly developed, engineered setup rich in interactions: a whole supple segmentarity that processes molecular energies and potentially gives desire a fascist determination.[177]

Conclusion

The diagram of development (and any diagram for that matter) is the immanent cause of concrete collectives or assemblages that secure differentiated effects, producing new composite bodies—natures, institutions, languages, technologies, and subjects—whose workings bear the trace of the aleatory: an irreducible indeterminacy.[178] *Things simply happen* despite the best of designs. Like any abstract machine development functions through connections—putting into relation—parts that are separate to enable improvements in the conditions of life. "What is development?" is a misleading question because "development" is a diagram, different-in-itself, of the desire for improvement. It is precisely the handling of this desire in different—and singular—ways by human actors that gives development its force. It is a force that is able to put human actors into new relations with other human *and* nonhuman actors; indeed it puts humans into new relations with their past and future "selves," providing a narrative to life. But relations are always flows, and the flows that make up an assemblage can always conjugate and multiply into new flows that undercut that assemblage.

These practices of human actors, their concrete handling of desire, have a shared modality. But they are also irreducibly singular. The error of postdevelopment scholarship lies in its failure to recognize these multiple handlings of development. It is the general yet singular *handling* of desires that constitutes "experience" and produces the effect— howsoever coherent or incoherent—of "self." I follow A. N. Whitehead on this point (and Raymond Williams), namely, "that consciousness presupposes experience and not experience consciousness." Indeed, "[Consciousness] is a special element in the subjective forms of some feelings. Thus, an actual entity may, or may not, be conscious of some part of its experience."[179]

The failure and decline of the developmental state is a common diagnosis of India's frayed polity from the 1980s onward. But the failure of the state to deliver is *not* the same as the failure of "development." Quite the contrary, it is the failure of the Indian state to *contain* the power of development. As we saw, for nineteenth-century British liberalism development was the suture that staunched the raw wounds of Empire: a suture that ultimately outlived its object of repair. Having supplied reason *for* Empire to liberal elites in the metropole and reason *against* Empire to anticolonial nationalisms across Africa and Asia, development was reactivated in the postcolony for a different conjugation: to join the several "minor" geographies that threatened to dissipate the nation's body. As with Empire, so with the democratic polity that succeeded it: development proved to be a poisoned suture. Over the long 1950s, the heydays of Nehruvian socialism and central planning, it furnished reason *for* "India," appearing to territorialize an assemblage with dizzyingly disparate and discordant parts. But by the mid-1960s the development machine had helped to set in motion an array of—at times, contradictory—de-territorializing forces that began to lacerate the uncertain fabrication called "India." The new forms of sociality that emerged in subsequent decades abolished neither Nation nor State—nor did they decisively decouple the two; but they significantly altered the modalities of State control and the Nation's itinerary. Many of the post-1965 transformations were turbulent. In Gujarat, where the communal war machine has captured the State apparatus to produce a "pure, cold line of abolition,"[180] they were bloody.

CHAPTER FOUR

Distinction

Leisure

Where there is growth, there is exudation. During my time in Matar Taluka, I was frequently surprised to encounter groups of male villagers who spent large parts of their day lounging on a *charpoi* (jute cot) in busy gossip, or hunched in small circles, playing cards, with the ubiquitous *beedi* (local cigarette) or *paan* (betel leaf smeared with condiments) close at hand. Had these village groups been merely seasonal occurrences whose emergence and disbandment corresponded to slack periods in agriculture, then my curiosity about them would have been considerably dimmer. But they were not. The size of the group varied, but lean agricultural season or busy, they endured—as if fixtures in the agrarian landscape. It soon became clear that the groups consisted mainly of landed and younger-generation farmers from the Lewa Patel caste. In conversations it also became apparent that several older-generation Patels disapproved of this malingering, which they saw as evidence of loose work habits. But many also seemed resigned to the generation gap and the waning interest of their wards in an agricultural future. S. N. Patel is a wealthy farmer, whom I met on a visit to the subdistrict in October 2004. He has been able to parlay his agricultural profits into a flourishing garment store in the village of Ambodi. S.N. told me with exasperation how his son—who had a diploma in electronics—wanted neither to farm nor work the store.[1] Instead, he had spent a large sum of family money on an ill-advised business venture: a machining foundry that would produce small tractor parts. But advance orders, necessary to secure subsidized industrial loans from local banks, never materialized and the workshop now lies half-finished on a plot of prime agricultural land that was converted with great difficulty—through well-directed bribes and cajoling—into NA (nonagricultural) status. The son now wants to go to the United States or Canada and was pressuring his parents to find him a girl with a green card. The father said they had explored possible marriage alliance at various times, but "there was too much competition for the girls."

S.N.'s story made me recall another encounter from the mid-1990s, during my initial spell of research in Matar. It was a meeting with another Patel, an engineer with Gujarat Refineries in the city of Vadodara who owned fifty *vighas*[2] of irrigated agricultural land in the village of Astha (where I undertook a survey). His nephew, the largest landowner in Astha, farmed the land on sharecrop in his absence. When he discovered that I was a student from the United States, he unleashed a story that was uncannily similar to S.N's.[3] Could I help him? he asked. He wanted my advice on how his son, Kamlesh, could immigrate to America. Kamlesh, he said, had completed an MSc in Computer Science from M.S. (Maharaja Sayajirao) University in Vadodara and had an excellent job with a well-known consulting firm—A. F. Ferguson Ltd. When a high-paying job in Dubai came along, Kamlesh resigned from A. F. Ferguson. But at the last minute, the Dubai offer fell through and Kamlesh was left high and dry. He was able to get admission into a Ph.D. program in the United States but was denied a visa by the American Consulate in Mumbai. Efforts to dig up relations *(saga-sambandhi)* who might be able to sponsor Kamlesh for a green card under the family reunification program had been unproductive. Kamlesh, according to his father, was now so obsessed with getting to the United States that he had become the local organizer in Vadodara for the Hare Krishna sect, in the hope that this might throw open a channel for entering America. I encountered several such stories of Patel males, in their twenties and thirties, heirs to often considerable land but disinterested in cultivation, intent on migrating to the United States, Canada, or Australia (and latterly to New Zealand). More curious, however, was that band of similarly placed young Patel men, who evinced no desire to leave farming but were almost never in their fields. They were instead to be found in scenes such as the one I described at the beginning of this chapter—lounging on a cot or clustered at a teashop, always in a public spot where they could monitor flows into and out of the village.

That young and affluent Patel farmers soaked in a consumerism which is now commonplace in rural India—and who, more importantly, can *afford* a life of idleness—were constituents of these village groups was not altogether surprising. After all, mainstream microeconomic theory offers a perfectly plausible explanation for idleness: provided leisure is a "normal" good (a property that would be reflected by the shape of the indifference curves that describe an individual's preference structure), it is feasible for the income effect to dominate the substitution effect and therefore for agents to consume more leisure—or equivalently, to work less—as their incomes rise.[4] A large body of empirical evidence suggests that larger incomes do, in fact, produce backward-bending supply curves of labor.[5] Thus, the behavior of younger-generation Patels could have been easily rationalized as confirmation of this result.

But what about the numerous, less well-to-do Patels, Panchals, Baraiyas, Kolis, and Rohits who also loitered in the village groups?[6] Could they afford to "squander" their time? Were they illustrative of elite stereotypes about them? The prevailing discourse of the propertied in Matar Taluka has a familiar refrain: the poor are lazy, indifferent parents, and produce too many children. I remember an instance, in Ashapuri, when R. P. Patel, a city-based engineer who returns to his village periodically, sidled up to me as I was talking one day to Dasarath, a seventeen-year-old Baraiya from a struggling family.[7] Dasarath was trying to make a go of it selling fresh vegetables (I recount his story in chapter 5). Gesturing toward the Baraiya quarters *(vas)*, R.P. began to lecture about the "ills" of population and illiteracy, which he claimed were undercutting the gains in production enabled by canal irrigation. "It's a failure in parenting if children don't finish at least tenth grade." He looked pointedly at Dasarath as he said this. Then rather imperiously he declared—I took this to be for my benefit—that people who chose to have too many children were selfish *(svarthi)*. "They don't realize they have a duty to the country, not just to themselves." By then a small crowd, mostly Baraiyas, had gathered around us. R.P. looked over and asked whether any of those present had bothered to count the average number of kids per household in the current generation. One thakur answered, "four or five," a response that was seconded. "In the current generation? Not possible!," shot back R.P. There was a murmur of assent. Then, as if to deflect attention from themselves, someone shouted the name of a *chamar* (Rohit) man in Ashapuri who had twelve children. "Doesn't anyone do family planning?," asked R.P. He looked clearly satisfied that his audience was with him. I argued with R.P. that asking children to drop out of school to enter wage labor or being inattentive to their performance in school wasn't irresponsible given the lack of networks and job opportunities that Baraiyas and Rohits routinely confront. "What good is higher education if it doesn't take you anywhere? At least casual labor brings in some income." And maybe, I ventured, more children are perceived as a source of security. After all, more working hands may imply larger family income. Agreeing with me, Dasarath rattled off a local proverb: "Three individuals means three annas, five individuals means five annas." R.P. shook his head in disgust. In his cost–benefit calculus, this was a "stupid" way to think.

R.P. irritated me, but I found myself sympathizing with his views whenever I saw poorer Patels, Panchals, Baraiyas, and Rohits idling with young, propertied Patels and Brahmins. Several of them, I would tell myself, *could* have used the income from daily wage labor instead of "wasting" their time. In their present economic conditions, the notion that they might be, like their prosperous Patel compatriots, on the backward-bending segments of their individual labor supply curves was absurd. I mentally trotted out a list of possible explanations for their behavior: sloth, indifference, physical infirmity, defiance, or aversion to field labor. A few months into my stay in Matar, I discovered that reluctance to take orders from employers and aversion to manual labor were the reasons that poorer villagers most frequently invoked in defense of idleness. Some, it transpired, were from previously wealthy households, now poor because of one or more male family member's addiction to alcohol or gambling, or due to economically crippling fragmentation of landholdings at inheritance. Such individuals considered supervised wage labor—indeed, the very idea of physical labor—degrading. Others, whose families had not experienced a sudden descent from affluence to poverty and who therefore attached no explicit stigma to wage labor, expressed dislike at being bossed over by employers. When I inquired from members of this poorer strata how they could afford to be idle, some simply shrugged that they were able to get by *(gamé te chalé chhé)*; others replied that they were not idle and were able to generate incomes by tending their livestock *(dhor)* or through various forms of petty enterprise *(amuk dhandha thi).* (Moonshining was apparently one, and lending small sums of cash for short terms at exorbitant rates of interest was another. Agricultural laborers, the group I most expected to be indebted, were usually *not* the most indebted in the villages I frequented—midsize cultivators with outlays and operating expenses were; and I was taken aback to learn that wage laborers were frequently the most active petty moneylenders.)

A few preliminaries, then, to situate my arguments in this chapter: Conventional economic theory, with its allegiance to an individual-centered model of rational choice, is neither able to account for backward-bending labor supply curves at low levels of income nor explain, in the case of the wealthy, why leisure should be a "normal" good. To pin it on the empty notion of "disutility" is to evade the task of explanation. As social beings, subjects make labor–leisure decisions within a relational and regulative *field* of meanings. Their individuality is formed through a cultural "logic of practice." These axioms, almost too obvious to warrant mention, compel an understanding of rationality—*conducts that are intelligible and optimal*—neither as discrete decisions nor the property of an abstract and *dis*placed creature of reason. Rather, rationality is restored as a spatial and distributive property of a subject's variable location within the latticework of connections that I have previously called an assemblage (see chapter 3). Optimality is no longer restricted to an economy of means to ends (net gain at the margin). Instead, it describes conducts which are in comportment with the meaningful ends that congeal within the latticework of relations a subject inhabits and conserve her ability to continue to realize those ends in the future. (Examples of ends could be food production, income, reputation, creditworthiness, or simply how one behaves.)

In short, rationality as normative conduct is relational. As the nature of connections changes—due to addition, subtraction, or modification of the human or nonhuman elements that are links in the diverse chains of connection, which traverse every individual—it transforms the universe of potential actions. Think, for instance, how war, drought, or death—or alternatively, access to new tools and ideas, infrastructures of movement, or social ties through marriage—redistributes individual possibilities. Yet we all know that a reorganization of possibilities does not automatically translate into altered practices. People's conducts exhibit considerable regularity and inertia (if society can be described as an agglomeration of patterned actions, it is precisely in this sense). The heterogeneous associations that endow them with "subjectivity" are channels of power. They exert a temporal hold on individual actions by continuously reactivating regulative grids of conduct. I use the term *cultural logic of practice* to name these regulative grids.

It is important to qualify my use of the term "cultural". My intention is not to anoint a domain of actions that stands separate from other domains like "economic" or "political" (to the contrary, this chapter hopes to trouble such demarcations). Nor is "cultural" intended to reference norms and ideals that exist on a plane of "consciousness," from where they can be excavated and codified by the enterprising ethnographer, historian, or economist. Instead, my use of the "cultural" has affinity to Louis Althusser's concept of "ideology." In his Pascalian (and nonpejorative) formulation, ideology serves as description for how people live and narrate their everyday existence: "Men 'live' their ideologies as the Cartesian 'saw' or did not see—if he was not looking at it—the moon two hundred paces away: *not at all as a form of consciousness, but as an object of their 'world'*—as their 'world' itself."[8] So why not simply use the term "ideological" instead of "cultural"? The short answer is that the concept of "cultural" does more analytical work for me. It also allows me to mark how two of Althusser's contemporaries (and protagonists)—Pierre Bourdieu and Michel Foucault—have inflected my reading of his oeuvre.[9]

Althusser's insights on the workings of "ideology"—its diffusion through "ideological state apparatuses" (ISAs) backed up by "repressive state apparatuses" (RSAs) and operation of subjects through the unconscious—are indispensable. He has far less to say about sources of change in ideological formations and their regional content and character. By comparison, Foucault provides a compelling archaeology of the cultural in *The Order of Things*. The "cultural" denotes *empiricities*—the "sayable" and the "visible"—that acquire a regional, stratified form and exert a generative "pull" on actions. Empiricities are *powerful*—they constitute a cultural field—in this precise sense of *affecting conduct*. Althusser's theory of subject formation, captured in his concept of "interpellation," has been justifiably influential in the human sciences. But Althusser is dismissive of the category of "experience," finding it a troubling remnant of humanist fictions. Yet, in so doing he has no way to think how the handling of experience by individuals within social contexts—as part of a process of interpellation—reproduces subjectivity: both a narrative sense of "self" as well as an awareness of the ability or inability to act. In *Outline of a Theory of Practice,* Bourdieu skirts humanist traps by positing conducts not as causal expressions of an organizing "consciousness" but as embodied dispositions, which show up as regularities in practice. These regularities, in turn, are retrospectively amenable to "explanation" in terms of certain structures of value, or normativities. (It is one subset of these that I gloss in this chapter as the "government of work.") I argue that this cultural logic, which is governmental, is consequential for understanding not only the microgeographical work practices of individual actors but also spatial agglomerations of labor arrangements within central Gujarat.

The Puzzle of Piecework Labor (Ucchakpratha)

In 1994–95 and again in 1997, over a period spanning roughly nineteen months, I undertook an ethnographic and census survey of three multicaste villages in Matar Taluka. But in this chapter I only draw upon information collected in two villages that were beneficiaries of canal irrigation from the Mahi Right Bank Canal (MRBC) project post-1962.[10] I interviewed 543 households in these two villages, collecting information on their demographics, a wide range of assets, and their transactions in labor, land, and credit markets. In addition, I was able to conduct open-ended interviews with key informants in at least a third of the eighty-two villages in Matar. My field investigation revealed that group-based and individual piecework *(ucchak)* arrangements were steadily becoming the modal form of payment for a variety of agricultural tasks—everything from tilling *(danti)* and leveling of land, to transplanting *(ropni)* and harvesting *(vadhaman)* of paddy, to application *(bharaman)* of fertilizers and pesticides for cereal and miscellaneous cash crops, like tomato, gourd, melons, and guava. Although lack of baseline data from earlier years impedes quantitative reconstruction of labor arrangements in the study villages, particularly on the changing incidence of piece-rate contracts, my ethnographic work in the villages, combined with findings from the 1965–66 survey of Matar Taluka[11] and the subsequent re-survey in 1974–75,[12] indicates that the incidence of piece-rate cash payments to farm workers (as contrasted to daily wage contracts and in-kind harvest shares) grew in scope enormously over the thirty-year period from 1965 to 1995.

For example, we know from the 1965–66 survey that at the time payment for transplanting rice seedlings was almost exclusively in daily money wage (two rupees per day, which at the time purchased three kilograms of paddy).[13] My surveys three decades later, in 1995, revealed that transplanting was almost exclusively piece-rated (commanding a lump-sum payment of Rs. 225 to 300 per vigha). Moreover, when compared to daily or half-day wage *(chhutak)* contracts, piece-rate *(ucchak)* payments for identical tasks invariably tended to be higher. Usually the difference was nominal, but in several instances payments were drastically higher. Hence, a *vigha* of paddy transplanted in *chhutak* cost an employer 125 to 150 rupees in 1995 (at twenty-five rupees per day for five to six laborers), as compared to the lower-bound *uchhak* payment of 225 rupees.

It is now clear that the rise of piece-rate contracts is not a regional aberration peculiar to central Gujarat. A number of village studies in India that have focused on changing agrarian relations corroborate the phenomenon.[14] In fact, the evidence indicates that piece-rate contracts were widely prevalent by the early 1980s. Hence, V. K. Ramachandran notes the growing prevalence of piecework in his study village of Gokilapuram in Madurai District, Tamil Nadu;[15] and Jan Breman, from his field observations in Bardoli District of south Gujarat, writes that the *udhad* system of piece-rate contract work has "gained greatly in popularity in recent years."[16] Similarly, John Harriss, based on an analysis of employment and wage data he gathered in several villages of North Arcot, Tamil Nadu, in 1973–74 and 1982–83, reports that "over the decade there has been a shift away from the standard daily payments that were still the norm in 1974/75 to much more employment of labor on the basis of various specific contracts."[17] But although the trend toward piecework is geographically widespread in rural India, it is by no means obvious that an identical set of underlying factors is driving it. In fact, in this chapter I shall argue that despite broad structural similarities (such as the availability of surface irrigation and use of modern varieties) between areas that reveal an employment trend in favor of task-based contracting, the emergence and consolidation of such arrangements is *conjunctural.* It hinges on a nondeterministic fusing of place-specific cultural, historical, and ecological processes with regional forces that buffet an agrarian economy (such as changes in technology, demand and supply conditions for labor and crops, and caste politics).

So, why have piecework or task-based contracts become increasingly common in Matar Taluka?

Seductions of Orthodoxy

No effort to interpret the phenomenon of piecework employment *(ucchakpratha)* can forego an encounter with two mainstream approaches—new institutional economics (NIE) and Marxist political economy (MPE)—that furnish the bulk of our social science vocabulary for analyzing the labor process. By invoking social science, I want to further indicate that NIE and MPE in their uptake within labor studies have been, with few exceptions, epistemologically realist. Realism comes in many forms, and this book is informed by the Spinozist variety (as filtered through Althusser and Deleuze)— structure or diagram as *immanent cause,* present only its effects.[18] The realism of NIE and MPE is different. It frequently approximates a Comtean positivism, where knowledge strives for fidelity to empirical observables.[19] The variables into which an empirical world is distilled and in which knowledge arrives *are* subject to scrutiny. But this is a methodological scrutiny that applies a "goodness of fit" criterion rather than one of "historical emergence." The principle of emergence understands categories not as neutral tokens that stage reality but, contrarily, as objects of force, which participate in the constitution of that reality. Hence, in NIE and MPE, labor contracts at large and the rise of piecework employment in particular are explained as the logical by-products of interaction between structures and economic actors, whose interests and identities are self-evidently available to theory. This in turn allows NIE and MPE to generate ordered predictions based on a relatively small number of variables, and abstract from messy geographical variations in "history, power, and ideology."[20]

The claim to certain knowledge is seductive for all the well-known reasons. But the certitude of NIE and MPE approaches is purchased by methodological abstraction, which effaces a series of necessary but dangerous supports that enable fictions such as the rational choice actor (NIE) or the rational class actor (MPE). Consider, for instance, how the force of *desire*—invisible in microeconomic theory—enables *rational choice.* Or how the work of the *unconscious* interrupts and sustains the *conscious.* Or how an elaborate weave of norms and rules underwrites even the most basic of economic transactions. Or how gender, caste, and other forms of difference striate and cement class. Jacques Derrida uses the terms "supplement" and "para-site" to describe the work of these necessary supports, which are the conditions of possibility of any system of knowledge, but dangerous to it because they subvert its explanatory power and sovereign claims to self-adequacy.[21]

In spite of these silences, NIE and MPE are socially and analytically powerful narratives that one cannot afford to cavalierly disregard. After all, words such as "economy," "society," "capital," "nation," "culture," and "nature"—or lately, "globalization"—are neither illusory nor innocuous. They are not *mere* words. They bear the dead weight of common sense and routinely bracket our actions. We live in their thrall. Yet, they are far from self-evident. And neither are the ancillary terms that support them. Each of the examples I have cited stakes out an operative domain and each has a complex (yet, often, banal) history of production that it must obliterate in order to function effectively. Once deposited, these categories discharge force fields (Ian Hacking calls them "interactive kinds"[22]) that organize *and* continuously transform the reality they putatively describe. To argue, ontologically, for the materiality of language—the messy entanglement rather than separable planes of "representation" and "reality"—is to embrace a mode of analysis where the accepted causal priors of social science are labored upon to unburden their biographies: the combination of forces and historical practices that have insinuated them as things in our lives: these concrete abstractions with planetary mass.

It is precisely because NIE and MPE truck in potent interactive kinds that we should be attentive to their claims. On a different register, while it is conventional to regard their world of "things" as mutually exclusive, this is neither desirable nor analytically justified. How *could* they be held separate given their fraught historical relationship? I therefore have qualified empathy for Andrew Sayer's proposal that although it is

> customary to think of these two approaches or modes of abstraction as mutually exclusive and contradictory, and there are indeed issues on which they flatly contradict each other, such as the nature of wages and the origin of profit . . . in some respects the concerns of the two modes of abstraction are no more contradictory than the concentric rings and parallel lines of wood grain; they are radically

different but complementary representations of different aspects of the structure of market economies.[23]

It will be apparent by now that the way in which I put theory to work is quite different from Sayer. But I am convinced, like him, that an encounter between NIE and MPE can be productive—at the very least for bringing into the open the shared understandings and misunderstandings that enable the analyses of scholars who inhabit these two powerful traditions of thought.

Studying Labor

While NIE and MPE furnish the bulk of our vocabulary for analyzing the labor process, the exchange of ideas between these two grand traditions of social science has, until recently, remained fairly cosmetic. Suspicious of each other's motives, models, and methods, the two camps have been more prone to trade in acrimony and misunderstandings than acknowledge their substantial, if unexpected, complementarities.[24] One curious similarity between NIE and MPE—and relevant to the argument of this chapter—is their shared silence on the role of language and meaning in the labor deployment decisions of social actors. Empirically, both approaches grant causal primacy to "economic" (and "political")—*hard, material*—explanations of workplace dynamics at the expense of—putatively *soft, idealist*—"cultural" accounts.

But is this type of separation of economic and political from cultural justified? I have already suggested not. In fact, it is a division based on two sorts of misconceptions: first, that the economic and political are somehow self-evident categories (like the Cartesian moon), whereas the cultural is an evasive realm of nonobservables; second, that rejection of the NIE and MPE brand of realism implies embrace of idealism and relativism. Far from it; as I have explained, the cultural does not mean that the concrete world of things (natural and social objects) ceases to matter or recedes into the background. Rather it directs us to the *materiality of words as things:* how certain meanings are geologically deposited on words and how these determinations (their "thingness," if you like) have the power to affect the conducts of social actors.[25] After all, on the subject of labor we only need to remind ourselves of Marx's insight that "'labor,' social activity in the material world, potentially comprises notions of self-expression, rational development, and aesthetic enjoyment.... What is distinctive about humans, according to Marx, is not simply that we depend on symbols but that we, in a sense, create ourselves through symbolically formed action in the world—'labor.'"[26]

But these insights appear to have been mislaid, albeit to different degrees. Whereas even the most economistic of Marxists seem to recognize that labor is a productive force unlike any other, most fail to theorize the *force of its significations*.[27] On the other end, neoclassical economists have, by and large, sidelined the cultural-ideological embeddedness of labor.[28] In general, the recognition that labor is a "pseudocommodity,"[29] not merely another input—and certainly not one that can be unproblematically inserted into a "production function"—has come rather belatedly to the discipline of economics. In fact, signs of change have appeared only with the relatively recent post-Walrasian shift within the discipline (with the "information economics" approach within NIE as its paradigmatic form).[30]

In order to concretely situate my review of NIE and MPE, and argue the merits of studying the cultural determinations of work, I focus on one well-researched area in labor studies: the impact of canal irrigation and green revolution technologies on agrarian labor relations. There is by now a vast and dated literature that examines the linked impacts of irrigation and biochemical innovations—a package consisting of modern crop varieties (MVs), chemical fertilizers, pesticides, and weedicides—on agricultural production and social relations.[31] Studies in production economics emphasize the dual role of irrigation: first, in reducing spatial and intertemporal variability in output (that is, objective risk within an agronomic system), and second, in increasing overall production. Companion studies, grounded in NIE or MPE, analyze how relative endowment shifts caused by irrigation alter social contracts and property relations, and thereby reallocate society's real income. The NIE and MPE approaches are methodologically similar in that that both analyze a pattern of change by examining (a) the technical attributes of irrigation and attendant biochemical and mechanical innovations, and (b) the institutional conditions—uniformity of access to means of production such as land, labor, information, and various forms of capital—under which a new technology is harnessed.

An early concern in the green revolution literature, raised by MPE scholars, was the potentially discriminatory nature of the new technology.[32] Two factors were mentioned: first, the scale nonneutrality of the technology itself (questions about its divisibility); and second, the nonuniformity of the institutional environment in which the technology would be used. The emergent consensus is that the biochemical innovations of the green revolution are, at least in principle, scale-neutral (although access to them may not be uniform); by contrast, mechanical innovations such as tractors, power-tillers, pumpsets, sprayers, threshers, and combine-harvesters, which are lumpy and indivisible, are not scale-neutral. They exhibit economies-of-scale in use. But since the biochemical package can be adopted without the mechanical package (which is to say, the two are not tied goods) it has been reasoned that small and medium cultivators can benefit from MVs in the same way, if not always to the same degree, as large farmers.[33]

However, when it comes to evaluating the impact of irrigation and green revolution technologies on labor market dynamics, the NIE and MPE approaches employ different sets of causal reasoning. The NIE literature models the advent of secure irrigation and the diffusion of MVs as a technical change, whose proximate outcome is a redistribution in the relative endowments of various production factors, particularly land and labor. Such movements in relative resource scarcity are expressed through an adjustment in relative factor prices, which in turn alter existing social contracts and norms (i.e., institutions) of income sharing.[34] The end result is a new institutional environment with a new allocation of society's real income. This argument, which presupposes that institutions respond in reasonably predictable fashion to relative price shifts in order to restore system equilibrium, is the well-known "induced innovation" hypothesis.[35] Whether or not the new allocation exhibits properties of static and dynamic efficiency have been the key concerns of NIE scholars. They have paid particular attention to the land- versus labor-saving biases of technology. Irrigation, for instance, is viewed as a land-saving endowment shift because a given production target can be met from less land. Similarly, MVs are also considered land saving.[36] But, unlike some types of farm machinery, MVs are not innately labor saving. In fact, they are typically labor absorptive, although to varying degrees.[37] Not only do MVs absorb more peak season labor than traditional varieties, they also induce a rise in cropping intensity that expands total labor demand and per capita employment, ceteris paribus.[38] The caveat, as Michael Lipton and Richard Longhurst point out, is that the labor-*using* characteristic of MVs may, in cases, prompt labor-*saving* interventions like mechanization. But they are quick to note that such interventions are the property of agents and social institutions, not the causal property of MVs; and, in any case, "labor-saving effects only partially offset the labor-using effects of MVs."[39] If MVs have an inherent limiting property, it is the degree to which their cultivation can be mechanized. Wheat, for instance, is more amenable to mechanization than paddy. Thus, a crop's gestational logic and ecological requirements may have significant implications for labor contracts.[40]

The approaches that I have collectively described as NIE are separable into two subcategories: the Walrasian and non-Walrasian. In the Walrasian world of competitive and perfect labor markets, the results of MV adoption on labor contracts are straightforward. Since MVs are labor absorptive, recipient areas would witness an initial surge in labor demand and decreased seasonal elasticity of demand, resulting in institutional changes that would benefit agricultural laborers.[41] Contractual changes might include an increase in daily or hourly real wages; in the quantity of customary perks, such as meals, cups of tea, cigarettes, and allowances of fuelwood and fodder; and a shift in the mode of payment from in-cash to in-kind if prices of wage-goods show an inflationary trend.[42]

The Walrasian scenario is readily identifiable as a subset of non-Walrasian analysis: a special case where different types of labor contracts are neutral with respect to the multiple costs associated with imperfect information and information asymmetry across employers and workers. In practice, employers and workers inhabit a non-Walrasian world of risk, hidden information, imperfect enforcement, and search costs, where dynamic outcomes are less certain because different contractual arrangements carry different transaction costs. Given that transactions costs—that is, efficiency losses measured as the sum of foregone production plus the opportunity cost of time spent in additional supervision or recruitment—inevitably rise with the increasing labor intensity of production, one should expect profit-maximizing employers to favor labor contracts that curtail costs from imperfect information and information asymmetry. Their menu of strategies might include piece-rate contracts for agricultural operations that minimize completion and supervision time; the hiring of farm servants; the use of interlinked labor contracts, which augment their abilities to sanction workers who shirk; or offers of higher than market wages to a group of preferred workers in order to optimize work effort.[43]

Whether or not employers succeed in implementing one or more of these contractual forms depends, of course, on an array of factors: including the nature of laborers' bargaining power under an MV regime, social norms of fairness, degree of ideological domination of subaltern groups by employers, the regional political milieu, and the relative abilities of workers and employers to overcome collective action problems that might impede coordinated class action.[44] These caveats are precisely the ones that MPE scholars like to point out, although they also take pains to evoke structural inequities in the control of assets and resources. These asymmetries, they argue, give employers considerable power to stifle or subvert growth in labor's bargaining position.[45] Jonathan Pincus, for instance, objects that far "too much emphasis has been placed [by NIE scholars] on the outward *forms* of labor arrangements as opposed to the *social bases* of these forms."[46] These objections draw to the forefront some key issues, namely, the ontological status and operations of "power," "freedom," and "exploitation" within the labor process.

Power, Freedom, and Exploitation

NIE and MPE regard these three important concepts very differently at the ontological level. For NIE, power lies in the relative abilities of individual transactors to affect economic outcomes in their favor, and is modeled either as a function of underlying supply and demand conditions (the notion of "market power"), or as the capacity of individual actors to "wait it out" and inflict "disagreement costs" on rivals (the notion of bargaining power).[47] NIE lacks a substantive (psychological, ethical, or juridical) concept of freedom or human agency. It assumes the ability of agents to enter into social contracts as innately sovereign and rational individuals, with or without perfect knowledge and anticipation of prospects.[48] Finally, exploitation for NIE describes a situation where a laborer (or, in general, a transactor) is paid below the value of her or his marginal product for services rendered.

MPE's empirical diagnosis of power as relative bargaining strength is strikingly similar to NIE's, but although supply and demand conditions are clearly proximate determinants of bargaining power in MPE models, their effects are ultimately derivative. According to MPE, unequal access to means of production is the "real" source of power. Moreover, "power," "freedom," and "exploitation" are an interlinked trinity grounded not only in a discriminatory system of private property rights but *also* an accompanying ideological condition that Marx identified as "commodity fetishism"—where "a relation between people takes on the character of a thing and thus acquires a 'phantom objectivity,' an autonomy that seems so strictly rational and all-embracing (in other words, so natural) as to conceal its fundamental nature."[49] Hence, in Marx's famous witticism in *Capital*, volume 1: "the sphere of circulation or commodity exchange . . . is the exclusive realm of Freedom, Equality, Property and Bentham," where buyers and sellers of labor-power contract as free persons, and "which provides the 'free-trader *vulgaris*' with his views, his concepts and standards by which he judges the society of capital and wage-labor."[50] But no sooner do we enter the sphere of production than we realize that although it is labor "as a living agent of fermentation" that gives form to the "lifeless constituents of the product,"[51] the product itself, the surplus labor it contains, and—for the duration of the working day—the embodied labor-power of the worker, belongs to the employer. These accounts clearly contain very different notions of power, freedom, and exploitation from those posited by NIE.

Take, once again, the case of agricultural work in green revolution tracts. It is generally the case that MVs have shorter gestation periods than the traditional crop varieties they displace. This biological fact is a mixed blessing for cultivators: although it allows greater cropping intensity, it also sharpens the need for timely completion of agricultural operations. Periods of peak labor demand, and correspondingly the risks of productivity losses from labor shortages in an agricultural year, mount. Profit-minded employers are likely to want more farm servants or attached laborers. They may try to attract such permanent workers by promising them not only secure wages but also a premium in the form of low-interest loans. These terms of contract are likely to appeal to workers who are risk-averse and unable to smooth their consumption streams due to credit constraints or credit rationing. Secure wage contracts, in this situation, become analogous to the certainty equivalent payoffs of lotteries. The key point, from the standpoint of NIE theorists, is that whatever the underlying social circumstances, employers and workers will find ways to negotiate mutually beneficial, hence, Pareto-improving, labor contracts (whether optimal or second-best).

An MPE scholar would explain the same outcome—the incidence of attached labor—in political terms. Take, for example, Tom Brass, an influential Marxist scholar of labor and agrarian change. According to Brass:

> [I]t is precisely when rural workers begin to exercise their freedom of movement or bargaining power to secure benefits such as higher wages, better working conditions, shorter working hours, etc. . . . that capital attempts to shift the balance of work-place power in its own direction once again by restricting labor mobility. . . . Employer response to worker mobility and/or militancy in a situation of labor scarcity consists . . . of converting free labor into unfree labor [through the mechanism of debt bondage].[52]

Here, the schism between the NIE and MPE approaches boils down to a single issue: the operation of power within the labor process.

Walrasian (that is, neoclassical NIE) economists model social contracts as voluntary transactions between self-interested agents who seek gains-from-trade at the margin (whether in the form of profits or greater utility). By assumption, neither employers nor workers are able to exert undue market power.[53] Non-Walrasian NIE, by contrast, does *not* assume that actors have equal bargaining power; although it does assume that they have clear, if probabilistic, perception of their current possibilities and preferences, and exercise sovereign choices based upon them when they make decisions. However, their choices are not autonomous (as in Walrasian theory) but, rather, interdependent. The outcome of interdependent choice—for instance, the payment structure and form of a labor contract—is typically modeled in one of two ways:

1. as a symmetric Nash bargaining game, where two or more actors negotiate a mutually beneficial outcome by agreeing to some division of an economic pie, the assumption being that disagreement would result in zero payoffs for all concerned;[54] or,

2. as a principal–agent problem, in which "an economically powerful entity, called the principal, attempts to devise contractual arrangements with one or more individuals, called agents, in a way that best serves the former's interest."[55]

The principal–agent game has obvious similarities to the Nash bargaining model. The major difference, as Clive Bell points out, is that the principal–agent framework assumes the existence of a principal who is so powerful (through the control of scarce production means) that he or she can unilaterally set the terms of the contract.[56] This premise hinges in turn on another implicit assumption: that the supply of agents is perfectly elastic, thereby implying that if the principal is unable to agree to a contract with one agent, he or she can costlessly (or at minimum cost) find another willing agent.

However, if the supply of agents is not entirely elastic, or if they are otherwise in a position to inflict a cost on a noncooperating principal, then the principal is in a bargaining game and must consider his or her "disagreement payoff" before making a contractual offer. The principal's threat to withdraw from negotiations, for instance, may not be viewed by the agent as a "credible threat" if it is inconsistent with the former's disagreement utility.[57] In short, as Peyton Young observes, "the outcome of a distributive bargain depends principally on the alternatives of the parties and their aversion to risk. A person who is risk neutral and has a good fallback position will tend to get a better deal than someone who is risk averse and has unattractive alternatives, all else being equal."[58] This diagnosis suggests that a rural laborer with few potential sources of income other than wage labor is likely to be risk averse[59] and likely to accept terms of contract that, on balance, favor the employer.[60] In short, the non-Walrasian NIE framework views power in positivist terms as *bargaining* power—a quantity measured by the ability of an agent, whether an individual or a class coalition, to inflict an economic cost on another agent by withholding cooperation.

The language of contracting and exchange at the margin is anathema to MPE scholars because, to them, it replaces a *substantive notion of personal freedom* (the freedom of labor from the *need* to labor[61]) with a *thin notion of contractual freedom* that diminishes its corporeal and psychological aspects. In their view, to work because you are compelled to for subsistence (as laborers are) or to starve is a rather empty notion of choice. By contrast, employers are under no such compulsion to submit control of their embodied labor-power if they choose not to; hence, it is legitimate to speak of their freedom. Karl Marx underscored this structural asymmetry between employers and employees in his *Economic and Philosophical Manuscripts of 1844:*

> The worker is not at all in the position of a *free seller vis-à-vis* the one who employs him. . . . The capitalist is always free to use labor,

and the worker is always forced to sell it. The value of labor is completely destroyed if it is not sold every instant. Labor can neither be accumulated nor even be saved, unlike true commodities. Labor is life, and if life is not each day exchanged for food, it suffers and soon perishes.[62]

In contrast to NIE, where power is the property of individuals, within MPE the origins of power are societal and its expression is at the level of class. Class power is sustained with the aid of a legal-juridical system of private property and an ideological apparatus that lends commodity exchange a phantom objectivity; and together they enable capitalist employers to extract surplus product from labor during the moment of production and recover it as surplus value in the realm of exchange. Implicit here is moral condemnation of a system where some (capitalists who control the means of production) are unduly and undeservingly rewarded at the expense of others (workers).[63] According to MPE and the "labor theory of value," the mere fact of asset ownership is no justification for control of the surplus product since, without "the living, form-giving fire"[64] of labor, there would be no surplus.[65]

The standard NIE response to this critique is that capital, like labor, is a factor of production, and that in *competitive* settings all factors are paid the value of their marginal product. Thus, in the absence of monopsony power, there is no such thing as the "exploitation" of workers. This particular rift between NIE and MPE is especially nettlesome because it is symptomatic of an ontological debate over the nature of wealth or surplus product under capitalism (what is it, and who creates it?). From this follows an equally contentious ethical and political debate over rights of ownership (who should legitimately control wealth?). Unless NIE and MPE can reach a consensus on ontology, which is hugely doubtful, the subject of exploitation will always remain an unbridgeable crevásse between them. Whereas the marginalists and their precursors variously invoke "reward for superintendence," "reward for abstinence," and "reward for risk-taking" as justifications for the legitimacy of capitalist profit, Marxists reject these claims on the grounds that since capitalists do not create wealth as surplus value in the first instance, they have no right to exert private property over it.[66]

Operational Similarities between NIE and MPE

Despite the sharp ontological divide between NIE and MPE, there are, as indicated, striking similarities in their empirical diagnosis of power, their schematic renditions of history (whether as eventful diachrony or the imagined pasts of different groups), and their peripheral attention to the cultural. Again, I employ a case study for clarity—the first, a study of contractual change in labor arrangements in Java from an NIE perspective; the second, a study of the same phenomena and in the same region from an MPE perspective.

In a study published in 1982, the Japanese economists Hayami and Kikuchi examined two separate contractual histories from Java via an NIE approach:[67] in South Subang, where rice yields had begun to stagnate and were outpaced by expansion in the workforce, they recorded a switch from the traditional *bawon* (open output sharing) harvest system to the *ceblokan* (closed or preferential) harvest arrangement, in which workers' right to harvest was made contingent on their participation in a range of pre-harvest tasks; by contrast in North Subang, where improvements in irrigation boosted crop productivity and where growth in demand for labor outstripped growth in labor supply, they claimed to witness retention of the more remunerative *bawon* system. A parallel study in central Java[68] registered an institutional change from the customary *bawon* system to the new *tebasan* (piece-rate) system, which by its authors' calculations represented a decline in workers' hourly real wages. The study attributed the adverse shift to "rapid changes in the labor supply caused by population pressures that outpaced the changes in the demand for labor."[69]

Based on a re-survey of the same villages in North and South Subang, Pincus argued from an MPE perspective that class bargaining provided a stronger account of observed contractual changes than demographic pressure.[70] His disagreement with the NIE approach was theoretical as well as empirical. He was critical of Hayami and Kikuchi for their "disregard [of] crucial differences in agrarian structure and class power," and it is precisely this neglect of geographical nuances, he suggested, that led to their misreading of empirical facts. Pincus claimed that laborers in South Subang had been able to "claim a larger share of the agricultural surplus than their counterparts in North Subang."[71] He attributed this to the presence of a "large population of smallholders in South

Subang,"[72] who, according to him, were instrumental not only for the initial appearance of *ceblokan* but also its retention in the 1980s, after the introduction of tractors.

These smallholders, who relied on cultivation as well as wage labor for a livelihood, evidently viewed *ceblokan* as a way to curtail participation by migrant workers in the harvest—in the process diluting both consumption and production risk (since sharing in the harvests of neighbors represented a form of informal risk pooling). Close kinship ties between small and middle farmers were important in generating class solidarity and consolidating the bargaining power of this semi-proletariat. Pincus claimed that the low incidence of *ceblokan* in North Subang—a fact noted as well by Hayami and Kikuchi—should have been properly attributed to the lack there of a conspicuous intermediate class; that in fact the continuation of the *bawon* system in which resident *as well as* migrant workers could participate indicates the relatively weak bargaining power of resident laborers—and not the converse as Hayami and Kikuchi suggest. Pincus took Hayami and Kikuchi to task for their neglect of "migrant farm work and off-farm employment" factors. This, he claimed, undermined the predictions of their demography-driven model, which assumed a closed (as opposed to an open) village community.

The preceding discussion reveals important dissimilarities *and* similarities between the NIE and MPE approaches. I begin with the similarities, which are empirical, not ontological. First, both Hayami and Kikuchi (NIE) and Pincus (MPE) view power in positivistic terms as *bargaining* power (that is, as the ability of agents, whether individuals or class coalitions, to inflict economic costs on other agents, either by withholding assets or cooperation). Second, both seem to concur that labor contracts are decided through a process of *bilateral* and *multilateral bargaining*.

The difference between the two approaches lies in how they characterize the bargaining *process:* Hayami and Kikuchi portray it as voluntary negotiations between asocial agents, who respond to structural changes in as efficient a manner as possible. In their demographic NIE model, they argue that observed changes in labor contracts occur in order to restore equilibrium to a system where, because of shifts in the ratio of land to labor, wages to labor no longer accurately reflect its marginal productivity; and where the inertia of custom precludes the emergence of certain institutional forms. By contrast, Pincus views the bargaining process as the expression of an underlying class struggle, informed by a history of class antagonisms and compromise. And whereas Hayami and Kikuchi predict a range of equilibrium outcomes, Pincus rejects the possibility of prediction on the grounds that outcomes depend on the local specificities of class relations.

Third, both Hayami and Kikuchi and Pincus underplay the role of cultural forces on the bargaining process and outcome: the actors who inhabit their accounts have pre-given identities as class agents, but otherwise remain culturally anonymous. Hayami and Kikuchi's token nod to the cultural is in their acknowledgment that certain equilibrium outcomes are foreclosed by custom. There is certainly no effort to understand contracting or labor deployment as activities embedded in a discursive universe and anchored to the embodied cultural identifications of actors.[73] Similarly, Pincus, having assumed that "class" is the most salient basis of affiliation, does not offer adequate justification why other types of social ties are less material to the analysis, or how class is constituted by nonclass identities.

Despite these operational similarities between NIE and MPE, we should not be blinded to their differences. For instance, although both Hayami and Kikuchi and Pincus seem to agree that shifts in relative factor endowments generate pressures for change in labor contracts, they disagree on the nature and direction of this change. NIE scholars like Hayami and Kikuchi believe that the direction of institutional change primarily hinges on realignments in relative factor prices. If the new technology makes labor less expensive relative to land, cultivators will increasingly opt for labor-intensive as opposed to land-intensive agricultural practices. This will eventually produce equilibrium labor contracts that work to the benefit of laborers *unless* countervailing forces inhibit their emergence. In general, NIE scholars are wedded to a methodological individualism, tend to subsume institutional context in the preference structures of agents, model social contracts as equilibrium (often "second-best") solutions to problems of missing markets, anoint price signals as the catalyst of change, and generally view contracts as voluntary transactions between self-interested agents who seek gains-from-trade at the margin (whether in the form of profits or greater utility).

MPE scholars like Pincus, meanwhile, abjure the idea of relative prices as deus ex machina, reject the language of exchange at the margin as a false depiction of human agency, and view methodological individualism with its focus on individual preference structures as blatant disregard of the fact that individuals are *social* actors and who, as such, have varying capacities to act and varying motivations.[74] From this perspective, contractual negotiations are episodic events in a continuous process of class bargaining, where the element of conflict or antagonism is always more salient than the prospect of mutual gain.

Let us return to the question that opened this chapter: How should we account for the growing incidence of piece-rate contracts in Matar Taluka? Within the labor studies literature, the rise of piecework within agriculture has been traced to a variety of causes. NIE explanations emphasize *efficiency* considerations:

I. The Incentive Hypothesis: Piece-rate regimes augment worker productivity and ease temporal constraints on agriculture. The theory predicts the diffusion of piecework in areas of capitalist agriculture where an expansion in cropping intensity has meant shorter and shorter time windows for the completion of agricultural operations. Employers keen to get operations completed on time will adopt piecework as a way of boosting the per-hour productivity of workers, since workers now have an in-built incentive to work faster in order to earn more.

II. The Lower Supervision Cost Hypothesis: Piece-rate regimes impose lower supervision costs on employers than conventional daily wage regimes. The theory predicts the diffusion of piece work in areas where (a) employers and their family members have high opportunity costs of time as a result of alternative employment; (b) wealthy landowners show a strong preference for leisure (as a result of being on the backward-bending portions of their labor supply curves); and (c) high operated land to family labor ratios, combined with tightening labor markets, compel adoption of piece-rate regimes, despite the problem of quality control ("moral hazard") associated with piecework.

MPE explanations are strikingly similar to the NIE ones, although, in contrast to the latter, they highlight *disciplinary* considerations (the opportunities for surplus extraction and social control of workers that piecework or task-rated regimes offer to employers):[75]

I. The Surplus Extraction Hypothesis: Piece- or task-rated work permits employers to expand absolute and relative surplus extraction through the internalization of work discipline. V. K. Ramachandran paraphrases Marx when he writes that under a "piece-work regime, it becomes the personal interest of the worker to work as intensively as possible and to lengthen the work day, since this means an increase in personal remuneration."[76] The theory predicts the diffusion of piecework in areas of capitalist agriculture with tightening labor markets.

II. Dual Labor Market Hypothesis: Since piecework is often more remunerative to workers than daily wage labor, employers can preferentially allot piecework as a way of stratifying the labor market and dividing workers (in short, as a worker-disciplining device). The theory predicts the diffusion of piecework in areas where class-conscious employers are confronted with seasonally or otherwise tight labor markets and growing worker unrest.

III. The Employer Deception Hypothesis: Piece-rate regimes may permit employers to circumvent minimum wage laws for agricultural work, since these laws apply with clarity only to daily, cash-rated work and not to task-based work. Piecework can also allow employers to cheat at the "margins": for instance, by contracting a group of laborers to harvest an acre of paddy on a plot that exceeds an acre in size by some small amount.

So where do we stand? I have made the case that both NIE and MPE offer persuasive, if different, points of departure for investigating labor arrangements.

My primary criticism so far is that despite political and philosophical disagreements and empirical overlaps, both NIE and MPE efface the importance of the *meaning*fulness of lived conduct[77] or, more exactly, how the cultural as the "visible" and the "sayable"—properties of the more-than-human assemblages that people inhabit—structures the way they "live the relation between them and their conditions of existence."[78] As a result, while both frameworks have the capacity to deductively anticipate system tendencies that seem to mirror observed phenomena (such as a shift from wage to piece-rate contracts), they

A. ONTOLOGY	NIE	MPE
Power	Relative abilities of transactors to affect economic outcomes in their favor. Two notions of power, one rooted in supply and demand conditions ("market power"), the other in differential capacity to inflict disutility in strategic interactions ("bargaining power").	Unequal access to means of production, rooted in a state-enforced system of private property rights, which compels some to sell their labor-power to asset owners in order to reproduce and, as a result, grants property owners asymmetric control over the lives of workers.
Freedom	Contractual freedom, specifically ability to transact in rational pursuit of self-interest as a sovereign actor.	Substantive freedom as physical freedom from drudgery and the need to labor, and psychological freedom from alienation.
Exploitation	Payment below the value of marginal product for services rendered.	Extraction of unpaid labor time in the form of "surplus value."
B. EMPIRICS		
Power	Individual or coalition bargaining power.	Class bargaining power.
Culture	Enumerable normative injunctions that truncate the preference set, operate as cognitive constraints on optimizing behavior, or produce interdependent utilities.	"Commodity fetishism" and ideology as a set of controlling ideas and institutional forms that generate a world of "appearances" that service dominant classes.
History	Evolutionary learning process and/or "path dependence."	Class struggle and its dialectical relations with the accumulative tendencies and contradictions of capitalism.

Figure 5. Ontological and operational aspects of NIE (new institutional economics) and MPE (Marxist political economy).

typically—although not always—do so without adumbrating the lived cultural facts that cause particular forms of work organization to crystallize in given time–space contexts. The reason, I think, is simple: strong functionalism (not to mention, a curiously deterministic voluntarism) in the case of NIE, and somewhat weaker structural functionalism in the case of MPE, enables them to generate universalizing predictions that can coincide with contextual realities, without necessarily identifying the processes that produce place-specific institutional trajectories and outcomes.[79]

While the efficiency and disciplinary considerations emphasized by NIE and MPE are clearly important influences on the labor process, I contend that specific institutional and contractual outcomes depend heavily on the cultural realities of actors' practices, and, as such, are onto-logically *conjunctural* rather than necessary.[80] I take issue with NIE and MPE explanations and their "epistemological assumptions of actors with stable identities performing actions with fixed meanings"[81] and argue, contrarily, that the recent surge in piecework employment in Matar Taluka has to be viewed as part of a historic tussle between two groups (the domi-nant Lewa Patel caste and the subordinate Baraiya/Koli castes) to alter their relative standings in the social order. Such groups, as I have previ-ously observed, have a *ruptural unity*. They are an articulation of *fractions*, or what Ernesto Laclau has called "demands."[82] In short, my invocation of groups is not intended as an endorsement of sociology and its modernist desire to render society legible as grid. Rather, I want to recognize that in their lived relations to the world, people come to handle experiences within "arrested" categories—such as caste identities.[83] "Caste" is a pow-erful example of an "interactive kind," which over time has achieved a factualness that allows it to loop back into and transform the reality it was initially only supposed to describe. It is a category that has *come to matter ontologically*. And it is "the active *pouvoir-savoir* or making-sense-ability [of such categories] . . . that provides the discursive field."[84] Language, to repeat, is immanent and material in *this* productive sense.

Labor as Social Theater

In *Learning to Labor*, his brilliant ethnography of working-class kids in Britain, Paul Willis writes: "Laboring is not a universal transhistori-cal changeless human activity. It takes on specific forms and meanings in different kinds of societies."[85] Another sociologist of work, Richard Biernacki, remarks: "It might seem that the expressions of labor and capital, as elemental and necessary constituents of commercial bour-geois culture, would take on the same meaning throughout indus-trializing Europe. But they appeared in varying guises and signified disparate features of human endeavor within the German and British economies."[86] These observations hint at the cultural logics that infuse the labor process.[87] The analytical implications are deep: laboring decisions have to be situated within the broader weave of *practice,* on the understanding that agents' intentions do not proceed from themselves but are instead bound up in the complex way in which structures are inhabited.

Caste is a particularly powerful inhabited structure, continuously present in its effects. In Deleuzian terms, caste identity is the *molar* articulation of *molecular multiplicities.* As molar entity, caste exerts a gravitational pull—*in the same way that a norm is centripetal*—on the conduct of subjects who are in its orbit. While the unmaking (or de-territorialization) of molar identities is always a possibility so, too, is their consolidation. In Matar Taluka, these efforts at consolidation (re-territorialization) have involved, among other tactics, shifting practices of work—with direct implications for labor contracts.

Take Lewa Patels. They exist as a unity of heterogeneous demands around a cultural nucleus, which not only summons certain conducts but also calls forth a certain self-narration. Hence, Patels will often describe themselves as a modern *(aadhoonik)* and progressive *(pragatisheel)* caste, endowed with superior abilities to recognize and take advantage of new economic opportunities. Their bravado can border on cultural arrogance. Hence, on visits to Matar (and elsewhere in Gujarat) I have been repeatedly told by Patel acquaintances that "villages where Patels reside are likely to be prosperous." Their acquired image as the quintessential modern caste predisposes them, for the most part, to a "severe practicality"[88] in the realms of household and farm economics. Their houses are usually large but functional, and lacking in superfluous possessions, their attires (except at weddings) are modest to the point of being nondescript; any household- or farm-related purchases and investments are made after careful deliberation. This normative life of economy *(karkashar)* is offset by a permanent drive for refinement—or more exactly, toward changing ideals of refinement. Patels are more fastidious about their food than any other caste group in the region. I frequently stay with Patel families on visits to Gujarat. But in the course of field research in Matar I also stayed and ate at the homes of Baraiya, Koli Patel, and Vankar families. When I would return to the homes of Patel hosts, I would be invariably asked: "What did you have to eat, Vinaybhai?," or "How much milk did the tea have?" Patel men, regardless of class, pride themselves on being gastronomes. They take great relish in eating the afternoon and evening meals, and their conviction of a discriminating palate often generates lavish and biting criticism of perceived deficiencies in women's cooking—as if they were the actual chefs and the women merely errant apprentices. Weddings are always judged, among other criteria, by the quality of food at the *jamanvaar* (wedding feast).

These are, I realize, suspiciously like sociological generalizations. They are not meant to be (in a trivial sense, it is possible, for instance, to find Patel families who do not conform to these norms). My intention, rather, is to underscore the power of the norm in producing regularities in the universe of conduct—or, what is the same, reducing variance or *ab*normality in conduct. *Normality is, after all, a certain order of normativity.*[89] Desire, anxiety, and fear of lack—in short, forces that work through the unconscious—are critical in securing a norm's effects. Thus, every Patel is in a strange repeating process of becoming-Patel "on the way to being determinately this or that."[90] The norm, always asymptotic, activates a process of self-fabrication that solders caste fractions into a caste unity. Patels would tell me how scrupulous they are in matters of finance (but as I have hinted, the logic of economy is always contaminated by an opposite logic of exudation). This self-audit has infected caste stereotypes that are in circulation in central Gujarat. I heard members of other caste groups say that Patels "maintain accounts carefully" or that "they live with great attention to economy." However, the nurtured austerity of Patels can clash with their desire to acquire social distinction *(abroo)* and be seen as a civilized *(sanskaari)* caste. Let me briefly illustrate how the efforts of Patels to acquire what they perceive as the marks of "civility" have influenced their deployment of labor.

Although Patels initially attempted to trace their lineage to Rajput clans in north India (and even hired local genealogists to construct fictive genealogies for them; see chapter 2), they soon abandoned the Kshatriya model of social development in favor of the Vania model, choosing to emulate the lifestyle of the affluent Thakkar and Jain trading castes instead. The most conspicuous adjustments were the adoption of practices that sought to refine the body: vegetarianism and public disavowal of alcohol; preoccupation with personal hygiene (seen most visibly in the insistence of Patel households—no matter how poor—on maintaining a latrine or toilet, while most villagers defecate in the fields); fastidiousness about eating *saatvik khorak* (loosely speaking, foods containing essential nutrients that will build virtue and strength); and the cultivation of an ideal of self-sufficiency (which circumscribed the ways in which Patels were willing to deploy family labor, especially women's labor).

The Patels' concerted effort at bodily cultivation, an ethics of the self, recalls analogous processes elsewhere, in sixteenth- and seventeenth-century Europe, documented by Norbert Elias in *The Civilizing Process: The History of Manners*. Elias shows the various sorts of moral injunctions that came to be attached to body habits (from sleeping, eating, and defecating to gender relations) and to the body's representation in public *and* private (through attire and etiquette), in the European upper-class quest for *civilité* or "civilized behavior"—a quest that greatly intensified after the second quarter of the sixteenth century.[91] In an equally stimulating study, Paul Willis has shown how working-class teenagers reproduce themselves as members of the working class, instead of moving upward into middle-class careers, by valorizing manual (particularly, factory) labor as masculine, liberating, and socially nonconformist—specifically, as a mark of their distinctive abilities to see through the authoritarianism and illusions of formal public school education. As Willis puts it: "The processes through which labor power comes to be subjectively understood and objectively applied and their interrelationships is of profound significance for the type of society which is produced and the particular nature and formation of its classes."[92] Both Elias and Willis draw our attention to a double process—a cultural logic of practice—where social regulation is secured through self-regulation.

The Management of Identity

"Who works without supervision?" retorted a young woman from the semiproletarian Baraiya caste when I posed to her the allegations of Patel employers, who were present at the interaction, that agricultural workers today are lazy, unreliable, and impertinent. The complaints of Patel employers in Matar Taluka are hardly unique. Scholars who study agrarian relations in India record employer disgruntlement with laborers as a matter of rote. It is a sign of the social tensions that always lurk within the employment contract and sometimes erupt into violent confrontation. The Baraiya woman's response was intriguing for its open defiance of her employers. On the one hand, she was unapologetic about her cavalier attitude to wage labor, which she clearly viewed as little more than "dull compulsion." On the other hand, she was making the less obvious point that if Patel employers today are less willing to engage in field supervision of work and more inclined to spend their time elsewhere, often in activities that would be described as "leisure," then why shouldn't laborers also be able to take a leisurely approach to work without inviting derision? The Patel employers read her remark as seditious and impudent, another illustration of the degenerate character *(boori daanat)* of present-day workers. But she was merely pointing out the skewed nature of the employment contract: the fact that workers and employers bring different moralities of time and effort to the workplace but are locked into a relation of uneasy interdependence (one for profit, the other for social reproduction) and where each is acutely aware of the shifting sands of power. How does this anecdote illustrate the cultural logic of practice that regulates the labor–leisure "choices" of elite and nonelite in Matar Taluka?

I propose to gloss this logic through the phrase "government of work"—to denote, simultaneously, the structural management *of* the labor process (achieved by controlling access to income-generating assets or means of production) and internalized management of work practices *within* it by members of a group. In invoking the figure of "government," I repeat with difference Michel Foucault's generative writings on the mode of power he calls "governmentality."[93] Two of Foucault's most important insights here concern, first, the upward and downward continuity of this mode of power, and second, its operation "according to the model of the economy."[94] Thus, caste categories as we know them in modern India are, in a *substantive* sense, *the precipitates of a governmentalized state, which has managed to distribute itself widely across a population.*[95] Caste exemplifies the downward continuity of the modern state. But like any state logic, the desire of the logic of caste is to unify. To recall Alain Badiou, a state logic is always technological, calculative, representational, and exclusionary: it seeks to connect disparate elements (a multiplicity) into a set of some thing—*to make them one.*[96] As such, the possibility of violence is omnipresent within caste government. The state logic of caste lacerates the "model of the economy" that also wants to govern caste. Here, we have to break with

Foucault to acknowledge a blind spot in his thinking of biopower: namely, improvements in the life of a population—its conditions of security—traverse a cultural field. Social hierarchy and distinction matter. Economic security is inseparable from cultural security. Thorstein Veblen was well aware of this in 1899, when he observed, in *The Theory of the Leisure Class,* that

> In order to gain and to hold the esteem of men it is not sufficient merely to possess wealth or power. The wealth or power must be put in evidence, for esteem is awarded only on evidence. And not only does the evidence of wealth serve to impress one's importance on others and to keep their sense of his importance alive and alert, but is of scarcely less use in building up and preserving one's self-complacency. In all but the lowest stages of culture the normally constituted man is comforted and upheld in his self-respect by "decent surroundings" and by exemption from "menial offices."[97]

Pierre Bourdieu puts it more precisely in his beguiling treatise on the social production of taste. He writes in *Distinction* that "economic power is first and foremost a power to keep economic necessity at arm's length ... [and this] is why it universally asserts itself by the destruction of riches, conspicuous consumption, squandering, and every form of *gratuitous* luxury."[98] This thinking can be extended to the labor process to show how an economy of life that recognizes the importance of excess—that is, a "general economy"[99] of waste and ostentation—is instrumental to the preservation of social hierarchy.

I offer four propositions. First, the quest for social distinction in agrarian societies is pursued primarily through the labor process. Where capitalist relations of production predominate, the key source of distinction for households is their ability to withdraw family labor power, either completely or partially, from the commoditized labor circuit, a process that I call "devalorization." I suggest, moreover, that the process of determining acceptable forms of labor deployment is also, inevitably, a process of inventing a work geography (spatially indexed work roles). Second, social distinction rests heavily on the fact that it is costly and therefore risky to attain. If mismanaged, it can lead to immiserization and to partial or total loss of any acquired distinction. Third, distinction by definition implies membership in an exclusive club, and since ease of entry into the club would diminish the value of the membership, it is necessary to erect barriers to entry. Specifically, I argue that membership in the club is constitutive of self-identity, and preservation of this identity is secured via structural domination.

Fourth, households that depend primarily on labor income for reproduction practice variations of the foregoing logic of distinction. They attempt to repudiate the economic necessity of wage work by being late for work; by displaying reluctance to take up wage work (for instance, by telling employers that they are tied up with "personal work"); by strategically shirking on the job; or by choosing alternative avenues of income generation, such as dairying, that exempt them from the compulsion of supervised wage labor (as discussed in chapter 3). Their ability to challenge the terms and conditions of work have been greatly augmented by favorable demand-side factors: on the one hand, an expansion in labor demand as a result of surface irrigation–induced changes in cropping patterns; on the other hand, growing opportunities for economic diversification through the diffusion of successful village-level dairy cooperatives and government affirmative action programs for economically and socially underprivileged groups. The cumulative effect of these developments has been to undermine the traditional control of the propertied upper castes over the labor process: And there lies its importance as a source of social distinction.

The aversion of the Lewa Patels to wage labor became increasingly prevalent after the 1860s and 1870s, a period of rapid agricultural growth in central Gujarat when production assumed a social form that was distinctly capitalist and displayed both rising demand for wage labor and rising real wages. In short, withdrawals from wage work grew precisely when the opportunity cost of withholding labor supply was rising. Based on his reconstruction of the social and economic histories of two villages in Kheda District, David Hardiman writes that although "about half the [Lewa Patels] in these villages were poor peasants [who owned less than 1.2 hectares] . . . almost no [Lewa Patels] hired themselves out as laborers, which was the essential mark of the poor peasant."[100] These observations second those of the economist J. C. Kumarappa, who in his 1929–30 survey of Matar subdistrict discovered only four Patel households in a total interview sample of 998 households that claimed to work as field laborers.[101]

When it was absolutely necessary for Patels to hire themselves out, they chose to work either for members of their own caste or occasionally for Vanias and Brahmins, who superseded them in the local caste hierarchy. Even so, they first attempted to redefine the manner in which their labor was valorized. Hence, a struggling Patel male preferred to be a sharecropper receiving some proportion of the harvest rather than a mere daily wage earner. Similarly, if he could muster money for rent, he would much rather be a tenant than a sharecropper. The motivations were always to reassert labor autonomy, to ease the shackles of outside control, and to alter the experience of laboring. To the extent that "the social and spatial are inextricably realized one in the other,"[102] the same type of work is apt to be seen differently depending on *where* it is performed. A Patel who engages in manual work on his own plot of land is far less likely to invite derision from members of his caste than a Patel who toils on someone else's land. Similarly, male members of poor Patel households express few compunctions about working as hired factory hands in urban industries, as salesmen in urban enterprises, or as tradespersons in commercial vocations; but ask them whether they would work as farm laborers and the answer is inevitably a "no."[103]

Disengagement from manual labor is a widely noted practice among upwardly mobile groups in agrarian societies. The Patels of rural Gujarat are no exception. Jan Breman writes that by the end of the nineteenth century "the large majority of [them] . . . succeeded in distancing themselves from the heavy manual labor accompanying the farmer's life" as part of the "transition to a new, more respectable life style."[104] Similarly, J. Tharamangalam describes the ways in which caste and status considerations impose constraints on labor deployment. His example, from the Kuttanad region in Kerala, exemplifies the hierarchy of "mental" over "manual" labor that seems commonplace to the labor process in rural South Asia:

> Among the higher castes in Kuttanad the Syrian Christians have been traditionally less affected by . . . [status] restrictions, especially as regards working in their own fields. Even among them, however, an upwardly mobile family will, at some point, stop working in the fields and start employing hired labor. This is seen as an important requirement for legitimizing its new status in the community. I came to know a Syrian Christian family which was to arrive at this stage and which was managing to send its eldest son to college. Although the father still worked in the field, the "college boy" not only stopped

participating in such work but also felt ashamed whenever his rough and blistered hands became visible to his college and hostel mates. In fact, he was attempting by various means to make his hands softer like those of his college friends from higher-class families.[105]

The privileged position of mental over manual labor is, needless to say, ideological. It is a telling example of the ways in which "labor" comes to be signified. Although mental and manual labors are *never* mutually exclusive, the *appearance of that separation* becomes critical. Thus Raymond Williams remarks that when the two are "categorically and practically" segregated in class societies, it not only results "in the degradation of what is marked off, in dominating and exploiting ways, as *mere manual labor,* deprived of its human conditions of conscious purpose and control, but in the false separation of *mental labor,* now held to be restricted to a certain class."[106] He proceeds to note that

> since the fact of the division of labor, in this basic class sense, is not just a matter of different kinds of work but of social relations which determine greater rewards and greater respect for *mental labor,* and of these relations as established in and protected by a specifically exploiting and unequal social order, the operations of *mental labor* cannot be assumed in advance to be exclusively devoted to *higher* . . . human concerns, but are in many or perhaps all cases likely to be bound up . . . with propagation, ratification, defence, apologia, naturalisation of that exploiting and unequal social order itself.[107]

While disengagement from manual labor is a widely noted practice among upwardly mobile groups in agrarian, among the Patels of Kheda it has been viewed as part of an evolving caste identity of civility and rationality. Mental work comes to be seen as, both, more cultured (*sabhya) and* more intellectually exacting (*buddhishaali)*—hence, in Patel discourse, as the proper undertaking of a genetically superior caste. When asked to contrast their affluence to its relative lack among other castes, Patels will often say that *"ame samajh thi kaam karye chhe"*—"we bring reason to our undertakings." The reference is to the deployment of instrumental or technical reason in decision making: an assessment of the most efficient means to an end, based on careful parsing of options. Instrumental rationality has become an end-in-itself for the Patel community. Reason (*samajh)* is reified by Patels as a sign of civilization in much the same way that the European nobility and bourgeoisie linked *kultur*—"cultivation"—to reason from the seventeenth century onward;[108] or, to invoke another European analogy, the way in which labor and profit accumulation are portrayed, in Weber's famous treatise on the Protestant work ethic, as "vocations" pursued for their own sake.[109] It is precisely this celebration of technical reason that prompts Patels to approach cultivation as a kind of "engineering" problem. The late Chandubhai Patel of Sandhana, who was twice hailed by the Government of Gujarat as the state's "best farmer" *(sarvottam khedut)*, is emblematic of Patel attitudes:

> Chandubhai is the epitome of the capitalist farmer, who takes obvious pride in his knowledge of the agricultural production process. To him production is not merely a question of the optimal allocation of physical capital, but human capital as well. The academic training of his sons reflects this. One of his sons has a degree in agronomy, and as a result is conversant with the latest agricultural technologies; the other son has a diploma in mechanical engineering, and is able to operate and fix all the farm machines. During our conversation, Chandubhai continually stressed the importance of timing in agriculture: water, fertilizer, pesticide, labor, and machines must all be applied at just the right juncture. This means that each must be available precisely when required. A good farmer cannot afford to have a machine or pump in disrepair. Chandubhai's view of himself corresponds more to that of an agricultural technician than of a farmer.[110]

The Patels of Kheda sought early on to differentiate themselves from other caste groups and from other members of their own caste. Virtually all historians of central Gujarat have noted the elaborate class layers that developed in Lewa Patel society, from the lowly Kanbi Patel (who was either an autonomous petty cultivator-cum-laborer or tenant of larger Patel farmers), to the lesser Patidar (the Lewa Patel farmer with midsize ownership holdings, whose cultivation was part-supervisory and who sometimes expanded his holdings by leasing-in land), to the *asal* (authentic) Patidar (the large estate owner, who either practiced supervisory cultivation with free or attached labor or simply leased out his land to sharecroppers and tenants).

As this hierarchy crystallized, it became the goal of every Lewa Patel to ascend to Patidari status (chapter 2). This was achieved in two ways: first, through the tradition of hypergamy, that is, the marriage of daughters to grooms from higher-ranked families; second, through accumulation that would permit replacement of physical farmwork by supervisory cultivation. Curiously, these strategies were often at counterpurposes because dowries or groomprice payments that were required to effect marital alliances with higher-ranked families were a severe drain on accumulated surpluses; there is frequent mention in historical accounts of Lewa Patels driven to financial ruin by extraordinary dowries. In a sense, then, the pinnacle of social achievement or distinction for the Lewa Patel became the ability to juggle costly dowries with potentially costly disengagement from the labor circuit. Together, these bespoke a surplus of material assets that was rare; hence, it announced the man who had arrived.

The practice of hypergamy that developed among Lewa Patels was founded at least partly on the premise that daughters married into wealthier households would neither have to sell their labor power nor work in the fields; in short, their work in *public* would be minimized. There was no guarantee, however, that their household work would diminish as well, but this really was not a decisive element for distinction. Ironically, then, the de-objectification of women's work (her dual withdrawal from commoditized work and public work) went hand-in-hand with women's objectification as status goods within the Lewa Patel community. Indeed, women's value as status goods seems to have become directly linked to the degree of withdrawal from the orbit of public work. It was as if public exposure of her labor, most profane when her labor power was sold to an employer, would compromise her femininity and sexual chastity.

Rutten, based on his fieldwork in Anand Taluka in Kheda District, offers a supporting commentary on the devalorization of women's work. He writes that

> as a result of their early economic rise and their aspiration to higher status, the Patidar farmers were among the first of the present-day entrepreneurial families to remove their women from direct involvement in field labor. For the wealthier Leva Patidars, this happened as early as the 1930s, while many members of the lower subcastes of Kanbi and Kadva [Patels] did not make this change until the end of the 1950s. . . . This tendency to withdraw the women from actual farming tasks has been extended . . . to other areas of work as well. . . . Until very recently, taking care of milch-animals was an important part of the day's work for the wives and daughters

of [large Patel farmers]. Along with the change in location of the animals—to separate stables near the farmhouse—jobs such as cutting the grass, milking the animals and cleaning the stables have been increasingly taken over by maid-servants and permanent laborers. . . . The overall outcome of these recent changes in working pattern for the women of entrepreneurial families is that housekeeping has become their main daytime activity.[111]

The past three decades have witnessed a fourth modification in labor deployment. As I described at the beginning of this chapter, younger generation Patels prefer to conduct agricultural operations from a distance. Like their fathers and grandfathers they exhibit a preference for supervisory labor, but unlike them are rarely willing to spend their days overseeing agricultural operations in the fields. Instead, supervision consists of ordering intermediaries from the comfort of the village, delegating tasks, or, occasionally, darting by motorcycle to monitor ongoing operations. Spending entire days in the field is now regarded with disdain. Once more, this new form of work distinction has come at a cost. It has altered the architecture of the local labor market because young Patel farmers now like to delegate agricultural work on piece rates, where they simply pay a team of workers a lump sum for completing a task. Since piecework regimes require minimal supervision it suits the younger Patels, who have added a new gloss to the meaning of civility. The blurring of boundaries between work *(kaam)* and leisure *(aaraam)* is now viewed as the mark of an adept and knowledgeable cultivator, whose supervisory acumen allows him remain on top of things even from a distance.

What's the evidence? My survey data and ethnographic notes (from two study villages in Matar that fall in the MRBC command area, combined with information gleaned in informal visits to thirty-nine other villages in the subdistrict) indicates a distinct trend in favor of piecework employment, away from in-kind—and to a much lesser extent, money-rated—daily wage regimes. Whereas the 1965–66 survey of Matar Taluka makes no mention of piecework employment in agriculture, it is evident that by the mid-1990s a piece-rate regime *(ucchakpratha)* was quite prevalent. While the proportion of cultivators who regularly hire workers on piece-rate contracts (that is, for the majority of agricultural tasks) is 20 percent for the village of Astha, and 13 percent for the village of Shamli, the more interesting fact from the perspective of this chapter is the apparently rising popularity of piecework hiring among Patel cultivators, who comprise the dominant caste in these villages. In Astha, 69 percent of Patel farmers, and in Shamli, 65 percent of Patel farmers hire workers regularly on a piece-rate basis—in striking contrast to cultivators from other major caste groups in these villages.

Table 9. Incidence of Piecework *(ucchak)* and Land Mortgage *(giro)* Contracts by Caste, in Two Villages of Matar Taluka, 1995

ASTHA Caste group	Total reporting households	No. who regularly hire on piecework	Percent	No. who have kept land on mortgage	Percent
Brahmin	6	2	33.3	0	0.0
Patel	22	15	68.9	9	40.9
Panchal	26	7	26.9	5	19.2
Baraiya/Koli	62	8	12.9	10	16.1
Bharwad	10	0	0.0	2	20.0
Muslim	0	0	Na	0	Na
Raval	0	0	Na	0	Na
Vankar	0	0	Na	0	Na
Rohit	18	0	0.0	2	11.1
Vaghri	1	0	0.0	0	0.0
Harijan	18	0	0.0	0	0.0
TOTAL	163	32	19.6	28	17.2

SHAMLI Caste group	Total reporting households	No. who regularly hire on piecework	Percent	No. who have kept land on mortgage	Percent
Brahmin	7	2	28.6	2	28.6
Patel	17	11	64.7	7	41.2
Panchal	2	1	50.0	2	100.0
Baraiya/Koli	105	21	20.0	12	11.4
Bharwad	55	4	7.3	10	18.2
Muslim	13	0	0.0	0	0.0
Raval	11	0	0.0	0	0.0
Vankar	23	1	4.3	1	4.3
Rohit	53	2	3.8	0	0.0
Vaghri	21	0	0.0	3	14.3
Harijan	14	0	0.0	0	0.0
TOTAL	321	42	13.1	37	11.5

Note: Caste groups are arranged in descending order by ritual rank. Only major caste groups are shown in the table.
Source: Fieldwork data gathered by the author in 1995.

Since Patels, on average, own more land than members of other castes,[112] it is perfectly plausible to explain the Patel preference for piece-rate hiring, which minimizes direct supervision, on their income-elastic consumption of leisure (this is the old "backward-bending supply curve of labor" explanation). Suffice to say that this standard neoclassical explanation would be an ethnographically "thin" account of what is a far more complicated—and historically continuous—process of caste consolidation and identity management. For instance, it would fail to answer the a priori question of how work preferences are formed, and why different forms of labor are non-uniformly ranked in different spatial contexts.[113]

There is also some indication from Table 9 that the preference for hiring on piece-rate may be linked to the incidence of in-mortgaging of land by households.[114] But this is entirely consistent with the government of work as a process of "self-regulation" that operates *in conjunction* with "social regulation." The Lewa Patels' cultivation of managerial reason, and attendant traits such as entrepreneurship *(saahas)*, progressiveness *(pragatisheelta)*, and accounting ability *(ganatri)*, as marks of caste civility and superiority, were remarkably effective in consolidating their economic and social dominance of rural central Gujarat over a period of 150 years; but so too were conjunctural factors such as their favorable treatment by colonial officials; and, the ability of Patels to accumulate mercantile, usurious, and—particularly after the 1930s—educational capital, over and above production surpluses from agriculture.[115] In fact, ownership was *never* the sole avenue by which Patels established control over primary means of production such as land and labor. In 1916, L. V. M. Robertson (we met him in chapter 2) observed that "a good many patidars who cultivate land also [used to] lend money."[116] Since a temporary transfer of usufruct rights to land was often demanded as loan collateral, borrowers ended up ceding de facto control over plots to Patel lenders, becoming sharecroppers on their own land. This practice of acquiring land as mortgage or loan collateral (a custom locally known as *giropratha*) continues to date. The mechanism of *giro* has been one of the most effective instruments that Patels have been able to harness in their effort to create a semiproletarian class that is dependent upon them for patronage and, additionally, augments the "reserve army of labor"—two factors that are critical to the social regulation of labor markets in agrarian settings.[117]

In seeking to explain the diffusion of piecework employment in Matar through a cultural logic of work I am not suggesting that we discount the repertoire of explanations that NIE and MPE offer. I am instead arguing that they are incomplete because they neglect the cultural universe in which work practices are embedded. Thus, the constant drive for refinement that has framed the actions of Patels over the past 150 years *has* to be recognized as a decisive factor in labor market dynamics.[118] The ongoing redefinitions of "work" that inform Patel identity are by no means smooth. The preference of younger-generation Patels for hiring on piece-rate sits poorly with older-generation Patels, who think that it makes poor economic sense. On one occasion, I heard an older Patel farmer angrily denounce the young son of a wealthy Patel landowner who had agreed to pay a group of workers Rs. 250 to spread organic manure over roughly two acres of land. He was aggrieved because according to him the same task, with supervision, could have been accomplished at a third of the labor cost, for about Rs. 80. In his opinion, decisions like the one taken by the young farmer were irresponsible because they encouraged laborers to raise their demands.[119] Even more objectionable to older-generation Patels is that their young wards assign on piecework not merely those agricultural tasks where performance quality can be reasonably gauged by the eye (such as tilling, leveling or, to a lesser extent, harvesting), and which therefore minimize the moral hazard problem inherent in piece-rated work, but also tasks such as transplanting, weeding, and fertilizer/pesticide application, where work quality is hard to monitor.

To fully appreciate the older farmer's concerns, they must be placed in the context of other transformations in Matar, such as those discussed in the previous chapter. Canal irrigation, since its arrival in the early 1960s, has had some unexpected effects. The expansion in the area under paddy by roughly forty thousand acres since 1965 has dramatically increased the supply of dry fodder, because paddy straw—a by-product of cultivation—is a nutritive food for livestock.[120] Correspondingly, the explosion of grass along the irrigation minors and subminors that furrow the landscape has created new grazing areas for open-grazed livestock and a steadier supply of green fodder for stall-fed milk animals like buffaloes and hybrid varieties of cows. Ecological spaces that were earlier economically marginal have become unexpectedly valuable. The unanticipated improvement in dry and green fodder availability has encouraged the spread of village-level dairy cooperatives in Matar and sparked rapid growth in the livestock sector. The number of village dairies in Matar escalated from thirty-two in 1965 to seventy by 1990, and membership in them increased fivefold.[121] In short, the growing importance of the milk economy created an alternative to wage labor for subordinate groups like Baraiyas and Kolis.

The resulting *decrease in the elasticity of labor supply* has to be juxtaposed against the *rise in labor demand* that has accompanied the massive expansion in paddy acreage—paddy being one of few commercial crops that has high tolerance to waterlogging and which cultivators in Matar could therefore safely adopt given the prevalence of water-retaining clay loam soils and the area's poor natural drainage. The net effect of expansion in paddy cultivation has been a significant augmentation in the bargaining power of rural working classes.[122] Employer efforts to blunt labor's bargaining power by resorting to mechanization of agricultural operations, through the use of tractors and/or combine harvesters, has been impeded by ecological factors: first, the labor absorptiveness of rice cultivation and the relative insubstitutability of labor by machines in the production process, and second, by the difficulty of maneuvering combine harvesters in the viscous, waterlogged soils of the subdistrict.

Just as the quest for civility has influenced the manner in which Patels regulate their work practices, it seems pertinent to enquire whether a corresponding cultural logic informs labor deployment by subordinated groups like the Baraiyas/Kolis and whether it has played a role in the rise of piece-rate contracts. My assessment, based on fieldwork, is that the proclivity of younger Patel cultivators to disengage from direct supervisory cultivation in pursuit of status, and growth in workers' bargaining power due to expansion in paddy cultivation and dairying, are the two factors most directly responsible for the trend toward piecework employment. However, it is clear that Baraiyas/Kolis, who form the bulk of the working classes in Matar Taluka, also have a *distinct preference* for group-based piecework. As I discuss further in chapter 5, the possibility of higher earnings is an obvious attraction; but discussions with Baraiya/Koli laborers reveal that a far bigger attraction for them is the fact that task-based contracts allow them to conduct work at their own tempo, and without constant interference and berating from Patel employers. Closely regulated forms of work such as supervised field labor and, especially, *mahinadari* (employment as a farm servant) are increasingly viewed as denigrating by younger Baraiyas and Kolis. In the village of Shamli, gangs of young Koli men, who have cultivated a reputation for hard work—and are, consequently, in constant demand as laborers—now insist on being hired only on piecework contracts. These observations echo those of Jan Breman, who reports from south Gujarat that "casual workers not only do not object but have a definite preference for piece-work. . . . Piece-work enables men and women in the prime of their working lives to free themselves of a direct tie to an employer which is felt as galling."[123]

To summarize, tightening labor markets and emerging opportunities for income diversification have effectively permitted previously wage labor–dependent households to practice their own forms of labor devalorizing strategies. As initially noted in my propositions, these include being late for work, sending messages to employers to say that they are tied up with "personal work," strategic shirking on the job, and the selection of alternative avenues of income generation, such as dairying, that exempt them from the compulsion of supervised wage labor. At the risk of repetition, it is perhaps worth asking once again why disengagement of labor from the commodity circuit—or, *if* trapped within the circuit, risky acts of defiance and disobedience—is a condition of distinction. I suggest that the answer lies in the element of anonymous compulsion disguised as freedom, which is the constitutive condition of labor transformed to commodity. This compulsion, far from being abstract, is often unbearably palpable. Picture the familiar scene of farm laborers suffering the abuse and goading of irate employers merely to secure a daily wage, which on the superficial level was voluntarily transacted, but which at a structural level was informed by the need of the employee to work and capacity of the employer to hire.

This structural truth is precisely the blot whose attempted erasure makes devalorization of labor by laborers an activity worthy of distinction. Devalorization, whether partial or complete, signals success in weakening the yoke of compulsion. Hence, the laborer who must continue to sell his or her labor power but is able to shirk (that is, foil the employer's gaze) or is otherwise able to frustrate and defy control by the employer, runs the risk of incurring the employer's ire—and in extreme cases can jeopardize his or her prospects for future employment. But these actions, which communicate to society a determination to resist standardization and control (thereby placing labor on a *distinct* footing from other means or inputs of production) can gain a laborer the admiration of fellow workers. Everyday expressions of labor disobedience constitute small attempts to devalorize labor, which invite distinction precisely because they entail a potential cost and because they establish the modest victory of choice (agency) over compulsion (script). The key word here is *artfulness:* the laborer who shirks does it not to acquire a reputation for indolence but rather to deny his or her docility.

Conclusion

I began this chapter by posing a concrete question: How should we explain the rise of piecework employment *(ucchakpratha)* in Matar Taluka? I then went on to examine whether it was possible to view labor arrangements, specifically piecework contracts in Matar subdistrict, as organizational strategies harnessed by profit-seeking employers. The existing NIE and MPE literatures on labor arrangements lend themselves to this functionalist narrative. And although both ultimately want to show how employers are able to extract labor effort from workers and augment profits, their strategic emphasis differs: NIE underlines the incentive, efficiency-enhancing aspect of labor contracts, MPE underscores the disciplinary effects of these contracts. I noted that both the incentive and disciplinary elements must be regarded as important factors in the rise of piecework employment in Matar Taluka. But I also argued that while the NIE and MPE explanations are parsimonious, they ultimately offer incomplete accounts of labor contracts and deployment.

By treating "labor" as a generic (acontextual and transhistorical) category and by neglecting the normative, signifying dimensions of labor, realist approaches—whether liberal or Marxist—are unable to produce a nuanced understanding of the labor process. I contend that place-specific cultural valences that become attached to work—in other words, the manner in which labor is differentiated on the basis of where and how it is performed, and the way it constitutes the identities of workers *and* employers—are critical in explaining the *process* of contractual change and caste consolidation. I make the case for a cultural political economy of workplace dynamics: the argument that abstract "labor" incarnates itself concretely as "work" within a lived cultural field that is regulative of individual conduct and rationality. Given that human agency is formed within a pre-individual universe of associations and meanings, we cannot afford to ignore the textuality of labor in theories of the labor process. Once we accept this stance, we have to reformulate the notions of "culture" and "power" that inhabit NIE and MPE.

In NIE, culture is reduced to norms and preference rankings, or in the guise of ideology, to misperceptions of relative prices or truncations of the preference set; meanwhile, power is reduced to bargaining strength or market power. In MPE, culture and ideology are, for the most part, coterminous and viewed as imposed inventions of the dominant class that effectively blind subordinate classes to their historical possibilities. Moreover, MPE—like NIE—operationalizes power as bargaining power, although—unlike NIE—it forcefully underscores the coercive elements and structural basis of power. In short, NIE and MPE theorize culture and power as external forces that facilitate the social regulation of subordinate groups by superordinate groups.

By contrast, the analytic "government of work," which I mobilize in this chapter as an alternative to NIE and MPE, combines "social regulation" *of* the labor process with the idea of "self regulation" *within* the labor process. By so doing, I want to draw attention to the *embodied* nature of power in labor practices. Power as corporeality instantiates itself in the ways individuals come to form certain kinds of self-perceptions and social identifications, and the dialectical way in which their forms of labor deployment are predicated on these identifications. After all, labor is not only the way each of us makes a living, it is also the way we create ourselves in relation to others through the meanings invested in forms of work. This is, as I readily acknowledge, not a new insight. It is borrowed from Marx and has been extensively developed by Hegelian Marxists and members of the Frankfurt School. The crucial point is that while work of some kind is a practical necessity, it is also a powerful instrument for establishing social distance.

When we reconstruct the history of local production relations in Matar Taluka from the mid-nineteenth century onward, we can trace the gradual emergence of a topology of work, where some forms of work came to be regarded as superior to others. These forms became sources of social distinction in the Patels' quest for civility. Over the course of the past 150 years, the Patels of central Gujarat have generated a symbolic economy of "work" to consolidate collective—particularly, class and caste—identities, and generate markers of social distance and rank that involve, among other strategies, the devalorization of women's labor and a blurring of the boundaries between "work" and "leisure." Patels display a preference for hiring workers on piecework not just because of the regulatory (incentive and disciplining) aspects of piece-rate contracts but also because, at this moment in history, the piecework arrangement meshes with their anxiety and desire to prosecute a particular self-image.

In each instance, the source of distinction lies both in the devalorization of labor and in the fact that it is costly to effect. The term "devalorization" refers to the withdrawal of labor power from the commodity circuit—an action whose partial result, but not always *overt* intention, is to assert the creative (animate and nonmechanical) dimension of labor, which, as Karl Marx explained, is alienated when labor offers itself as labor power within capitalist exchange. Thus, devalorization within the context of rural labor deployment seeks the restitution of use value over exchange value.[124] The subtext it broadcasts is the ostensible replacement of need by desire, compulsion by choice, and the rebuttal of external control over one's labor.[125] Put simply, no one likes to be bossed over. But, on the other hand, not every one can aspire to be the boss either. In an agrarian economy, where the majority of men and women must sell their labor power in order to reproduce themselves and their families, the ability to partially or wholly disengage from the commodity circuit presumes either a degree of financial security and surplus that is normally unavailable, or bravado that is risky in the utmost. I suggest that devalorization confers distinction on social agents for three reasons. First, it conveys to society at large an individual's actual (or, if false, then cleverly disguised) state of financial security. Second, it entails some foregone material benefit (in the language of economics, an opportunity cost) that newly adopted forms of labor may or may not offset; for instance, a productive laborer may be a poor sharecropper or tenant, supervisory agriculture with hired labor may be more prone to productivity losses from moral hazard, and the sequestration of women in households may make liquidity and labor constraints more binding during peak agricultural periods. Finally, the inevitable element of risk in devalorizing strategies implies a positive likelihood of impoverishment (or at the very least, loss in accumulated wealth) for households that practice them. This is perhaps most evident in the case of the younger-generation Patels, who in their pursuit of "leisured work" risk productivity losses through lack of adequate oversight in cultivation.

To restate my point, precisely because devalorizing strategies are potentially costly, they must either be offset by alternative sources of surplus generation, or else must inevitably aggravate the risk of losing acquired distinction. This is so because a façade of financial security projected to society at large may attract distinction in the short run, but in the long run, the bluff must be backed up by real evidence of wealth. A poor man who pretends to be wealthy but is caught in the act suffers derision as a *khokhla manas* (hollow man) and cannot cling to his distinction. *Here lies the paradox of distinction: it has to be costly to count as distinction, but should it prove too costly—that is, should it visibly result in financial degeneracy—it may backfire and corrode distinction.* Hence the preservation of distinction, far more so than its initial acquisition, demands accomplished gamesmanship—indeed, brinksmanship: the artistry to juggle too acute a cost (which would erode distinction) against too modest a cost (which would fail to earn it, because it would be too *common*place).

CHAPTER FIVE

Interruption

Concrescence

Capitalism is a "one" that is a "many": a more-than-human concrescence. To be exact, it is a constantly repeating concatenation of uncountable concrescences—*different-in-itself in space and time.* It has no essence. But it has a structural logic, which is diagrammatic. Let's call it the "law of value." Capital is becoming-value. It does not matter how or where. It is utterly disinterested in normativities—forms of life—that differ from *its* norm of value, unless those forms can be conscripted to its self-expansionary end. Its myriad fractions want, above all, to never rest. To stop is to confront the prospect of death. To keep moving is to grow and survive. There is not only raw energy and daring here but also barely contained anarchy. The human and nonhuman joinings that hold together capital's countless circuits each have different georhythms and lifecycles. They can erode, contort, break, or vanish—arresting movement. Capital is in a permanent struggle against entropy. The work of repair and replacement is unstopping, and there are other hazards. In its blind desire to expand, one fraction of capital might undermine the conditions of existence of another, or that fraction might cannibalize its own conditions of existence. The travels of capital are chaotic, continuously remaking the latticework of connections that animate accumulation. Precisely because capital is heterogeneous, composed of a dizzying multiplicity of fractions, moving at different velocities, the terrains of difference produced and exploited by it can lead to booms in one place and, via entirely unforeseen connections, crises in other places.

Here is such a tale of booms and crises from Matar Taluka. But, first, some narrative background is necessary. In Gujarat, three agencies—the Gujarat Industrial Development Corporation (GIDC), the Gujarat Industrial Development Board (GIDB), and the Gujarat Industrial Investment Corporation (GIIC)—are charged with development planning in the state, a mandate that includes attracting investment and promoting the establishment of large and small industries. GIDC describes its ethos as a "win-win business philosophy," and it aims to provide entrepreneurs turnkey industrial infrastructure. In sentiments reminiscent of Ayn Rand, it sees this as furnishing "a solid base for the natural outcome of growth and prosperity."[1] In considerable part due to the deliberate efforts *and* oversights of GIDC, the primary of the three industrial bodies, large stretches of the national highway from Ahmedabad in north Gujarat to Valsad in south Gujarat are now thick with a haphazard mix of industries that include textile and dyestuff production, tanneries, cold storage warehouses, dairy processing, pharmaceutical industries, light engineering works, gem polishing and jewelry-making firms, food processing units, petroleum storage and refinery complexes, and plastics and petrochemical (particularly fertilizer and pesticide) manufacturing plants. In October 2002, there were 272,397 officially registered Small-Scale Industries (SSIs) in the state (of which 75 percent were functioning) and another 2,100 Medium and Large Industries (of which 76 percent were operational).[2] Air, water, and soil pollution are rife with unforetold health consequences. But the Government of Gujarat with its longstanding probusiness (and antilabor) stance has resolutely neglected ecological and occupational safety concerns.[3]

There is continuity in this modus operandi. The region that now takes the name "Gujarat" has long histories of sovereign power and (particular fractions of) capital supplementing each other, sometimes violently.[4] From the vantage point of this supplementary logic, sectarian violence in Gujarat in the postcolonial period enacts a repetition with difference. This is not a return to economism. It does not deny the singularity of events by, say, reducing episodes of communal violence to the interests of a capitalist class. Instead, it recognizes that events are always overdetermined, the fusion of multiple logics—in which the supplementary relation of sovereignty (as state of exception) to capital is an important force. Thus, one effect of the 2002 Gujarat pogrom was to secure the futures of certain urban capitalist fractions

(Hindu businesses) by elimination of (Muslim) rivals. While evidence shows that violence was both selective and enabled by graduated uses *or* suspensions of state power, it does not transitively imply that violence was engineered by interested fractions of capital. Furthermore, because capitalism is a collective of different fractions that operate at different scales, violent events—particularly those in which a state is complicit—are fraught with risk. They may drive away potential investors. The timing and content of the ongoing, media-intensive "Vibrant Gujarat" campaign is far from innocuous in this respect. It is a thinly secular attempt to showcase the Narendra Modi government's accomplishments to those captains of industry whose desire to invest in Gujarat might have wavered in the aftermath of March 2002.

The account of Matar Taluka that follows is not about sectarian bloodshed but other, more banal, forms of violence that striate the fitful movements of capital. A year or two after a 1974–75 re-survey of the subdistrict was completed, the northern tract of Navagam started to experience an economic downturn. Conflicts with upstream users of the Khari River had been a recurring phenomena since the Khari system's inception in the late eighteenth century, and they had intensified after the construction of the Khari-Cut Canal in 1878, an upstream diversion from the Khari River that was meant to supply water to villages in adjacent Ahmedabad District that were off the river's main course. Although an 1895 decision by the Bombay High Court had affirmed the superior riparian rights of the eleven Kalambandhi villages in the region of Navagam, de facto these rights continued to be undermined by upstream users through unsanctioned withdrawals from the Khari River.

In 1948, the Government of Bombay (of which Gujarat was then part) attempted to remedy the conflict by approving a new irrigation scheme, the Meshwo project. The plan was to channel water from the Meshwo River into the Khari in order to irrigate the Kalambandhi villages, thereby freeing the Khari's flow for diversion into the Khari-Cut Canal. In a meeting of representatives from the Kalambandhi and upstream villages with government officials, it was agreed that the Kalambandhi villages would forego their legal entitlement to kharif irrigation from the Khari River provided they were assured a minimum discharge of seventy cubic feet per second (cusecs) from the Meshwo. Any deficit below seventy cusecs was to be made up by supplements from the Khari, with the exception of severe drought years in the region.[5]

A plan that sounded reasonable on paper began to falter in the 1960s because supply from the Meshwo became increasingly irregular. Upstream users of the Khari, who were obligated to make up the deficit, continued to resist the riparian rights that had been granted to Matar's Kalambandhi villages. In 1969, ten upstream villages in Ahmedabad District filed a case in the Gujarat High Court, challenging the water rights of the Matar villages. The court once more upheld the Kalambandhi entitlements, prompting a group of upstream villages to file an appeal with the Supreme Court. The Court refused to hear it. Meanwhile, 1974 was a terrible rainfall year. The measuring station at Matar recorded only 8.64 inches of rainfall, against the expected average of 30 inches. Tempers flared upstream and downstream. Representatives of the Kalambandhi villages in Matar met with aggrieved upstream users in order to reaffirm the voluntary sharing arrangement negotiated in 1948, which stipulated provisions for diverting the Khari's flow to Matar in the event of deficit supply from the Meshwo. Although the agreement was reaffirmed in principle, informants in Matar claimed that upstream villages subsequently reneged on their commitments. They continued to divert the Khari's flow into the Khari-Cut Canal, and sank numerous wells into the ground along the canal embankment, thereby circumventing the prohibition on direct appropriation of water from the canal but greatly reducing downstream flow.

In 1978, newly resurgent dyestuff industries in Ahmedabad's Vatva-Narol industrial complex began dumping untreated effluents into the Khari-Cut Canal, thereby polluting its downstream flow. The heavy acid content of the effluents imparts to the waters of the Khari a reddish tinge and an almost unbearable stench in the non-monsoon months, when the river's flow is weak. Villagers in the area recounted stories of water in their wells turning red after 1980, early incidents of injury and mortality among cattle watered at the canal, and an epidemic of stomach ailments that chemists at Maharaja Sayajirao (M.S.) University in Vadodara attributed to the ingestion of tainted drinking water.[6] The persistent use of polluted Khari water has proved damaging, particularly to paddy, whose yields, according to Navagam cultivators, is deeply sensitive to water quality (many claimed that application of contaminated water nearly halves productivity).[7] Although *bajri* (millet) is more resilient in comparison to paddy to poor water quality and spotty water flow, returns from it are too low for households to base livelihoods exclusively on its cultivation. Hence, unless heavy monsoonal flows sufficiently dilute the pollutants in the Khari, or unless cultivators have access to groundwater low in salinity, paddy—the economic mainstay of the Navagam region for over two centuries—cannot be cultivated.[8]

As if conflicts with upstream villages and water pollution were not enough, Matar Taluka—and most of Gujarat State—recorded six years of subnormal rainfall between 1982 and 1992. Flows in the Meshwo River declined. As a result of poor recharge in the Prantij–Bokh reservoir (which regulates water volume in the Khari), the Khari's flow also diminished sharply. The rice economy of Navagam collapsed. Land values fell precipitously. In 2004, it was not unusual to find a *vigha* (0.59 acres) of land in the Navagam area to be put for sale at 10,000 to 15,000 rupees (US$220 to 330) and face difficulty locating buyers. There have been several governmental and private attempts to develop bore-well and tube-well irrigation in the Navagam division, but the results have been mixed because of well malfunctions as well as saline ingress across much of the region.[9]

Several Patel families from Navagam have emigrated: some to urban centers like Ahmedabad, Nadiad, or Bombay, and others—with more far-flung family networks—to the United Kingdom and the United States. A walk through the Patel *falia* (neighborhood) reveals several houses lying empty, or, when occupied, with families dependent for reproduction on remittances from one or more migrant relatives. Households from the semiproletarian layer (mainly Baraiyas, Muslims, Nayaks, Rohits, and Harijans, who had small holdings to begin with and lacked viable migration prospects) have been worst hit. The few among them who are in salaried employment—either at the regional Central Desalter Plant of the Oil and Natural Gas Commission (ONGC), in various sub-district bureaucracies, or as government school teachers—have managed to prosper, frequently by doubling up as moneylenders to credit-squeezed households.[10] The rest lead a tenuous existence, many with remarkable stoicism, surviving through a combination of animal husbandry for milk sales to the village dairy, hourly labor at nearby brick kilns, by collecting and selling *Prosopis juliflora* twigs as firewood to tea stalls and restaurants on the nearby Mumbai–Ahmedabad national highway, or by commuting daily to Ahmedabad for piecework wages in the very same dyestuff industries whose disposal of untreated effluents has decimated their area's agriculture. Capital has profited from desperation in odd and cruel ways.

Take the brick kilns that have erupted across the ragged Navagam landscape. Run by a regional network of entrepreneurs frequently from the Prajapati caste, they tend to be gouge-and-run operations. In return for a loan, a landowner temporarily transfers his usufruct and soil rights to the entrepreneur (usually for a year or two), who in turn excavates four to five feet of the topsoil for on-site baking of bricks. Once the pliable upper soil layers are exhausted the operation moves to another field. It was not unusual to find a landowner and his family members ripping up their *own field* as wage laborers for the entrepreneur who lent them money. Or, take the toxic dyestuff industries on the fringes of Ahmedabad. Their profits have come at the expense of livelihoods in parts of Navagam, which, as a consequence, now function as a reservoir of surplus labor. One man in his thirties, whom I met in the village of Pinglaj in 1995, was suffering from an undiagnosed respiratory ailment. His fingers shook and he could barely go a minute without convulsing into a spasm of coughing. He told me it was due to the acids he was forced to breathe every day on the shop floor of the dyeing unit in Vatva/Narol, where he worked. "Why do you do it?" I asked. He gestured around him. It was a scene of poverty and disrepair. He said the polluted water in the Khari had put an end to agriculture. I pressed him: "How much do you make?" He said he was paid on piecework basis and on a good day he was able to bring in thirty to thirty-five rupees (approximately seventy to seventy-five cents at the time). He spent ten rupees from his daily earnings for the roundtrip commute by bus to Vatva/Narol. The trip took him an hour each way, not counting the three-kilometer walk from the village to the highway. His job had no security. In order to evade labor legislation mandating that employees receive certain job-related benefits, the dyestuff industry owners, he said, rehired their workers daily, thereby showing them on the rolls as temporary laborers, not permanent employees. Labor officers from the government were fully aware of the practice but were paid off by owners to look the other way. Workers received no training, no benefits, and none of the minimal occupational safeguards necessary in such a hazardous line of work. Since agricultural work in adjacent Bareja was paying twenty-five rupees at the time (and was far less hazardous), I asked him why he didn't do that. He responded that he was a Rajput, his family was a large landowner in Pinglaj, and to work as an agricultural laborer would be utterly degrading for him. Evidently, no such stigma attached to industrial work.

Such are the shiftless trajectories of capital. By the 1980s, Matar had witnessed a brutal reversal of core and periphery. The previously rain-fed villages of Limbasi Division—whose agricultural labor force once used to flock to the *daskosi* (Kalambandhi) tract of Navagam for employment—by then had managed to supplant the daskosi area as the rice bowl of Kheda District.[11] In 2004, when I last visited Navagam, it had an agricultural regime that was part rain-fed, part riverine, part groundwater driven and well supplied by surface irrigation from the Meshwo and Khari rivers *only* in exceptional rainfall years.[12]

Dialectic, or Not?

In his 1972 essay, "Différance," Jacques Derrida pointedly observes that the entangled logic of (spatial) difference and (temporizing) deferral that circulates within the word *différance,* "although maintaining relations of profound affinity with Hegelian discourse" also operates "a kind of infinitesimal and radical displacement of it."[13] This subversive fidelity to Hegel's thought, particularly the dialectic, emerges at various points in Derrida's writings. But few have the vivid and characteristically playful quality of a 1996 interview with Maurizio Ferraris, where Derrida declares: "I have never *opposed* the dialectic. Be it opposition to the dialectic or war against the dialectic, it's a losing battle. What it really comes down to is thinking a dialecticity of dialectics that is itself fundamentally not dialectical."[14]

What *is* a "dialecticity of dialectics that is … not dialectical"? Is it "love"? Can love be a political act—the source of revolution—that ends the unitarian terrors of sovereignty and authoritarianism globally and ushers in its place a new humanity, a "democracy of the multitude"? This is exactly the nondialectical salve that two eminent left theorists, Michael Hardt and Antonio Negri, recommend in their recent book, *Multitude.* They write: "People today seem unable to understand love as a political concept, but a concept of love is just what we need to grasp the constituent power of the multitude."[15] This is not a naïve summons to sentiment. Following Spinoza in Part V of *Ethics,* it is an urging to "love" as that highest form of knowledge, which strives to know God/Nature—that is to say, matter-substance—in all its concrete modes of being, without prejudice.[16] It is therefore a call to engagement and connection, indeed to probe the limits of "self," as the basis of politics. In issuing this call, Hardt and Negri refuse to inhabit the plane of antinomy, because it risks becoming the dialectical moment of negation that labors in the service of the same. Their nemesis is no less a figure than Hegel, that preeminent philosopher of sublation, who, in the famous Preface to *Phenomenology of Spirit* (1807), declares: "Mediation is nothing but the self-identity which moves itself; in other words, it is reflection into itself *[in sich selbst]*, the moment of the I as being-for-itself, pure negativity, or—when reduced to its pure abstraction—it is simple becoming."[17] Because "self-identity" is the barely disguised S/subject of "Europe,"[18] Hegel effectively consecrates history as the outcome of Europe's self-mediation, scission and self-motion.

Within the "speculative philosophical economy" of the Hegelian *Aufhebung,* a process of simultaneously lifting up, conserving and negating (the English translations "sublation" and "supersession" struggle with these contradictory meanings), a restrictive strategy of opposition maintains the accumulative logic of profit.[19] Think of narratives where capital advances by co-opting or superseding that which stands in opposition. Think of descriptions of history as an expansionary (and unmistakably colonizing) movement toward progressively higher spheres of meaning—Hegel, for instance, anoints history as the *circulation* of Spirit or the One returning to itself as an ever richer and higher unity. Here, the logic of profit finds its intellectual cognate. Gilles Deleuze captures the unease we experience: "It is not difference which presupposes opposition but opposition which presupposes difference, and far from resolving difference by tracing it back to a foundation, opposition betrays and distorts it."[20] Consequently, Hardt and Negri's summons to "love" is a deliberate rejection of imperial forms. Far from absurd, it can serve as a provocation to examine the disaffection of many left intellectuals with the dialectic and their efforts to articulate a politics that wriggles around it. When Hardt and Negri proclaim love as a political concept, we should ask, what are the itineraries of thought that give it this public form? Should we understand affirmation of love as rejection of the dialectic, or as a certain parsing and reclaiming of it for a necessarily heterogeneous left politics? These are admittedly sprawling questions, but I pursue them with an unrelenting eye to the concrete: specifically, how can debates around the dialectic illuminate the global and local articulations of capital (as "one" that is "many") and prospects of resistance to it.

The dialectic has a long and polyvalent biography going at least as far back as Buddhist/Hindu and Greek philosophy.[21] But its modern figuration as a *logic of content* that enables Western modernity's self-understanding—and from the standpoint of postcolonial critique, misrecognition—as a perfected, universal set of ideas, ideals and institutions is most closely associated with Hegel's thought, particularly the interconnected development of history and human consciousness (which he alternatively calls Spirit or Reason). Here is Hegel:

> The process whereby its [spirit's] inner determination is translated into reality is mediated by consciousness and will. The latter are themselves immersed at first in their immediate natural life; their primary object and aim is to follow their natural determination as such, which, since it is the spirit which animates it, is nevertheless endowed with infinite claims, power, and richness. Thus, the spirit is divided against itself; it has to overcome itself as a truly hostile obstacle to the realization of its end. That development, which, in the natural world, is a peaceful process of growth—for it retains its identity and remains self-contained—is in the spiritual world at once a hard and unending conflict with itself. The will of the spirit is to fulfill its own concept; but at the same time, it obscures its own vision of the concept, and is proud and full of self-satisfaction in this state of self-alienation.[22]

In this passage, Hegel anticipates a mode of thinking that Marx will appropriate in generative ways in the *Grundrisse:* the limits of Being [Spirit, Capital] repeat with difference, they are internal and immanent to it, and the drive to overcome them—Being as becoming—is the motor that drives history. Contrary to standard interpretations, Hegel does not claim inevitability for development. The prospect that Being could remain in an alienated state of "self-satisfaction" is an open possibility (Hegel's predecessor Immanuel Kant had stated as much in his 1784 essay, "What is Enlightenment?"[23]). Marx displaced the Hegelian narrative. He left open the possibility of capital existing in a state of endless recycling ("simple reproduction"), or withering away from *stasis* ("devaluation").[24] But both forms of being, he argued, were diminished forms of a vital entity that desires to grow—Being as becoming: value as mediation: capital as value in motion: expanded reproduction. Hegel again:

> Development, therefore, is not just a harmless and peaceful process of growth like that of organic life, but a hard and obstinate struggle with itself. Besides, it contains not just the purely formal aspect of development itself, but involves the realisation of an end whose

content is determinate. And we have made it clear from the outset what this end is: it is the spirit in its essential nature, i.e., as the concept of freedom.[25]

So, here we have it. The telos of development is freedom, as self-realization of Being's potential to be free. This proposition can serve as the bulwark of neoconservative or neoliberal politics, or of a politics of love. Hegel lends himself with equal ease to various factions of the Right and the Left.

Wilhelm Halbfass provides an instructive appraisal of Hegel's system of thought:

> The history of philosophy is the unfolding of philosophy itself, and Hegel's own system is designed as the consummation of the historical development of philosophy. . . . We are what we have become in and through history. History shows us the genesis and evolution of present state of being and knowing . . . [Furthermore] [i]n and by the process and progress of historical development, what is prior is integrated in what is posterior. It is—in Hegel's suggestive and ambiguous terminology—"aufgehoben," i.e., cancelled, suspended, preserved and moved upward all at once.[26]

Here we find another read of Hegelian philosophy. It is a philosophy of the present that is hemmed in by its time: that is to say, it can neither anticipate beyond its time nor return to the past which it has sublated within a superior, more comprehensive system of being and knowing. It can only recollect the past because there is no way back in history. More emphatically, history is History: the single and continuous time of unfolding of the Hegelian Spirit, a sequence of synchronic moments or presents defined by the contemporaneity of this essence with its determinations. Or, as Louis Althusser remarks:

> [T]his conception of historical time is merely a reflection of the conception Hegel had of the type of unity that constitutes the link between all the economic, political, religious, aesthetic, philosophical and other elements of the social whole. Because the Hegelian whole is a "spiritual whole" in the Leibnizian sense of a whole in which all the parts "conspire" together, in which each part is a *pars totalis*, the unity of this double aspect of historical time (homogeneous-continuity/contemporaneity) is possible and necessary.[27]

Althusser is not a generous reader of Hegel. But let us take for granted that this is a tenable rendering of Hegel's thought (if not the only possible one).[28] In that case, we are in a position to apprehend the unease of a long line of illustrious scholars with the *Aufhebung*—the dialectical process that lends metaphysical purpose to Hegelian history (history *as* development) and, in a repeating crime of guilt by association, to Marx's putative propositions about capitalist development. I will return to the issue of whether or not Marx's dialectic is a simple materialist analog of Hegel's dialectic; and more generally—the proximate source of disquiet—whether the movement of the dialectic metonymically implies synthesis, sameness, unity, and identity as conventional wisdom has it, or whether it can be reclaimed for antitotalitarian projects as a figure of nonidentity and difference (but *not* nonrelation).

In its usual uptake as the operative figure of Marxist thought, the dialectic has been viewed in one of three interconnected ways: as a method for deciphering the historical geography of capital (in which guise it is also a constitutive proposition about capitalism's ontology); as a claim about the epistemological organization of Marx's texts; and as a characterization of the relationship between theory and praxis.[29] Precisely because of the iconic stature granted to the dialectic—so much so that Marx's innovation in thought and renovation of philosophy is often reduced to a materialist inversion of Hegel's dialectic—those who feel unease with Marxism often express it as an allergy to dialectical thinking given its synthesizing embrace and supposed logical complicity with two disturbing propositions. The first is the image of social existence as a "totality" organized around a dominating logic that functions by imposing uniformity upon heterogeneity (Nazi Germany and Stalinist USSR being the paradigmatic examples).[30] The second is the specter that this totality, trapped in the deadly grip of dialectical determination, is moving compulsively (and tragically) toward a destination where all will become same. This ominous portrait of the dialectic opens it up for condemnation from virtually every ideological quarter. Liberals mistrust it for its summary dismissal of free will and its apparent unwillingness to concede the empirical reality (capitalism's self-evident triumph). Conservatives despise it for its disdain of "tradition" and its temporal nominalism vis-à-vis questions of morality. And what might be (hazardously) termed the poststructural Left assails it for leaving no apparent room for "difference." Common to each of these critiques is a supposition that the pincer movements of dialectic, totality, and telos anticipate and assimilate "alterity" in the disparate forms that liberals, conservatives, and poststructuralists would like to see it ordained. But is it correct to conclude, as these critics do, that dialectic, totality, and telos are always bound together as accomplices? Is the relationship of these three figures a necessary one, or are they potentially separable? If separable, how are they to be pried apart?

These are, I want to suggest, neither arcane nor innocuous concerns. They speak forcefully to how we imagine and write about the social formation called "capitalism"; and how we can begin to think more expansively about sites and strategies of political action to contest its varied degradations of humans and nonhumans, which in molar and molecular ways undercut the conditions of possibility for collective life. The implication for intellectual practice is to think *at the limits of necessity*: identifying those fractures and play of forces that can transform the pasteurized pessimism of necessity—the seemingly inexorable logic of global capitalism—into particulate possibilities of lives lived not merely as "use-value for capital" but rather for their infinite other, *non-* or *a-*capitalist affective capacities and potentials. This would encompass forms of association that are not subjugated to the "pathological normality" of capitalism.[31] The Grundrisse is a vital political text in this regard.

In *Grundrisse* Marx unpacks the process of production as a fraught space-time of *non-circulation* that capital must traverse before reentering the realm of circulation. And it is in this domain outside circulation, where capital directly encounters the other it must subsume as its own moment if it is to continue to exist, that we are offered *Grundrisse's* new understanding of capitalism as a two-sided whole: value-for-itself (capital) pitted against use-value-for-itself (labor). There is one vital passage in Notebook III of the *Grundrisse* that fitfully encapsulates my normative claims in this chapter. Marx writes:

> Labor posited as *not-capital* as such is: (1) *not-objectified labor [nicht-vergegenständlichte Arbeit], conceived negatively* (itself still objective; the not-objective itself in objective form). As such it is not-raw-material, not-instrument of labor, not-raw-product: labor separated from all means and objects of labor, from its entire objectivity. This living labor, existing as an *abstraction* from these moments of its actual reality (also, not-value); this complete denudation, purely subjective existence of labor, stripped of all objectivity. Labor as *absolute poverty*: poverty not as shortage, but as total exclusion of objective wealth. Or also as the existing not-value, and hence purely objective use value, existing without mediation, this

objectivity can only be an objectivity coinciding with his immediate bodily existence.

Several key elements of Marx's oeuvre make cameo appearances here. We meet living labor in an abstracted existence as "immediate bodily existence": pure potentiality that has not yet become an instrument or raw material for capital; that has not as yet been captured and consumed for the production of value—the objective form of wealth under capitalism. In this unmediated *capacity* (and in this sense only) living labor can be described as "purely objective use value," that is, use value *for-itself*. As it stands, Marx has only opened a breach. Its emancipatory force awaits explanation. He gives us this in the second segment of the passage in question:

> *Not-objectified labor, not-value,* conceived *positively,* or as a negativity in relation to itself, is not the not-*objectified,* hence non-objective, i.e., subjective existence of labor itself. Labor not as an object, but as activity; not as itself *value,* but as the *living source* of value. [Namely, it is] general wealth (in contrast to capital in which it exists objectively, as reality) as the *general possibility* of the same, which itself exists as such in action. Thus, it is not at all contradictory, or, rather, the in-every-way mutually contradictory statements that labor is *absolute poverty as object,* on one side, and is, on the other side, the *general possibility* of wealth as subject and as activity, are reciprocally determined and follow from the essence of labor, such as it is *presupposed* by capital as its contradiction and as its contradictory being, and such as it is, presupposes capital.[32]

Here, Marx tells us that in the raw state of *"[n]ot objectified labor, not value,* conceived *positively," living labor as activity* is the *possibility*—the irreducible prospect—of multiple actualizations or becomings. In this reading, one possible actualization (indeed, the global condition these days) is for living labor to become *"the use value* of capital"[33]: the "form-giving fire" that sustains and extends capital. But conscripted as capitalism's *"general possibility* of wealth" labor is hurled into forms of life that hem, or denude, its creative possibilities. The latter half of the passage is notable for Marx's emphasis on labor as *activity*. Hence, "[l]abour not as an object, but as activity; not as itself *value,* but as the *living source* of value." On this reading, capital has an ultimately molecular existence. It names an immensely powerful structure, capitalism, that is however no more *and* no less than the combinatorial effect of spatially diffuse and iterative practices that enable the capture of labor's use value. Capital, one might say, has a virtual materiality, its diagrammatic powers over planetary existence continually activated *in action* through apparatuses for the capture of living labor that are vast and ingenious: encompassing the spheres of production, distribution, and consumption.

But so captured, labor is "*presupposed* by capital as its contradiction and as its contradictory being, and such as it is, presupposes capital." One could read into this fragment the proposition that capture is not merely a question of foreclosing freedoms—for instance, employment choices—by divesting labor of property or means of production as the classic Marxist argument would go. It is also the work of inciting individual desires in ways that are useful for capital, not to mention critical in its relentless drive for self-expansion. Thus, identities of various sorts—validated in the name of "freedom" as vessels of emancipation—are easily annexed to the commodity logic of capital, becoming its spectacular productions.

But the electric buzz of hope never vanishes. The Marx of *Grundrisse* is intent on producing political knowledge charged with a kinetic potential for subversion. Thus, in spite of capital's incursions (its ingenious forms of capture) labor remains "its contradictory being." Marx in fact hints that labor remains, at some deep level, *unintelligible* to capital. Its possibilities to be otherwise, not-for-capital, are therefore an omnipresent source of fear and peril. *Grundrisse* leaves us with a looming political question: will capital use this viral contradiction that suffuses its existence to discover new strategies of survival and accumulation (as it has been doing), or will the virus short-circuit its host?

In another register, the passage from *Grundrisse* that I have just analyzed lends itself to a thinking of *difference in capital*: both, how capitalism is different-in-itself and how difference exists under (the reign of) capital. Capital does not have a single template for accumulation. As a (more-than-human) social formation it is a spatial articulation of interlaced value-producing activities—"normativities"—that are *structured-in-dominance to economy*. Or, as Althusser visualizes it in one particularly vivid passage in *Reading Capital*: "[T]he structure of the whole is articulated as the structure of an organic hierarchized whole. The co-existence of limbs and their relations in the whole is governed by the order of a dominant structure which introduces a specific order into the articulation *(Gliederung)* of the limbs and their relations."[34]

What is this dominant structure? It is "economy": the diagram of capitalist value,[35] which continuously strives to enroll labor in a rationalized (abstracted) form to maintain—or, if possible, exceed—some necessary rate of profit. It *is* a form of normativity in conduct, but a restrictive one. Labor *is* enabled a certain freedom and creativity. But only in service of the bottom line. Althusser is quick to caution that the "dominance of a structure ... cannot be reduced to the primacy of a centre, any more than the relation between the elements and the structure can be reduced to the expressive unity of essence within its phenomena."[36] Capitalist production dominates the universe of human (and nonhuman) activity, but activities are not reducible to—*not mere expressions of*—capital. Instead, we confront a "complex whole" *where production activity oriented to profit-taking for accumulation interdigitates with other value-creating practices:* in short, labor realizing its potential for varied life-becomings in activity—in disperse places, at disperse moments. It is moreover a "complex whole" comprising countless circuits of human and nonhuman joinings that capitalist value as self-canceling mediation must traverse—in the garb of product, commodity, and then money—in order to be reaffirmed as capital. Finally, it a "complex whole" that operates in heterogeneous and nonlinear time—what Althusser once called "a time of times."[37]

Such a move is critical and generative in a number of important ways. First, it enables us to think differently of the terms that inhabit the dialectic-totality-telos trinity and the ostensibly ironclad relationship between them; second, it raises questions about the adequacy of postcolonial studies' uptake and critique of Marx and capitalism; third, it opens up the possibility, as suggested, for thinking capitalism as a geographically uneven social formation where heterogeneous value-creating practices ("labors") are sutured together in lesser or greater degrees of repair (but where the wounds of that suture are never completely effaced); and, fourth, it therefore allows for the prospect that labor politics does not have to take the archetypical forms of labor union and labor party in order to stake out opposition to capital. Instead it points to forms of political action, and prospective articulations between them, that could be as extensive or subtle as the movements of capital's "value."

In order to incite what is at stake in theorizing capitalism as this sort of ontological multiplicity, I veer away briefly from abstract analysis in order to report on the molar and molecular geographies of capitalism and the forms of existence and existential politics, some interruptive, that sprout in the nooks and crannies of the capitalist assemblage. This, I hope, will bring clarity to my preceding claims as well as pave the way to understanding what Derrida, earlier in this chapter, enigmatically described as a "dialecticity of dialectics that is itself fundamentally not dialectical."[38]

A Rhizome of Stories

"[T]he book," Gilles Deleuze and Félix Guattari tell us, "is not an image of the world. It forms a rhizome with the world."[39] I take this to be a statement about the immanence of language, indeed, the radical materiality of the corpus of words that constitute and are territorialized through social practices in the form of a book. Moreover, to claim the immanence of language is to abjure correspondence or representational theories of knowledge, where language is external to and descriptive of the world, in favor of a materialist theory of knowledge, where language is entangled within and transformative of that world (see chapter 4). Put another way, the book is an effect of multiple forces and practices that secures its own multiple effects. The "rhizome" describes the dense, intertwined, heterogeneous, *and* contingent connections between elements that make up a "whole": whether that whole is experienced as a book, a human body, a caste community, a village, a society, a nation, or capitalism. Each of these is a "multiplicity"—a combination of diverse elements—that is grasped within empiricist or rationalist epistemologies as an "entity," something that coheres as a "thing" because of its allegedly internal properties and can be represented within an arboreal logic of hierarchies and taxonomies. The figure of the rhizome not only shuns these epistemologies it also shuns the conventional view of dialectic, a binary logic of us/them or self/other that is normally attributed to the Hegelian *Aufhebung*. The rhizome instead seeks to be a concept of interrelations and connectivity that is nonclassificatory and nondialectical: that is to say, a generative and *experimental* "line of flight." Taking this cue, I assemble, without further ado, a narrative about social relations in central Gujarat that experiments with a rhizomatic form of exposition in the hope that it will secure some useful effects for the debates at hand.

Hasmukhbhai

My first introduction to Ajibhai Samabhai Solanki, on June 21, 1994, was summary. The first rains of the monsoon had arrived exactly a week ago and preparations for the kharif paddy crop would be in full swing soon. I was trying to make the most of the remaining time before the tempo of life accelerated and the swarms of mosquitoes, which I had been warned about, proliferated. Hasmukhbhai Jani and I were chatting on a cot in front of Nirmalbhai Patel's house in Astha.[40] Although Hasmukhbhai, a Brahmin, is principal at the local secondary school, I almost never saw him go to work. More often than not he could be seen whizzing in and out of Astha on his Hero Honda motorcycle, with his younger brother Ghanshyam or one of the younger Patels in tow. I could never quite figure out what kept him so busy. But I was told by friends in Astha that Hasmukhbhai had many "connections" in the area—at the irrigation department, in the police, at the local branches of various banks, and within the Taluka bureaucracy at Matar.[41] He was also an insurance agent for LIC (the Life Insurance Corporation of India), an agent with the Post Office authorized to issue National Savings Certificates (NSCs) and Kisan Vikas Patras (KVPs),[42] as well as a broker licensed to buy and sell stocks in the Ahmedabad share bazaar. His government job as schoolteacher was simply a channel of guaranteed income. When I expressed surprise at Hasmukhbhai's rather casual attitude toward his job at the *pathshala* (school) my friends in the village had scoffed, "He paid good money to get the job, now he is recouping his investment."[43] I wasn't particularly keen to talk to Hasmukhbhai about village matters. He had deflected my attempts to engage him in conversation on several previous occasions.[44] But friends in Astha kept urging me to talk to him—"he knows a lot," they insisted. So, finally, I had managed to snag Hasmukhbhai that June morning and we sat down to discuss a range of issues connected to the impact of canal irrigation on the village's economy, on the prospects of nonfarm employment, on cultivators' cash needs, on moneylending practices, and on intercaste relations. Ajibhai happened to pass by just as I had asked Hasmukhbhai to explain why the condition of Thakur (Baraiya) households in Astha was on the whole so abject. A recent encounter had jolted me to the knotted workings of power and left deep, unsettled questions about the ethics and political economy of ethnographic research. I could anticipate Hasmukhbhai's answer: he would blame the Thakurs for their condition. But I had to confirm.

Ranchhodbhai and Laxmanbhai

Ashapuri is a multicaste village like Astha, about twelve kilometers to the southeast, in which I had been hoping to do research. There too Baraiyas are a numeric majority, but where political control—like in Astha—vests with the Patels and their caste allies (Brahmins, Thakkar Vanias, and Panchals). My first introduction in Ashapuri—back in March—had been to a wealthy Patel farmer, Kashibhai, who is the brother-in-law of a retired Gandhian politician, also a Patel, who lived in a nearby town and whom I had come to respect and like. At the time I had no idea of Kashibhai's affluence and only a minimal appreciation of political dynamics in Ashapuri. On that very first meeting Kashibhai had invited Nandubhai Mehta, a Brahmin—and as it happened, also a schoolteacher!—to join us. I was also introduced that same day to a person called Rajatbhai. The entire afternoon had been spent in the Patel khadki. When it had come time to leave I had been cornered by seven to eight Patel farmers who interrogated me at length—who I was, where I came from, why I was here in Ashapuri, what I planned to do, how long I intended to spend, and so on.

Early introductions, particularly when new and unfamiliar to an area, can have lasting consequences. The strong element of path-dependence in fieldwork means that getting off on the wrong foot with an individual or a community can make it difficult to repair or salvage relations down the road. Power-holders within a village—always alert to contingencies and determined to preserve control—exert a gravitational pull on outsiders, particularly unknown quantities like researchers (I elaborate on this point in the afterword). To fast forward, I was never able to gain the trust of the Baraiya community in Ashapuri. Yes, a few individuals did eventually come to accept my presence and even engaged me in discussions, but these were, inevitably, the better-off members of the Baraiya community who perhaps had less reason to be skeptical of me or feel threatened. Poorer Baraiyas either avoided me or displayed thinly concealed hostility when I tried to approach them. In the fourteen-odd months I would spend visiting Ashapuri on a fairly regular basis, on only two occasions did members of poor Baraiya households acquiesce to talk to me.

One of these had been just a few days earlier when, acting on impulse, I ventured into the Baraiya *vas* (living quarters) in Ashapuri. Several quizzical and a few resentful eyes followed me as I walked through the vas not quite sure what to do next. Two men sipping a cup of tea in their mud hut stopped me and invited me to join them. I set down my *jhola* (shoulder bag) and entered their hut. They introduced themselves as Ranchhodbhai and Laxmanbhai, brothers. We began talking. In marked contrast to the Patel farmers in Ashapuri, they never bothered to ask me who I was and why I was there. They seemed to assume that I had a right to be there. Our conversation touched on familiar themes:[45]

> *Why were so many Baraiyas impoverished?* The now-familiar reasons had been trotted out: ceremonial debts, drinking, gambling, low education levels, not enough cash to buy adequate inputs for cultivation, being bilked out of lands by Patels and Thakkars.
>
> *Was farm employment ample?* Yes, except in April and May when cultivation grinds to a halt . . . some larger farmers are now using combine harvesters for the wheat crop and this is beginning to hurt.
>
> *How easy was it to get loans for agriculture or for social and ceremonial obligations?* Small loans of a few hundred rupees are usually obtained from near relatives *[saga-sambandhi]* or a well-to-do farmer who is a regular employer . . . sometimes Ashapuri's grain merchant—a Thakkar Vania, who has managed to amass a large amount of land through trade and moneylending—provides petty loans . . . for larger loans it all depends on one's *abroo*,[46] those with good *abroo* can get loans at 3 percent per month, others have to pay as much as 5 percent or put up jewelry as collateral . . . often it becomes necessary to mortgage land for a large loan.[47]
>
> *Were they paid the agricultural minimum wage for farm labor [khet majuri]?*[48] [They seemed surprised to hear of a legal minimum wage] We aren't sure what it is, we get twenty five rupees per day without a meal or twenty rupees with a meal . . . the Patels are always try to overwork us, and they bring in Bhil *adivasis* [tribals] from the Panchmahals to try and keep down the wages of local workers.

And so on the conversation had gone for about forty-five minutes until one of them asked me, "When can we get a loan?" at which point I realized with utter dismay that they thought I was a government loan officer of some sort. Embarrassed, I repeated my name and who I was—I had explained at the start of our discussion but evidently they had not understood. Just then another Baraiya who had been passing by their hut said, "Arre, he's that one, the one who has come to study, he stops over at Kashibhai's house." The effect had been electric. My hosts had immediately stopped talking to me, and seemed upset that I had wasted their time (which I had, given their interest in me) and perhaps because they felt compromised by the information they had been sharing so candidly. I left hurriedly after that, apologizing.

The memory of this encounter had come flooding back as I was talking to Hasmukhbhai—perhaps prompted by the obvious disparity in my terms of engagement with him, as contrasted to Ranchhodbhai and Laxmanbhai in Ashapuri. He answered my question as expected. Pointing to Ajibhai he said: "That man going there, you see him? His forefathers were large land owners, his father used to drink, he also got into drinking, has no interest in working, he has been getting rid of his land little by little and become a pauper, now he has started distilling liquor . . . this is the condition of *thakurs,* lazy people to begin with, on top which their bad habits kill them."

Dasarath

On subsequent visits to Astha, I crossed paths with Ajibhai several times. We would nod to each other but were never introduced. In the meantime my research in Ashapuri had continued, and one of the Baraiyas I got to know quite well was a seventeen-year-old boy named Dasarathbhai Solanki. Until 1993, Dasarath had operated a fledgling provision store from premises which Ramabhai Solanki's sparsely stocked shop now occupies. The premises, Dasarath explained, belonged to Ramabhai's father, who, over a period of several years, had mortgaged or sold off thirty-six *vighas* (twenty-one acres) of the family's original holdings of forty vighas. Dasarath claimed (and I had no basis for judging the valid- ity of his claim) that when his business started becoming successful, some envious members of the Baraiya community persuaded Ramabhai's father to cancel Dasarath's lease and start his own shop instead. It was evident from the inventory at hand that Ramabhai's store was struggling. Dasarath contrasted his now defunct business to Ramabhai's. According to Dasarath, when he was running his store he would purchase from cultivators up to five hundred *maunds* (ten thousand kilograms) of *dan- gar* (paddy) in a single *chomasu* (monsoon, or *kharif*) season. Because of his cordial relations with traders in nearby Limbasi, he was able to get sixty to seventy thousand rupees in credit from them. He would use some of the funds to make direct paddy purchases and recycle the remainder as loans within Astha's Baraiya community. The loans were paid back in kind. Rice that would ordinarily command a market price of ninety to one hundred rupees per maund was sold to him at sixty rupees by debtors. This enabled him to generate a tidy profit *(saro nafo)* on the rice trade.[49] By late 1994, when our acquaintance grew, he was operating a small vegetable and petty groceries store from a *lari* (handcart) parked on an empty flat of land that belonged to Sivabhai Thakkar, Astha's largest grain merchant. He was paying a small monthly rent to Sivabhai for the privilege. Dasarath's makeshift store was not open regularly, and he admitted that it wasn't doing well. He would talk off and on about relocating it next to the newly built dairy on the western fringe of Astha. "Don't you think I would get more customers there?" he would ask me. And not knowing the answer to this, I would say that he ought to speak to Shamabhai Solanki, the village dairy's secretary, about it.

In the time I was in Astha, one of Dasarath's brothers, barely out of high school, left for Rajkot to join the diamond-polishing trade. Rajkot and Surat are the major diamond-polishing centers in India. The trade is dominated by Kutchhi Patels, who operate polishing units that are little more than sweatshops. At the time, new workers were paid two thousand rupees (US$44) per month for ten to twelve hours of cramped and grueling labor. But to a struggling household, a regular income of two thousand rupees was a boon. In comparison to a monthly intake of nine hundred rupees ($20), which a fully employed agricultural laborer would have earned back then in *peak* agricultural season, when work is readily available, two thousand rupees was clearly not a sum to be lightly disregarded. After subtracting for meals and lodging, Dasarath's brother's income was closer to fifteen hundred rupees. But not everyone could get a job as a diamond polisher, Dasarath explained. And not everyone wants it. His brother was able to avail of the opportunity, Dasarath told me, because they had an uncle in Rajkot who was already working in a polishing unit. Connections matter. But some younger people, even if they have the opportunity, refuse to go because they know its hard work and don't like the idea of living away from home.

Dasarath described his family as one of the few undivided Thakur families in the village. He said this proudly. His father and uncles had been able to avoid the discord *(khichpich)* that typically culminates in partition. According to Dasarath, the main reason his family had managed to remain together was because all the brothers were hard-working and none had bad habits *(vesan)*. Why was an undivided family *(sanyukt kutumb)* a good thing, I asked? Because, Dasarath said, it was stronger. There were always enough hands to work in their fields, so they didn't have to worry about getting laborers on time or supervising them. And the brothers help each other out financially *(jyaare paisa ni jarurat padé)*. The sense of mutuality *(madad ni bhavna)* is much deeper among brothers who are together than those who have separated.[50] Moreover, Dasarath continued, expensive social expenditures *(mohnga samajik kharch)* can be scaled back without loss of face or reputation *(abroo)*. For example, two wedding ceremonies could be performed simultaneously but only one wedding feast *(jamanvaar)* would have to be organized. There are also benefits in cultivation *(kheti ma pan labh chhe)*. He rattled off a few examples: supervision of laborers and guarding crops from cattle *(dhor)* and other animals *(beeja jaanvar)*; application of water, when water has to be drawn from an irrigation subminor to a field with the help of a hose and diesel engine; tilling by tractor, because a divided plot is sometimes too small to justify the cost of hiring a tractor; transportation of harvested crops from fields, because tractor-operators prefer large jobs to small ones. Then there's the comparative ease in defraying wedding expenses. For instance *(dakhla tariké)*, take my family, said Dasarath. In 1993 *(teranu ma)* we spent one lac and five thousand rupees (US$2,333) on three marriages—two boys *(be chhokra)*, one girl *(ek chhokri)*. Because of the wedding expenses, we were not able to pay back the twenty-five thousand rupees in loans we had taken from the [village] credit society *(dheeran mandli)*.[51]

I was a bit flabbergasted to hear this because it meant that year Dasarath's family did not have the security of a low-interest government loan to defray their cultivation costs. When I said so, Dasarath deflected my concern. He told me that his family had thought through this whole thing carefully. "We calculated the marriage expenses a year in advance and came up with a strategy to finance them. If we had borrowed twenty-five thousand rupees privately, we would have paid at least 3 percent on the money, 36 percent for the year. With the credit society, even with the penalty, we only pay half that amount." Dasarath was evasive when I asked where the remaining eighty thousand rupees for the weddings had come from (through savings? through private loans? by mortgaging some of their land?), or how his family had paid for cultivation expenses that year. He told me he supports the social reforms *(sudhaar)* within the Baraiya *qum* (community) advocated by Shamabhai, the secretary of the dairy. But wedding expenses were unavoidable. If they had spent less than what they did their standing within the community would have suffered—"We have to maintain social relations, no?"

Shamabhai

As it turned out, Dasarath knew Ajibhai of Astha—he was a distant relative—and promised to introduce me. But first, a bit about Shamabhai, who represents a small but influential strand within the Baraiya community: Shamabhai Vaghjibhai Solanki is thirty-three years old and the secretary of the successful dairy in Astha. He is a college graduate with a B.Com. (Bachelor of Commerce) degree. His job as dairy secretary pays six hundred rupees per month. Although he owns only three vighas of land, he has kept an additional ten vighas on mortgage from people in his community. As a devout follower of the Vadtal Swaminarayan sect, he stays off liquor, opium, and gambling. He is also at the vanguard of a reform movement that seeks to eradicate bad habits *(vesan)* from the Baraiya community. He told me that fondness for liquor and gambling are the main weaknesses of Thakurs. Their tendency to spend heavily on social obligations is another: "You won't believe it, Vinaybhai, one man sold off his house in order to get his daughter married off in style . . . he now lives in a hut . . . this is the condition!" He also complained about widespread superstitions *(anshraddha)* among Thakurs, particularly their belief in *matas* (local female deities). A lot of money is wasted in chicken and goat sacrifices to please or appease a mata, he said.

Shamabhai told me that he had been partially successful at stopping the rite of *barmu,* which is the custom of feasting members of the community on the twelfth day after the death of a family member. Depending on the number of people invited, the cost of the meal can run from one or two thousand rupees to well over ten thousand rupees. The larger the meal the more accolades it brings *(vah-vah thai)* for the host. It's seen as sign that he has spared no cost in honoring a departed family member. Since money for the feast has to be generated at short notice, it is common practice among Thakurs, who are normally strapped for cash, to raise money by mortgaging a parcel of land. A vigha can bring anywhere between 5,000 and 12,000 rupees depending on its physical location and quality, the borrower's *garaj* (degree of need), and the calculations *(ganatri)* of the lender. When I asked Shamabhai how he had managed to do so well, compared to some of his neighbors, he said by keeping unnecessary social expenditures down, circulating surplus money *(vadharana paisa)* as credit, and controlling his family size (his four-member household, in addition to himself, consists of his wife, his son, and his widowed mother). "Baraiyas don't keep their population in check, that's also a major problem," he lamented.

Shamabhai's economic wellbeing, amicable demeanor, and reputation as an ambitious and responsible *(jawabdar)* dairy secretary have made him an *agevan* (leader) in the village, and within Baraiya *samaj* (society).[52] He maintains close ties with the large Baraiya community of Limbasi, as well as merchants there. He told me that because of his reputation he has no trouble mobilizing funds, whether for personal use or to sponsor community events—such as the Navratri festivities.

Ajibhai

Dasarath finally introduced me to Ajibhai the following year.[53] I had been reminding him and one day he said Ajibhai had invited us to his field to have *tuver na ponkh*.[54] Ajibhai's field was about a kilometer away from the road that connects Astha to State Highway 16, the main trunk road that runs from the town of Tarapur to the town of Kheda, bisecting Matar Taluka. When we arrived at about 11 A.M., the *ponkh* was already ready. Ajibhai and his wife and three children greeted us warmly. Neither he nor the four other men who were present, plucking pods *(fali)* off the thin, tall stems of the tuver plant, ever asked where I was from or why I was there. They either knew or did not seem to care. We talked about the tuver crop. It looked full, and I said so. Ajibhai explained that it had been a good year. There had been no pest attacks. When I asked whether pest outbreaks were common, he said that because of the extension of irrigated crops after the arrival of the canal, the humidity in the environment had risen, and as a result, pest outbreaks had increased. Tuver, he explained, is particularly susceptible to insect pests in the flowering and podding stages in the field. But, this year, we got lucky, he said. Why do you plant tuver, I asked? He told me that on elevated *goradu*—sandy silt—plots like his, it's the most reliable crop. And it's very useful. It can withstand water shortages and its peas are good for eating. He gestured toward the ponkh as he said this. In addition, the plant itself can be fed to livestock as green and dried fodder. It improves their milk output. Breaking off a stem, he said it was also of use within the home as a substitute for (fuel) wood. And the best part—he smiled as he said this—it doesn't demand as much effort as other crops.

I took this as a cue for other questions I wanted to ask him. I inquired how much land he owned. He told me twenty vighas: half is goradu like this, and the rest is *kali jamin* (low-lying black clay soil on which paddy is grown). How is the paddy crop this year? I asked. He said he had given up his kali jamin on mortgage *(giro)*. I asked him why. He shrugged and told me there had been some social expenses *(samajik kharch)* that he could not stave off. And, who knows, he said, I might even make some money off mortgaging. How will you do *that?* I asked, a bit dubious. Ajibhai said there was lot of demand for *giro jamin*. People want to lend money on land. They hope that the borrower won't be able to pay the loan back and they will get to keep the land. But if you are clever, he said, you can play one lender off against another and get them to bid up the price of land. That way, you can pay off your old loan and make something extra *(vadharanu)* on top. So that's how you survive? I asked. He said he and his wife worked as farm laborers here and there. They sell milk to the dairy. They have their goradu lands. And, there are other things. He was vague. When I asked what, he smiled and gave a shrug—"You won't understand." I decided to be direct and asked Ajibhai about the allegations some people had made about him—that he had bad habits, didn't like working, drank a lot, brewed liquor. Ajibhai was unapologetic. Yes, I drink, he said, I enjoy myself. If people don't like it, it's their problem. I am not anybody's servant. I work when I want to and rest when I want to. We live. We don't hurt anyone.

A Visit to the Rohit Vas

I want to offer one final ethnographic instance before turning to some explicitly theoretical concerns.[55] When I revisited the village of Ashapuri in late March of 1994, Kashibhai D. Patel once more extended a warm welcome to me. Over the mandatory cup of tea, I informed K.D. of my desire to visit the lower-caste quarters. He seemed bemused, as if unsure what there was to gain from such a visit. But as a good host, he indulged my request. We walked over to the Rohit vas. The Rohits were surprised to see us. They ushered us into the courtyard that runs the length of their vas. A cot was quickly pulled out. We were asked to sit on it. The Rohits, including the elderly ones, sat down in a semicircle around us, on the ground. I was deeply embarrassed but didn't protest. One Rohit *agévan* (luminary), clearly taken aback by K. D. Patel's presence, dryly remarked to him that the last time he had visited them was two years ago when he was in urgent need of field laborers. The Rohits flooded K.D. with questions about the *mehman* (guest) he had brought to their *vas*. K.D. explained that I was a student from America, here to study the impact of canal irrigation. The children stared at me quizzically, the grown-ups skeptically. K.D. nudged me to ask my questions. Acutely conscious of the unequal basis of this exchange, I directed an apologetic stare at everyone and then inquired in hesitant Gujarati whether their *aarthik paristhiti* (economic condition) had improved with the advent of the canal. Most of the elderly Rohits nodded assent. But there were murmurs of dissent from some of the younger Rohits. They said wage increases had been offset by *monghwaari* (inflation). Work was unevenly available, with pronounced slack periods. K.D. retorted that work was always available to anyone who cared to work, although—he conceded—it was not always the preferred, physically less-demanding sort of work. He admonished the younger Rohits, stating that laborers these days were lazy, did not care to work, and expected to be paid for minimum effort. He vehemently denied there was any *berozgaari* (unemployment).

"I am always on the lookout for laborers *(majoor)*, but often I have trouble finding any one willing to work. Laborers think I make them work too hard." K.D. continued: "I am not ready to pay a fat wage *(moti roji)* for a day's work, but I pay what's fair *(vyaajbi)*. All I demand is proper effort. But you laborers no longer want to work, so you don't like an employer who demands work."

A tidily dressed man in the back, sporting a Gandhi cap, *tilak,* and white *dhoti,* bristled at this deprecation of laborers' work habits. "How would you feel if you had to work in the field each day of the year for a living *(kamaani)?*" he asked. "Wouldn't you feel tired, wouldn't you want to rest occasionally too, if your body was beaten in the fields day after day?"

"Don't laborers need rest? You big farmers only stand in the field and give orders . . . it's easy for you to criticize the work habits of labor-ers." The younger Rohit men and women murmured in support. The older Rohits seemed embarrassed. They tried to tell the man to be quiet, that this was a village matter. The man defiantly refused. He said it was a matter that concerned the Rohit *qum* (community). K.D. asked one of the elderly Rohits who the man was. It transpired that the man was a schoolmaster from a distant village, who was visiting one of his relatives in Ashapuri. We left the Rohit vas after some more discussion. On the way out, a few Rohit elders told me to come back again—but alone. I promised. K.D., who had retained his equanimity in face of the schoolmaster's accusations, simply said, "This is what happens when outsiders who do not understand village matters interfere."

Ethnography as Affect

Consciousness presupposes experience, not experience consciousness. We are social beings entangled in relations of affect with our more-than-human world. At times we enter into connections that open us, revealing ways of being that were unimagined. At other times we are thrown into connections that restrict our capacities for becoming. Ethnography is a peculiar mode of knowledge. As an instrument of domination in the imperial arsenal of Anthropology, it has been ferociously and deservedly critiqued.[56] But do we have to abandon ethnography because of its sordid past? Can't it instead name a mode of knowledge, which opens our capacities to be affected in ways that are not possible within other modes? Let me turn briefly to a passage from Paolo Virno's *A Grammar of the Multitude* that has left a deep mark in this respect. Virno is describing Gilbert Simondon's ideas of individuation:

> *[I]ndividuation* is never concluded . . . the pre-individual is never translated into singularity. Consequently, according to Simondon, the *subject* consists of permanent interweaving of pre-individual elements and individuated characteristics; moreover, the subject *is* this interweaving. It would be a serious mistake according to Simondon, to identify this subject with one of its components, the one which is singularized. The subject is, rather, a composite: "I," but also "one," unrepeatable uniqueness, but also anonymous universality.[57]

Ethnography intensifies the capacity for precisely this sort of productive dislocation of the ethnographer as subject of knowing. There is no centering subject, ethnographer as Cartesian "I." Instead, the subject learns to see itself as enabled effect. Knowledge is rendered radically immanent as an uncertain and always connected production: more or less intimate, depending on connective intensities (which are rarely within the ethnographer's control). It says nothing about whether that knowledge is "quantitative" or "qualitative." This pernicious divide loses relevance. Nor does it sanction a puerile relativism, which says any representation is possible and tenable. It is not. The "*conditioned* indetermination" of our pre-individual reality ensures against this. Brian Massumi offers a compelling vision of the sort of ethnographic theory of knowledge that I am endorsing. Consider this provocative account of the situated, bodily, and overdetermined *practice* of knowledge making:

> Take wood. A woodworker who sets out to make a table does not pick just any piece of wood. She chooses the right piece for the application. When she works it, she does not indiscriminately plow into it with the plane. She is conscious of the grain and is directed by it. She reads it and interprets it. What she reads are signs. Signs are qualities (color, texture, durability, and so on). And qualities are much more than simply logical properties or sense perceptions. They envelop a potential—the capacity to be affected, or to submit to a force (the action of the plane; later, the pressure of salt shakers and discourteous elbows), and the capacity to affect, or to release a force (resistance to gravity; or in a nontable application, releasing heat when burned). . . . The presence of the sign is not an identity but an envelopment of difference, of a multiplicity of actions, materials, and levels. In a broader sense, meaning even includes the paths not taken. It is also all the forces that could have seized the thing but did not. . . . Interpretation consists in developing what is enveloped in the sign. The woodworker brings the qualities of the wood to a certain expression. . . . Although the activity of the woodworker may seem to occur on a conscious level as a "will" or "intention" translated into action, it is no more subjective than the sign was merely objective. . . . *Interpretation is force, and an application of force is the outcome of an endless interplay of processes natural and historical, individual and institutional.*[58]

Even self-representation is an interpretation in the sense outlined above. In short, knowledge works its power by being *affective*. Its truth-effects are to be measured by its force of dispersion; not by its efforts to confirm the known and the given, or the said and the seen. These latter are *also* functions of knowledge—but not as levers of critique, rather as sentries of the status quo. Knowledge functions critically when it *releases* thought ("thought" understood here as the potential to arrest, trouble, alter, even shatter, the barnacle-like deposits of accustomed or encrusted thinking). Perhaps what I am speaking about, at the risk of appearing disingenuous, is knowledge as the capacity for becoming otherwise. Michel Foucault has offered a description of this critical stance with admirable directness:

> This philosophical ethos may be characterized as a *limit-attitude*. We are not talking about a gesture of rejection. We have to move beyond the outside-inside alternative; we have to be at the frontiers. Criticism indeed consists of analyzing and reflecting upon limits. But if the Kantian question was that of knowing *[savoir]* what limits knowledge *[connaissance]* must renounce exceeding, it seems to me that the critical question today must be turned back into a positive one: In what is given to us as universal, necessary, obligatory, what place is occupied by whatever is singular, contingent, and the product of arbitrary constraints? The point, in brief, is to transform the critique conducted in the form of necessary limitation into a practical critique that takes the form of a possible crossing-over *[franchissement]*.[59]

Non-Dialectical Dialectics

What, then, are we to make of the ethnographic instances presented above? One obvious inference is that they speak to both the "politics of labor," conventionally understood, as well as (to effect a distinction) a "politics of work."[60] The politics of labor names the dialectical struggle between two principal antagonists—"capital" and "labor"—within and outside the labor process, around conditions of work and wages. These antagonisms are extraordinarily important. But, within most narratives, they appear as episodes in the development and attendant movements of capital. They may reveal capital's limits but ultimately end up demonstrating its relentless ingenuity and capacity to overcome barriers through power of sublation.

Theodor Adorno once remarked that the "name of dialectics says no more, to begin with, than that objects do not go into their concepts without leaving a remainder, that they come to contradict the traditional norm of adequacy."[61] Therefore, when I attempt to separate "work" from "labor," I am trying to reclaim for that term its heterogeneous and irreducible sense of meaningful fabrication—*labor as potentiality: potentiality as activity*. It should be clear that I am not merely gesturing to labor's existence as a transhistorical form of activity (a metabolic interaction with nature, necessary for human existence) or as the antithetical force that animates capital and/or is its foreordained nemesis within an eschatological scheme. The move I am proposing—that of disentangling "work" from "labor"—approximates the sense of *labor as use value for-itself*: the potential for multiple becomings that exceed the plan(e) of capital.[62] These becomings have antagonism as their motive force in that they want not to be actualized as *the use value of capital*. However, rather than constitute around an identity that is merely the negative of "capital"—hence, still within *its* force field and *its* terms of engagement— they explore other, affirmative, forms of becoming. In contrast to the politics of labor, the politics of work, as I am calling it here, begins from a "negative dialectics"—the tense and fecund moment of contradiction, negativity—and breaks capital's flow by making affective connections that are based upon a refusal to be dialectically defined by capital as "not-capital." Here is the way to take Hegel from behind, to think "a dialecticity . . . that is non-dialectical."[63]

Concretely, Ajibhai most closely fits the bill of affirmative, non-dialectical politics as described. He chooses to operate by criteria that frustrate the recuperative desires of capital (manifested in the person of capitalist farmers who function as bearers, *Träger,* of the social relations represented by this category). He arranges to use his labor and his activities of consumption in time and space at *his* pleasure.[64] Of course, this is not always possible because he is *not* outside the gravitational pull of capital. But he seems to be trying to put together a mode of existence that is not readily conducive for the circulation of value, and so earns the ire of an agrarian elite that wants to conscript his land and labor. The allegations they parade about Ajibhai's drinking follow a universal script. Drinking is wasteful, an economy of excess without meaning. It recalls Antonio Gramsci's trenchant observations on Fordism: the drives by American industrialists to police the private lives of factory workers—to ensure, in puritanical manner, that alcohol consumption and sex did not corrode or destroy their "muscular-nervous efficiency."[65] Ajibhai is not mounting a frontal assault against capital—an individual in any case does not have that kind of capacity—but he is producing a crisis in one molecular point through which capital as value must pass. Call it a counterforce. It is resistance in *that* sense.

More intriguing is the case of Patels who engage in practices of labor devalorization (chapter 4). Don't they too practice a "politics of work"? Once again, their arrangement of labor use in time and space can also dissipate, or at least slow down, the accumulative logic of value. What are we to make of their associations of commoditized labor (particularly women's) with bodily contamination? Their actions, on the one hand, appear to militate against their class interests. On the other hand, the sense of distinction that their class position demands seems to hinge precisely on doing what is *not*, on the face of it, economically rational.

Then, we have the Rohits in Ashapuri—some resigned to their condition, others defiant. They occupy more readily a politics of labor. Their mix of accommodation and opposition remains on capital's terrain, within its zone of familiarity—and hence can be dialectically overcome. But there is body politics at work among Rohits too. The schoolmaster who turned on K. D. Patel—did you notice how he was dressed? His Gandhian attire and assumption of moral authority from the vantage point of that ideology was an unmistakably political statement. And, wouldn't you know it, he was unknowingly echoing Marx's denunciations of capitalism in the *Grundrisse* in the way he launched his critique. In *Grundrisse,* Marx interrupts the discourse of "self-denial" that capitalists enjoin upon workers: namely, that in order to stave off economic crises, workers ought to deny themselves even ordinary pleasures. Here is Marx:

> The most he [the worker] can achieve on the average with his self-denial is to be able to better endure the fluctuations of prices—high and low, their cycle—that is, he can only distribute his consumption better, but never attain wealth. And that is actually what the capitalists demand. . . . That is, the demand they should always hold to a minimum of life's pleasures and make crises easier to bear for the capitalist etc. Maintain themselves as pure laboring machines and as far as possible pay their own wear and tear. . . . [That he deny himself] participation in the higher, even cultural satisfactions, the agitation for his own interests, newspaper subscriptions, attending lectures, educating his children, developing his taste, etc.[66]

In short, the instances I have posed do not have to fit cleanly into one of two boxes—"politics of labor" *or* "politics of work." They bear a contaminated logic, which troubles this dualism. In an earlier chapter, I discussed the proliferation of piecework *(ucchak)* contracts in Matar Taluka. It is clear that the Baraiya and Tadbda Kolis (hereafter, Kolis), who form the bulk of the working class in Matar Taluka, have a *distinct preference* for group-based piecework. The possibility of higher earnings is an obvious attraction. But discussions with Koli laborers reveal that a far bigger attraction for them is the fact that task-based or piecework contracts allow them to conduct work at their own tempo, and without constant interference and berating from Patel employers.

V. K. Ramachandran is, of course, correct in noting that "[w]orking for piece-rates does not . . . make the hired laborer any less a hired laborer (or the proletarian any less a proletarian)."[67] But his argument does not undercut my central claim that piecework markedly alters the *experience* of time *and* space for laborers by permitting them to vary the tempo of work, and to work in relative autonomy from employers toward whom they nurture a history of antagonism or aggrievement. In fact, the first aspect is clear from an interview that Ramachandran himself conducted with Ramasami Pallar, who was fronting for a group of low-caste contract laborers in Ramachandran's study village. According to Ramasami, members of his group preferred piece-rate work because, although "the work may last for longer hours, we [the work party] can arrange the work time to our preference. For instance, during harvest time, from 10 A.M. to 12 noon, I may send [the women in the work group] home; they go home, do any housework that they may have on hand and look to the children, and work again when the sun is not as hot." Ramachandran also makes the important point that although there is competition for jobs *between* work groups (a point to which I return below), *within* a group one can occasionally observe the "germs of collective labor": in short, a situation where—to recall a now famous article by E. P. Thompson—the disjuncture of work from social life is partly attenuated, thereby diluting an individual laborer's sense of alienation.

Georg Lukács and Bertell Ollman have powerfully emphasized that psychological fragmentation—the separation of the worker's labor-power from his or her total personality, and the consequent loss of creativity—is a key aspect of alienation in the labor process. This sense of alienation is heightened when, under supervised and rationalized conditions of production, "time sheds its qualitative, variable, flowing nature . . . [and] becomes space"[68]—in other words, when the passage of time is reduced to measures of physical productivity and the experience of work loses its social character. Group-based piecework restores, to an extent, not only the social character of work but also the variability in rhythm that embellishes the experience of work. It is not, strictly speaking, a politics of work as I have defined it above; nevertheless, it exhibits flashes of this within a conventional politics of labor.

What about Dasarath and Shamabhai, the other two individuals who figure prominently in my ethnographic examples? Shamabhai is easier to diagnose. His advocacy for social reforms among the Baraiyas of Ashapuri and his entrepreneurial work ethic identify him as the bearer of social relations who will, or ought to, take the name "capitalist." Gauging from his economic trajectory, this is exactly the identity he is in the process of assuming. Dasarath also desires to be an entrepreneur. But he is caught between multiple forces, not all of which draw him inexorably into the embrace of capitalist "value."

The Provenance of "Capital"

What is at stake, intellectually and politically, in theorizing interruptions to capital—or to its philosophical cognate, the imperial logic of Hegel's *Aufhebung?* And how might one go about doing this? The readings of ethnographic text are suggestive, but by themselves inadequate for the "limit-attitude" that can (although will not inevitably) produce the "crossing-over" Michel Foucault urges. One admittedly contrived way of pushing the limit is to set two figures, who have each thought through the workings of capital carefully but differently, into engagement with each other—and see what emerges from that aleatory encounter. It is a wager, like this book. In putting David Harvey's *Limits to Capital* into engagement with the historian Dipesh Chakrabarty's book, *Provincializing Europe: Postcolonial Thought and Historical Difference,* I proceed in the spirit of Marxist heterodoxy, hoping to spur a "symptomatic reading" of Marx and his interlocutor, Harvey.[69] I focus on Marx's categories of "labor" and "value" in order to identify those moments of interruption in the circuits of capital that can further elucidate the tasks of resistance for political action and writing (taking for granted that these are interrelated).

Chakrabarty's *Provincializing Europe* is not a book that is in direct conversation with Harvey. For one, the books were published at different times: *Limits* in 1982 and *Provincializing Europe* in 2000. But the books deserve to be put in engagement precisely because Chakrabarty foregrounds a problem that neither the Harvey of *Limits* nor, I would argue, the later Harvey adequately confronts: the consequences of theorizing within the epistemic space of capital. Chakrabarty's analytic device of History 1 and History 2s illuminates this claim. To write within the space of History 1, according to Chakrabarty, is to produce the "universal and necessary history we associate with capital,"[70] or equivalently, the history of "the reproduction of the logic of capital."[71] By contrast, History 2s are those "multiple possibilities [or] pasts" that "may be under the institutional domination of the logic of capital and exist in proximate relationship to it, but . . . do not belong to the 'life process' of capital." The task of History 2s, then, is both epistemological and ontological: on the one hand, to function as a strategy of writing that constantly interrupts "the totalizing thrusts of History 1"; on the other hand, to write those pasts and presents that reveal "the human bearer of labor power [as having the capacity] to enact other ways of being in the world"[72]—other than, that is, being the bearer primarily of labor power, the use value of capital.

Limits operates firmly within the ontology and scope of History 1, with the result that it writes back dispersed geographies of life into the expansionist narrative of capital's becoming—as variations in a singular, relentless process of capitalist development. In so doing, it effectively recoups a diversity of struggles and modes of being into the unifying dialectic of capital.[73] Although Harvey never succumbs to the seductions of teleology in describing capitalist dynamics—he is far too alert to geographical contingencies, the unevenness of capital's movements, and the creative powers of workers to commit that error—the optic of "capital" is so totalizing in *Limits* that it renders improbable the possibility of non-capitalist political identifications and logics of organizing. One is either complicit with capital, in a class compromise with capital, or in opposition to capital.[74] This is exactly the prison-house of a politics of labor.

My critique of Harvey's *Limits*, then, is, two-pronged. First, I want to draw attention to the epistemic limits of the dialectic in general and the dialectic of capital in particular, and in so doing, foreground the question of representation; second, I want to discuss the political and ethical consequences of always rendering difference in a relationship of actual or prospective assimilation to capital. Agrarian studies and post-colonial studies offer logical vantage points for this critique. Despite their disciplinary heterogeneity, both have been acutely sensitive to contingency and conjuncture in processes of change; conscious of capital's hegemonizing operations, yet unwilling to reduce history to its logic; and, lastly, skeptical of capital's ability to assimilate all forms of life that oppose its aspirations. This is not the place to elaborate the convergences and divergences between agrarian studies and postcolonial studies.

Suffice to say that I judge them as potentially complementary modes of critique.

By putting political economy into engagement with anthropology and ecology the Marxist branch of agrarian studies has produced a rich empirical scholarship demonstrating the limits of capital's reach.[75] In these accounts, "culture" and "nature" operate as signifiers that cordon off regions of "life"—in the figure of the "peasant," for instance—that exist in a relation of marginality and subordination to capital yet manage to remain, in some fundamental way, "exterior" to it. Put differently, culture and nature designate logics that are, to varying degrees, ontologically autonomous of the capital's law of value and insert an element of radical contingency into its workings in space and time. From the perspective of agrarian studies, then, *Limits* is prescient in diagnosing the expansionist, uneven geography of capitalist accumulation but wrong to imply that the differences that culture and nature code exist merely or primarily because they are functional to the circulation of capital.[76]

Unlike agrarian studies, which generates an epistemological and ontological critique of *Limits* by summoning an "outside" to capital, postcolonial studies mounts a similar critique from the "inside." Its motivation, aptly summarized by David Scott, is "a cognitive-political demand for the decolonization of representation, the decolonization of the West's theory of the non-West."[77] This places it in opposition not only to the putative Eurocentrism of capital-centered narratives such as *Limits* but, fairly or not, also to a prospective ally, agrarian studies, for invoking "culture" and "nature"—categories that postcolonial criticism views as discursive bulwarks of European imperialism—in unproblematized ways.[78] Not surprisingly, capital enters postcolonial critiques as a constitutive force of Empire. There is no effort, unlike agrarian studies, to locate an "exterior" to capital. Instead, the attempt is to force an epistemic rupture in narratives that organize themselves through capital's optic—and, by metonymic association, through the universalizing optic of Europe's (provincial) modernity. Capitalism, it is claimed, effaces difference by rendering the "singular" as just a particular form of the universal.[79] These effacements—which amount to a systematic erasure of possible subject-effects in text and practice—can be gathered under the name "subaltern." This usage remains faithful to Gramsci to the extent that it designates subordinated elements of society. But since these subordinated elements are heterogeneous and always fragmented, the signifier "subaltern" becomes "not the container of a presence but the placeholder of an absence"[80]—a catachrestic, anti-universal universal that urges an ethic of responsibility to the dominated.[81]

The interventions of Dipesh Chakrabarty are consequential here. Beginning with his 1989 book, *Rethinking Working-Class History,* and through a series of articles that culminate in *Provincializing Europe,* Chakrabarty develops a compelling critique of the category and practice of history and the implications of Marx's legacy for postcolonial scholarship. His critique revolves around the violence of abstraction that is constitutive of capitalist modernity and inscribed within "capital" by its inseparable linking of abstract time and abstract labor. In *Limits,* David Harvey famously describes capital "as value 'in motion.'"[82] The unrelenting emphasis on various processes of capital circulation—variable, constant, finance, landed, merchant, credit, and industrial—each with different turnover times and different effects, is one of the searing insights of the book. It also exposes one of the presuppositions of capital: that for "value" to expand, it must be possible to measure its complex movements within a time of equivalence. Chakrabarty names this homogenous, secular time "the time of history." Unless time is uniformly measurable across space—everywhere an identical precise continuum—how can capital realize its universalizing imperative? No one perhaps has driven this point home more forcefully than E. P. Thompson in his remarkable article, "Time, Work-Discipline, and Industrial Capitalism," where he describes how traditional conceptions of time held by laborers in England had to be systematically subordinated to "clock time" in order for industrial capital to flourish.[83] In other words, the logic of capital demands that diverse temporalities—which pose potential limits to capital—be sublated to the abstract time of "history." Since workers can embody multiple senses of time in their practices, it follows that their concrete labors must be regulated, either through factory discipline (as E. P. Thompson or, later, Michel Foucault describe) or via de-skilling by technology (as Harry Braverman argues), in order for abstract labor—the "substance of value"—to become operative "as a guiding force within capitalist history."[84] Harvey provides a characteristically exact account of this process:

> All labor is concrete in the sense that it involves the material transformation of nature. But market exchange tends to obliterate individual differences both in the conditions of production and

on the part of those doing the laboring. . . . What happens in
effect is that the commensurability of commodities achieved
through exchange renders the labor embodied in them equally
commensurable.[85]

Moreover,

> [t]he existence of money [as a social measure able to represent value
> materially] is a necessary condition for the separation and distillation
> of abstract out of concrete labor. . . . Social relationships are expressed
> as relationships between things. On the other hand, the things
> themselves exchange according to their value, which is measured
> in terms of abstract labor. And abstract labor becomes the measure
> of value through a specific social process . . . [within which the]
> existence of money—the form of value—conceals the social meaning
> of value itself.[86]

Harvey's elucidation of Marx emphasizes that abstract time and
abstract labor, which are co-constitutive, congeal in the mysterious
figure of the commodity. There is also an implicit argument here
about space: namely, that the move from concrete to abstract labor
entails a binding of distant events into a common, interdependent
capitalist space-economy, with money as the key intermediary.[87] But
Limits's capital-centric analysis has little or no room to admit multiple
temporalities and noncapitalist forms of value production as integral
regions within the complex whole of capitalism. Instead, it is either
forced to confront them as "outsides" whose relationship to capital
remains unclear; or domesticate them within a suspect anthropology as
precapitalist, premodern survivals.

As a scholar who is constantly mindful of Marx's legacy for postcolonial studies, Chakrabarty's intellectual project has straddled the
uneasy divide between capital's global aspirations and impacts and
the Eurocentrism of historical knowledge, including Marx's theory of
capitalism. Thus, a fuller understanding of how Chakrabarty's work
constitutes a critique of Harvey's *Limits* requires wading into the deeply
unsettled debate on the putative Eurocentrism of Marx. There are two
lines of critique in this debate.

The first approach renders Marx as a historicist who advocates a
stagist theory of historical development that situates Europe "as the site
of the first occurrence of capitalism, modernity, or Enlightenment,"[88]

and as the cultural referent by which development in all other societies ought to be evaluated. There is certainly room to read Marx this way, for instance, his claim in the *Grundrisse* that "[b]ourgeois society is the most developed and the most complex historic organization of production."[89] At the same time, there is enough contrary evidence to suggest that Marx was a supple and open dialectical thinker who, faced with changing historical circumstances, was able to revise—even reject—the Eurocentrism of his earlier views. Pranav Jani, for instance, makes a compelling argument that the Revolt of 1857 in India led Marx to critique both his notion of an Asiatic Mode of Production and the progressivism of British Rule (a rejection that was strengthened by accounts of British atrocities in post-Revolt India and the brutal suppression of Fenian republicanism in Ireland).[90] Similarly, August Nimtz argues that after the failed revolutions of 1848–49 in Europe, Marx and Engels gradually discarded their belief in the European working class as the revolutionary vanguard and increasingly came to view "the entire globe as their theater of operations."[91] However, neither Nimtz's defense nor (to a lesser degree) Jani's confronts the criticism that Marx's theory of capitalism is Eurocentric *not in the parochialism of its spatial imaginary but rather in the presuppositions from which it derives epistemic warrant.*

Here we come to the second line of critique, namely that there are certain underlying assumptions of a distinctly European provenance without which Marx's theory of capital cannot function. Hence, in *Rethinking Working Class History,* Chakrabarty argues that workers in the jute mills of Calcutta were never able to muster a working-class consciousness or politics because they were divided by ties of community and by the "hierarchical and inegalitarian nature of the relationships of power" within the mills.[92] That is, Marx's notion of human emancipation presupposes a notion of juridical and political "equality" and "citizenship"—indeed, an abstract concept of the "human"—that was simply not available to workers in Calcutta's jute mills. As such, a socialist politics was not only *not* possible but also, more emphatically, to write a labor history of the jute mills within the prefabricated categories of Marxism would be patently false.

While we should appreciate the founding gesture of this critique— the intertwined problem of translation/representation in explanation— the premise of Chakrabarty's critique, namely, the impossibility of class analysis or class politics because the "power relationships that made up . . . [workers'] everyday life arose out of a culture that was hierarchical and inegalitarian, subordinating the individual to imagined communities of a distinctly precapitalist character,"[93] borrows straight from the same sociological meta-narrative of modernity that Chakrabarty is intent on displacing. How else can Chakrabarty speak in naturalistic terms of "precapitalist communities" or of "a culture," as if there were such autonomous objects of knowledge? One could also ask why post-colonial critics like Chakrabarty disregard the possibility that Marxist ideas might have traveled, along with capital, from the metropole to the peripheries?

Chakrabarty acknowledges some of these shortfalls in *Provincializing Europe*.[94] Steadied by an autocritique of his earlier work and a more sophisticated reading of Marx, Chakrabarty proceeds to unpack the category of "abstract labor" upon which the process of generalized commodity exchange is premised. He observes that "Marx's philosophical category 'capital' is global in its historical aspiration and universal in its constitution,"[95] then gestures to what I consider his book's central question: What does the logic of capital implicated in the idea of "abstract labor" mean for historical difference (both lived difference and the writing of histories of difference)? This question could be alternatively posed as follows: What does the universalizing geography of capitalism imply for the plurality of "lifeworlds" and their "representation" within Western academy?

Chakrabarty's answer is precise:

> As is well known, the idea of "history" was central to Marx's
> philosophical understanding of "capital." "Abstract labor" gave
> Marx a way of explaining how the capitalist mode of production
> managed to extract from peoples and histories that were all different
> a homogenous and common unit for measuring human activity.
> "Abstract labor" may thus be read as part of an account of how the
> logic of capital sublates into itself the differences of history.[96]

In short, abstract labor serves a mediating function in a process of translation. It is the common term—not an empirically verifiable "thing" but rather a "social substance" with "phantom-like objectivity"[97]—that allows qualitatively different and otherwise incommensurable activities of work, sometimes inhabiting nonsecular temporalities outside the time of "history," to be brought into commerce *and* conversation with each other.[98] In an evocative passage on "commodity fetishism" in *Specters of Marx*, Derrida describes the

> phantasmagoria of *commerce* between market things . . . when a piece
> of merchandise *(merx)* seems to enter into a relation, to converse,
> to speak *(agoreuein)*, and negotiate with one another, corresponds
> *at the same time* to a naturalization of the human *socius*, of labor
> objectified in things, and to a denaturing, a denaturalization, and a
> dematerialization of the thing become commodity, of the wooden
> table when it comes on stage as exchange-value and no longer as
> use-value.[99]

The denunciation here of the objectification of living labor in the commodity-form; the "violence" of a process of translation and representation that institutes relations of abstract equivalence, permitting radically different social use-values to truck with each other as commodities; and the subtle jab at Hegel's concept of identity, all bear directly on Chakrabarty's critique of capitalist modernity. Chakrabarty relies heavily on theoretical openings in Marx's *Grundrisse* and the displacement of Hegelian dialectics in Derrida's notions of "différance" and "trace" to make his argument. He contends that although capital sublates "difference" (Chakrabarty variously invokes "History 2s," "concrete/real labor," and "subaltern pasts" as examples) into its Being, these continue to "inhere in capital and . . . interrupt and punctuate the run of capital's own logic."[100] He makes much of the fact that Marx, in describing bourgeois society as "the most developed and the most complex historic organization of production" in *Grundrisse*, then goes on to add that

> [t]he categories which express its relations, the comprehension of its
> structure, thereby also allows insights into the structure and relations
> of production of all the vanished social formations out of whose
> ruins and elements it built itself up, whose *partly still unconquered
> remnants are carried along with it,* whose mere nuances have
> developed explicit significance within it, etc.[101]

Chakrabarty reads Marx's claim about "unconquered remnants," along with other instances in *Grundrisse*, as an opening for History 2s—those traces of other ways-of-being that continue to dwell within capital.

Derrida's notion of "trace" also provides an important corrective, although Chakrabarty does not explicitly flag this, to the logic of double negation that is both the power and failing of Hegel's logic of identity—and whose suffocating embrace Chakrabarty must renounce in order to sustain his thesis. Why? In a trenchant critique of Hegel, Deleuze writes:

> Hegelian contradiction does not deny identity or non-contradiction: on the contrary, it consists in inscribing the double negation of *non-contradiction* within the existent in such a way that identity, under that condition or on that basis, is sufficient to think the existent as such. Those formulae according to which "the object denies what it is not," or "distinguishes itself from everything that it is not," are logical monsters (the Whole of everything which is not the object) in the service of identity. . . . Difference is the ground, but only the ground for the demonstration of the identical. Hegel's circle is not the eternal return, only the infinite circulation of the identical by means of negativity.[102]

It is precisely because negativity is incorporated into the definition of identity that Hegel's legacy is so difficult to repudiate. What is *not* is incorporated into the constitution of what *is*.[103] But Hegel reveals himself in this formulation as the philosopher of unity—of "I" (the presupposition) that returns to itself, *non-identically* and *repeatedly*, as "I" (the result). This is precisely where Derrida's notion of "trace" (or "difference-itself," "reserve," "différance") enters.[104]

As Spivak points out in her translator's preface to *Of Grammatology*, "Derrida . . . gives the name 'trace' to the part played by the radically other within the structure of difference that is the sign."[105] For Chakrabarty, then, the "trace" is that ineffable element—the "unconquered remnant" of the *Grundrisse*, the "radically other" of Derrida, the "History 2s," the "subaltern"—that constantly challenges from within capital its "claims to unity and universality."[106] As such, his critique of capital is both ontological and ethical: ontological because it is a critique of the Hegelian *Aufhebung* that negates difference and leaves no room for the affirmation of diversity; ethical because it demands that historical narratives, rather than translate all forms of life into the abstract, formalized categories of capital following the logic of generalized exchange, find writing strategies that evade the pull of equivalence. And it is on these ontological and ethical grounds, then, that Chakrabarty finds fault with Harvey's *Limits*.[107] He upbraids Harvey for asserting that "from the standpoint of capital, workers are indeed objects, a mere 'factor' of production—the *variable form* of capital—for the creation of surplus value."[108] This seems to leave no room for workers to constitute forms of existence, identification, opposition and *affirmation* that are independent of the law of "value."

Is Chakrabarty's criticism valid? On the face of it, it would appear so because Harvey here seems to ignore Marx's statements to the contrary. Consider, for example, this passage from *Grundrisse:* "Labor is not only the *use value* which confronts capital, but, rather, is *the use value* of capital itself. As the not-being of values in so far as they are objectified, labor is their being in so far as they are not-objectified; it is their ideal being; the possibility of values, and, as activity, the positing of value."[109] Now it is true that in subsequent sentences Marx qualifies that it is only "through contact with capital"—that is, through its objectification—that labor becomes "really value-positing"; even so, this objectification, Marx goes on to suggest, is not of a permanent character but rather one of repeated suspension of living labor as it enters the process of production.[110] In short, *there is a living, creative potential in labor that is irreducible;* that persistently survives objectification by capitalist social relations. More provocatively, labor's potential to produce surplus—capitalist and otherwise—provides a spinozist understanding of capitalism as a distinct regime of value that has taken hold through a logic of contingent necessity; and whose facticity consists of aleatory joinings of matter-substance that harness labor's potential for producing surplus with historically unparalleled intensity.

In a curiously nostalgic formulation in the afterword to *Limits* that is at odds with the magisterial analysis that precedes it, Harvey gives credence to Chakrabarty's critique by gesturing to the unassimilable aspect of labor: "[T]hough susceptible to all manner of influence through bourgeois institutions and culture, nothing can in the end subvert the control workers exercise over certain very basic processes of their own reproduction. Their lives, their culture, and, above all, their children are for them to reproduce."[111] Coming on the heels of a rigorous exposition of the "extraordinary power of capital to adapt to the varying circumstances in which it finds itself—circumstances that include tremendous diversity 'in nature' as well as in 'human nature'" and which relegates worker militancy to a "noble rearguard action fought here, the specific resistance offered there, [that] may be important for understanding the uneven development of world capitalism ... [but that] fade into insignificance, become irrelevant, when judged against the broad sweep of the history of capitalist accumulation,"[112] Harvey's belated invocation of the sphere of reproduction as a bastion of worker autonomy and hope is, at once, odd, charming, and inadequate.

Harvey's summoning of workers' "lives, their culture, and, above all, their children" as domains beyond the remit of capital nicely captures the predicament of left politics—namely, where to find and how to construct spaces of resistance that can evade the insidious reach of capital. I have argued so far that the question of the "outside," as a prolegomena to politics, can be pressed by unsettling Marx's interlinked categories of "labor" and "value" in one of two ways. The first is from the vantage point of agrarian studies, which foregrounds the cultural politics of economy, society, and nature and their conjunctural articulations *and* disarticulations with capital. The second is via postcolonial studies, which strives to de-sediment the West's representations of the non-West. It does so by textualizing universalizing narratives, such as those of capital, which emerge from the geographic and epistemic space of "Europe."[113] Rather than seek an ontological "exterior," as agrarian studies does, postcolonial critics expose those moments of crisis within the "text" that make visible the contingency of its meanings and how an "outside" is inscribed "within" the text at the moment of its founding. Their deconstructive method pries open radical alterity: the irreducible "traces" of other ways-of-being within categories like "labor" and "value" that constitute capital and enable its circulation as structuring social force *and* academic master-narrative (more on this in the afterword).

Chakrabarty critiques both forms of capital in *Provincializing Europe*. However, before I render a final verdict on the success of his project and its implications for *Limits*, it is useful to situate his intervention within the wider landscape of Left critique. Schematically, Left politics has emerged from one of two positions:[114] a critique of capitalism *from the standpoint* of labor and a critique *of labor* in capitalism. The former, characteristic of Marxist scholars like Georg Lukács, Henri Lefebvre, Enrique Dussel, and the Harvey of *Limits*, identifies the working class as the agent of capitalism's transcendence by virtue of its privileged epistemological and ontological position within the capitalist system. The latter—a more loosely arrayed set of positions—associated with Spinozist Marxists like Antonio Negri, Michael Hardt, Paolo Virno, and Gilles Deleuze (to name but a few), post–Frankfurt School Marxists like Moishe Postone, Althusserians like Warren Montag and Jason Read, and postcolonial critics like Gayatri Spivak and Dipesh Chakrabarty tries to pry loose "labor's" heterogeneity and creativity from its abstract domination under capital by "value" *and* from the "speculative philosophical economy" of the dialectic, which constantly negates difference in service of higher meaning/unity/profit.[115]

Chakrabarty, as indicated, inhabits the second group of Left scholars. His critique calls for resisting the epistemic pull of capital, which he does by foregrounding the politics of translation and by affirming the singularity of diverse forms of life within capitalist modernity. By contrast, the Harvey of *Limits* remains firmly within—indeed, consolidates—the epistemic space of capital. At one point he makes this telling declaration:

> It should be noted that Marx was indeed deeply influenced by Hegel's *Logic,* and that we should therefore not be surprised to find that the concept of value contains its own negation in the form "not-value." ... Quite simply, we can say that if value is interpreted as human labor in its social aspect under capitalism, then "not-value" can be interpreted as human labor that has lost its social meaning owing to processes *that are also unique to capitalism.*[116]

Here, "not-value" remains in a binary and dependent relation to capital. So pervasive is the optic of capital that not-value as a prospective space of difference or alterity *not contingent on the logic of capital* is simply never registered. In short, Harvey appears to preclude a politics of work as I earlier defined it.

The Becoming-Being of Capital

Let me reiterate at this point—perhaps a limit-point in the encounter between Harvey and Chakrabarty?—that I do not pose the politics of labor and the politics of work as mutually exclusive forms of opposition to capital. They function differently. Furthermore, despite my disaffections with Harvey, the virtue of *Limits* is to render "capital" as a multiplicity of forces (different fractions of capital, different types of capital, different circuits of capital with different tempos of circulation—all held together by mobile connections between human and nonhuman actors). There is a layered spatiality in this imagination of capital that is, oddly enough, missing in Chakrabarty. Despite his otherwise incisive, even brilliant, denouements of capital-centric narratives, his own understanding of capital remains quite flat and schematic. For example, Chakrabarty's problematic artifice of History 1 and History 2s would be unnecessary if capital were understood to be, in agreement with Whitehead, as a "one that is many"—that is to say, a concrescence of multiple fractions and forces that are territorialized by power/knowledge to produce the effect of an expressive whole—a dialectical, interior unity—that takes the name "capitalism." Incongruously, then, Chakrabarty ends up repeating a dualism—and with it, an impasse—that made its appearance years ago. Indeed, in the very first volume of *Subaltern Studies*, in Ranajit Guha's inaugural essay on subaltern historiography. In staking out as this alternative historiography's point of departure the structural dichotomy that differentiated elite politics from subaltern politics, Guha had famously declared:

> There were vast areas in the life and consciousness of the people
> which were never integrated into [the Indian bourgeoisie's]
> hegemony. . . . Such dichotomy did not, however, mean that these
> two domains were hermetically sealed off from each and there was
> no contact between them. On the contrary, there was a great deal of
> overlap arising precisely from the effort made from time to time by
> the more advanced elements among the indigenous elite, especially
> the bourgeoisie, to integrate them. Such effort when linked to
> struggles which had more less clearly defined anti-imperialist objects
> and were consistently waged, produced some splendid results.[117]

The unresolved conflict in Guha's text—its failure to adequately theorize *how* subaltern consciousness manages to remain ontologically autonomous ("outside" as it were) of elite conceptions of the world—carries over into Chakrabarty's analysis almost twenty years later. Indeed, this lacuna is the site of an ironic convergence between the Marxist intellectual, Harvey, and his postcolonial critic, Chakrabarty. And it is precisely at this juncture where the merits of Althusser's rendering of capital as a "complex whole" become apparent.

Althusser's theory of structural domination, with its logic of overdetermination, offers a generative way out of the impasse. The "economy" (or, if you prefer, the law of value) is revealed as the ordering, diagrammatic structure of capitalism. Like development, it repeats with difference in its concrete effects. It has an absent presence and its domination of other regions of life follows the strange causal logic of "contingent necessity." Importantly, domination does not operate by instrumentally subordinating diverse regions to "economy." Rather, it articulates them within a coexisting whole in the same loose but essential manner that the trunk of a body joins limbs as part of a functional whole. The limbs can't function without a trunk, but the trunk is useless without limbs. Capitalism as a social formation is an articulated hierarchy, but hardly one that can be reduced to the primacy of a center. Moreover, what historically becomes the trunk and what takes the shape of limbs is an aleatory outcome within this formulation. Who knows what the capitalist body may become in future articulations? It should not surprise us that this question is an open possibility in Althusser's thought, or that it is reminiscent of Spinoza. Spinoza was, after all, one of Althusser's favorite philosophers.

Let us return, then, to the figures of History 1 and History 2s. Why do I claim that these might be redundant devices were capital to be recognized as different-in-itself? In Chakrabarty's narrative History as the Time of Capital (or Capital as History) implicates the continuing imperialism of Europe. More than merely a geographic entity, "Europe" is the colonizing desire of modernity itself. In its quest to universalize, Europe systematizes and gives coherence—even synchronicity—to the discontinuities and textures of time. But can capitalism be annexed with such ease to the imperial projections of Europe? Is there a "Time of Capital"? I suggest not. Its temporality has always been a "time of times." With its heterogeneous fractions enabled by variegated circuits of human and nonhuman joinings, capital has always led a para-sitic existence. It has always contained multiple histories. And each of these histories, *even when life is structured-in-dominance to capitalist value,* has remained an interlacing of multiple value-productions that are not-capital. Thus, there can be strictly speaking no single "Time of Capital."

What does all this imply for forms of politics as previously described? It does *not* mean capital's effects are not powerful. Quite the contrary, it means that they are multiply powerful and molecular, but also fissured. To the extent that the value-form of labor is the starting point of capital and abstract labor the defining aspect of the value-form, this ontological move vastly expands the terrain of labor geographies and the mandate of labor politics. Furthermore, it leaves no room for renderings of capitalism as an expressive unity that coheres around an inexorable, interior logic such as the law of value. What are instead dragged to the forefront are a series of diffuse and disparate normative practices—effaced labors, strivings—struggling to make *life in common* possible.

Geographies and politics of work, then, pull our attention to the acts of fabrication that sustain life and species being. But they also direct us to sites where *work* is enrolled as *value* through various modalities of power. These enrollments are, by any reckoning, fraught—even violent—processes that involve the constantly iterated suspension of living, creative, concrete labor and its objectification as abstract labor. It is precisely in these iterative, enacted and immanent geographies of abstracting that any "law of value" resides.

In *The Limits to Capital* David Harvey, as mentioned earlier, felicitously portrays capital as "value 'in motion.'" The unrelenting accent on various networks of capital circulation, each with different turnover times, none necessarily complementary to the other, is one of the book's gripping insights. It also exposes one of the presuppositions of capital: that for value to expand it must travel—restlessly—through different phases. Moreover, like a passenger its travels entail out-of-pocket expenses (deductions from surplus-value),[118] and like any passenger, it faces the constant threat of an accident or breakdown (even death, *negation*) that can bring the journey to an abrupt halt. The simile of value as passenger precisely conveys one of the principal themes in a politics of work: namely, never losing sight that value is contingently enabled within and by more-than-human networks of circulation.

Caveats to the Politics of "Zero-Work"

Gayatri Chakravarty Spivak observes that if "the critique of political economy were simply a question of restoring a society of use-value, this would be an aporetic moment."[119] I take this remark to mean that Left politics can neither afford to lose sight of the singular importance of use-values in immanent projects of emancipation; nor can it afford to naively celebrate use-values without paying careful attention to the international—and highly unequal—division of labor. On the one hand, expanding the realm of needs (or use-values) of workers and for workers is clearly an important task for labor politics. In *The Communist Manifesto,* Marx and Engels scorn "bourgeois society" for its merely instrumental regard of workers' lives (where "living labor is but a means to increase accumulated labor"). Denouncing the "bare existence" of workers under capitalism, they press the case for a communist society where "accumulated labor . . . [will be] a means to widen, to enrich, to promote the existence of the laborer."[120] This agenda, in varying forms, has been zealously promoted by a bevy of scholars associated with the Frankfurt School: Alfred Schmidt, Herbert Marcuse, and, most recently, Moise Postone. But others in the Frankfurt School, most prominently Max Horkheimer and

Theodor Adorno, warned of the dangers of this politics dissipating into an unbridled consumerism, with an accommodationist stance towards capital.[121]

The debate around a politics of use-values can be sliced another way. Hence, the Italian *Autonomia* tradition, associated most popularly with the writings of Antonio Negri, presses a manifesto for nondialectical Marxism that revolves around the practice of "self-valorization." In *Marx Beyond Marx,* Negri's provocative reading of *Grundrisse,* he advances a program of resistance to capital through a continual expansion of "*the sphere of non-work,* that is, the sphere of their own needs, the value of necessary labor. . . . *the ontological broadening of* [workers'] *use value, through the intensification and elevation of their own needs.*"[122] To the extent that this political program impedes the realization of "value," it interrupts and ultimately short-circuits the dialectic of capital. Spivak's response to this radical agenda is worth reproducing. She writes:

> If a view of *affectively* necessary labor (as possible within the present state of socialized consumer capitalism) as *labor* as such is proposed without careful attention to the international division of labor, its fate may be a mere political avant-gardism. This, in spite of sincere evocations of the world economic system is, I believe, a possible problem with Antonio Negri's theory of zero-work.[123]

The message is clear. While a politics of use-values that scrupulously attends to both labor as the use-value of capital at one end of the value chain and to the consumption of use-values at the other end can vastly expand the terrain and scope of progressive politics—generating new possibilities for articulating "diverse commonalities" and synthesizing "politico-ethical alliances"—it can also dissipate into reactionary consumerism, righteous militarism, economic and moral imperialism, or simply political avant-gardism. In short, it is a politics fraught with openings *and* contradictions.

Earlier I insisted that a commitment to geographies and politics of work entails analyzing value as an assemblage and that, by so doing, the remit of labor politics is vastly enlarged. Why? Because, at the most rudimentary level, it compels attention to the quotidian actions that produce humans as part of more-than-human societies.[124] If we take "subaltern" to be those marginalized but ever-present forces that cannot be dialectically integrated to capital because they are, in some critical way, unintelligible to it (think Ajibhai), then a politics of work is necessarily a subaltern politics. Specifically, it names practices of living and connecting that are transgressive of the established order and that shame and expose its hermetic and depoliticized grids of Difference as *political relations* of difference. Rejecting the sacred and secular motifs of tolerance and multiculturalism, it views participation in society neither as rights-borne privilege nor as charity, but as irrevocable claim to what Georges Canguilhem described as "normal" life—which is to say, *not a life reduced to the norm of self-preservation (which is a pathological normality, a reduced and diminished life) but the opposite—a life of "normativity," of health: the capacity to creatively confront risk and inconstancies in the environment, and court error.*[125] In short, a life of possibilities that is able to deviate from (the constancy of) norms in order to flourish.

A life that can dare to "love"?

AFTERWORD

Aporia

October 1993: I was at the Tribal Research and Training Centre (TRTC) at Gujarat Vidyapeeth, in the city of Ahmedabad, India, trying to track down the original survey forms from a landmark rural survey conducted by the Gandhian economist J. C. Kumarappa and his team in 1929. The survey of 998 households, in the economically deprived subdistrict of Matar in central Gujarat, resulted in a publication called *A Survey of Matar Taluka in Kheda District.*[1] The publication is both a singular early contribution to the emerging field of agricultural economics in India and a stinging indictment of colonial economic policies in then British Gujarat. But its arguments rely on aggregated statistics, and ethnographic detail on agrarian life is markedly absent—almost as if it might compromise the factual gravity of the claims. But it is precisely what is missing that interested me: disaggregated information on the individual households that were surveyed, as well as any ethnographic and margin notes that might have been left out in the formal publication. Was it possible that the actual survey forms had survived the tribulations of time? I was dubious, but an academic colleague in Gujarat recalled using the original forms in the early 1970s, boosting my hopes. I should note that I wasn't interested in a re-survey. My research objectives were both more modest and more ambitious.

I had arrived for fieldwork in Gujarat strongly influenced by a rich and eclectic peasant studies literature, particularly the theories of agrarian change associated with Karl Kautsky, V. I. Lenin, A. V. Chayanov, L. N. Kritsman,[2] and, more recently, Eric Wolf and Teodor Shanin.[3]

But like Kumarappa's survey, these otherwise exemplary studies suffer from lack of ethnographic and structured historical insight into intra- and interhousehold interactions and how they influence patterns of agrarian differentiation. By contrast, Tom Kessinger's monograph *Vilyatpur, 1848–1968*[4]—a book that along with Arvind Das's remarkable biography of the village of Changel[5] has left an indelible impression—reconstructs agrarian change in a single place via the innovative use of archival materials and family genealogies. Understandably enough, its considerable microeconomic and micropolitical insights come at the expense of theoretical exactness. Was it possible, I wondered, to combine the analytic rigor of Kautsky and others with the methodological virtuosity of Kessinger to put to "test" the former's longitudinal predictions?

If I could trace descendants of a representative subsample of households from Kumarappa's original survey and be privy to the household-level information gathered by his team in the 1929 survey, then there was a distinct possibility, I thought, of pulling this off. So there I was on a scorching October morning, waiting for the gates of TRTC to open. It was a moment of anticipation and excitement, one of those singular markers by which the uncertain arc of fieldwork gets inscribed in memory. I had good reason to be hopeful that Kumarappa's surveys were within grasp.

Gujarat Vidyapeeth, the site of TRTC, was established in 1920 by Mohandas Karamchand (Mahatma) Gandhi as an alternative institution of higher education for Indian students. Gandhi imagined that the Vidyapeeth would pursue an anticolonial pedagogical and political mission by emphasizing, among other things, a non-orthodox curriculum to be taught in the Gujarati vernacular rather than the colonizers' English. Here, serendipity steps in as the guiding hand of fieldwork. Gandhi, as it happens, had asked my grandfather, Assudomal Gidwani, to serve as the first *Acharya* (vice-chancellor) of Gujarat Vidyapeeth. This fact emerged incidentally when I mentioned to a relative that I was about to visit the Vidyapeeth. Once aware, I casually—even opportunistically—assumed that this information would help me navigate the bureaucratic hurdles of a government institution. I was wrong. My lineage meant absolutely nothing to the head clerk at TRTC. On the other hand, the fact that I was a researcher based in the United States who at the time spoke fledgling Gujarati and had the audacity to assume that I could waltz in expecting to gain ready access to *his* records room meant everything. Over the course of the next few days he repeatedly rebuffed me: first, I needed permission from the Director of TRTC; when I brought such a letter, the key to the records room was missing; when I kept returning, he declared that the records room had been flooded this past monsoon thanks to a broken window. That it was doubtful that the materials I wanted could be salvaged. When I asked if I could nevertheless check, he looked at me with contempt and said, "I am the head clerk, don't you believe me?" His undisguised hostility (which at the time I could not fathom) mutely challenged me to do something about it. He bargained on the fact that in practice there was little I *could* do. He was right.

My deeply anticipated research project was defeated before it started. I had to scramble to recover from the setback, and for many years thereafter I would revisit my encounter with the head clerk with an amalgam of savage regret and resentment—and bafflement.

It took me a while to accept another narrative of those pivotal events: why the head clerk at TRTC had responded so sharply to me despite what I took to be my unassuming manner. What I thought was a straightforward request to view available records may have struck him—in the absence of initial mediation and proper acknowledgment of his authority—as an affront. His hostility could be read as a subaltern critique of both my class privilege (my assumption that I had the *right* to access what I took to be public records at a government institution) and northern academic production (that I could use this information to advance *my* goals and career in the United States).

The rudiments of this critique, which can come in varying styles, are not particular to place but rather to the gradient that connects researchers in the north to global field destinations in the south. The anthropologist Hugh Raffles describes this incidental conversation with Moacyr, a skilled and deeply knowledgeable Brazilian research assistant:

> At one point—we were talking about foreign researchers—Moacyr asked me how it was that foreigners could come here, get to know maybe one or two places, perhaps a couple more if they stayed a long time, and then return to their universities, stand it front of roomfuls of students, and teach about somewhere called Amazonia. What he asked, with a mixture of bafflement, irony, and refusal, allows them to make such a claim: to pretend that they know *Amazonia?*[6]

Here Moacyr displays wonder at how his knowledge of Amazonia, vastly more detailed and nuanced than that of the foreign researchers who hire him, is undervalued in the global political economy of knowledge production. Although the tenor of his critique differs from the TRTC head clerk's their responses reveal shared subaltern disquiet about capitalist circuits of knowledge, where those who control means of production—credentialized northern researchers—profit most heavily.

I can now state my two principal claims. First, knowledge is produced as a commodity within a spatial division of labor that characteristically profits researchers in the metropole. Second, this production is indelibly marked by another connective geography: *a politics of translation that is at once a politics of transportation.*[7] To count as "knowledge," information must be moved from the peripheries to a metropolitan location and be given recognizable form within prevailing disciplinary protocols and debates.[8] These claims throw up a third and corollary argument, that research conducted from the north in the global south is necessarily *aporetic:* it must proceed but in order to proceed it must navigate blockages or nonpassages, which I gloss as the "ethicopolitical."[9] The ethicopolitical marks zones of *liminality* where the prior certitudes of theories and methodologies are confronted by demands that cannot be anticipated or resolved a priori.[10] As scholars we encounter the liminal at various junctures: when formulating a research problem, during field-work, and when translating field research into written product.

By likening researchers in the north (including myself) to capitalist entrepreneurs in a global knowledge economy I do not seek to doubt their sincerely held intellectual and ethical convictions. That would be simplistic and disingenuous. Rather, I suggest that we researchers in the north are bearers of social relationships that are capitalist. To recall Marx via Laclau, "capitalist relations of production consist of a relationship between *economic categories,* of which social actors only form part insofar as they are *Träger* (bearers) of them."[11] Thus, capitalists do not count as concrete persons, of flesh and blood, but as agents of capital. This capitalist, within a mode of production geared to the accumulation of value, has no choice but to relentlessly pursue profit or perish. The advice given to young scholars, "publish or perish", seems to capture precisely this imperative.

Within the northern academy, a researcher's academic survival depends in large measure on the exchange value of her written product, which—like any commodity—depends for its "realization" on its social use-value to the academic community. It must be "consumed." If the social use-value is judged slender or if there is over production (too many similar papers in circulation), then the researcher's product is in a very precise sense, *devalued.* Use-value is always *social* and in the academic context what counts as use-value is governed by the regulative ideals of the prevailing academic canon. As in the corporate world, so in academia; risk-taking can never be completely autonomous from the exigencies of capitalist "value." If anything, nonconventional work—a new approach that bucks orthodoxy or collaborative scholarship that tries to restore authorship to those based in the global south—always runs the danger of being recuperated as avant-garde commodity: the latest novelty on the academic scene.

Where, then, should we look for the liminal moments of the ethico-political? Nowhere—and least of all in textbooks or fieldwork manuals. Eluding anticipation and hence domestication as *knowledge,* they are only instantiated in the practice of research and achieve significance precisely in relation to the problematic of "value." They can only be recognized after the fact. Heuristically, I propose that these moments can be conceptualized as border crossings in two epistemological senses:

First, ethicopolitical moments designate unforeseen ruptures within academic circuits of "value," which jeopardize its production or else realization in circulation. Every researcher encounters liminal moments in the course of research, which put his finely (or crudely!) wrought enterprise of information gathering and production into crisis.[12] At these junctures the circuits of value that garner academic merit or profit are threatened. They can break down. Thus the term "ethicopolitical" struggles to signify those moments when reason finds itself unable to furnish the normative criteria for a decision. But some decision *must* be taken—this is what makes it *aporetic.* The moment must be passed in face of a nonpassage. And depending on its unpredictable effects it may become impossible to continue with the research enterprise in its previously envisioned form.

Second, in the course of processing and re-presenting the field research for circulation and publication, the researcher may arrive at a critical realization—if he has not already—of the regulative ideals that operate him; indeed, of the political economy of uneven development that enables him to profit within the academy. Again, this is a potential moment of crisis, of liminality, where the future trajectory of value is placed into question. The researcher may start to ask what it would mean to write with a primary commitment to extra-academic social use-values that diverge from—even actively reject—the circuits of exchange and academic reward.[13]

Let me partially illustrate these claims. As I have noted earlier in the book, I carried out approximately seventeen months of field research in Matar Taluka of central Gujarat in the mid-1990s. In April 1995, campaigning for the Taluka elections was in full swing. Three candidates were in the fray: the first, a politically experienced and reputedly crooked incumbent from the Congress-I Party, belonging to the affluent but numerically small Rajput caste; the second, a locally powerful *sarpanch* (head of village panchayat) from the landed Patel caste, who was supported by the Bharatiya Janata Party (BJP); and the third, an ex-*shikshak* (teacher) of the Gujarat Vidyapeeth, belonging to the numerically preponderant Baraiya caste, who was waging an improbable campaign for Taluka panchayat chairman as an Independent. His main campaign pledge was to eliminate corruption and, in order to build his identity as "one with the masses" (in contrast to his well-heeled opponents), he had cleverly chosen the bicycle as his election symbol. *"Cycle ne vote aapo"* (Vote for the Cycle) was his improbable refrain. Somehow, that year, his message—which villagers ordinarily might have dismissed as a disingenuous election promise—plucked at the lurking resentment of many villagers, particularly those from subordinate classes, who either felt disenfranchised by an unresponsive and corrupt taluka bureaucracy (small and middle peasants from the so-called *Kshatriya*—Baraiya and Koli Patel—castes); betrayed by the unfulfilled pledges of development by the Congress-I (Kshatriyas, Muslims, and Dalits); or threatened by the Hindu nationalist BJP (Muslims and Dalits). Local elections in India, like their national counterpart, are games of patronage that fracture constituencies into interest groups—which then have to be soldered into new hegemonic blocs. In this kinetic process, neither tactics of hegemony nor interests and subjectivities are constant.

One of the villages where I was doing fieldwork became bitterly divided. The unlikely coalition of Brahmins, Patels, Kshatriyas, Muslims, and Dalits that had emerged during the village (*gram panchayat*) elections in 1993 to prevent a rival coalition of Bharwads and miscellaneous castes (including dissenters from the majoritarian Kshatriya castes) from capturing the seat of sarpanch fell apart during the Taluka election campaign. The Brahmins and Patels defected from their coalition and formed a new alliance with the Bharwads to campaign for the BJP candidate. Meanwhile, the Kshatriyas, Muslims, and Dalits put their weight behind the Independent candidate. During this election fray, I was seated one afternoon at the *galla* (petty store) of a Patel acquaintance discussing the various candidates when a young Muslim laborer walked over to purchase *beedis*. My Patel acquaintance asked him whom he was planning to support in the Taluka election. The youth mumbled an evasive answer, saying he wasn't sure. The Patel shop owner, a village-level BJP organizer, asked again. He was again rewarded with an inconclusive answer. At this point a young Brahmin landowner and self-styled BJP leader walked over to the galla. He confronted the clearly intimidated Muslim youth and pointedly asked him why the Muslims in the village were supporting the Independent candidate, and not the BJP one. Giving the youth no chance to respond, he went on to accuse Muslims at large of being unpatriotic and seditious, parading the familiar allegation that during televised cricket matches between India and Pakistan, the Muslims in the village, as elsewhere, always cheered for Pakistan. (The Muslim boy protested that he barely watched television.) Then, with unexpected vehemence, he proclaimed that all Muslims (*miyan lok*) in Gujarat should have been "put on the train to Godhra in 1947." The frightened Muslim boy shuffled uneasily, avoided our gaze, and quietly walked away.

There are many inferences one could extract from this story, not the least of which is the way in which majoritarian ideologies operate by generating negative stereotypes of minority groups within regional and national borders. The Brahmin landowner's tirade stemmed from anxiety about the Taluka election in which the BJP candidate appeared to be trailing behind the Independent, in large part because, like the Congress-I incumbent, he had a reputation for being corrupt and parochial (the Independent candidate eventually won the election). But this anxiety about local politics and economics quickly became a communal discourse about the lack of reliability of Muslims in India, an indictment of their absent patriotism. It never struck him to consider that his candidate might be lagging in the elections because of questionable character; or that Baraiyas and Kolis in the village—his recent allies—were the primary vote bank of the Independent candidate. Significantly, he would have never thought of questioning the patriotism of the Kshatriyas, because his tirade contained the unsaid and taken-for-granted supposition that Hindus are, definitionally, loyal Indians.

But I was unclear about the allusion to Godhra, so I asked. The Brahmin BJP organizer told me that his reference was to an incident during the Partition, when Muslims attempting to flee by train to the Pakistani border from troubled areas in Gujarat were slaughtered in large numbers at Godhra Junction in north Gujarat. This was a liminal moment for me. The Brahmin landowner was an influential presence in the village in which I was doing fieldwork, and opposing him in public could have imperiled my ability to continue with field research in a village where I had already "invested" six-odd months. I had no idea what those consequences could be, but at *that* moment I could not stand by without taking a stand—either to let the moment pass by in silence or to confront my Brahmin interlocutor. In that instant I experienced neither the epiphany of the protagonist who, at a critical juncture in the novel, proclaims—"I knew then what I had to do!"—nor the steadfastness and prescience that is the gift of those with unshakeable convictions. I felt timid and alone, consumed by guilt, and acutely conscious of the looming decision. I decided to object to the Brahmin landowner's words, at which point he turned to me and told me that I was exactly the sort of weak and unpatriotic *Gandhivaadi* (follower of Mahatma Gandhi's ideas) who had done most damage to the country, by tolerating and thereby stoking Muslim sedition.[14] My research was not severely impaired, although my interactions with the Patel shopkeeper and the Brahmin landowner subsided considerably thereafter.

On another occasion, in another village, the consequences of a decision were different. As I have previously indicated in the book, early introductions—particularly when new and unfamiliar to an area—can have lasting consequences. Getting off on the wrong foot with an individual or a community can make it difficult to salvage relations down the road. Jan Breman, a Dutch anthropologist who has done pioneering work on labor politics in Gujarat, notes that members of the dominant caste—ever keen to maintain control—exert a gravitational pull on outsiders, particularly unknown quantities like researchers. They approach them, invite them, query them, monopolize their time, try to plumb their purpose, attempt to fix their social coordinates, and if the outsider shows undue interest in village affairs, endeavor to influence him to their points of view and limit his mobility within the village. In this instance, I was hoping to pursue survey and ethnographic research in a multicaste village, where

Baraiyas are the most numerous but where political control lies with the Patels and their caste allies (Brahmins, Thakkar Vanias, and Panchals).

My first introduction in the village was to one of the wealthiest Patel farmers, Kashibhai, the brother-in-law of a retired Gandhian politician, also a Patel, who lived in a nearby town and whom I had come to respect and like. I allowed myself to be introduced this way—it was a moment of decision, when I saw fit to get a toehold in a village where I was interested in working by the entry route just described. On that very first meeting, Kashibhai had invited Nandubhai Mehta, a Brahmin teacher in the village's middle school, to join us.[15] That same day I was also introduced to a person called Rajatbhai. The entire afternoon was spent in the Patel khadki. When it was time to depart, I was surrounded by several Patel farmers who quizzed me at length—who I was, where I came from, why I was here in Ashapuri, and so on.

I was never able to gain the trust of the Baraiya community in Ashapuri. A few individuals did eventually come to acknowledge my presence and even engaged me in discussions. But, as mentioned in the previous chapter, these tended to be the better-off members of the Baraiya community who, understandably, had less reason to be apprehensive or to feel threatened by me. Poorer Baraiyas either avoided me or displayed thinly concealed hostility when I tried to approach them. In the fourteen-odd months that I regularly visited Ashapuri, members of poor Baraiya households only acquiesced to talk to me twice, and under very revealing circumstances. It will suffice to describe one of them. Walking to Ashapuri along the metaled road one day, I saw a youth—he must have been fifteen or sixteen—sitting by the roadside eating a simple lunch of *bajri rotlis, shaak,* and *dungri.* On impulse, I asked whether I could sit down with him. He shrugged his shoulders, so I sat down. I asked him in whose field he was working. With a turn of his head, he indicated an adjacent rice field (which I later discovered belonged to Shamabhai Makwana, one of the few landed Baraiyas and secretary of the village dairy cooperative in Ashapuri). The youth—call him Kanu—was shy but seemed willing to entertain my questions. We talked about his family's economic situation (used to be good, but debts have piled up), relations between Baraiyas and Patels (seeing no one around, Kanu informed me that Ashapuri's Patels always played at dividing the Baraiya community and taking over their lands), sources of credit (the aforementioned Rajatbhai is the largest moneylender in the village, almost half the Baraiya households were in debt to him, Rajatbhai borrows money at low interest from traders in Nadiad and circulates it in Ashapuri at high rates of interest), and so on our conversations went until a motorcycle with two riders—Nandubhai Mehta in the driver's seat and one of the Patel farmers on the pillion—slowed down as they passed us. Nandubhai, looking at Kanu but speaking to me, said, "What's up, Vinaybhai, having a chat?" Kanu, who had been glancing around furtively all throughout, clammed up. Soon thereafter he got up and said he had to go home. I asked whether we could meet again the next day. He nodded uncertainly. We fixed a time and place. He never showed up (and I never tried to chase him down).

As a final illustration, I ask you to recall the events that transpired during my first visit to the Rohit vas in Ashapuri (chapter 5). In that visit, a visiting Rohit schoolmaster had publicly upbraided my escort—the wealthy farmer, K. D. Patel—for his insensitivity to workers' need for rest. I had stayed mostly silent during the exchange that occurred in the Rohit vas, despite agreeing with the sentiments of the visiting schoolmaster. I could have interjected while the exchange was occurring or raised the matter later with K.D.—who, despite his frequently retrogressive views on matters of caste (he once despaired that the caste system was breaking down and wondered, very earnestly, who would clear animal carcasses from village byways if Bhangis rejected their designated function within society), was otherwise an honest, extremely industrious man, who rarely dabbled in village politics. But I let the episode pass by unremarked upon. Why? I am not sure. Perhaps because right then I didn't feel entitled to an opinion on "village matters" that I grasped only lightly (as K.D. had implied for the Rohit schoolmaster); or perhaps because I was afraid it would strain my relationship with K.D., who had taken pains to teach me the details of *kharif* (monsoon) and *rabi* (winter) agriculture (an avocation for which he had a genuine passion and gift). In retrospect, the early associations with Nandubhai Mehta (the local schoolteacher who, I later came to know, was notorious for dishonesty and corruption) and Rajatbhai Patel (the moneylender who sometimes charged usurious rates of interest from borrowers) probably impaired my ability to gain the confidence of the Baraiyas of Ashapuri far more than my association with Kashibhai.

This brings me to the second operative sense of liminality: the ethicopolitical conundrums that mark the translation and re-presentation in abstracted value-form the lived labors of collaborators from the South. Two short clarifications are necessary here. First, when I invoke the term "value" it is not as a labor theory of value that stands—and falls—on labor being the physical substance of value. Instead, as elucidated previously, I draw upon a reading of Marx's theory of value made by Diane Elson. I take "value" to imply that set of rationalizing and normative practices enacted by capital, whereby concrete labor is continuously enrolled and represented in abstracted form through the medium of money, as exchange-value. There is also an implicit argument here about space, as earlier noted: namely, that the move from concrete to abstract labor entails a binding of distanciated events and occurrences into a common, interdependent capitalist space-economy, with money as the key intermediary. What is the academic correlate? It is precisely the "truth" that a work of scholarship must not only circulate as exchange-value but also, in order for its value to be actualized, must be consumed as use-value (by journal referees, conference audiences, faculty colleagues, graduate students, etc.: how else should we account for the importance placed, for instance, on counting citations?).

Second, "representation" implies for me not only the active and inevitable processes of interpretation, translation and writing entailed in the scholarly enterprise (re-presentation); but also the fact that representations that come to count as "value" in the northern academy involve textual and territorial displacement from the subjects and subject matter re-presented. The researcher–producer is a representative who is necessarily dislocated from the subjects he claims to represent.

As mentioned initially, I embarked on thesis field research saturated in Marxist theories of the peasantry and pioneering Indian historical scholarship on place-based agrarian change, intending to carry out a genealogical investigation of social differentiation. Thwarted by a resolute head clerk at TRTC, my research morphed into an ethnographic and historical study of caste formation, agrarian relations and agroecological transformations. Reluctant to jettison my passion for and fixed investments in Marxist theories of agrarian change, I sought to combine the theoretical insights of Marxist geography with marxissant theories of cultural practice and rational-choice models of land, labor, and credit contracts based in the so-called New Institutional Economics (NIE) approach.

What exactly did I expect to achieve? Earlier in that year, I had carefully read Lenin's *fin de siècle* masterpiece *The Development of Capitalism in Russia,* where he set out to investigate the transformation of a simple commodity economy into a capitalist one. The book's core thesis is established early when Lenin observes that the "basis of the commodity economy is the social division of labor."[16] Through an analysis of 1895–96 *Zemstvo* data, he identified four key mechanisms of economic differentiation within agrarian economies: the ability of large farmers to exhibit greater *technical efficiency* because of superior and more timely access to draught cattle, implements, and other capital inputs; to reap economies of scale in production; to circulate cash surpluses as *usurious capital,* extracting interest rents from borrowers; and to *extract surplus value* from wage-workers and utilize it to improve cultivation practices and further accumulate land. He never formally spells out the microeconomics of agrarian interactions. New institutional economics on the other hand does, choosing to understand contractual and social arrangements within agriculture as the outcomes of strategic interaction between rational agents under conditions of imperfect information and/or incomplete markets. Yet neither Leninist political economy nor NIE is much concerned with "cultural practices"—that is, the complex productions that give sense to the everyday lives of people.

Around that time, I had also carefully read Pierre Bourdieu's book, *Outline of a Theory of Practice,*[17] coming away deeply impressed by his exposition of a culturally saturated theory of action. Bourdieu manages to stitch together a Marxist–Weberian analysis of capital as a structuring field of power together with a devastating critique of Levi-Strauss' structural anthropology. He offers an ingenious recuperation of rational choice theory that gathers inspiration from diverse sources: notably, Maurice Merleau-Ponty's phenomenology of perception and Erving Goffman's brilliant forays into the "microsociology" of public interaction. Bourdieu provides a rich tapestry of life in Kabylia—a rugged region of Algeria inhabited by Berbers—where social actors tacitly know how to act and interact in ways that serve to maximize their accumulation of "symbolic" and "material" capital. Actions are not analyzed as discrete units but as embodied practices that emerge from agents' "generative dispositions" and are expressions of *habitus.* Bourdieu makes the provocative claim that these practices are disinterestedly rational: optimizing without agents necessarily being conscious of it. I thought, why not take Bourdieu's propositions and try to fill in the gaps in Marxist/Leninist political economy and NIE? This was easier said than done, and I distinctly remember one incident—having returned to the United States for mid-research consultations—where an advisor, a noted development economist, looked at me as if I had gone mad when I told him, with great excitement, that I was trying to combine Bourdieu's practice theory of rational action with NIE analyses of agrarian arrangements in order to come up with a fuller account of agrarian change. Bourdieu was foreign to his disciplinary canon and he plainly disapproved. It was a moment of passage when I realized that some disciplinary fences were going to be harder to cross than others. A decision loomed. I passed over into Bourdieu's territory, and although I remained on good terms with that particular advisor, his interest in my project waned noticeably.

When I finally returned to the United States and, after a break, revisited my field notes, I was struck by one particular entry from June 1995. It was a simple question: "What am I doing here in Matar?"

That question contained, as I now realize, the germ of this meditation. Without consciously apprehending, I was already beginning to sense the limits of the stabilizing epistemologies to which I was then prone—deductivism and historicism, each of which mistakenly eases the task of research by positing historical change as a logical, unified process. I was also beginning to experience acute disquiet around the conundrums of Northern research, where the demands of formalized, disciplinary knowledge generates an imperative to abstract and repair disjointed instances of the concrete into a coherent narrative that will be judged academically worthy. And yet, here it is.

I offer you this, commodity.

Acknowledgments

I remember a visit to the village of Khada, where my host graciously offered me the "guest toothbrush" (I accepted after a stunned moment of indecision). I remember squatting on toilets so clogged with shit that my hosts had sticks ready at hand in the bathrooms to clear a path into the drain. I remember days so thick with mosquitoes that my body blurred into a vast, continuous itch. I remember when two eight-year-olds showed me a stalk and then giggled in amazement when I said rice instead of wheat ("And you are in college?," they asked). I remember the meeting with an aspiring local politician, a Muslim, who explained his BJP candidacy by saying that it was pro-India, not anti-Muslim. I remember Koli friends asking with morbid fascination whether I could imagine marrying a Harijan girl, and then laughing nervously at my answer. I remember long days tilling the plot of a Raval friend and thinking how I wasn't tough enough to handle his life. I remember a monsoon day when the rain came down in sheets, filling the front room in the house of my hosts, and the daughters-in-law dispatched to clear the water with buckets while the men sipped tea and delivered instructions. I remember the startling generosity of friends and strangers who could ill-afford it. I remember moments of laughter, wonder, knowledge, and seduction. I am formed of these myriad memories that have settled into the detritus of experience.

The debts that underwrite this book are achingly large, and to imagine that I can remember—let alone repay—them all is a conceit I can't begin to entertain. Why I ended up in the sleepy subdistrict of Matar in central Gujarat for fieldwork rather than elsewhere is a tale of several accidents. In early 1992, I accidentally ran across J. C. Kumarappa's 1929 survey of Matar Taluka in the South Asia library at Berkeley. It piqued my interest because at the time I was exploring early-twentieth-century village and regional studies in India. I was doing this to find out whether any of them could provide me sufficiently detailed benchmark data to "test" (with the help of a re-survey) the causal mechanisms embodied in certain theories of agrarian change. My interest in these theories, stoked by two redoubtable scholars at Berkeley, Michael Watts and Gillian Hart, was the culmination of a quite accidental introduction to the field of agrarian studies. The erudite and utterly persuasive Ramachandra Guha is the initial culprit in the story. Ram was sojourning at the School of Forestry and Environmental Studies at Yale University as I was trolling through a long list of graduate programs. I was thinking economics or public policy, but Ram challenged me to be different: why not environmental studies, he asked. Why not, I thought. I wasn't about to argue with the author of *The Unquiet Woods,* a book that made such a gripping argument for the political and environmental sources of poverty. Ram suggested I enroll in a graduate seminar on peasants and resistance that a friend of his, James C. Scott, was teaching in the Department of Political Science at Yale. I gamely agreed. A chance introduction to agrarian studies bloomed into a lasting engagement. At the time, I was feeling disaffected with the mechanical, unitary world of rational-choice economics, and the messy universe of agrarian studies, rich in struggle and contention, was the perfect antidote. Jim Scott reeled me in with the passion and precision of a missionary. Even as my thinking over the years has departed from his, Jim has remained a constant reminder of the possible: an exemplary teacher who is also an exemplary scholar and person.

Once hurled into the field of agrarian studies, it was difficult for me to leave. It would have been decidedly odd had I not found my way to Michael Watts, Gillian Hart, and Alain de Janvry at Berkeley. They are, after all, stalwarts in the field of agrarian studies. No such accusations would have ensued had I not found my way to Jeff Romm. Jeff as Ph.D. advisor was chance discovery. A friend had praised his unorthodox thinking, and as I asked around I heard corroborating testimony from students at Berkeley. I wrote to Jeff, he showed interest, and once again I said why not. Now that the years have passed it's easy to see that Jeff suffered at my hands. But I suffered at his, so I suppose we are even. I can't capture Jeff's contributions in words: his was the underlaboring that enables thought but is effaced by it. He never once allowed me to take leave from critical thinking behind the comforting wall of abstractions. Every time I thought I had given all he coolly demanded more. And in spite of our repeated intellectual disagreements he insisted that I find my own directions rather than meekly follow the paths laid down by scholars before me. These other directions were made possible by the formative influence of some additional figures at Berkeley, each noteworthy: George Akerlof and Pranab Bardhan, whose wide and acute engagements outside economics demonstrated why transgression from disciplinary norms is such fecund practice; as well as Louise Fortmann, Ann Hawkins, and Nancy Peluso, who gave me new tools to think about the entanglements of state, society, and nature.

So there I was, in Matar Taluka, carried by accidents that had somehow traced a line of necessity. I remember my first night in Matar, in a cold, spartan room at the Jain temple *dharamshala,* equipped with mangled Gujarati, a small duffel bag, and acute loneliness. The window to my room opened into a narrow alley with an open sewer. January wasn't enough to dispel the ripe smell of excrement. The dogs howled all night in that alley, and I felt like howling with them. Two days later, I was a guest in Ramankaka's house in Limbasi—invited to stay with his joint family of eighteen (at the time) for as long as I wanted, all on the strength of an uncanny connection. I had planned to stay four months; I ended up staying seventeen.

I first stumbled into Ramanbhai Narsibhai Patel at the Labor Cooperative in Matar. He cut an eccentric figure: dressed in khadi, armed with a thick walking staff, his face wrapped in a coarse brown scarf. Without invitation—hesitation is unknown to the man, I later came to recognize—he started interrogating me in a rapid mix of Gujarati, Hindi, and English. An hour later, he was asking me to pack my bag and come live with his family. Why? At some point in the conversation, perhaps to explain my association with Gujarat, I happened to mention that I was the grandson of Assudomal Gidwani. It was an electric moment. He knew of my grandfather's work at Gujarat Vidyapeeth and in the freedom movement (some of it in nearby Kheda, where my grandfather had set up a school for Harijan children in the 1920s). That was enough to establish my credentials. I can't imagine a more serendipitous encounter.

Ramankaka is a peasant intellectual par excellence, as conversant with Vedic philosophy as he is with Einsteinian physics, as saturated in Gujarati politics as he is in Gujarat literature. Over the past thirteen years, he has shared his incomparable knowledge of the area and its people, doused me in trivia, freely introduced me to acquaintances and strangers across Kheda, and severely tested the limits of any theory that I have claimed to hold. He has done all this with the gruff affection of a father. To Ramankaka, Ba, and their extended family—now mine—I owe more than I can measure.

This immeasurable debt extends to several friends in Matar, who each in their singular ways have made this fitful book possible. Tyebbhai Zamindar (Tyebkaka) and Suresh, whom I leaned on for support on innumerable occasions, deserve special mention; also Rameshbhai, Ambubhai Makwana, Master, Kanubhai Somabhai, Somakaka, Maheshbhai Bharwad, Bhikabhai Patel, Dinubhai Mehta, Kanukaka, Kaki and Jignesh, Dilipbhai Patel, Vasantbhai Jani, Yogeshbhai, Poonambhai Raval, Bhikubhai Makwana, Dasarathbhai, Chotabhai Shanabhai Dabi, Rameshbhai, Leelaben, Arjibhai, Natubhai Brahmbhatt and his associates at the Majoor Sahkaari Mandali in Matar, Jagdishbhai Patel in Hadeva, Mafatbhai Patel in Garmala, Ajaybhai Rathod in Bherai, Gordhanbhai Shambhubhai Patel (now deceased) of Navagam, and numerous other individuals who shared their lives and insights with me in staggering acts of generosity. I remember with gratitude the selfless deed of a remarkable but anonymous individual at the subdistrict Registrar's Office in Matar, who spent hours guiding me through fat books with barely legible entries of land sales and purchases. Thanks also to Albertbhai Christian, Sunilbhai, and Govindbhai for introducing and throwing open the Kheda Collectorate Record Room. Now that time has dulled the discomfort of scorching heat, I can fondly replay days when I combed through dusty files under a lazy fan dangling from a livid tin roof.

I was a novice at fieldwork when I began research in Matar. V. K. Ramachandran and Madhura Swaminathan, then at the Indira Gandhi Institute for Development Research (IGIDR), welcomed me into their home, shared their furrowed knowledge of agrarian issues, and taught me how to write a good survey questionnaire. Anil Gupta at the Indian Institute of Management–Ahmedabad (IIMA) N. S. Jodha who was then at ICIMOD, Kathmandu, and M. V. Nadkarni at the

Institute for Social and Economic Change (ISEC) in Bangalore served as mentors and sounding boards for my initial and sometimes unlikely ideas. Anil Gupta's attentiveness to the connections that hold together a rural economy was particularly important to what I subsequently did. Rakesh Basant, Keshab Das, Sudershan Iyengar, B. L. Kumar, R. Parthasarthy, Amita Shah, Pravin Sheth, and Jeemol Unni at the Gujarat Institute of Development Research (some are now elsewhere) listened, advised, assisted, and fine tuned my thinking of socioeconomic issues in Gujarat. A series of gifted Gujarat scholars inspired through vim and words: Ambubhai S. Patel (then at the Department of Sociology in Vallabh Vidyanagar), R. B. Lall (then director of the Tribal Research and Training Centre, Gujarat Vidyapeeth), Ghanshyam Shah (then at the Center for Social Studies, Surat), S. P. Punalekar (also at CSS, Surat), A. M. Shah (now in Vadodara, retired from the Department of Sociology at Delhi University), and M. B. Desai (retired from the Department of Economics at M.S. University, Vadodara). Professor Manubhai Shah and his family in Ahmedabad were a home away from home, and Deepak, Mauli, and Shraddha Gidwani in Vadodara *were* home, as were Pushpa aunty, Nirma aunty, and Sarla aunty.

The author is a convenient fiction, a one who is many. Geography is written into scholarship through multiple "sites" of authorship—indeed, the weave and span of social relationships that produce the effect of *an* "author." Friends who have adulterated my thinking in unmistakable ways and must therefore bear some responsibility for the book they have enabled (warts and all) include Mark Baker, Cesare Casarino, Sharad Chari, Ben Crow, Navroz Dubash, Marcia Frost, Jim Glassman, Ashok Kotwal, Geoff Mann, Richa Nagar, Anand Pandian, Marty Olson, K. Sivaramakrishnan, Michael Thoms, Joel Wainwright, Melissa Wright, and Darren Zook. Some (Ashok, particularly) will wince at what they read. If I had a caption to detain your unique contributions I would, but, alas, each of you demands a mini-essay, which I have neither time nor patience to write.

At the University of Minnesota, I have had the luck of being surrounded by shockingly talented scholars and friends who have pushed my thinking to the limit: Josh Barkan, Bruce Braun, Cesare Casarino, Arjun Chowdhury, Michael Goldman, George Henderson, Qadri Ismail, Helga Leitner, Arun Saldanha, Abdi Samatar, Simona Sawhney, Rachel Schurman, Eric Sheppard, and Ajay Skaria. Several of these individuals are regular interlocutors who painstakingly commented on draft manuscripts, in part or full. To Josh, Bruce, George, Qadri, Eric, and Ajay, I owe far too much to capture in words. At times I wonder whether my ideas are separable from yours.

A few other individuals, who I deeply admire, were dragooned into reading versions of the manuscript and inspired through their scholarship (in some instances, also friendship): Arun Agrawal, Noel Castree, David Hardiman, John Harriss, Timothy Mitchell, Geoff Mann, Jamie Peck, Vicki Lawson, Gerry Pratt, and K. Sivaramakrishnan. Arun Agrawal and Noel Castree subsequently revealed themselves as reviewers for the University of Minnesota Press; without their incisive comments this book would have been far less.

Thanks also to a set of stellar undergraduate and graduate students at Minnesota, who over the years have challenged me, taught me, and incited the arguments that inhabit this book. Josh Barkan has exceeded the call of duty in this regard. So, too, the talented Sula Sarkar, who produced the maps in the book.

Carrie Mullen, erstwhile editor at the University of Minnesota Press, endorsed the book in its nascent form; Jason Weidemann, my editor at the Press, has stewarded it since. Along the way, he has suffered my vacillations and repeated reneging of deadlines with stoicism, never once wavering in his support for the project. Adam Brunner, editorial assistant, was a model of alarming efficiency and partially offset my writing delays. Nick Maier and Patricia A. Mitchell steered the book through the copyediting (Nick even beyond), and vastly improved its style.

Thinking demands time and resources. The American Institute for Indian Studies, the Population Council, the Izaak Walton Killam Foundation, the College of Liberal Arts at the University of Minnesota, the McKnight Foundation (which underwrites McKnight Land-Grant Professorships at University of Minnesota), and my home departments (Geography and Institute for Global Studies) at the University of Minnesota generously provided these for various segments and iterations of the book. Thanks especially to Evelyn Davidheiser. Donald Clay Johnson, Curator of the Ames Library at the University of Minnesota, was an anchor with his encyclopedic knowledge of South Asia scholarship, intellectual acumen, and friendship.

Who knows when books begin and end? They seem to defy endpoints. This book, among other provocations, is an effort to come to terms with diverse inheritances and quarrels—economic geography, rational-choice theory, post-Walrasian economics, agrarian studies, anthropology, environmental studies, postcolonial criticism, and multiple strands of Marxism. I take the idea of an "inheritance" from political theorist Sheldon Wolin's essay "Contract and Birthright" in *The Presence of the Past: Essays on the State and Constitution* (1989). This essay has been formative for many reasons, but one, the importance of accepting and seizing one's inheritance, stands out. Inheritances have the distinctive quality that they can be ignored but not forsaken. In some undeniable way, we are born into them. They exert a force over us. My birth as a scholar has come with inherited entailments I have since tried to forget, reject, pare, parse, or render compatible. Ultimately, I have come to see that I cannot—and should not—abdicate my birthright. Rather, my task is to reinterpret its elements (some commensurable, others not) for particular intellectual and political projects. The only way to do this is through continuous application of mental and physical labors. Critique, then, is less the practice of sifting, sorting, and judging; it is far more a work that generates, affirms, and reclaims—and along the way transforms.

We are sustained within communities of affect. Aside from friends and family members already mentioned, I would remiss not to recognize the sustenance I have claimed from: Ashish Andley, Shireen, Ajay, and Ajesh Bhargava, Sarina and Kamal Bose, Roshan and Bharati Gidwani, Francis Harvey and Anna Piasecka, Sharad, Sonia, and Tappi Koppikar, Nikhil and Varsha Kripalani, Chander Lall, V. Arivudai Nambi, Deepti and Satyendra Rana, Regina Sadilkova, Rohit Salve and Helena Brykarz, Shreen Saroor, Saroj Sivaramakrishnan (Bala), Shiney Varghese, Navendu Karan, and my in-laws, Karan Singh Verma and Sarla Verma. Thank you all. (I know the book will be unintelligible to some of you, and for others, disagreeable.) My uncle, Vasant Koppikar, never fails to astonish with his talent, fortitude, and thirst for life. A few years ago, when this book was critically ill, he let me stay at his cottage in the Himalayan foothills for a month. 'Mirandella'—sylvan, serene—was a magical antidote. The book recovered.

My final words are reserved for four people. They don't necessarily understand what I do. But they understand that it is important to me and so let me do it—sometimes willingly, often grudgingly. What they possibly don't understand is that they are its conditions of possibility. Pushpa aunty, Divya, Aseem, and Aman: I can't explain what you bring to my life. It's enough to say that without you all this would be meaningless. You are ever mine, and I am ever yours.

Notes

Introduction

1. Stuart Hall, "The Supply of Demand," in *Out of Apathy*, ed. Edward Thompson (London: New Left Books/Stevens and Sons, 1960), 56–97; and Stuart Hall, "The Meaning of New Times," in *New Times: The Changing Face of Politics in the 1990s*, ed. Stuart Hall and Martin Jacques (London: Lawrence and Wishart, 1989), 116–34. Hoggart and Williams, along with E. P. Thompson, are widely acknowledged as the founders of cultural studies.

2. Hall's intellectual trajectory and the criticisms generated in the wake of his *New Times* article are admirably covered in Colin Sparks, "Stuart Hall, Cultural Studies, and Marxism," and Angela McRobbie, "Looking Back at the New Times and its Critics," in *Stuart Hall: Critical Dialogues in Cultural Studies*, ed. David Morley and Kuan Hsing-Chen (London: Routledge, 1996).

3. An expressive theory of causality is inevitably a "historicism," as Louis Althusser has so meticulously analyzed. Historicism is always teleological and always presupposes an underlying unity of elements, that is, a totality. It can take a materialist form (a Second Internationalist mechanicism, where a totality driven by the structural "laws of movement" of capitalism determinately moves toward its final destination) or an idealist form (for right Hegelians, an underlying essence—*Geist* or Spirit—which progressively unfolds as a cumulative process of rational self-understanding, culminating in the perfection of the State; or, for left Hegelians—including Lukács—an arrival of self-awareness on part of the Proletariat as the Subject of History and, by implication, universal emancipation). Two of Althusser's chapters are particularly important in this respect: "The Errors of Classical Economics: An Outline for a Concept of Historical Time" and "Marxism Is Not A Historicism," both in Louis Althusser and Étienne Balibar, *Reading Capital*, trans. Ben Brewster (London: Verso, 1997 [1968]), 91–118, and 119–44, respectively.

4. Sparks, "Stuart Hall, Cultural Studies, and Marxism," 97.

5. See Colin Gordon's instructive commentary on Foucault's thesis that the Chicago School's genius lies in its re-activation and radical inversion of the economic agent as conceived by the liberalism of Hume, Smith, and Ferguson;

see Gordon, "Governmental Rationality: An Introduction," in *The Foucault Effect*, ed. Graham Burchell, Colin Gordon, and Peter Miller (Chicago: University of Chicago Press, 1991), 42–44. The agent of choice who inhabits the Chicago School doctrine of economics is no longer a sovereign, free-willed entity driven by interior "natural laws"; rather, he or she is a creature who responds to environmental conditions by engaging in incremental, often implicit, calculations of benefit and cost. This behavioralism vastly opens up the terrain of analysis of economic theory, and is entirely consistent with an understanding of governmentality as the "conduct of conduct."

6. See Barbara Harriss-White, "India's Socially Regulated Economy," *QEH Working Paper Series,* Working Paper Number 133 *(QEHWS133)* (Oxford: Queen Elizabeth House, Oxford University), 14–16.

7. There are now several books that document the career of Hindutva in Gujarat. See, for example, Radhika Desai, *Slouching Towards Ayodhya: Three Essays* (New Delhi: Three Essays Press, 2002); Siddhartha Varadarajan, ed., *Gujarat: The Making of a Tragedy* (New Delhi: Penguin Books, 2002); Asghar Ali Engineer, ed., *The Gujarat Carnage* (New Delhi: Orient Longman, 2003); Achyut Yagnik and Suchitra Sheth, *The Shaping of Modern Gujarat: Plurality, Hindutva and Beyond* (New Delhi: Penguin, 2005); and Ornit Shani, *Communalism, Caste and Hindu Nationalism: The Violence in Gujarat* (Cambridge: Cambridge University Press, 2007).

8. As Karl Marx so clearly recognized in *The Eighteenth Brumaire of Louis Bonaparte* (New York: International Publishers, 1963).

9. There is no better account of the crisis that contingently produces the theoretical concept of hegemony in the writings of Lenin than the first two chapters of Ernesto Laclau and Chantal Mouffe's acute study, *Hegemony and Socialist Strategy* (London: Verso, 1985).

10. In his glossary to Althusser's *For Marx,* Ben Brewster makes the useful observation that Lenin was opposed to the "ideology of spontaneity" of the Social Democrats, but had enormous regard for the "*real* spontaneity, capacity of action, inventiveness and so on, of the 'masses'"; see Brewster, "Glossary," *For Marx* (London: Verso, 1977 [1969], 254. Here Lenin, like Althusser, reveals the influence of Spinoza, who, *contra* Hobbes, affirmed the force of the multitude. The works of the Italian *Autonomista* Marxists, especially Antonio Negri and Paolo Virno, have been instrumental in the recent revival of interest in Spinoza. Meanwhile, Lenin's attack on "spontaneism" is most forcefully enunciated in his tract, "What Is to Be Done?" There, equating advocates of Economism and (non-Social Democratic) terrorism, he writes: "The Economists and terrorists merely bow to different poles of spontaneity: the Economists bow to the spontaneity of the 'pure and simple' labor movement, while the terrorists bow to the spontaneity of the passionate indignation of the intellectuals, who are either incapable of linking up the revolutionary struggle with the labor movement, or lack the opportunity to do so" (quoted in Henry M. Christman, ed., *The Essential Works of Lenin* [New York: Dover, 1987], 109).

11. Laclau and Mouffe, *Hegemony and Socialist Strategy,* 20. Hall's uptake of this point of view clearly owes to his engagement with Althusser in the early 1970s.

12. Brewster, "Glossary," 250.

13. Notably, Perry Anderson, "The Antinomies of Antonio Gramsci," *New Left Review* 100 (November 1976–January 1977); and Christine Buci-Glucksmann, *Gramsci and the State,* trans. David Fernbach (London: Lawrence and Wishart, 1980).

14. Laclau and Mouffe, *Hegemony and Socialist Strategy,* 48.

15. On this point, see Antonio Gramsci, "Some Aspects of the Southern Question," in David Forgacs, ed., *The Antonio Gramsci Reader* (New York: New York University Press, 2000), esp. 173–74. See also Lenin's remarks from "What is to Be Done?" in Christman, *The Essential Works of Lenin,* 113.

16. Michèle Barrett, "Ideology, Politics, Hegemony," in *Mapping Ideology,* ed. Slavoj Žižek (London: Verso, 1994), 249.

17. Forgacs, *The Antonio Gramsci Reader,* 261; also see Forgacs's entry on hegemony in the same volume, 423.

18. See the editorial, "Not a People's Plan," *Economic Weekly,* June 18, 1955.

19. Ramachandra Guha, *India After Gandhi: The History of the World's Largest Democracy* (New Delhi: Picador, 2007), 223.

20. Karl Kautsky, *The Agrarian Question,* 2 vols. (Winchester, Mass.: Zwan Publications, 1988 [1899]), 1:1–2. It should be pointed out that the "agrarian question" had been the subject of debates within the German Social Democratic movement for years prior to the publication of Kautsky's book, as Kautsky himself acknowledges in the foreword to his study. The great German sociologist Werner Sombart had also given a face to the problem in his *Sozialismus und Soziale Bewegung* (Jena: Verlag von Gustav Fischer, 1905 [1896]).

21. Kautsky, *The Agrarian Question,* 1:10 (italics mine).

22. Michel Foucault, "Nietzsche, Genealogy, History," in *Essential Works of Foucault, 1954–1984,* 3 vols., Vol. 2: *Michel Foucault: Aesthetics, Method and Epistemology,* ed. James Faubion (New York: The New Press, 1998).

23. Michel Foucault, "What Is Enlightenment?," in *Essential Works of Foucault 1954–1984,* 3 vols., Vol. 1: *Michel Foucault: Ethics, Subjectivity and Truth,* ed. Paul Rabinow (New York: The New Press, 1997).

24. Benjamin, quoted in the introductory essay by Rolf Tiedemann, "Dialectics at a Standstill: Approaches to the *Passagen-Werk,*" in Walter Benjamin, *The Arcades Project,* trans. Howard Eiland and Kevin McLaughlin (Cambridge, Mass.: Harvard University Press, 1999), 941.

25. See Timothy Mitchell, "Can the Mosquito Speak?," in *Rule of Experts: Egypt, Techno-Politics, Modernity* (Berkeley: University of California Press, 2002). My characterization of capital's "para-sitic" being paraphrases Mitchell.

26. According to a 2007 United States Census Bureau report, Patel was the most common Indian surname in the United States (and the 172nd most common surname in the country). See David L. Word, Charles D. Coleman, Robert Nunziata, and Robert Kominski, "Demographic Aspects of Surnames from Census 2000," available at http://www.census.gov/genealogy/www/surnames.pdf [last accessed November 24, 2007].

27. Ranajit Guha, *Dominance Without Hegemony: History and Power in Colonial India.* (Cambridge, Mass: Harvard University Press, 1997).

28. See Partha Chatterjee, *The Nation and its Fragments* (Princeton, N.J.: Princeton University Press, 1993), chap. 8 ("The Nation and its Peasants") and chap. 10 ("The Nationalist State").

29. Jacques Derrida interviewed by Maurizio Ferraris; Jacques Derrida and Maurizio Ferraris, "I Have a Taste for the Secret," in *A Taste for the Secret* (Cambridge: Polity, 2001), 33.

1. Waste

1. My synopsis of the Jadunathji Maharaj libel case is based on B. N. Motivala's biography *Karsondas Mulji: A Biographical Study* (Bombay: Karsondas Mulji Centenry Celebration Committee, 1935) and Usha Thakkar's excellent article "Puppets on the Periphery: Women and Social Reform in 19th-Century Gujarati Society," *Economic and Political Weekly*, January 4–11, 1997, 46–52. Karsandas Mulji's newspaper article, which was at the center of the libel case, went by the title, "The Original Religion of the Hindus and the Present Heterodox Opinions"; see Motivala, *Karsondas Mulji*, 106–11, and also Karsandas Mulji, *History of the Sect of Maharajas, or Vallabhacharyas, in Western India* (London: Trübner and Co., 1865).

2. The sect of Vallabharcharya, also known as Pushti Marg (literally, "the way of enjoyment"), emerged in the sixteenth century and distinguished itself from other Hindu sects by preaching the worship of god—specifically the amorous, playful Balkrishna, whose exploits with the *gopis* (female cowherds) dominate the tenth book of the *Bhagvat Purana*—"with pomp and abundance of flowers, food, and items of luxury" (Thakkar, "Puppets on the Periphery," 47). Pertinently, the Maharajas (of whom there were sixty to seventy dispersed throughout India at the time of the libel case) were regarded by their followers as incarnations of Krishna, to be worshipped and indulged with favors including, apparently, sexual ones—just as one would Krishna.

3. Motivala, *Karsondas Mulji*, 366; quoted in Thakkar, "Puppets on the Periphery," 51.

4. Mulji, *History of the Sect of Maharajas*, Appendix, 103–4; quoted in Thakkar, "Puppets on the Periphery," 51.

5. Mulji, *History of the Sect*, 81; quoted in Thakkar, "Puppets on the Periphery," 51.

6. Tellingly, Motivala's centennial biography of Karsondas Mulji carries the following dedication: "DEDICATED TO THE SACRED MEMORY OF SIR JOSEPH ARNOULD, Kt., The noble Judge of the Supreme Court of Bombay, whose lucid judgment in the Maharaja Libel Case thoroughly vindicated the righteousness of the crusade, in the cause of Truth and Purity in religion, against the moral immoral practices prevalent in the Vaishnava Sect of Vallabhacharya, wages to vehemently against heavy odds, with the help of a band of zealous and earnest reformers of all communities by KARSONDAS MULJI . . . "; see Motivala, *Karsondas Mulji*.

7. For reasons that will become evident it is "development" rather than its cognate "progress" (the more commonly used term in the writings of liberal philosophers) that I believe better describes liberalism's problematic.

8. Few scholars have illuminated this as clearly as James Ferguson and Timothy Mitchell. See Ferguson's *The Anti-Politics Machine* (Minneapolis: University of Minnesota Press, 1994) and Mitchell's *Rule of Experts: Egypt, Techno-Politics, Modernity* (Berkeley: University of California Press, 2002), esp. chaps. 3 ("The Character of Calculability") and 7 ("The Object of Development").

9. The antidevelopment manifesto that lurks in the pages of this literature is, however, considerably more naïve and nettlesome and fully deserves to be taken to task. I have attempted to do so, in retrospect somewhat unsatisfactorily, in my

article, "The Unbearable Modernity of 'Development'?" *Progress in Planning* 58, no. 1 (2002): 1–80.

10. Althusser, in turn, adapts it from his close friend and colleague Jacques Martin to whom his *For Marx* is dedicated; see Louis Althusser, *For Marx*, trans. Ben Brewster (London: NLB, 1977 [1969]), 32. Martin, as Althusser points out, employs the concept "to designate the particular unity of a theoretical formation and hence the location to be assigned to ... [the] specific difference" that distinguishes one theoretical formation from another.

11. Althusser, *For Marx*, 67 n. 30 (italics in original).

12. The Hegelian whole or expressive totality is a "spiritual whole" in the Leibnizian sense of a whole in which all the parts "conspire" together, in which each part is a *pars totalis,* that is to say, where each part is the image of both the other parts and of the ensemble, as if it were a set of mutually reflective mirrors. It is precisely this conception of totality that enables Hegel to present human history as the march of Spirit *(Geist),* reducing the multitude of phenomena to expressions of this essence. See Althusser, "The Errors of Classical Economics," in Louis Althusser and Etienne Balibar, *Reading Capital,* trans. Ben Brewster (London: Verso, 1997 [1968]), 96 (and the extended discussion from 93–101).

13. Ben Brewster, "Glossary," in Althusser, *For Marx,* 253.

14. Althusser, *For Marx,* 67 n. 30 (italics in original).

15. Althusser, "From 'Capital' to Marx's Philosophy," in Althusser and Balibar, *Reading Capital,* 26. The intersections between Althusser and Foucault—despite their commonly accepted differences—are striking. Compare Althusser's remarks on the "problematic" that I quote in the text, first published in 1968 as *Lire le Capital* (Paris: Maspero, 2 vols.), to Foucault's observations on "discourse" in *The History of Sexuality,* vol. 1 (New York: Random House, 1978), first published in French in 1976: "[W]e must not imagine a world of discourse divided between accepted discourse and excluded discourse, or between the dominant discourse and the dominated one; but as a multiplicity of discursive elements that can come into play in various strategies. It is this distribution that we must reconstruct, with the things said and those concealed, the enunciations required and those forbidden, that it comprises" (100). Warren Montag's article, "'The Soul Is the Prison of the Body': Althusser and Foucault, 1970–1975," in *Depositions: Althusser, Balibar, Macherey, and the Labor of Reading, Yale French Studies,* no. 88 (1995): 53–77, is remarkably insightful in tracing the congruities and incongruities between the bodies of work that take the proper name "Althusser" and "Foucault."

16. Althusser, "From 'Capital' to Marx's Philosophy," 25 (italics in original).

17. It would be exhausting and pointless to attempt to summarize the debates generated by Althusser's writings. Interested readers can consult, among others, the following English-language references: E. P. Thompson, *The Poverty of Theory and Other Essays* (London: NLB, 1978); Perry Anderson, *Arguments within English Marxism* (London: Verso, 1980); Gregory Elliot, *Althusser: A Detour of Theory* (London: Verso, 1987); Terry Eagleton, *Ideology: An Introduction* (London: Verso, 1991), esp. chap. 5; E. Ann Kaplan and Michael Sprinker, eds., *The Althusserian Legacy* (London: Verso, 1993); Gregory Elliot, ed., *Althusser: A Critical Reader* (Cambridge: Blackwell, 1994); Antonio Callari and David F. Ruccio, eds., *Postmodern Materialism and the Future of Marxist Theory: Essays in the Althusserian Tradition* (Hanover, N.H.: Wesleyan University Press, 1996); and Warren Montag,

Louis Althusser (New York: Palgrave Macmillan, 2003). Also see Foucault's oblique critique of Althusser's distinction between "ideology" and "science" (Althusser goes unnamed) in his *The Archaeology of Knowledge*, trans. A. M. Sheridan (New York: Harper, 1972), 184–86. Althusser acknowledges (this time Foucault goes unnamed) in *Essays in Self Criticism*, trans. Graeme Lock (London: NLB, 1976), esp. 101–61.

18. On this aspect of ideology, see Louis Althusser, "Ideology and Ideological State Apparatuses," in his *Lenin and Philosophy*, trans. Ben Brewster (London: NLB, 1971), 171–72.

19. It should be said in all fairness that Althusser offers these clarifications on the distinction between "science" and "ideology" in response to criticisms that he reifies these categories, thereby committing an idealist (worse, bourgeois!) error of claiming to be able to authenticate Truth; and that he seems to accord primacy to theory over political struggle. For Althusser's acknowledgment of these criticisms and his response, see his *Essays in Self Criticism*, 132–50.

20. Althusser, *Essays in Self Criticism*, 160.

21. Here again we witness a congruity between Althusser and Foucault; both invoke the concept of "epistemological break" or "rupture" (*coupure epistémologique*) and both borrow it from Gaston Bachelard. See Bachelard, *La Formation de l'esprit scientifique* (Paris: Vrin, 1996 [1938]).

22. Althusser, *Essays in Self-Criticism*, 112–13 (italics in original).

23. Montag, *Louis Althusser*, 48.

24. Montag, *Louis Althusser*, 49.

25. Althusser, *Lenin and Philosophy*, 162.

26. Althusser, *For Marx*, 233.

27. Montag, *Louis Althusser*, 62. Althusser gives warrant to Montag's claim in his *Essays in Self-Criticism*, 135–38. Michele Barrett is one example of a careful theorist who has charge-sheeted Althusser on the question of the "imaginary," on the grounds that Althusser misappropriates Lacan's concepts. See her "Althusser's Marx, Althusser's Lacan," in Kaplan and Sprinker, eds., *The Althusserian Legacy*, 169–82.

28. This point deserves a much longer analysis, examining, among other things, Althusser's greater affinity for Lenin than Gramsci (although he acknowledges strong debts to both). Perhaps Althusser's clearest statement on philosophy's partisanship is to be found in his *Essays in Self-Criticism*, 142–50.

29. Also notable are Neil Rabitoy's incisive articles on the forging of British administration in Gujarat. These articles, "Administrative Modernization and the Bhats of British Gujarat, 1800–1820," *Indian Economic and Social History Review* 11, no. 1 (1974): 46–73, and "System v. Expediency: The Reality of Land Revenue Administration in the Bombay Presidency, 1812–1820," *Modern Asian Studies* 9, no. 4 (1975): 529–46, both show the gap between theoretical doctrine and on-the-ground policies, and the uncertain transition to governmentality.

30. David Scott, *Refashioning Futures: Criticism after Postcoloniality* (Princeton, N.J.: Princeton University Press, 1999), chap. 1. Scott also clarifies that although the category "modern" here signifies a *break* it neither implies sympathy for the false pieties of developmentalism or modernization theory nor a judgmental periodization of history into the "traditional" and the "modern." Rather, in keeping with Zygmunt Bauman's formulation, Scott employs the term "modern" to signify an "alteration of grounds, of fundamental bases—that it is important to speak of the

modern as forming a break with what went before, a break beyond which there is no return, and in which what comes after can only be read in, read through, and read against the categories of the modern" (34). Cf. Bauman, *Modernity and Ambivalence* (Oxford: Blackwell, 2004; first published by Polity Press, 1991).

31. Scott, *Refashioning Futures,* 34 (italics in original).

32. The complicity between Foucault's notion of "governmentality" and the liberal doctrine of government is not incidental. But whether or not Foucault was *endorsing* liberal government via the backdoor is moot (unlike Derek Kerr, for instance, I happen to think not). What *is* clear is that Foucault wants to shift our attention to the micrology of governance—to underscore that liberal philosophers like Montesquieu, Smith, Rousseau, Bentham, Ricardo, and J. S. Mill, among others, who explicitly associated "government" with the liberty of "self-government" were foregrounding a new modality of power. Take, for instance, J. S. Mill, whose treatise on liberty (*On Liberty* [London: Longman, Roberts, & Green, 1869]) bears the marks of Adam Smith's market doctrine, with some important differences. Mill's understanding of government entailed, first, the cultivation of the self as the cultivation of civilizing reason (hence, Mill's ability to justify colonial rule as a "civilizing mission") coupled with an understanding that the duty of the state was to provide for conditions (which included a very expansive notion of "education") that would further this civilization of individuals; and second, the reinforcement of a generalized system of individual exchange—in short, markets—and private property rights as the means that would best enable individuals who constitute a population to pursue their welfare in accordance with their interests, and by so doing ensure the welfare of the state. For assessments of Mill's philosophy of government, see S. Ambirajan, *Classical Political Economy and British Policy in India* (Cambridge: Cambridge University Press, 1978); Quention Skinner, *The Foundations of Modern Political Thought,* 2 vols. (Cambridge: Cambridge University Press, 1978); James Tully, *An Approach to Political Philosophy: Locke in Contexts* (Cambridge: Cambridge University Press, 1993); Lynn Zastoupil, *John Stuart Mill and India* (Stanford, Calif.: Stanford University Press, 1994); Uday Singh Mehta, *Liberalism and Empire* (Chicago: University of Chicago Press, 1999); and Martin I. Moir, Douglas M. Peers, and Lynn Zastoupil, eds., *J. S. Mill's Encounter with India* (Toronto: University of Toronto Press, 1999).

33. Michel Foucault, "Governmentality," in Graham Burchell, Colin Gordon, and Peter Miller, eds., *The Foucault Effect: Studies in Governmentality* (Chicago: University of Chicago Press, 1991), 99. Also important here is Pasquale Pasquino's article, "Theatrum Politicum: The Genealogy of Capital," in *The Foucault Effect,* 105–18. Pasquino traces the rise of the cameralist science of police, where the term "police" denotes not the punitive institution for maintaining law and order in civil society that we commonly associate it with today but rather its original German sense, which is closer to the English word "policy." He shows that the idea of "police," which clearly influences Foucault's formulation of governmentality, was inaugurated at the beginning of the seventeenth century by Georg Obrecht, a high official of the city of Strasbourg and the Rector of Strasbourg University. Obrecht's use, according to Pasquino, marks the first departure from the political language of prince and his principality—that is, from a theory of sovereignty, to the language of population and *Obrigkeit,* a term that means authority but also public power or government. Obrecht is writing just before the start of the Thirty Years' War (1618–48), and his

attempt is to address a very practical problem of maintaining state power: namely, that wars are expensive and require the reliable generation of revenues to fight them. Armies must be equipped, replenished, and augmented, troops must be paid wages, and populations must be provided some basic measure of security. There is a relentless demand for money, and the old theory of sovereignty emblematically associated with Machiavelli's *The Prince* no longer seems workable. Instead of a juridical system of power that coerces and extracts through taxes and levies, there has to be a set of measures designed for the development of wealth. Accordingly, Obrecht enumerates three tasks of "police": "First, information, conceived as a sort of statistical table bearing on all capacities and resources of population and territory; second, a set of measures to augment the wealth of the population and enrich the coffers of the state; third, public happiness" (Pasquino, "Theatrum Politicum," 113, paraphrasing Obrecht). Here we already see the difference in the political rationality of government as opposed to older, sovereign, forms of power. Obrecht is taking the first steps in redefining the state from a purely sovereign creature that exerts its power by wielding the threat of physical punishment to an "economic pastorate," which tends to its population as a pastor might to his flock and where its power takes an increasingly biopolitical form. Eventually, as Foucault details in his essay "Governmentality," it becomes the task of government through assistance, tutelage, and medicalization to enable the individuals who constitute a population to enrich themselves and the state.

34. On these points, see Mary Poovey, *A History of the Modern Fact* (Chicago: University of Chicago Press, 1998), chap. 5.

35. Francis G. Hutchins, *The Illusion of Permanence: British Imperialism in India* (Princeton, N.J.: Princeton University Press, 1967), esp. chaps. 1–3. Charles Grant, cofounder of the influential Clapham sect, along with John Shore, was the primary mover behind the early nineteenth-century evangelicalism that sought to improve Indian society by reforming its morals.

36. Adam Smith, *Wealth of Nations,* new edition (Amherst, N.Y.: Prometheus Books, 1991), 325.

37. Poovey, *A History of the Modern Fact,* 239.

38. Some of the similarities and differences between British and French liberalism are recorded in F. Rosen, "Eric Stokes, British Utilitarianism, and India," in Moir et al., *J. S. Mill's Encounter with India,* 18–33.

39. Thus, a system of civil servants rigorously trained in the science of government was established for India (with the founding of the East India Company's Haileybury College in 1804) well before a similar system of administrators was proposed for Britain itself in 1854. William J. Barber in *British Economic Thought and India, 1600–1858* (Oxford: Clarendon Press, 1975) notes in a similar vein that the land taxation scheme implemented in India under the ryotwari settlement was based on the Ricardian political-economic principle of rent. However, the same principle could not be applied in Britain itself because the political clout of the landed gentry, who dominated the House of Lords, was insuperable.

40. Civil servants were expected to train for two years at the East India College in Haileybury.

41. James Mill's treatise was also intended as a sharp repudiation of Orientalists like Warren Hastings, William Jones, and William Robertson, who had celebrated the achievements of Indian civilization and sought its restoration; and of their

conservative supporters in the British Parliament, most notably Edmund Burke, who had vocally sought to minimize the harm caused by British intervention in India and instead allow Indian institutions to develop of their own devices. The transformative zeal radiant in Mill's *magnum opus* faithfully echoes Bentham's commitment to "reformation in the moral" domain, expressed most forcefully in his *A Fragment on Government*, ed., J. H. Burns and J. L. A. Hart (Cambridge: Cambridge University Press, 1977).

42. S. Ambirajan, *Classical Political Economy and British Policy in India* (Cambridge: Cambridge University Press, 1978), 12.

43. David Livingstone, *The Geographical Tradition* (Malden, Mass.: Blackwell Publishers), 112.

44. As Spinoza did, even though Locke and his intellectual inheritors—who considered Spinoza a heretic—would have never recognized this affinity.

45. Hans Blumenberg, *The Legitimacy of the Modern Age*, trans. Robert M. Wallace (Cambridge, Mass.: MIT Press, 1983), 30, 32.

46. My argument here, on the displacement of the "political" under liberalism, is a modification of Sheldon Wolin's original claim made in *Politics and Vision: Continuity and Innovation in Western Political Thought*, expanded edition (Princeton, N.J.: Princeton University Press, 2004). However, Wolin never entertains how liberalism was transformed by empire. This is symptomatic of a larger failure—in an otherwise brilliant book—to problematize the "West": to see it not as a self-contained, coherent entity, but as an epistemic space constituted through colonialism.

47. See John Locke, *The Second Treatise of Government*, ed. Thomas P. Peardon (Indianapolis: Bobbs-Merrill Company, Inc., for The Library of Liberal Arts, 1952). My analysis is also indebted to Bhikhu Parekh's essay, "Liberalism and Colonialism: A Critique of Locke and Mill," in *The Decolonization of Imagination*, ed. Jan Nederveen Pieterse and Bhikhu Parekh (London: Zed Books), 81–98, but esp. 85–87.

48. Harold J. Laski, *Political Thought in England: Locke to Bentham* (London: Oxford University Press, 1920), 52.

49. Scott, *Refashioning Futures*, 43.

50. On the emergence of the "social," see Jacques Donzelot, *L'Invention du Social* (Paris: Fayard, 1984) and Donzelot, "The Mobilization of Society," in Burchell et al., eds., *The Foucault Effect*, 169–80.

51. Foucault, "Governmentality," 93. Notably, Foucault goes on to liken this government of society to the government of a ship and a household, and elsewhere, the government of the self—indicating the upward and downward continuity of this mode of power. "Upward continuity" refers to the coextensiveness between self-government and the government of the state, hence, the collective welfare of state and society begins with responsible self-conduct. "Downward continuity" means that a well-run state "disposes things" in a manner that enables individuals who constitute a population to conduct themselves in a manner that serves their interest and those of the state (91–92).

52. An analogous double imperative is palpable in the post-1830 writings of J. S. Mill. Previously an ardent advocate of progressive change, Mill shifted his views from the 1830s onward under the influence of the ideas of the French Saint-Simonians and Samuel T. Coleridge (particularly, the latter's *On the Constitution of the Church and State*), as well as the experience of administrative work at India

House dealing with matters concerning the affairs of native states. He begins to argue for a balance between the forces of "permanence" and "progression." On Mill's evolving philosophy, see Zastoupil, *John Stuart Mill and India* and Mehta, *Liberalism and Empire*, chap. 3.

53. Little wonder, then, that the principal theorists of liberalism from the seventeenth to nineteenth centuries—Locke, Montesquieu, Hume, Helvetius, Beccaria, Bentham, Smith, Rousseau, Ricardo, and Mill—felt compelled to supplement their economic and political treatises with commentaries on human nature.

54. Capt. C. J. Prescott, Superintendent of Revenue Survey and Assessment for Goozerat, to J. W. Hadow, Collector of Kaira (No. 542 of 31.12.1862), in Selections from the Records of the Bombay Government, New Series [hereafter SRBG (NS)], *Correspondence Relating to the Introduction of the Revenue Survey Assessment in the Talookas of Matur (Now Mehmoodabad) & Muhoonda in the Kheda Collectorate* (Bombay: Education Society's Press, 1864), 5 [hereafter *Matar R.S.A.*].

55. J. W. Hadow to C. J. Prescott (No. 77 of 23.1.1863), SRBG (NS), *Matar R.S.A.*, 31–32.

56. C. J. Prescott to J. W. Hadow, *Matar R.S.A.*, 4.

57. B. H. Ellis, Revenue Commissioner for Northern Districts, to J. W. Hadow, Collector of Kaira, *Matar R.S.A.*, 37–38.

58. Michel Serres, with Bruno Latour, *Conversations on Science, Culture and Time* (Ann Arbor: University of Michigan Press, 1995), 63, 65.

59. C. J. Prescott to J. W. Hadow, *Matar R.S.A.*, 5.

60. Portions of this argument have been adapted, in extensively revised form, from my article, "'Waste' and the Permanent Settlement in Bengal," *Economic and Political Weekly* 27, no. 4 (January 25, 1992): PE-39–PE-46.

61. Mehta, *Liberalism and Empire*, makes a stronger claim about liberalism's response to the encounter with the singularity and newness of India. Building on Homi Bhabha's statement that the texts of Empire disclose "the repeated threat of the loss of a 'teleologically significant world,'" Mehta contends that "if the particularities and trajectories of the histories to which the empire exposed liberals did not somehow already align themselves with . . . [their universalistic] vision, then either that vision had to be acknowledged as limited in its reach or those recalcitrant and deviant histories had to be aligned to comport with it. Liberals consistently opted for the latter—that is to say, 'reform' was indeed central to the liberal agenda and mindset. To that end they deployed a particular conception of what really constituted history along with a related view of what counted as progress" (77).

62. In this articulation also lies the explanation for why contemporary neoliberals are able to assert a causal link between "human rights" and "democracy" and the spread of the "free market." For a suggestive exploration of this, see Talal Asad, "Redeeming the 'Human' through Human Rights," in his *Formations of the Secular* (Stanford, Calif.: Stanford University Press, 2003), 127–58.

63. Walter K. Firminger, ed., *The Fifth Report on East India Company Affairs, 1812*, 3 vols. (Calcutta: R. Cambray and Co., 1917).

64. Locke, *Second Treatise*, 53–54.

65. Philip Francis, the key architect of the Bengal settlement, was greatly influenced by the economic theories of the physiocrats (Quesnay, Turgot, and the older Mirabeau) and in his Plan of 1776 had proposed that assessments on landowners be fixed in perpetuity. The decision to scale this down to a "lifetime" was taken in

1784 at the instance of John Shore, a member of Governor General Macpherson's Supreme Council and an influential voice in the Bengal settlement debates (Shore was to succeed Cornwallis as Governor General of India in October 1793). For a superb analysis of the permanent settlement, including the Plan of 1776 and its aftermath, see Ranajit Guha, *A Rule of Property for Bengal* (Durham, N.C.: Duke University Press, 1996 [1963]).

66. Cornwallis's Minutes in the preamble to Regulation II of the Bengal Code of Regulations of 1793, quoted in Eric Stokes, *The English Utilitarians and India* (Oxford: Clarendon Press, 1959), 6.

67. In *The English Utilitarians and India* Stokes popularized the notion that Munro was, at the end of the day, a Romantic and a Benthamite, who favored government under the benign oversight of a single, powerful, local executive. The first part of Stokes's assertion has not been challenged. But the second has been, vigorously, by scholars such as John Roselli, Frederick Rosen, and Burton Stein. They have questioned Stokes's characterization of Utilitarianism as an authoritarian strand of thought in uneasy coexistence with liberalism's principle of liberty, as well his untenable clubbing together of diverse figures such as James Mill (a confirmed Benthamite), Montstuart Elphinstone, William Bentinck, and Thomas Munro, etc., under the label Utilitarians. See, for example, Burton Stein, *Thomas Munro: The Origins of the Colonial State and his Vision of Empire* (Delhi: Oxford University Press, 1989), esp. 345–53.

68. Here the question arises how Lockean and Benthamite principles could be adduced in favor of large landowners. The typical defense took two forms. First was the argument advanced by those like Arthur Young in 1770 (and taken up by others after him) that the large landowners of Britain were more entrepreneurial and liable to make much more productive use of their land than, say, small cultivators in Scotland or peasants in France. Since Locke had enjoined that the most productive use of nature was what God had intended of man, this was sufficient to establish the moral basis of large landownership. The second argument was a weaker variant of the first, that large landowners, particularly aristocrats, were entitled to their estates on the basis of public service rendered to society. See Arthur Young, *Rural Economy, or Essays on the Practical Parts of Husbandry* (Doublin: J. Exshaw et al., 1770). These arguments are considered—and dispensed with—in a fascinating exegesis, compiled in the *Fifth Report*, on the comparative merits of the zamindari and ryotwari settlements; see Mr. Thackeray's report of August 4, 1807, in Firminger, ed., *Fifth Report*, 3:562–95.

69. W. W. Hunter, *Bengal MS Records, 1782–1807*, 4 vols. (London: W. H. Allen, 1894), 1:86.

70. Governor General's Minute, September 18, 1789, in Firminger, ed., *Fifth Report*, 2:512. See also H. Colebrooke's Minute (no date), para. 14, in *Selection of Papers from the Records of the East India House*, 4 vols. (London: Printed by order of the Court of Directors, 1820), 1:420 (microfiche).

71. Even Orientalists like William Jones, Warren Hastings, and James Rennell, who celebrated the achievements of Hindu civilization (and were the target of acid critiques by figures as diverse as James Mill and Karl Marx), saw its glories as a thing of the past.

72. Any form of empiricism that grounds knowledge in the transparency of sense data amounts to verisimilitude. This does not mean that statements attached

to empiricist methodologies are untrue or unreal. To the extent that they exert force and have effects, they are real. The task of philosophy—what Foucault has called "archaeology"—is to re-create the archive of implicit premises and reattach statements to their conditions of emergence.

73. See Noyes's magisterial treatise, *The Institution of Property: A Study of the Development, Substance, and Arrangement of the System of Property in Anglo-American Law* (London: Longman, Greens and Company, 1936), 264.

74. See particularly the section entitled "Property" in Locke, *Second Treatise*, 16–30.

75. Locke, *Second Treatise*, 23.

76. Locke, *Second Treatise*, 21.

77. Locke, *Second Treatise*, 26. It is worth mentioning that although Locke remains within the paradigm of sovereignty he has already taken steps that render the prince an immanent entity, hence: "If a controversy arise betwixt a prince and some of the people in a matter where the law is silent or doubtful, and the thing be of great consequence, I should think the proper umpire in such a case should be the body of people; for in cases where the prince has a trust reposed in him and is dispensed from the common ordinary rules of the law, there, if any men find themselves aggrieved and think the prince to act contrary to or beyond that trust, who so proper to judge as the body of people (who, at first, lodged that trust in him) how far they meant it to extend?" (*Second Treatise*, 139).

78. Locke, *Second Treatise*, 20: "God gave the world to men in common; but since he gave it them for their benefit and the greatest conveniences of life they were capable to draw from it, it cannot be supposed he meant it should always remain common and uncultivated. He gave it to the use of the industrious and rational." We saw previously how, on these grounds (albeit an unscrupulous recreation of them), Locke was able to deny the rights to property of Native Americans. Given his belief in a system of natural rights, he was not in a position, however, to deny them the right to exist; hence, could not—and did not—sanction explicit settler violence against them.

79. Ibid., 28.

80. And Marx gleefully derides this line of reasoning in the chapter on "Primitive Accumulation" (chap. 26) in *Capital*, Vol. 1: *A Critique of Political Economy*, trans. Ben Fowkes (London: Penguin, 1976 [1867]).

81. Locke, *Second Treatise*, 18.

82. We might say, drawing from Michel Serres, that Smith functioned as a *clinamen*. For Serres, "the clinamen marks the moment when an atom [or any other entity] in laminar flow deviates from its path, collides with another atom, and initiates the formation of things and ultimately of worlds." More generically, the clinamen stands in for a point of condensation or equilibrium, the common measure, the logos of analogy, the chain of mediations, etc. See Serres, *Hermes: Literature, Science, Philosophy* (Baltimore: The Johns Hopkins University Press, 1982), 51–52, and 51 n. 13.

83. William J. Barber, *British Economic Thought and India, 1600–1858*, 175.

84. Hence, according to Terence Hutchison, "Smith was a historical economist not only in the sense that he was empirical, but in that the theme of *progress through natural stages of development* runs all through his *Inquiry into the Nature and Cause of the Wealth of Nations*. Smith, in fact, like Hume, Ferguson and Millar,

belonged to 'the historical age' and 'the historical nation.' He did not claim to have discovered 'laws' of economic development, or indeed, *any* economic laws, and so might not be describable as 'historicist' in the fullest sense. But, especially in the often rather neglected volume III of The *Wealth of Nations,* 'Of the Natural Progress of Opulence,' Smith seeks to lay down 'the natural course of things' or 'an order of things which necessity imposes in general'" (italics in original). Hutchison, *Before Adam Smith: The Emergence of Political Economy, 1662–1776* (Oxford: Basil Blackwell, 1988), 357–58.

85. Michel Foucault writes that whereas "in Classical thought trade and exchange serve as an indispensable basis for the analysis of wealth (and this is still true of Smith's analysis, in which the division of labor is governed by the criteria of barter), after Ricardo, the possibility of exchange is based upon labor; and henceforth the theory of production must always precede that of circulation." Foucault, *The Order of Things: An Archaeology of the Human Sciences* (New York: Vintage Books, 1970), 254.

86. Cf. Marquis de Mirabeau, *La Philosophie Rurale* (Amsterdam, 1763) and Francois Quesnay, *Tableau Economique* (London: Macmillan, 1972 [1758]).

87. Ranajit Guha, *A Rule of Property for Bengal,* 99. Given the distinction the physiocrats drew between the value of labor power and the value created through its use, we can understand why Marx was able to speak of them as "the true fathers of modern economics."

88. It is worth mentioning that the physiocrats were greatly impressed by the transformation and successes of capitalist agriculture in England following the Enclosures.

89. Quoted in Foucault, *The Order of Things,* 194.

90. See Ross Harrison, *Bentham* (London: Routledge and Kegan Paul), chap. 9 ("The Benthamite State"), esp. 258–60. According to Harrison, "police" had come to be used "in a looser or wider sense at the end of the eighteenth century, particularly in France and Germany, to mean the more general prevention of mischief." But when Bentham employs the term his "chief concern . . . is that 'for the power which takes for its object the introduction of positive good, no peculiar name, however inadequate, seems yet to have been devised'" (259).

91. Jeremy Bentham, *A Fragment on Government,* ed. J. H. Burns and H. L. A. Hart (Cambridge: Cambridge University Press, 1988), 25–26 (italics in original).

92. Eric Stokes, in *The English Utilitarians and India,* follows the reading of Elie Halévy in rendering Bentham as the creator of an authoritarian doctrine of jurisprudence that was to give British liberalism—especially its colonial manifestations—a hard, almost military edge. Clearly, Stokes has not been entirely fair to Bentham, given his commitment to radical democracy in the latter part of his career. That said, Althusser's observation that an ideology must be responsible for its effects, is apropós: Bentham cannot be completely absolved of the deployments of his core principle.

93. Alexander Dow, "A Dissertation Concerning the Origin and Nature of Despotism in Hindostan," in *The History of Hindostan,* 3 vols. (London, 1770), 1:vii.

94. Robert Orme, *Of the Government and People of Indostan* (Lucknow: Pustak Kendra, 1971 [1782]), 42.

95. James Grant, "An Historical and Comparative Analysis of the Finances of Bengal," in Firminger, ed., *The Fifth Report,* 2:276 (italics mine).

96. In Book 8, Montequieu examined the "Distinctive Properties of Despotic Government."

97. Minute of John Shore, June 18, 1789, in Firminger, ed., *The Fifth Report*, 2:40 (paras. 168, 169).

98. Firminger, ed., *The Fifth Report*, 2:83.

99. Governor General's Minute, September 18, 1789, in Firminger, ed., *The Fifth Report*, 2:512.

100. James Mill, *The History of British of India*, 6 vols. (New York: Chelsea House Publishers, 1968 [1817]), 1:332–33.

101. Samuel Smiles, *Self-Help: with Illustrations of Conduct and Perseverance*, abridged and edited by Sauvik Chakraverti (New Delhi: Liberty Institute, 2001). The Board of Advisors of the Liberty Institute includes that famous nemesis of *dirigisme*, the UCLA-based Indian economist, Deepak Lal.

102. Gurcharan Das, "Foreword," ibid.

103. See Timothy Mitchell, *Colonizing Egypt* (Berkeley: University of California Press, 1988), 109.

2. Birth

1. A *khadki* is a neighborhood or cluster of houses in a village that trace its origins back to a common founding ancestor. Ambodi has two khadkis, corresponding to the two brothers who are said to have established domicile in the village. Members of a khadki are considered kin.

2. The narrative I recount is drawn from fieldnotes taken in Ambodi, dated November 1, 2004. Where appropriate, names of places and persons have been altered here and elsewhere in the book.

3. A brief note on the subject of "nature": in my conversations during fieldwork, whenever allusions to nature surfaced (and they were frequent)—in their local noun or adjectival attire, as *kudrat/i, prakriti/k, svabhav/ik, danat, vatavaran*—the implication seemed to be not that nature is that which is unchangeable or beyond the scope of human intervention but rather that nature denotes inherent and inherited traits that are plastic up to a point. Hence, the inherent properties of land (*jamin na gun*) can be transformed through techniques of cultivation, but only up to a point. A person's conduct can also change, through education or proper guidance, for instance, but, again, up to a point. *Daanat* is an interesting word because it designates not an acquired attitude but rather an intrinsic or genotypic orientation. It indexes a certain predisposition that one is born into and that has a determining influence on all subsequent conduct. Upbringing and guidance can modulate the effects of daanat, not erase them.

4. Conventionally speaking, neither the Patels nor the Baraiya Kolis constitute castes. They are, rather, subcastes or *jatis*. The Patels of Ambodi (who now call themselves Patidars) belong to the subcaste of Leva Kanbis. In order to eliminate the common confusion between castes and subcastes and to underscore that inter- and intracaste differences take the form of both vertical hierarchies and lateral divisions, the sociologist A. M. Shah developed the schematic of ordered divisions to clarify differences. Hence, the Leva Kanbis are represented as one of five second-order divisions of the first-order caste category "Kanbis," the other four being Kadva, Anjana,

Bhakta, and Matia. Of the five, the Leva Kanbis have been (and continue to be) regarded, ritually and economically, as superior. The Kolis have two second-order divisions that, interestingly, distinguish between indigenous and outsider status. Within this division fall several specific second-order groups: Chumvaliya, Khant, Patanvadiya, Baraiya, Thakarda, Thakor, Talabda, Pagi, Kotwal, Palia, Matia, and Gulam. Of these, the Patanwadia (those who immigrated from Patan in north Gujarat), Chumvaliya (who immigrated from the Chumval tract in north Gujarat), and Baraiya are considered immigrants. Although in most cases households in the second-order divisions freely arrange marriages across group boundaries, a geographic hierarchy continues to operate, with Kolis to the north or from the north being preferred in marital alliances. Thus Crispin Bates points out that by the 1920s Talabda Kolis, who, in general, appeared to be better off than members of other Koli divisions in Kheda, had initiated efforts to "cut themselves off from their poorer caste mates" (Bates, "The Nature of Social Change in Rural Gujarat: The Kheda District, 1818–1918," *Modern Asian Studies* 1, no. 4 [1981]: 801).

Similarly, Alice Clark's investigations on Koli marriage patterns in Brahmvasi village of Padra Taluka, Baroda District, in the mid-1970s revealed that in contrast to caste information presented in the kalambandhi record for the village from the 1820s—where the appellation "Koli" was employed in an undifferentiated manner—there were three distinct marital groups among the Kolis, consisting of a small number of Solanki households at the top, a large number of Baraiya households in the middle, and another large group of Parmar households at the bottom. In my ongoing conversations in Matar Taluka, members of non-Koli caste groups apply the terms *kshatriya, thakur,* or *dharala* (the last less than the two former) as a generic address for Kolis writ large. As I have suggested, this wrong usage not only signals the often blurred subcaste boundaries but also a continuation of the tendency, formalized under British rule, to lump out of ignorance (and sometimes disdain) often consequential social boundaries. For example, the Talabda Koli Patels in one of my study villages (Shamli) view themselves as culturally different from and superior to the Baraiya Kolis of Limbasi, a large village approximately ten kilometers away as the crow flies. For more on caste orders in central Gujarat, see A. M. Shah, "Division and Hierarchy: An Overview of Caste in Gujarat," *Contributions to Indian Sociology* (NS) 16, no. 1 (1982): 1–33. Other studies, in addition to Bates's cited above, that document processes of change in caste formations in central Gujarat include David Pocock, "Inclusion and Exclusion: A Process in the Caste System of Gujarat," *Southwestern Journal of Anthropology* 18 (Spring 1957): 19–31; Ghanshyam Shah, *Caste Association and Political Process in Gujarat* (Bombay: Popular Prakashan, 1975); and Alice Whitcomb Clark, "Central Gujarat in the Nineteenth Century: The Integration of an Agrarian System," Ph.D. diss., University of Wisconsin–Madison, Ann Arbor, 1979.

5. The practice of attributing one's wealth and domination to past labors is not confined to the Patels of central Gujarat. In his superb book, *Fraternal Capital: Peasant-Workers, Self-Made Men and Globalization in Provincial India* (Stanford, Calif.: Stanford University Press, 2004), Sharad Chari demonstrates how the Gounder owners of knitwear units in Tiruppur, Tamil Nadu, mobilize an agrarian past underscoring their toil to explain—indeed, justify—their status quo.

6. Karl Marx, *Capital,* vol. 1: *A Critique of Political Economy,* trans. Ben Fowkes (London: Penguin Books/NLR, 1976 [1867]), 873.

7. The word *charotar* is a conjugation of *charu*, meaning "golden" and *tad*, meaning "land," indicative of the area's fertile soil.

8. Anjana N. Patel and Natvarbhai D. Patel, *The Leva Patidar Patels of Charotar: A Community History* (London: Charotar Patidar Kutumb, 2001), 8 (italics in original). The copyright page of the book states: "The logo of Charotar Patidar Kutumb represents a 'Dhow,' a type of Arab sailing boat which was the means of travel for people leaving Gujarat for East Africa during the early part of the 20th century."

9. This characterization of historiography is Michel de Certeau's. See his *The Writing of History*, trans. Tom Conley (New York: Columbia University Press, 1988), xxv. Rudimentary to the possibility of historical narrative is an explicit "relation to a social body and an institution of knowledge," in addition to its textual figuration by writing—understood as "the construction of an écriture (in the broad meaning of the organization of signifiers)" (Certeau, *The Writing of History*, 86). I take these premises for granted in my presentation.

10. Clark, "Central Gujarat in the Nineteenth Century," 38–39, citing Pamela Nightingale's argument from her *Trade and Empire in the Western India, 1784–1806* (Cambridge: Cambridge University Press, 1970). My discussion of economic and political transformations in nineteenth-century central Gujarat draws extensively on Clark's research. In addition, I have found the following secondary materials very helpful: John Wilson, *Suppression of Female Infanticide in Western India* (Bombay: Smith, Taylor and Co., 1855); Alexander Rogers, *The Land Revenue of Bombay* (Delhi: B. R. Publishing, 1985; original publication London: W. H. Allen, 1892), vol. 1; Alexander Kinloch Forbes, *Ras Mala, Hindoo Annals of the Province of Goozerat in Western India*, 2 vols. (London: Oxford University Press, 1924); M. B. Desai, *The Rural Economy of Gujarat* (London: Oxford University Press, 1948); Kenneth A. Ballhatchet, *Social Policy and Social Change in Western India, 1817–1830* (London: Oxford University Press, 1958); R. D. Choksey, *Economic Life in the Bombay Gujarat, 1800–1939* (Bombay: Asia Publishing House); David Pocock, *Kanbi and Patidar: A Study of the Patidar Community of Gujarat* (London: Oxford University Press, 1972); Neil Rabitoy, "System v. Expediency: The Reality of Land Revenue Administration in Bombay Presidency, 1812–1820," *Modern Asian Studies* 9, no. 4 (1975): 529–46; David Hardiman, *Peasant Nationalists of Gujarat: Kheda District, 1917–1934* (Delhi: Oxford University Press); Bates, "The Nature of Social Change in Rural Gujarat"; Cathy Chua, "Development of Capitalism in Indian Agriculture: Gujarat, 1850–1900," *Economic and Political Weekly* 21, no. 48 (1986): 2092–99; N. den Tuinder, "Population and Society in Kheda District (India), 1819–1921," Ph.D. diss., University of Amsterdam, 1992; and L. S. Vishwanath, *Female Infanticide and Social Structure: A Socio-Historical Study in Western and Northern India* (New Delhi: Hindustan Publishing Corporation, 2000).

11. Clark, "Central Gujarat in the Nineteenth Century," 40.

12. The Haribhakti house of Poona, which opened their branch in Baroda c. 1775, was to emerge as one of the most influential business-cum-banking entities in the Gaikwad State, playing "a vital role in the shaping of State Financial Policy on the one hand and galvanising rural resources on the other" to build an urban-centered commercial economy in Gujarat. See C. D. Sharma and M. A. Patel, "State and Indigenous Business in the Urban Economy of Gujarat, c.1770–c.1810: A Study of the Haribhakti Records," in *Urbanization in Western India: A Historical*

Perspective, ed. Makrand Mehta (Ahmedabad; Sarvoday Press/Gujarat University, 1988), 59.

13. Ballhatchet, *Social Policy and Social Change in Western India,* 1.

14. See, for instance, B. H. Baden-Powell, *The Land Systems of British India,* 3 vols. (Oxford: Clarendon Press, 1892), 3:207–10; and G. D. Patel, *The Land Revenue Settlements and the British Rule in India* (Ahmedabad: Gujarat University, 1969), 380–86.

15. Quoted in Choksey, *Economic Life in the Bombay Gujarat,* 14.

16. Quoted in Clark, "Central Gujarat in the Nineteenth Century," 52.

17. Bruno Latour, *We Have Never Been Modern,* trans. Catherine Porter (Cambridge, Mass.: Harvard University Press, 1993), 73. On the same page, Latour writes: "They [the moderns] consider everything that does not march in step with progress archaic, irrational or conservative. And as there are antimoderns who are delighted to play the reactionary role that the modern scenario has prepared for them, the great dramas of luminous progress struggling against obscurantism . . . can be deployed, all the same, for the greater pleasure of the spectators."

18. Capt. C. J. Prescott to J. W. Hadow (No. 542 of 31.12.1862), in Selections from the Records of the Bombay Government, New Series [hereafter SRBG (NS)], *Correspondence Relating to the Introduction of the Revenue Survey Assessment in the Talookas of Matur (Now Mehmoodabad) & Muhoonda in the Kheda Collectorate* (Bombay: Education Society's Press, 1864), 6 [hereafter *Matar R.S.A.*].

19. Henry W. Diggle, after serving as Assistant Resident to Alexander Walker (the original British Resident at Baroda), was appointed the first Collector of Kheda when, in 1805, the central Gujarat territories of the Bombay Presidency were administratively distributed between three collectorates—Kheda, Broach (hereafter referred to as Bharuch), and Surat. John Morison served as the first Surat Collector (and for nearly twenty years) even though he had no knowledge of any Indian language and regarded by his superiors as a mediocre administrator. William Steadman, who was appointed the first collector of Bharuch, managed to pass an examination in Gujarati only with the assistance "of a native with whom he is in habit of transacting business." In Rabitoy, "System v. Expediency," 539 (also see the extended discussion on 539–44).

20. Rabitoy, "System v. Expediency."

21. Rabitoy, "System v. Expediency," 541. In the same article, Rabitoy also points out that John Morison, the Surat Collector, operated by relying on his "head clerk" Sukaram Moroji, a man who was repeatedly accused of corruption and oppression (540).

22. Thus, Alexander Walker himself depended primarily on a Brahmin named Gangadhar Shastri for information and advice. In a note written in 1820, Walker confessed that "almost every European Servant has a favourite native, and it is astonishing what power and ascendancy he soon obtains" (ibid., 543).

23. Details of the decision taken by the London-based Board of Control and the debates that preceded it are documented in the famous *Fifth Report,* which I discussed in chapter 1; see Walter K. Firminger, ed., *The Fifth Report on East India Company Affairs, 1812,* 3 vols. (Calcutta: R. Cambray and Sons, 1917).

24. Choksey, *Economic Life in the Bombay Gujarat,* 15.

25. Hardiman, *Peasant Nationalists of Gujarat,* 16.

26. Bates, "The Nature of Social Change in Rural Gujarat," 774.

27. According to inherited practice, cultivators owed the Gaikwad state one-half of output from the rainy season *(kharif)* crop and one-third of output from the dry season *(rabi)* crop if grown by irrigation. This principle of sharing meant that absolute revenue payable varied from year to year.

28. For historical documentation of the thriving regional economies of Gujarat in the pre- and early colonial eras see, for instance, the collection of papers in Makrand Mehta, ed., *Urbanization in Western India*.

29. David Pocock says that the title of *patidar* "refers to a particular form of land tax instituted by the Mogul government" and that certain Kanbi families received this title toward the end of the seventeenth century; in Pocock, "The Movement of Castes," *Man* 55 (May 1955): 71. Meanwhile Bates, "The Nature of Social Change in Rural Gujarat," 776, claims in complementary fashion that the *narwa* tenure was established in Mughal times as an extension of the revenue bureaucracy. Den Tuinder offers a different interpretation. He hypothesizes, pace Bates, that "peasants in many villages of the Charotar founded *narwa* corporations in response, as a means to preserve solidarity against both tax-farmers [contracted by the government] and the lower classes" ("Population and Society in Kheda District," 41). Both Bates and den Tuinder (and other historians of Kheda, such as Alice Clark, David Hardiman, and Marcia Frost) agree that the narwa system was basically one of joint responsibility for payment of a village's taxes. The state assessed a lump-sum revenue demand on the village, which was distributed across various shares called *pati* or *bhag*. The originary shares were further subdivided as per conventions of inheritance. If a sharer or subsharer was not able to meet his share of the revenue demand, it was the responsibility of other sharers to make up the arrears. A few things are notable about this system: first, sharers clearly had an incentive to pass on tax demands to tenants if they could get away with it; second, they had an incentive to both extend and/or intensify cultivation as well as alienate land, since they controlled any surpluses generated beyond their share of the lump-sum revenue demand; third, it reinforced a form of corporatism that was to prove enormously profitable to narwa villages as agricultural conditions and prices in Kheda improved after the 1860s. For a very useful discussion on the tenures prevailing in Kheda in the early 1820s, see den Tuinder, "Population and Society in Kheda District," 41–48.

30. "[Patels] were held most responsible for the extensive alienations of government land. . . . They were furthermore accused of destroying or altering village accounts, of concealing the amount of government or revenue-paying land, and of charging their private expenses to the village accounts" (den Tuinder, "Population and Society in Kheda District," 97).

31. This link was continuously reiterated during my field research in Matar Taluka. Also see Hardiman, *Peasant Nationalists of Gujarat*, 281, for a supporting observation.

32. The three stalwarts of the Lewa Kanbi community, who summoned the 1815 protest meeting in Chaklasi, were Ajoohbai Prabhudas, Ragubhai Vallabbhai, and Ajoobhai Kishandas. The congregation condemned the Resolution of 1814, which would station an official agent of the government in their villages, as a violation of local custom. It is important to clarify that is was *not* unusual to find a village Patel or even a Patidar from one of the Koli denominations. But most Patels and Patidars in Kheda claimed affinity to the subcaste of Lewa Kanbis.

33. Vinayak Chaturvedi, *Peasant Pasts: History and Memory in Western India* (Berkeley: University of California Press, 2007), 40. Chaturvedi's imaginative book recounts, among other regional dynamics, the 1815 protest action and its aftermath.

34. Hardiman, *Peasant Nationalists of Gujarat,* 16.

35. The Gujarat Revenue and Topographical Survey, as it was termed, was implemented under the supervision of Captain Monier Williams, Surveyor General of Bombay Presidency (and, subsequently, India). Survey operations commenced in Bharuch in 1812, Surat in 1815, and Ahmedabad and Kheda in 1820, effectively ceasing in 1827. Marcia J. Frost summarizes the three principal charges of the survey in an instructive article on the drought of 1824–25 in Kheda; see her "Coping With Scarcity: Wild Foods and Common Lands: Kheda District (Gujarat, India), 1824/5," *The Indian Economic and Social History Review* 3, no. 3 (2000): 295–329, esp. 299–302.

36. According to Frost, Talatis earned on average Rs. 100 per year, which in early 1820s prices was the equivalent of 5,000 *seers*—approximately 5,000 pounds—of *bajri* (Frost, "Coping with Scarcity," 302). This was a considerable sum, which was no doubt meant to dissuade corruption. Even so, Patels did not cease their efforts to influence Talatis. Bates, "The Nature of Social Change in Rural Gujarat," 777, notes that "in villages such as Chuklasi and Kambaluj the *nurwadars* were able effectively to bribe and obstruct the government *talatis.*"

37. Bates, "The Nature of Social Change in Rural Gujarat," 774.

38. Letter from J. Sutherland, Second Judge of Circuit, to L. R. Reid, Acting Secretary to Government, October 20, 1826. Quoted in Chaturvedi, *Peasant Pasts,* 42.

39. Clark, "Central Gujarat in the Nineteenth Century," 80.

40. Soon after taking up office, Elphinstone issued a caution to district officials against too zealous an implementation of ryotwari management; see Rabitoy, "System v. Expediency," 536. These sentiments are confirmed in a letter Elphinstone wrote in 1822 to his friend Edward Strachey, who, in 1819, had been appointed to the powerful post of Assistant Examiner at East India House (at the same time as James Mills's appointment to the same post). Said Ephinstone, "I am not democratic enough to insist on a ryotwar system: I think that the aristocracy of the country whether it consists of heads of villages or heads of zemindarees should be kept up but I also think its rights and the opposite rights of the ryots should be clearly defined and the latter especially effectually defended"; quoted in Ballhatchet, *Social Policy and Social Change in Western India,* 32. Plainly, ryots' rights were not "effectually defended" in the original Kheda settlements.

41. Hardiman, *Peasant Nationalists of Gujarat,* 38.

42. Alexander Rogers, *The Land Revenue of Bombay,* 1:87. Rogers's two-volume compilation from 1892 summarizes land survey operations in Bombay Presidency; unfortunately, he fails to name the 1826 report he cites. Den Tuinder, "Population and Society in Kheda District," 46–47, describes the close similarity between narwadari and khatabandhi tenures.

43. Hence, contrasting the nonshared *senja* villages to sharehold villages, Rogers writes that "[r]yots in villages managed on this system were, as a rule, not so substantial as those in Narva or khatabandi village" (*The Land Revenue of Bombay,* 1:88). Correspondence pertaining to the revised surveys that were undertaken in

Kheda in the 1860s, which Hardiman invokes, also tend to use the terms *khatabundy* and *narwadari* interchangeably; while simultaneously discussing khatabundy tenures under the heading of directly managed ryotwari villages.

44. Quoted in Bates, "The Nature of Social Change in Rural Gujarat," 784–85 (italics mine).

45. According to den Tuinder, "Population and Society in Kheda District," 101–2, there were 69 narwa villages in Kheda by 1825–26 and Collector Williamson of Kheda, who actively sought to restore narwa tenures in villages where it had dissolved, also succeeded in granting raiyatwar leases for 411 villages by 1829–30.

46. Hardiman, citing evidence from *Gazetteer of the Bombay Presidency, Vol. III, Kaira and Panch Mahals,* claims that "[u]ntil the 1860s, the British collected most of their revenue from urban bankers, who in turn made agreements with local moneylenders, landlords, and rich peasants to collect the revenue from the peasants" (*Peasant Nationalists of Gujarat,* 16).

47. One vigha in Gujarat equals 47/80ths of an acre.

48. The steep decline in the status of talukdars is acutely captured in the following observations by a colonial official named Lely: "Since 1814 the relations between proprietors and tenants have greatly changed. I have heard an old Girasia complain bitterly at his loss of position. . . . Formerly if a Kanbi, or even a Vania, trimmed his whiskers or tied his turban in martial Rajput fashion . . . he would have had his clothes pretty soon torn off his back and himself probably well kicked. And now one does not know a Vaghri from a Kanbi, or a Kanbi from a Sipahi, and a Dhed may twist his moustachios and swagger about with the sword of a Girasia" (quoted by Bates, "The Nature of Social Change in Rural Gujarat," 774). Lely's remarks are revealing in several ways. First, they indicate that in the talukdari areas Kanbis and Vanias (Jain and Thakkar merchants, who are regarded as upper caste in Gujarat) held clearly subordinate positions to Rajputs. They continue to do so today in many parts of Saurashtra, where the dismantling of talukdari privileges was less assiduously pursued and less effective. Second, they show that the leveling of differences between castes was deeply ignominious to the Rajput and Koli elite. To accuse a person of behaving like a Vaghri is, even today, a severe form of insult. It suggests that he is of low morals, untrustworthy, unclean, and ill-mannered. To call him a Dhed is to accuse him of being meek, subservient, or fawning.

49. SRBG (NS), *Papers Relating to the Revision Survey Settlement* [hereafter *R.S.S.*] *of 76 Villages of the Dholka Taluka of the Ahmedabad Collectorate* (Bombay: Govt. Central Press, 1888), 154.

50. E. C. Ozanne to the Chief Secretary to Government (No. 854 of 1.4.1893), SRBG (NS), *R.S.S. of Matar Taluka of Kaira Collectorate* (Bombay: Govt. Central Press, 1895), 80 [hereafter *Matar R.S.S.*].

51. Eric Stokes, "Dynamism and Enervation in North Indian Agriculture: The Historical Dimension," in his *The Peasant and the Raj* (Cambridge: Cambridge University Press, 1978).

52. See, for instance, Bernard Cohn's insightful essays, "Structural Change in Indian Rural Society: 1596–1885" and "The British in Benares," in his *An Anthropologist Among the Historian and Other Essays* (Delhi: Oxford, 1987).

53. Gilles Deleuze and Félix Guattari, *A Thousand Plateaus: Capitalism and Schizophrenia,* trans. Brian Massumi (Minneapolis: University of Minnesota Press, 1987), 385.

54. Hence, the potential of land is its fertility, of labor its capacity for surplus labor, and of money its capacity to promote exchange by bringing into relations of equivalence products of different quality.

55. Louis Althusser, "*Une philosophie pour le marxisme: 'La ligne de Démocrite,'*" in his *Sur la Philosophie* (Paris: Gallimard, 1994), 40–42, translated by and reproduced in Cesare Casarino, *Modernity At Sea: Melville, Marx, Conrad in Crisis* (Minneapolis: University of Minnesota Press, 2002), 150.

56. One loud silence in colonial documents is the paucity of mention of the economic condition of dalit groups.

57. Figure obtained from den Tuinder, "Population and Society in Kheda District," Table 4.1, p. 95, who notes that cultivated area in Matar Taluka increased from 94,188 bighas in 1806–7 to 123,409 bighas by 1818–19.

58. Marcia Frost, "Coping With Scarcity," 303; thanks to her interpretive labors, we now possess suggestive insights into the 1824–25 drought.

59. Frost, "Coping with Scarcity," 306.

60. Frost discusses the importance of this coping strategy in her paper, see esp. 316–29.

61. Den Tuinder, "Population and Society in Kheda District, 114."

62. It was the short supply of British coin that was partly responsible for depressed grain prices in Kheda and elsewhere in the 1820s. The escalating cost of the Burma war led to severe cost cutting within the Company's Indian administration and was the direct reason for the premature termination of the Gujarat Survey in 1827.

63. The best articles on the subject still are A. M. Shah and R. G. Shroff, "The Vahivanca Barots of Gujarat: A Caste of Genealogists and Mythographers," in *Traditional India: Structure and Change,* ed. Milton B. Singer (Philadelphia: American Folklore Society, 1959), 41–70; and Neil Rabitoy, "Administrative Modernization and the Bhats of British Gujarat, 1800–1820," *Indian Economic and Social History Review* 11, no. 1 (1974): 46–73.

64. Rabitoy, "Administrative Modernization and the Bhats," 49–50.

65. See Hardiman, *Peasant Nationalists of Gujarat,* chap. 2.

66. Karatani points out that accumulation of capital—mercantile or industrial/production—always depends on its ability to take advantage of differences between two or more value systems. Whereas mercantile capital takes advantage of spatial differences, industrial capital continuously produces new values systems temporally. See Kajin Karatani, *Transcritique: On Kant and Marx,* trans. Sabu Kohso (Cambridge, Mass.: MIT Press, 2003), chap. 6, esp. 234–41. Karatani's claims are an elaboration on Marx's arguments in *Capital,* vol. 3 (particularly parts 4 and 5).

67. Gyan Pandey points out that, on the whole, "the evangelical belief in 'improvement' faded as north India broke out into the Great Rebellion . . . of 1857. The government's energies, concentrated as they were in any case in building a vast authoritarian edifice organized around law and order even during the heyday of the civilizing mission, lost their reformist impulse. The lesson that the British drew from the rebellion was that, if anything, India needed to be ruled with a stronger hand, that what the natives required was a productive and secure empire fashioned with modern technologies of rule" ("The Colonial Genealogy of Society: Community and Political Modernity in India," in *The Social in Question: New Bearings in History and the Social Sciences,* ed. Patrick Joyce [London: Routledge, 2002], 85). However,

as we saw in chapter 1 with the Maharaja libel case, and see in this chapter with regard to female infanticide, regional projects of moral/ethological improvement continued to be pursued—but at the individual behest of colonial officials, not as matter of policy.

68. Den Tuinder, "Population and Society in Kheda District," 141.

69. Tuinder, "Population and Society," 142.

70. According to den Tuinder, "[b]y the end of the 1870s, all major towns of the district had been connected by road to the railway. Furthermore, the Anand-Pali feeder had been converted into a branch railway"; ibid., 131.

71. Karl Marx, *Capital,* vol. 3, trans. David Fernbach (London: Penguin Books, 1981), 449.

72. Den Tuinder, "Population and Society," 134.

73. See, for instance, the compilation in Gujarati, *Patidar Jatini Sanskaarik Reetrivaajnu Aekikaran* ("Compilation of the Cultural Customs of the Patidar Caste"), which was based on a write-in survey of Patidars conducted by the Government of Baroda (Baroda: Baroda Printing Press, 1910).

74. Also, L. S. Vishwanath, *Female Infanticide and Social Structure* (New Delhi: Hindustan Publishing Corporation, 2000).

75. H. R. Cooke, *Report on the Repression of Female Infanticide in the Bombay Presidency* (Bombay: Govt. Central Press, 1875), 40.

76. Cooke's aforementioned *Report on the Repression of Female Infanticide* documents Mr. Fawcett's and Mr. Webb's concerns. Wilson's *Suppression of Female Infanticide in Western India* reveals an obsession with female infanticide among native rulers and gentry dating to the early days of company rule in Gujarat.

77. *Correspondence Relating to the Introduction of the Revenue Survey Assessment in the Kheda Collectorate of the Province of Gujarat* (No. 3859 of 9.11.1867) (Bombay: Govt. Central Press, 1869) [hereafter *Correspondence R.S.A.*].

78. Mr. Fernandez to the Collector of Kheda *Matar R.S.S.,* 7 (italics mine).

79. This is documented in several papers collected under in Gyan Prakash's edited volume, *The World of the Rural Laborer in Colonial India* (Delhi: Oxford, 1990), as well as in Sugata Bose's edited volume, *Credit Markets, and the Agrarian Economy of Colonial India* (Delhi: Oxford, 1994). See also I. J. Catanach, *Rural Credit in Western India: 1875–1930* (Berkeley: University of California Press). Malcolm Darling was almost the sole voice of dissent in this tirade against sahukars; see his *The Punjab Peasant in Prosperity and Debt,* 4th ed. (Delhi: 1947).

80. *Correspondence R.S.A.,* 9.

81. L. V. M. Robertson to the Collector of Kaira (No. 268 of 1.7.1916), 7, in SRBG (NS), *Papers Relating to the Second Revision Survey Settlement of Matar Taluka of the Kaira District* (Bombay: Govt. Central Press, 1920) [hereafter *Matar S.R.S.S*].

82. See D. N. Dhanagre, *Agrarian Movements and Gandhian Politics* (Agra: Institute of Social Sciences, Agra University, 1975), esp. 30–41; and Hardiman, *Peasant Nationalists of Gujarat.*

83. Rainfall figures in the text are culled from L. V. M. Robertson's memo to the Collector of Kaira (No. 268 of 1.7.1916), Appendices A and A-1, 28–29, *Matar S.R.S.S.*

84. Robertson, memo to Collector of Kaira, 5. A comparison of census population data for seven subdistricts of Kaira [Kheda] District between 1891 and 1921 shows that the male and female populations of the district declined secularly between 1891

and 1901 (the period that brackets the *chhapanio dukal*—the Great Famine of 1900, or *Samvat* 1956), with *proportionately* larger declines in the male populations of the subdistricts as well as in the male and female populations of Kapadvanj, Thasra, Matar, and Mehmedabad subdistricts—in that order. Nadiad subdistrict, the most prosperous in the district, was least affected (although absolute mortality was high). Borsad and Anand subdistricts were also considerably less affected than Kapadvanj, Thasra, Matar, and Mehmedabad. The statistics are not surprising given that the latter four subdistricts were agriculturally (and, in general, economically) the most vulnerable in the district. By contrast, Nadiad, Borsad, Anand, and Petlad (which was then part of adjoining Baroda State) form the Charotar, which is—and was at the turn of the century—the most fertile and well-diversified agricultural region in Western India. By 1911, there were signs of muted recovery in Anand, Borsad, and Kapadvanj subdistricts, but nowhere else. The district as a whole continued to reel under the impact of a series of indifferent rainfall years and lingering morbidity compounded by malaria, plague, and cholera outbreaks. It was not until 1921 that census data registers a secular recovery in the population of the district. In accompaniment of this trend, it is also possible to observe without postulating a causal connection an increase in the prices of jowar, bajri, paddy, wheat, and cotton, as well as an increase in the real daily wages of field laborers. Whereas crop prices escalated after 1918—on the heels of World War I and famine across most of Bombay Presidency—and managed to retain an upward momentum until 1925; real wages, which began rising in 1918, continued to climb until 1932.

85. Robertson, memo to Collector of Kaira, Appendix D, 32.

86. Robertson, memo to Collector of Kaira, Appendix F, 32.

87. Quoted in Chaturvedi, *Peasants Pasts*, 104.

88. L. V. M. Robertson to the Collector of Kaira (No. 268 of 1.7.1916), 14 and 6, *Matar S.R.S.S.*

89. Chaturvedi, *Peasant Pasts*, 105, notes: "Large numbers of Dharalas died in these camps as a result of exhaustion and malnutrition, but others also perished from communicable diseases like cholera and dysentery. Many who survived the relief camps simply preferred to return to their respective villages during the famine as a way to escape the labor demands established by the government."

3. Machine

1. Some recent notable books include M. P. Cowen and R. W. Shenton, *Doctrines of Development* (London: Routledge, 1996); Jonathan Crush, ed., *Power of Development* (London: Routledge, 1995); Arturo Escobar, *Encountering Development* (Princeton, N.J.: Princeton University Press, 1994); James Ferguson, *The Anti-Politics Machine: "Development," De-Politicization and Bureaucratic Power in Lesotho*, new edition (Minneapolis: University of Minnesota Press, 1994); James C. Scott, *Seeing Like a State* (New Haven, Conn.: Yale University Press, 1998); K. Sivaramakrishnan, *Modern Forests* (Stanford, Calif.: Stanford University Press, 1999); Gillian Hart, *Disabling Globalization: Places of Power in Post-Apartheid Africa* (Berkeley: University of California Press, 2002); Timothy Mitchell, *Rule of Experts: Egypt, Techno-Politics, Modernity* (Berkeley: University of California Press, 2002); Donald Moore, *Suffering for Territory: Race, Place, and Power in Zimbabwe* (Durham, N.C.: Duke University

Press, 2005); and Christine Walley, *Rough Waters: Nature and Development in an East African Marine Park* (Princeton, N.J.: Princeton University Press, 2004).

2. Gilles Deleuze and Félix Guattari, *A Thousand Plateaus: Capitalism and Schizophrenia,* trans. Brian Massumi (Minneapolis: University of Minnesota Press), 142. In the same passage they note that an abstract machine "plays a piloting role."

3. I have opted here for the description "out-of-caste" rather than equivalents like Scheduled Caste (SC), *dalit* ("downtrodden" or "broken"), Untouchable, or *asprushya* (Gujarati, "unclean") because in my meetings with Kanubhai he resolutely refused these terms as self-identifiers. "Out-of-caste" does not bear the pejorative sense of "outcaste"; at the same time it is technically accurate in conveying that Nayaks fall outside the four formal *varnas* (Brahmin, Kshatriya, Vania, and Sudra) of the Hindu caste system. In other instances in the book, where an interlocutor explicitly claims an SC or dalit identity, I have used the appropriate term.

4. Conversation with Kanubhai Nayak and his mother, Pinglaj, March 31, 1995. The Gujarati word *dosi* is a generic and more or less respectful term of address for an old woman. It carries the connotation of "grandmother."

5. Her election was invalidated on two corruption charges in the conduct of her poll campaign in the parliamentary elections of 1971. She was accused of violating the Indian law, first, by using an officer of her government to make campaign arrangements, and second, by using other state officers to put up speaker's stands in her constituency and supply electricity to her amplifying equipment.

6. Pravin Sheth, *Political Development in Gujarat* (Ahmedabad: Karnavati Publications, 1998), 21.

7. Alfred North Whitehead, *Process and Reality* (corrected edition), ed. David Ray Griffin and Donald W. Sherburne (New York: Free Press, 1978), 53. French neostructuralist philosophers (Althusser, Foucault, Derrida, to name three) have also moved "the subject from a constituting function to a constituted position." But their project was not the same as Whitehead's. As Etienne Balibar, "Althusser's Object," *Social Text* (1994): 157–88, notes, none of the prominent neostructuralists were satisfied with disqualifying the subject. Rather they wanted to ask how it was that classical philosophy and modern political theory installed the "subject" in a foundational position.

8. Thus, the activated capacity of "labor-power" is a desiring production. But labor-power is not the attribute of pre-given "individuals." As Marx notes in *Grundrisse* and *Capital,* labor-power as pure potential to produce exceeds individuals; cf. Karl Marx, *Grundrisse,* trans. Martin Nicolaus (London: Penguin Books, 1973 [1858]) and *Capital,* Vol. 1: *A Critique of Political Economy,* trans. Ben Fowkes (London: Penguin Books/NLR). Or, as Paolo Virno puts it, "[L]abor-power does not designate one specific faculty, but the entirety of human faculties in as much as they are involved in productive praxis." See Virno, *The Grammar of the Multitude* (Los Angeles: Semiotext(e), 2004), 84. As I discuss in chapter 5, capitalism tries to appropriate and discipline this constituting *potential* as use-value for itself; but there lies the rub: as potential it can be harnessed for other, noncapitalist, uses (which may or may not include revolutionary desire)—a reality that capital is acutely cognizant of.

9. The italicized phrase is from Nicholas Georgescu-Roegen, *The Entropy Law and the Economic Process* (Cambridge, Mass.: Harvard University Press, 1999 [1971]), 13. It is an obvious reference to the process philosophy of Alfred North

Whitehead, particularly his concept of "concrescence"; cf. Whitehead, *Process and Reality.*

10. This motto painfully describes majoritarian violence against Muslims and Christians in Gujarat today. Deleuze and Guattari, *A Thousand Plateaus,* 216.

11. Bentham's writings are sufficiently complex to stymie any easy rendering of them. They can be read, as James Mill apparently did, to sanction a disciplinary form of government. Moreover, Mill attempted to purge the hedonistic implications of Utilitarianism—namely, the equation of "utility" to "pleasure"—by associating "utility" with "usefulness." This translation, first, made it acceptable as a moral philosophy to the evangelical stream within Liberalism and, second, gave warrant to a range of colonial interventions into Indian society on the grounds these would promote "usefulness" of conduct, in the two senses discussed in chapter 1. In contrast to this "authoritarian" interpretation of Bentham (which Eric Stokes also perpetuates) lies the argument that Bentham's principle of utility was ultimately an endorsement of democracy, because democracy alone could enact the checks and balances that would ensure government committed to "the greatest happiness" of society. Indeed, on this reading Bentham becomes a key inspiration for the modern welfare or social democratic state—that is, the state of "police" in the older sense. On this latter point, see Ross Harrison, *Bentham* (London: Routledge and Kegan Paul, 1983), esp. 225–62. On Bentham and democracy, see Bhikhu Parekh, "Introduction," in Parekh, ed., *Bentham's Political Thought* (London: Croom Helm, 1973), 13–44; Harrison, *Bentham,* 195–224; and Allison Dube, "The Tree of Utility in India," in *J. S. Mill's Encounter with India,* ed. Martin I. Moir, Douglas M. Peers, and Lynn Zastoupil (Toronto: University of Toronto Press, 1999), 34–52.

12. Eric Stokes, *The English Utilitarians and India* (Oxford: Clarendon Press, 1959), 67.

13. Ranajit Guha, *Dominance without Hegemony: History and Power in Colonial India* (Cambridge, Mass.: Harvard University Press, 1998).

14. Antonio Gramsci, "Passive Revolution, Caesarism, Fascism," in *The Antonio Gramsci Reader: Selected Writings, 1916–1935,* ed. David Forgacs (New York: New York University Press, 2000), 261.

15. My use of the term "people" rather than "masses" or "multitude" is deliberate. As Paolo Virno clarifies, the notion of "people" is historically inseparable from the contemporary State and public sphere. Invoking Hobbes, he writes: "For Hobbes, the decisive political clash is one which takes place between multitude and people. The modern public sphere can have as its barycenter *either* one *or* the other. Civil war, always threatening, has its logical form in this alternative. The concept of people, according to Hobbes, is strictly correlated to the existence of the State; furthermore, it is a reverberation, a reflection of the State: if there is a State, then there are people. In the absence of the State, there are no people." Virno, *The Grammar of the Multitude,* 22.

16. Sir John Shore, Minute of June 18, 1789, in the appendices to Walter K. Firminger, ed., *The Fifth Report on East India Company Affairs, 1812,* 3 vols. (Calcutta: R. Cambray and Co., 1917).

17. For an instructive discussion of the banal practices through which the category "economy" is produced—as an autonomous and self-regulating domain of transactions—see Timothy Mitchell, "The Character of Calculability," in *Rule of Experts* (Berkeley: University of California Press, 2003). While I am persuaded by

Mitchell's analysis of "economy" as the effect of practices, I am less swayed by his claim that its emergence as a self-adequate entity must be dated to the early twentieth century. Certainly with the rise of increasingly sophisticated statistical techniques and mathematical models, juxtaposed to the power of science, the economy-effect becomes dramatically more pronounced and pervasive in the twentieth century. But to claim that seventeenth- and eighteenth-century mercantilism, eighteenth-century physiocratic thought, or eighteenth- and nineteenth-century classical economics did not produce an economy-effect strikes me as untenable. On one issue I have no dispute with Mitchell: that seventeenth- through nineteenth-century doctrines were doctrines of political economy that were tied to governmental power and whose image of the economy was that of a super-aggregated household whose wealth had to be wisely supervised.

18. Quoted in Sunil Khilnani, *The Idea of India* (New Delhi: Penguin Books, 1998), 69.

19. On these aspects of colonial rule, see U. Kalpagam, "Colonial Governmentality and the 'Economy,'" *Economy and Society* 29, no. 3 (August 2000): 418–38; Manu Goswami, *Producing India: From Colonial Economy to National Space* (Chicago: University of Chicago Press, 2004); and Rohan D'Souza, *Drowned and Damned: Colonial Capitalism and Flood Control in Eastern India* (New Delhi: Oxford University Press, 2006).

20. MISA was passed by Parliament in 1973 under Indira Gandhi's administration, and repealed in 1977 by the Janata Government.

21. On January 10, 2007, the activist Medha Patkar was arrested in Singur, West Bengal, under Section 144, which "bans the assembly of people." Singur is the slated site of a new Tata vehicle manufacturing facility. It will be built on 900+ acres of land that the State of West Bengal intends to acquire by eminent domain from villagers for around 130 crore rupees and lease to Tata Industries for ninety-nine years at a paltry rent of Rs. 10 lacs per month. A parallel agitation against land expropriation in Nandigram, West Bengal, for a proposed chemical cluster to be operated by an Indonesian multinational, has led to several deaths and police detentions.

22. McKenzie Wark, *A Hacker Manifesto* (Cambride, Mass.: Harvard University Press, 2004), 261.

23. Donald Moore, *Suffering for Territory*, 9.

24. David Scott, *Refashioning Futures: Criticism After Postcoloniality* (Princeton, N.J.: Princeton University Press, 1999), 38.

25. Uptakes of governmentality that underplay the role of violence are understandable: with few exceptions, Foucault had little to say about the violence of colonial (or postcolonial) rule and how imperial encounters might have been linked dialectically to changing configurations of power. Foucault's 1975–76 lectures at the College de France, "*Society Must Be Defended*," trans. David Macey (New York: Picador, 2003) are a notable exception. But contrast Foucault's writings with Michael Taussig's, particularly his *Shamanism, Colonialism, and the Wild Man* (Chicago: University of Chicago Press, 1987), in which he demonstrates the brutal coupling of sovereignty–discipline–governmentality (without naming these modes of power as such). On newly innovative forms of violence, I think of the flexible logic of colonization practiced by the Israeli Defense Forces (IDF) in the Occupied Territories. Older modes of colonization, including apartheid regimes, which relied on segmentation of people, spaces, and things to control colonized populations.

By comparison, the IDF combines a segmentary logic (the Wall) with a mobile logic. The latter includes ad hoc closures and openings of border crossings; shifting criteria of documentary evidence (to prove one's "identity," for instance); arbitrary house demolitions and assassinations; wanton shelling of Palestinian habitations; repeated "accidental" deaths of Palestinian children by sniper fire; erratic permission for entry of foreign funds, food and other commodities into the Occupied Territories; refusal to recognize inalienable property rights of Palestinians to their lands or water resources; and so on. A mobile logic of control wants to produce the effect of radical uncertainty—of not knowing what codes apply to life. And by such uncertainty it seeks to dissipate resistance—indeed, the will to resist.

26. Michel Foucault, "Governmentality," in *The Foucault Effect: Studies in Governmentality*, ed. Graham Burchell, Colin Gordon, and Peter Miller (Chicago: University of Chicago Press, 1991), 95. In that same essay, Foucault writes: "[W]e need to see things not in terms of the replacement of a society of sovereignty by a disciplinary society and the subsequent replacement of a disciplinary society by a society of government; in reality on has a triangle, sovereignty–discipline–government, which has as its primary target the population and its essential mechanism the apparatuses of security. . . . I wanted to demonstrate the deep historical link between the movement that overturns the constants of sovereignty in consequence of the problem of choices of government, the movement that brings about the emergence of the population as a datum, as a field of intervention and as an objective of governmental techniques, the process which isolates the economy as a specific sector of reality, and political economy as the science and technique of intervention of government it that field of reality" (102).

27. This distinction is from Michel Foucault, *A History of Sexuality, Vol. 1* (New York: Vintage Books, 1978), esp. 135–59, where he elaborates the consequences of these different modalities of power.

28. One of the best and most comprehensive recent analyses of development planning and its aftermath, extending up to the present, can be found in Stuart Corbridge and John Harriss, *Reinventing India: Liberalization, Hindu Nationalism and Popular Democracy* (Cambridge: Polity Press, 2000), esp. chaps. 3 and 4. Also see Akhil Gupta's fine book, *Postcolonial Developments: Agriculture in the Making of Modern India* (Durham, N.C.: Duke University Press, 1998), for a lucid discussion of agricultural policy and agrarian populism. Other excellent examples, though more narrowly focused, include Sukhamoy Chakravarty, *Development Planning: The Indian Experience* (Oxford: Clarendon Press, 1987), from a roughly centrist perspective; Jagdish Bhagwati, *India in Transition: Freeing the Economy* (Oxford: Clarendon Press, 1993), from a right-liberal perspective; M. L. Dantwala, ed., *Dilemmas of Growth: The Indian Experience* (New Delhi: Sage Publications, 1996), from a neopopulist perspective; and Byres, ed., *The Indian Economy: Major Debates Since Independence* (Delhi: Oxford University Press, 1998), from a left perspective.

29. The planning debates began in earnest in 1938 with the inception of the National Planning Committee (NPC) of the Congress Party. Jawaharlal Nehru, the Chairman of the NPC, and Subhas Chandra Bose, then President of the Congress Party were instrumental in its creation. As committed socialists, who were impressed by the apparent success of socialist economic planning in the Soviet Union, both Nehru and Bose came to see planning as crucial for ameliorating poverty and inequality in India. For informative discussions of the NPC and other

precursors to the post-Independence planning process, see Hanson, *The Process of Planning*, 27–49, and Pramit Chaudhuri, "The Origins of Modern India"s Economic Development Strategy," in Mike Shepperdson and Colin Simmons, *The Indian National Congress and the Political Economy of India 1885–1985* (Aldershot, U.K.: Avebury, 1988), 272–81. Also Khilnani, *The Idea of India*, chap. 2.

30. Chakravarty, *Development Planning*, 9–10.

31. Jawaharlal Nehru, *The Discovery of India* (Calcutta: The Signet Press, 1946), 665.

32. Nehru, *The Discovery of India*, 658–59.

33. This sentiment is forcefully expressed by Jawaharlal Nehru, the architect of India's post-Independence development path, in his autobiography: "Our final aim," he writes, "can only be a classless society with equal economic justice and opportunity for all, a society organised on a planned basis for the raising of mankind to higher material and cultured levels"; Jawaharlal Nehru, *An Autobiography* (London: John Lane, The Bodley Head, 1936), 551–52.

34. Michael Kidron, *Foreign Investments in India* (London: Oxford University Press, 1965).

35. P. C. Mahalanobis, *Papers on Planning*, ed. P. K. Bose and M. Mukherjee (Calcutta: Statistical Publishing Society, 1985), 197–98; English translation of an article originally in Russian.

36. Mahalanobis, "The Need of Scientific and Technical Man-Power for Economic Development," in *Papers on Planning*, 205.

37. For a discussion of Nehru's intellectual influences, including Lenin, see his *An Autobiography*, 19–26; also Francine Frankel, *India's Political Economy, 1947–1977* (Princeton, N.J.: Princeton University Press, 1978), 13–14.

38. Chakravarty, *Development Planning*, 14. The influence of the Bombay Plan of 1944, sponsored by a consortium of Indian industrialists led by J. R. D. Tata and presented as a template for post-Independence economic policy, has been the subject of some debate. In predictable fashion, mainstream economists (including left-centrists like Chakravarty) acknowledge that it played a part in planning debates but discount its overall influence; left economists, by contrast, tend to claim that the economic vision of the Bombay Plan was realized in the initial Five-Year Plans, which granted domestic capitalists substantial protection from foreign competition and an effective monopoly over the value-added light-manufacturing sectors. A. H. Hanson in his *The Process of Planning: A Study of India's Five-Year Plans 1950–64* (London: Oxford University Press, 1966), 41–44, concludes that the Bombay Plan had a decisive structural influence on the First Five-Year Plan, but that the Second Five-Year Plan was more sympathetic to the vision of socialist People's Plan promoted by M. N. Roy and the Indian Federation of Labor.

39. Dual-economy models were the rage in the nascent field of "development economics" during the 1950s and 1960s. The basic premise of these models—mathematically formalized through the construct of a two-sector economy, hence, the name—was that the development paths of Third World countries could be analyzed as an evolving relationship between a (capitalist, modern, high-productivity, high elasticity of consumption) urban-industrial sector and a (backward, traditional, low-productivity, low-elasticity of consumption) agricultural sector. It was a mostly one-sided relationship, with agriculture as handmaiden to industry. On the one hand, it served as a site for "primitive surplus

accumulation" through transfer of labor, agricultural products, raw materials, and savings (or, in the most general sense, surplus product); on the other hand (but less prominently), as a domestic market for manufactured goods. Whereas the (classical) Lewis and Ranis-Fei models assumed zero marginal product of labor in agriculture until a certain threshold, thereby ensuring that labor migration to industry did not negatively affect agricultural output; in the neoclassical Jorgensen model labor's marginal product in agriculture was assumed to be positive all along. Accordingly, Jorgensen placed great emphasis on the role of technological change in agriculture that would increase labor's marginal productivity and offset the negative impact of population migration to the urban-industrial sector. The Lewis and Ranis-Fei model foresaw agriculture transforming itself—by an unspecified process—from an "average product" regime (cultivators devoted to maximization of total returns) to a "marginal product" regime (cultivators devoted to profit maximization). Both types of dual-economy models predicted an eventual downsizing and modernization of the agricultural sector and increasing importance of the urban-industrial sector (in terms of share in GDP and population concentration).

40. See Chakravarty, *Development Planning,* 94, where he excerpts from Sen's December 1959 speech.

41. Chakravarty, *Development Planning,* 7; also see Patnaik, "Some Debates on Planning," 159. The views of these authors is at variance with the assessment offered by Frankel, who maintains that Indian planning was a compromise between the modernization and Gandhian socialist wings of the Congress Party; cf. Frankel, *India's Political Economy,* 14–16.

42. Partha Chatterjee's provocative argument that Indian nationalist thought at its moment of arrival or synthesis—embodied in the figure of Nehru—represents the victory of "capital" in engineering a "passive revolution" that serves its interests is a strong form of this claim. Although Chatterjee does not want to be voluntarist (his innovative deployment of Gramsci and Hegel is in an objectivist mode) he tends to lapse into voluntarism when, for example, he depicts Nehru as a calculating figure who enrolls Gandhi as a mass leader for nationalism's anticolonial moment of maneuver primarily as a matter of strategy. See his *Nationalist Thought and the Colonial World* (Delhi: Oxford University Press, 1986), 152.

43. Louis Althusser, *For Marx,* trans. Ben Brewster (London: Verso), 232.

44. One thinks here of Engels's famous discussion of Marx's recuperation of the "theory of value" from the floundering wreckage of Smith's and Ricardo's predecessor labor theories of value; see Frederick Engels, "Preface," in Marx, *Capital,* vol. 2, trans. David Fernbach, introduction by Ernest Mandel (London: Penguin Books), 83–102 (but particularly 97–102). Engels's preface had a formative impact on Althusser's concept of the problematic as evident from his *Reading Capital;* see Louis Althusser and Étienne Balibar, *Reading Capital,* trans. Ben Brewster (London: Verso, 1978), 19–28. Chatterjee, *Nationalist Thought and the Colonial World,* 143–45, also notes that the Gandhian plan was a nonstarter from the outset.

45. See Nehru, *An Autobiography,* esp. 509–52. On a different note, I should clarify that the issue here is not whether the Gandhian approach would have been more "correct" than the Nehruvian approach adopted in the Five-Year Plans. As a child of India's path to modernization—and one able, retrospectively,

to perceive its errors but nevertheless unable to endorse a system built around traditions as the more desirable—I am, in any case, hardly in a position to sit judgment. Instead, my continuing if conflicted affirmation of development as a "good" and dogged resistance to Gandhian economics—its image in my mind as an anachronistic, moralizing system—is compelling testimony to the power of development.

46. Jawaharlal Nehru, "The Big Machine," in *The Essential Writings of Jawaharlal Nehru*, ed. S. Gopal and Uma Iyengar (Delhi: Oxford University Press), 1:679–80.

47. For a highly readable account of the Nehruvian model of centralized planning, see Ramachandra Guha, "The Conquest of Nature," in his *India After Gandhi: The History of the World's Largest Democracy* (New Delhi: Picador, 2007), 201–25. Guha observes that B. R. Shenoy was "the sole economist on the panel of experts who disagreed with the basic approach of the second five-year plan" (221). Shenoy appeared to nurture reservations about the wisdom of nationalization and to be committed to laissez-faire methods. But his main criticism of the plan, notes Guha, was that it was overambitious and "seriously overestimated the rate of saving in the Indian economy"—and, as such, would precipitate a shortfall in funds that "would have to be made up by deficit financing, contributing to greater inflation" (222). Another economist, B. V. Krishnamurti, objected to the second plan on different grounds—its neglect of education and the "absurdly low" sums allocated to this constitutional priority (222–23).

48. Mahalanobis, "The Need of Scientific and Technical Man-Power for Economic Development," 205, 207 (italics mine).

49. The Plan document included a chapter titled "Land Reform and Agrarian Organization."

50. Cf. Sudipta Kaviraj, "On the Crisis of Political Institutions in India," *Contributions to Indian Sociology* 18 (1984): 223–43, and Kaviraj, "The Modern State in India," in *Dynamics of State Formation: India and Europe Compared*, ed. Sudipta Kaviraj and Martin Dornboos (New Delhi: Sage, 1997); Partha Chatterjee, *Nationalist Thought and the Colonial World: A Derivative Discourse?* (Minneapolis: University of Minnesota Press, 1986), esp. chap. 5. Also see C. J. Fuller and John Harriss, "For an Anthropology of the Modern Indian State," in *The Everyday State and Society in Modern India*, ed. Christopher John Fuller and Véronique Bénéï (London: C. Hurst and Co., 2001).

51. According to Frankel, *India's Political Economy*, 23, "The Congress party, which had dominated politics since the turn of the century, mastered the art of political accommodation to its highest degree. They succeeded by adapting local power structures, using the natural building blocks closest at hand. Within each region, they recruited from among those who were typically members of the dominant landowning castes and who were the leading members of the large land-owing caste. Such local notables put together the basic units of the Congress Party organization. The units were composed of the leader's kin, caste fellows, and economic dependents. The wider district, state, and national party organizations represented a complex pyramiding of these vertical (multicaste and multiclass) alliances. Indeed, the majority of Congressmen retained primary loyalty to their faction, or, if the party dissolved, to the kinship and caste groupings at its core." See also Corbridge and Harriss, *Reinventing India*, chap. 3.

52. Wark, *A Hacker's Manifesto*, 263.

53. See Joseph Buttigieg, "Gramsci on Civil Society," *boundary 2* 22, no. 3 (1995): 1–32. Also, in the Indian context, Fuller and Harriss, "For an Anthropology of the Modern Indian State."

54. Jawaharlal Nehru, "Building India," in *The Essential Writings of Jawaharlal Nehru*, ed. S. Gopal and Uma Iyengar (Delhi: Oxford University Press), 2:148.

55. Gilles Deleuze, *Foucault*, trans. Séan Hand (Minneapolis: University of Minnesota Press, 1988), 33.

56. See Bruno Latour, "Visualization and Cognition: Thinking with Eyes and Hands," in *Knowledge and Society: Studies in the Sociology of Culture Past and Present*, ed. H. Kukli and E. Long (Greenwich, Conn.: JAI Press), 6:1–40.

57. Hence, in his classic 1966 study of Indian planning, A. H. Hanson observed that "the [Planning] Commission"s approach, as revealed in the three [Five-Year] plan reports, suggests a tendency to regard political factors as tangential rather than central. The planners come up with certain ideologically inspired or economically calculated proposals that are then modified or deflected by a variety of group pressures. The result is compromise, inconsistency, and lack of realism. Much of this could be avoided if the whole constellation of sociopolitical circumstances were treated as basic data. 'Politics' could then be built into the plan itself, rather than being left to impinge upon it. . . . Instead, the Indians have adopted what might be described as a "planning orthodoxy," consisting of a series of assumptions about Indian society on which approach to planning is based. The assumptions involve the necessity of unanimity and the irrelevance of "politics"; Hanson, *The Process of Planning*, 262. A parallel example of how certain assumptions trump others in the rendering visible of the terrain that is to be transformed by development planning see Timothy Mitchell's provocative essay, "The Object of Development," in his *Rule of Experts: Egypt, Techno-Politics, Modernity* (Berkeley: University of California Press, 2002), 209–43. On the technicization and attempted evacuation of politics from development planning, see also James Ferguson, *The Anti-Politics Machine* (Princeton, N.J.: Princeton University Press, 1991).

58. Terry Byres, "Introduction," in *The Indian Economy*, ed. Byres, 15, and Prabhat Patnaik, "Some Indian Debates on Planning," in the same volume, 159–64.

59. For more, see Mary Poovey, *The Making of a Social Body* (Chicago: University of Chicago Press, 1995); also Deleuze, *Foucault*, 75–77. In his Spinozist rendering of Foucault, Deleuze characterizes power as "unformed affects," specifically the potential affects of "unformed matter" (the field of receptivity or visibility, which has the ability to be *affected*) and "unformalized functions" (the field of spontaneity or statements, which has the ability to *affect*). Knowledge actualizes power by giving form to or stabilizing these two kinds of affects. Knowledge and power are mutually presupposing because one cannot operate without the other. To elaborate: the concrete assemblages that make the relations of a diagram *visible* and *sayable*—clinics, schools, factories, banks, various agencies and departments that comprise "the State," and less obviously, the individual "subject"—hinge on a "double articulation." On the one hand, they organize (or form) *matter* into fields of visibility; on the other hand, they finalize (or form) *functions* into fields of articulability. Combinations of things and statements, connected *in* (practices of) knowledge, demarcate historical strata as *formations*. Thus, assemblages are formations that are sutured, and thereby granted a modicum of consistency, by knowledge: their power to act and the

knowledge that would enable power to become action (the "conduct of conduct," for instance) are mutually presupposing. Consider the various disciplinary knowledges that are organized around development: development anthropology, development economics, development planning, development sociology, political economy of development, development studies, even postdevelopment. Each deploys things *and* words—technologies and empiricities to "see" development and mechanisms and sign regimes to "talk" about it—through concrete institutional sites. These deployments in turn diagnose and/or prescribe development interventions.

60. This way of characterizing the agonism of planners versus peasants owes to Chatterjee, *Nationalist Thought and the Colonial World*, 145.

61. On the connections between religious notions of progress and salvation and secular doctrines of development, see M. P. Cowen and R. W. Shenton's extraordinary, *Doctrines of Development* (London: Routledge, 1995).

62. These were, of course, sectors complementary to both industry and agriculture—the staple of dual-economy models that dominated planning for two decades after Independence.

63. On various forms of capital, and the importance of production time and circulation time to capital accumulation, see Karl Marx, *Capital*, vol. 2, trans. David Fernbach (London: Penguin, 1978). Also see Ernest Mandel's "Introduction" to the volume, particularly 18–26; and on the topic of "simple" versus "expanded" reproduction, Étienne Balibar, "Reproduction," in Louis Althusser and Étienne Balibar, *Reading Capital* (London: Verso, 1997 [1970]), 254–72.

64. It is worth pointing out that in characterizing governmentality this way Foucault plays "on the double meaning in French of the verb *conduire* (to lead or to drive) and *se conduire* (to behave or conduct oneself)—whence *la conduite*, conduct or behavior." See endnote 2 by translator in Michel Foucault, "The Subject and Power," in *Power: Essential Works of Michel Foucault, 1954–1984*, vol. 3, ed. James D. Faubion (New York: New Press, 2001): 348.

65. On this theme, see Partha Chatterjee, *The Politics of the Governed: Reflections on Popular Politics in Most of the World* (New York: Columbia University Press, 2004).

66. An interesting sidebar here, connected to the "ideological state apparatuses" that constitute key instruments of government, is the phenomenal growth in post-Independence India in the profession of economics. Marking the beginnings of passage from sovereign power to governmentality, Edmund Burke—the enormously influential late eighteenth-century conservative English politician—lamented in his *Reflections on the Revolution in France*: "[T]he age of chivalry is gone. That of sophisters, economists, and calculators has succeeded; and the glory of Europe is extinguished for ever" (quoted in Byres, "The Creation of 'The Tribe of Pundits Called Economists,'" in his *The Indian Economy*, 20). From barely existing in 1947, the discipline of economics within a decade had begun to attract the country's most talented students. The Delhi School of Economics had risen to international prominence, attracting several famous visitors (including left-liberal economists such as Albert Hirschman, Joan Robinson, Nicholas Kaldor, and John Kenneth Galbraith, as well as right-wing economists like Milton Friedman and P. T. Bauer); and theoretical advances within the still young field of development economics, as the eminent development economist Hla Myint observed on several occasions, had soon accumulated a formidable debt to Indian planning. Of course, planning is now out of fashion (the "reformists," it seems, are on top for the time being) but governmental

power, far from being on the wane, has simply revised its distribution of tactics, giving freer rein, as the early British liberals would have wanted, to the "invisible hand" of the market. In this process, the conduct of the nation-state has itself become the object of governmental power—its welfare and that of its citizens now hegemonically linked to "responsibilized conduct" in the global market, in accordance with the rules of competition, private property, human rights, and democracy. In all of this, the continued visibility and influence of Indian economists on the domestic and international fronts, and their contributions to the "reform" debates, confirms that the interpellation of this important segment of the population—those who, in the very practice of their professions, endorse and elaborate techniques of government (as the "conduct of conducts") through education, scholarship, and policy—remains as important as ever.

67. Chakravarty, *Development Planning*, 21–22.

68. S. R. Sen's speech at the All-India Agricultural Economics Conference, Baroda, December 1959, excerpted in Chakravarty, *Development Planning*, 94.

69. Mellor listed three phases of agricultural modernization: Phase I, an initial stage of technological stagnation; Phase II, an intermediate stage of technological dynamism with low capitalization; and Phase III, the final stage, combining technological dynamism with high capitalization of agricultural operations. The details of his agricultural development approach are presented in John W. Mellor, *The Economics of Agricultural Development* (Ithaca, N.Y.: Cornell University Press, 1966). Also see John W. Mellor, *The New Economics of Growth: A Strategy for India and the Developing World* (Ithaca, N.Y.: Cornell University Press, 1976); and John W. Mellor and Gunvant Desai, *Agricultural Change and Rural Poverty* (Delhi: Oxford University Press, 1986).

70. Dale Jorgensen, "The Development of a Dual Economy," *Economic Journal* 71 (1961): 309–34.

71. For an overview of the economics literature that was influenced by Mellor's work in the 1960s, see Nirvikar Singh, "Some Aspects of Technological Change and Innovation in Agriculture," in Kaushik Basu, ed., *Agrarian Questions* (Delhi: Oxford University Press, 1994). The importance of access to credit as a means of negotiating consumption and production risk and, thereby, in creating conditions for differential household accumulation, is one the main planks of this thesis. Culturalist explanations that highlighted the absence of a particular attitude or mentality, such as "a spirit of entrepreneurship," to explain low levels of savings and investment—in short, the "backwardness"—of countries like India, were popular among development economists in the 1950s. See most notably Bert Hoselitz, "Non-Economic Barriers to Economic Development," which first appeared in 1952 in the journal *Economic Development and Cultural Change* and is reprinted in Stuart Corbridge, ed., *Development Studies Reader* (Oxford: Oxford University Press, 1995), 17–27; and Albert O. Hirschman, *The Strategy of Economic Development* (New Haven: Yale University Press, 1958), whose account is considerably more nuanced and multifaceted than Hoselitz's. Nevertheless, these sorts of explanations consolidated an anthropology of development based around "the denial of coevalness" (to use Johannes Fabian's felicitious expression). In the narratives of Hoselitz, Hirschman and others, *cultural difference*—wittingly or unwittingly—came to function as an index of *temporal distance;* tautologically, then, those in industrialized nations of the West were held to be "developed" because of their entrepreneurial instinct for

capital accumulation, whereas those in backward countries like India lagged behind (remained "underdeveloped") because of the lack of such attitude. The irony does not end here. Those like the economist T. W. Schultz, who rejected culturalist explanations to argue that traditional agriculturalists were every bit as rational as their counterparts in the West—on the face of it, a progressive move—ended up committing a different fallacy. They smuggled in a particularism masquerading as universalism, namely, the assumption that individuals universally exhibit a calculative rationality that is "always, already" geared toward capital accumulation. What was missing then, in their estimation, was simply the proper set of incentives; see Schultz's famous statement, *Transforming Traditional Agriculture* (New Haven: Yale University Press, 1964). Mellor, it would appear, was influenced by Schultz in his formulation of the agricultural development approach, with its underlying model of peasant rationality. But, both, the cultural economists and the rational-choice economists could have usefully engaged with Marx, who, in the *Grundrisse* and in *Capital*, vol. 3, observed that "capitalists"—broadly understood now as those who engage in production primarily for the sake of profit—do not come ready made. They are products of a definite conjuncture of historical factors and have to be continuously reproduced. The participation of individuals as capitalists is, as such, never guaranteed, as I will show in chapter 5. In this sense, to assume a capitalist rationality as the universal predisposition is simply folly. Note, however, that I do not reject out of hand the arguments of either the cultural economists or the rational-choice economists: because, between them, they produce a "truth"—namely, the nominalism of "rational" conduct. Unfortunately, they dent this truth by asserting in their models a pre-given rationality, without justifying its material basis. What is the spectrum of rational actions within a particular time-space context and how does it come to be so are the prior and difficult questions that have to be confronted. Some instruction on these matters can be found in Pierre Bourdieu, *Outline of a Theory of Practice*, trans. Richard Nice (Cambridge: Cambridge University Press, 1977); the various essays by Michel Foucault gathered in *Power: Essential Works of Michel Foucault, 1954–1984*, vol. 3; and Donald Donham, *History, Power, Ideology* (Cambridge: Cambridge University Press, 1990).

72. Deleuze and Guattari, *A Thousand Plateaus*, 433.

73. Peter Hallward, *Badiou: A Subject to Truth* (Minneapolis: University of Minnesota Press, 2003), 96. There is (perhaps intentional) proximity between Badiou's thinking on the state and Deleuze and Guattari's given Badiou's conflicted affinities with them; there is also unintended proximity with James C. Scott's, *Seeing Like a State*, where he diagnoses modern state control as a combination of two interlinked logics: "legibility" and "simplification." See Deleuze and Guattari, *A Thousand Plateaus*, esp. chaps. 12 and 13; and James C. Scott, *Seeing Like a State* (New Haven: Yale University Press, 1999).

74. Giorgio Agamben, *Means without End: Notes on Politics* (Minneapolis: University of Minnesota Press, 2007), 87.

75. Giorgio Agamben, in asking "What is a camp?," refuses to identify it with an empirical location. Rather he approaches the question ontologically, observing that the "camp is the space that opens up when the state of exception starts to become the rule." Cf. Agamben, "What Is a Camp?," in *Means without End: Notes on Politics* (Minneapolis: University of Minnesota Press, 2000), 39. Elsewhere in that essay, he describes "the birth of the camp as in our time ... [as] an event that marks in a decisive way the political space itself of modernity" (41).

76. Gilles Deleuze and Félix Guattari, *A Thousand Plateaus: Capitalism and Schizophrenia*, trans. Brian Massumi (Minneapolis: University of Minnesota Press, 1987), 385.

77. Paul Veyne, "Foucault Revolutionizes History," in *Foucault and His Interlocutors*, ed. Arnold I. Davidson (Chicago: University of Chicago Press, 1997), 150–51.

78. On this, see Jawaharlal Nehru, "Development of River Valleys," in *The Essential Writings of Jawaharlal Nehru*, 2:78–81.

79. For a short overview of the Khari system, see T. K. Jayaraman, "Farmer"s Organisations in Surface Irrigation Projects," *Economic and Political Weekly* 16, no. 39 (Review of Agriculture, September 26, 1981), A-89–A-98.

80. V. N. Asopa and B. L. Tripathi, "Command Area Development in Mahi-Kadana," *CMA Monograph No.78* (Ahmedabad: Indian Institute of Management/CMA, 1975), 11.

81. According to the economist A. Vaidyanathan "between 1950 and 1997, the central and State governments together ... directly invested nearly Rs. 540 bn. [approximately, US$12 billion] on irrigation and flood control works, which is by far the largest single item (accounting for a little under four-fifths) of the total public sector plan outlays on development of agriculture and allied activities." See A. Vaidyanathan, *Water Resource Management* (Delhi: Oxford University Press, 1999), 56.

82. The total cultivable area of Gujarat is 12.48 million hectares, which means that the projected irrigation potential for the state is 52 percent. This is, in all likelihood, an overly optimistic appraisal given the continuing vicissitudes of the Narmada irrigation project. See N. B. Desai, O. T. Gulati and K. G. Rathod, "Performance Overview of Mahi-Kadana Project," mimeo (Anand: Water and Land Management Institute, n.d.), A-2, from where the figure of 52 percent was computed. According to Wood, Gujarat continues to remain a food-deficit state despite the large expenditures on irrigation development; John R. Wood, "Changing Institutions and Changing Politics in Rural Water Management: An Overview of Three Zones in Gujarat," paper presented at the conference on *Community Water Management in South Asia, Institute for Asian Research, University of British Columbia*, December 15, 1997.

83. Hydraulic development exemplifies a by now well-trodden insight of Foucault's: "The things with which ... government is to be concerned are in fact men, but men in their relations, their links, their imbrication with those other things which are wealth, resources, means of subsistence, the territory with its specific qualities, climate, irrigation, fertility, etc." Foucault, "Governmentality," 93. The colonial state also pushed hydraulic development as a means of forging economic and social relations that would abet capitalist production. See, for example, David Gilmartin, "Scientific Empire and Imperial Science: Colonialism and Irrigation Technology in the Indus Basin," *The Journal of Asian Studies* 53, no. 4 (1994): 1127–49; and D'Souza, *Drowned and Damned*.

84. S. S. Ray, V. K. Dadhwal, and R. R. Navalgund, "Performance Evaluation of an Irrigation Command Area Using Remote Sensing: A Case Study of Mahi Command, Gujarat, India," *Agricultural Water Management* 56, no. 2 (2002): 82.

85. Anonymous, "Irrigation Development and Performance of MRBC Project," mimeo (Nadiad: Mahi Right Bank Canal Authority). Internal MRBC documents provided to author.

86. The term "dislocation" is from Ernesto Laclau, *New Reflections on the Revolution of Our Time* (London: Verso, 1990).

87. Ray et al., "Performance Evaluation of an Irrigation Command Area Using Remote Sensing," 86–90.

88. These branches were, first, the Matar Branch with a current culturable command area (CCA) of 13,272 hectares; second, the Limbasi Branch with a CCA of 31,073 hectares across Petlad and Matar Talukas; and third, the Cambay Branch, which waters a few villages in the extreme southwest portion of Matar Taluka. The source of this information is a 1995 unpublished in-house report on the performance of the MRBC project made available to the author by MRBC authorities.

89. This figure was computed from C. H. Shah, Vimal Shah, and Sudershan Iyengar, *Agricultural Growth with Equity* (Delhi: Concept Publications, 1991), Table 4.1, p. 83.

90. Records obtained in 1995 from the MRBC Authority, Nadiad.

91. Theodor Adorno, *Negative Dialectics,* trans. E. B. Ashton (New York: Continuum Publishing, 1973), 43.

92. Michel Foucault, *The History of Sexuality,* 3 vols., *An Introduction* (New York: Vintage Books), 1:144.

93. See Vimal Shah and C. H. Shah, *Re-Survey of Matar Taluka* (Bombay: Vora and Co., 1974).

94. See Shah, Shah, and Iyenger, *Agricultural Growth with Equity.* The second re-survey in 1974–75 revealed an increase in labor absorption from 19.79 man-days per acre of crop production in 1965–66 to 31.11 man-days per acre in 1974–75. Real wage for a typical agricultural operation—the weeding of rice beds—rose from Rs. 2.00 per day in 1965–66 to Rs. 3.60 per day in 1974–75. The Gini ratio for asset distribution (valued in real terms) across land-size classes diminished from 0.43 in 1965–66 to 0.33 in 1974–75. The disparity in average per capita expenditure in real terms of occupational groups declined over the same period. Since 1974–75 was also a subnormal rainfall year, like 1965–66, we may assume that employment, consumption and production statistics were biased in the same direction in both survey years and are, therefore, comparable. However, I have other reservations regarding the 1974–75 survey data. Based on firsthand interviews with research assistants on the survey team and one of the co-authors of the published report, I have reason to believe that the numbers gathered contain large measurement bias for two reasons: first, because interviewers were ill-trained and second, because the survey was conducted so rapidly (998 households were interviewed in an astonishingly short period of three months) that there was insufficient time to establish the requisite rapport with respondents and confirm the accuracy of their responses through cross-checks and re-visits. Additionally, the survey form was forty-four pages long, divided into twelve sections, and demanded well over one thousand pieces of information. It must have been a nightmare to fill—for the interviewer as well as the interviewee. Based on my field experience, it is inconceivable how villagers would have (or should have) exhibited the level of patience that a proper response to all items would have required. Hence, any comparison of the 1965–66 and 1974–75 data demands caution. For instance, I am inclined to trust the data on wages, agricultural prices, employment (with the usual caveats concerning recall), and production; I am less confident about the data on income, assets, and consumption.

95. The exceptions were those years when the entire state was hit by a drought and the Kadana reservoir—the primary catchment for MRBC—failed to fill to capacity.

96. Robert Chambers, *Managing Canal Irrigation: Practical Analysis from South Asia* (Cambridge: Cambridge University Press, 1989).

97. Terminologically, the emergent distribution of aggregate output, combining steps 1 and 2, is said to exhibit first- and second-order stochastic dominance (henceforth, FOSD and SOSD) over the historical (pre-irrigation) distribution of output. This means that such a distribution, if available, would be preferred, both, by risk-neutral farming households who maximize expected returns, as well as risk-averse farming households who maximize expected utility.

98. Few have more powerfully repudiated Eurocentric versions of the claim that Europe as alibi for the West has exclusive claim to instrumental reason than Pierre Bourdieu. See, for example, his *Outline of a Theory of Practice* (Cambridge: Cambridge University Press, 1977). Enrique Dussel, meantime, makes a compelling case that the managerial reason which Europe claims as the distinctive and autonomous hallmark of its modernity is in fact the "culture" of a center/core that emerged from the imperative to control, administer, and exploit colonized margins. Reason, in short, was an *effect* and not the internal cause of European domination and universality. Dussel, "Beyond Eurocentrism," in *Cultures of Globalization,* ed. Masao Miyoshi and Fredric Jameson (Durham, N.C.: Duke University Press, 1997), 1–37. Reactivating the observations of the eighteenth-century Scottish philosopher David Hume, Gilles Deleuze notes that the art of calculation is not peculiar to modern times. It has been always underwritten the emergence of subjectivity. Hence, "The subject is the entity which, under the influence of the principle of utility, pursues a goal or an intention; it organizes means in view of an end and, under the influences of principles of association, establishes relations among ideas. Thus, the collection becomes a system. The collection of perceptions, when organized and bound, becomes a system." Deleuze, *Empiricism and Subjectivity* (New York: Columbia University Press, 1991), 98.

99. The French term *dispositif,* encountered in the writings of Michel Foucault, has no single translation into English: it means, simultaneously, "mechanism," "device," "apparatus," "functions" and "institution"—in short, a "sociotechnical assemblage." On how the social exceeds human association, see Bruno Latour, *Reassembling the Social* (London: Oxford University Press, 2005).

100. Consider the popularity of recent books like Steven Levitt and Stephen Dubner's *Freakonomics: A Rogue Economist Explores the Hidden of Everything* (expanded and revised edition) (New York: William Morrow, 2006). Levitt's Chicago colleague, the economist Gary Becker, was the first to stake the imperial claims of marginal value analysis; but never garnered the same popular recognition (although he exercised as immense influence on economics and its allied fields). On the notion that ideas follow an epidemiological logic, see another bestseller: Malcolm Gladwell, *Tipping Point: How Little Things Can Make a Big Difference,* reprint edition (New York: Back Bay Books, 2002).

101. This is consistent with overall productivity trends in Gujarat between 1960 and 1980: thus the annual compound rate of growth in agriculture was 2.27 percent in the period 1960–61 to 1970–71 and 4.15 percent over the period 1970–71 to 1980–81, with trend line turning negative in the subsequent (1980–81 to 1990–91)

decade. Most Gujarat economists attribute the early growth to an expansion in irrigation facilities and gross cropped area, followed up by the seed-fertilizer (Green) revolution. The stagnant growth thereafter is blamed on "technological limitations" such as saturation of water supplies, loss of genetic potential in HVYs, and diminution in soil fertility as a result of input overuse. Adverse prices (primarily, terms of trade with manufacturing) are not considered a significant contributing factor; as such, the call to resuscitate Gujarat agriculture revolves around the urgent need for a "technological breakthrough." See, for example, Bhupat Desai and N. V. Namboodiri, "Developing Agriculture in Gujarat: A Strategic Perspective for Ninth Plan," *Economic and Political Weekly* (Review of Agriculture: March 29, 1997): A-31–A-40; and Indira Hirway and Piet Terhal, "The Contradictions of Growth," in *Development and Deprivation in Gujarat*, Ghanshyam Shah, Mario Rutten, and Hein Streefkerk, eds. (New Delhi: Sage Publications, 2002), 37–58. As a point of comparison, we might note that the lower and upper bound per-acre yields for paddy in Matar Taluka of 2088 kgs. per acre compare favorably with per-acre paddy yields in Java, which in 1976 were 1696 kgs. under an intensified wet-paddy regime and 1252 kgs. under a nonintensified regime (in Anne Booth and R. M. Sundrum, *Labor Absorption in Agriculture* [Delhi: Oxford University Press, 1984], 124, Table 5.10).

102. The coefficient of variation (C.V.) is a unit-free measure, calculated as the ratio of standard deviation to mean for a given series. As such, it effectively measures the spread of the distribution, i.e., how wide or narrow a distribution is. Since a wider distribution (with a higher cumulative probability of extreme outcomes) is considered a riskier distribution, a higher C.V. value signals a riskier spread. Because C.V. is a unit-free measure it permits comparison between sets of observations measured in different units.

103. Keep in mind that because employment or labor-utilization statistics are difficult to measure they can be quite unreliable. Hence, the figures in Table 5 should be read as broadly indicative rather than exact. Finally, since 1965 and 1974 were poor rainfall years, the data probably overstates the magnitude of change between these survey years and 1982.

104. B. Nanjamma Chinnappa and W. P. T. Silva, "Impact of the Cultivation of High-Yielding Varieties of Paddy on Income and Employment," in *Green Revolution?* ed. B. H. Farmer (Cambridge: Cambridge University Press, 1977).

105. IRRI, *Changes in Rice Farming in Selected Areas of Asia* (Los Banōs: International Rice Research Institute, 1975), vol. 1.

106. See, for example, Francesca Bray, *The Rice Economies: Technology and Development in Asian Societies* (Oxford: Basil Blackwell, 1986), on Southeast and East Asia; V. K. Ramachandran, *Wage Labor and Unfreedom in Agriculture: An Indian Case Study* (Delhi: Oxford University Press, 1990) from Madurai District in Tamil Nadu; and Anindita Mukherjee, "Labor," in *Economic Development in Palanpur Over Five Decades*, ed. Peter Lanjouw and Nicholas Stern (Oxford: Clarendon Press, 1998) from Palanpur village in Uttar Pradesh.

107. Gujarat Institute of Area Planning (GIAP), *Survey of Matar and Nadiad Talukas, Kheda District*. Mimeo (Gota: GIAP, now Gujarat Institute of Development Research [GIDR]), Table 14, p. 41.

108. Actual names of villages have been altered.

109. Since I did not collect data on area planted to modern varieties, I am unable to pronounce on the level of adoption of modern varieties across size class.

In 1974–75, *average* area planted under modern varieties across *all* cultivators were as follows: paddy 47 percent; wheat 49.1 percent; bajra 65.8 percent; and cotton 43.3 percent (cf. Shah et al., *Agricultural Growth with Equity*, Table 7.2, p. 122). My poll of cultivators (owner operators and tenants) on the varieties they had planted in the 1994–95 rice *(kharif)* and wheat *(rabi)* seasons revealed that, barring a few instances, they mostly used improved varieties in the case of rice, and high-yielding varieties or improved varieties in the case of wheat.

110. The figure in the text is obtained as follows: (Increase in paddy acreage) × (Avg. person-days of labor per acre of irrigated paddy) ÷ 365 = (42,013) × (45.6) ÷ 365 = 5,248 person-years. The average person-days employed in Matar Taluka per acre of irrigated paddy (45.6) was taken from column labeled "Irrigated, 1974–75," in Table 5 of the main text.

111. This is because the reduction in *bajra* acreage masks a shift from unirrigated *bajra* that absorbs, on average, 21.4 person-days per acre to irrigated bajra, which absorbs roughly twice the number of person-days per acre (Shah, Shah, and Iyengar, *Agricultural Growth with Equity:* Table 10.2, p. 150).

112. Cropping intensity, an index of how intensively a unit of land is used, is defined as gross cropped area (GCA) divided by net cropped area (NCA) × 100.

113. Pulses are sown in sandy-loam soils called *goradu* (or, if situated on river banks, *bhatha jamin*) locally. Paddy and wheat are sown in low-lying clay-loam soils called *kali* (black) *jamin*, where water tends to sequester.

114. Cropping intensity increased from 1.08 in 1965–66 to 1.15 in 1974–75 to 1.18 in 1979–80.

115. Kheda Jilla Panchayat, *Kheda Jilla ni Ankdakiya Rooprekha, 1989–90.* It should be qualified that although Table 7 suggests a significant rise in net sown area, it cannot be concluded that this change is permanent. The monsoons in 1983 and 1984 (one of the data years), were particularly good: the measuring station at Matar recorded annual precipitation of 938mm in 1983 and 988mm in 1984, against a 117-year normal of 750mm. More important, rains in June, July, August, and September—the four months that are most crucial in terms of water stress for paddy development—were not only adequate but well distributed and probably inspired cultivators to extend paddy cultivation to lands which they might ordinarily have left fallow. In the 1985–86 agricultural year, when precipitation was only 58 percent of normal (with no rain in June, when rice seedlings are prepared), net sown area declined sharply to 82,137 acres from 137,902 acres in the previous year. This prompts the caveat that comparisons of crop acreage and yield based on discrete (single-year) data, rather than a continuous time-series, can be broadly indicative but should not be taken as evidence of monotonic time-trends. The volatility of year-to-year data, in light of acreage and yield sensitivity to environmental factors, is sharply emphasized by Vaidyanathan, *Water Resource Management*, 19–20.

116. On the ecology of rice cultivation, see D. J. Greenland, "Rice and Rice-based Farming Systems," in *Agriculture in the Tropics*, 3rd ed., ed. C. C. Webster and P. N. Wilson (Oxford: Blackwell Science, 1998).

117. Nicholas Georgescu-Roegen, *The Entropy Law and the Economic Process*, 15, 16.

118. Raymond Williams, "Ideas of Nature," in his *Culture and Materialism* (London: Verso, 2005 [1985]).

119. Sandra Postel, *Pillar of Sand: Can the Irrigation Miracle Last?* (New York: W. W. Norton, 1999), 91–92.

120. Postel, *Pillar of Sand,* 92.

121. Whitehead, *Process and Reality,* 21–22.

122. Whitehead, *Process and Reality,* 23.

123. K. A. Bhagwat,"Monitoring of Crop Production in Saline and Sodic Soils of Gujarat with the help of Remote Sensing," mimeo (Ahmedabad: ISRO-RESPOND Project, 1989), 7.

124. See P. C. Raheja, "Aridity and Salinity (A Survey of Soils and Land Use)," in *Salinity and Aridity: New Approaches to Old Problems,* ed. Hugo Boyko (The Hague: Dr. W. Junk Publishers, 1966), 43–127; and Bhagwat, "Monitoring of Crop Production in Saline and Sodic Soils of Gujarat with the help of Remote Sensing."

125. Anions are ions that carry a negative charge (and therefore characteristically migrate toward the positive electrode in electrolysis), whereas cations are ions that carry a positive charge (and move toward the negative electrode in electrolysis).

126. See the excellent collection of papers in Boyko, *Salinity and Aridity,* and in Dan Yaron, ed., *Salinity in Irrigation and Water Resources* (New York: Marcel Dekker, Inc., 1981). Yaron estimates that one-third of all irrigated land in the world is affected by soil salinity problems.

127. Narmada and Water Resources Department (NWRD), "Mahi Right Bank Canal Project: Report on the Behaviour of Sub-Soil Water Table, 1991–92," mimeo (Gandhinagar: NWRD, n.d.).

128. Whitehead, *Process and Reality,* 89.

129. On this topic, see Chambers, *Managing Canal Irrigation.*

130. Robert Wade's South Indian case study, *Village Republics: Economic Conditions for Collective Action in South India* (Cambridge: Cambridge University Press, 1988) is an exemplar on this subject.

131. In 1991–92, total annual expenditure on the MRBC system at the Mahi Irrigation Circle, Nadiad, was Rs. 345.72 lacs (Mahi Irrigation Circle, internal documents), which at an exchange rate of 44 rupees to US$1 translates to US $785,727. Assuming 70 percent of this was "eaten away" by corrupt officials and contractors, it would put the misappropriated amount at US$550,009—a huge annual loss!

132. ISRO is the acronym for the Indian Space Research Organisation, a Government of India agency controls all remote sensing and outer space initiatives.

133. Deleuze and Guattari, *A Thousand Plateaus,* 453 (italics in original).

134. Ibid., 441–46.

135. Ibid., 453.

136. Ibid., particularly chaps. 9 and 12.

137. Ibid., 216.

138. See, for example, the collection of reports and essays in Siddhartha Varadarajan, ed., *Gujarat: The Making of a Genocide* (New Delhi: Penguin Books, 2002); Parita Mukta, "On the Political Culture of Authoritarianism," in *Development and Deprivation in Gujarat,* ed. Ghanshyam Shah, Mario Rutten, and Hein Streefkerk (New Delhi: Sage Publications, 2002); the investigative compilation *Crime Against Humanity,* 2 vols., by Concerned Citizens' Tribunal—Gujarat 2002, available online: http://www.pucl.org/Topics/Religion-communalism/2002/crimes.htm (last accessed 11 December 2007); Asghar Ali Engineer, ed., *The Gujarat Carnage* (New Delhi: Orient Longman, 2003); Achyut Yagnik and Suchitra Sheth, *The Shaping of Modern Gujarat: Plurality, Hindutva and Beyond* (New Delhi: Penguin, 2005); and

Ornit Shani, *Communalism, Caste and Hindu Nationalism: The Violence in Gujarat* (Cambridge: Cambridge University Press, 2007).

139. For an instructive analysis of the Congress Party split in 1969 into Congress–(R) (where "R" stood for "Requisition," the Indira faction) and Congress–(O) ("O" for "Organisation," the old guard); and the 1971 general election, see Frankel, *India's Political Economy*, chaps. 10 and 11.

140. The very same image of the village that Dr. B. R. Ambedkar, inspiration for the modern dalit movement, so bitterly denounced in the debates that led up to the framing of the Indian Constitution.

141. R. K. Amin, Rural Renaissance and Shri Bhailalbhai, *Dr. Bhailalbhai Patel 75th Birth Souvenir* (Vallabh Vidyanagar: Charotar Vidya Mandal, 1963), 17–18, quoted in Ghanshyam Shah, "Caste and Land Reforms in Gujarat," in *Land Reforms in India, Vol. 8: Performance and Challenges in Gujarat and Maharashtra*, ed. Ghanshyam Shah and D. C. Sah (New Delhi: Sage Publications, 2002). Shah's article gives a useful summary of the land reform process in Gujarat.

142. It is worth noting here that Morarji Desai, the enormously popular Gujarati leader, who had been deposed as Deputy Prime Minister by Indira Gandhi in 1969, contributing to the Congress party split, was resolutely and proudly anticommunist. A practicing Gandhian and a man of great ability and integrity, he nevertheless exemplifies the latent Hindu normativity of Gujarat's social formation.

143. Mario Rutten, *Farms and Factories: Social Profile of Large Farmers and Rural Industrialists in West India* (Delhi: Oxford University Press, 1995).

144. See J. C. Kumarappa, *Survey of Matar Taluka* (Ahmedabad: Gujarat Vidaypeeth, 1931), Vimal Shah and C. H. Shah, *Re-Survey of Matar Taluka* (Bombay: Vora and Co., 1974); and M. L. Dantwala and C. H. Shah, *Evaluation of Land Reforms: With Special Reference to the Western Region of India* (Bombay: Department of Economics, University of Bombay, 1971). To the extent that access to land is an accurate index of economic well-being in an agricultural economy (and it need not always be), a comparison of the 1929–30 data with the 1965–66 data for Matar Taluka shows that Scheduled Caste (SC) households suffered severe economic setbacks over the thirty-six-year period, whereas Kolis as a group were able to consolidate their economic position. When tenancy reform was initiated in Gujarat in 1954, Kolis, it appears, were more aggressive in claiming possession of the plots they held as tenants of Patel landlords than SCs in a similar position. SCs (especially members of the Bhangi and Vankar castes) have historically had a subordinate and strongly clientilist relationship with Patels—although this is now changing. But until fifteen years ago it was common, even for a moderately well-off Patel cultivator, to maintain one or more SC farm servant. These farm servants were provided two meals a day, a set of new clothes and a pair of new shoes every year, petty loans when required, a cash allowance of sixty to hundred rupees a month, and finances (in cash and kind) on ceremonial occasions. Frequently, they were also given land to sharecrop. Although the custom of maintaining servants addressed the need for farm labor as and when required, it was also and continues to be a mark of social status among Patels. As in other parts of rural India, the farm servant serves as an emblem of social rank. SCs seem not to have been able to convert sharecropping rights into ownership rights as effectively as other castes because of their inability to press claims for ownership with landlords, who were also their patrons. Of course, some Patels voluntarily gave away plots to SC households, but such cases were few. The economic vulnerability

of households from various caste groups is starkly apparent when agricultural labor households in the 1965–66 re-survey are partitioned by caste. From 119 agricultural labor households sampled, 58 percent were SCs, 21 percent were Kolis/Baraiyas, 10 percent were Bharwads only 10 percent, and a mere 4 percent Patels.

145. Some Bharwad families I came to know in Astha and Shamli owned thirty or more heads of livestock and at the time (1994–95) were earning up to two hundred rupees ($4.50) daily—a considerable sum—from milk sales to the village dairy.

146. David Hardiman, *Peasant Nationalists of Gujarat: Kheda District, 1917–1934* (Delhi: Oxford University Press, 1981), 44, makes a parallel observation. Also see David Pocock, *Kanbi and Patidar* (Oxford: Oxford University Press, 1972).

147. Figures obtained on August 28, 1995, Sub-District Registrar's Office, Matar.

148. The phrase is from David Harvey, *The New Imperialism* (Oxford: Oxford University Press, 2003).

149. P. G. Shah, *Vimukta Jatis: Denotified Communities in Western India* (Bombay: Gujarat Research Society, 1967) and S. B. Rajgyor, ed., *Kheda District Gazetteer* (Ahmedabad: Government Printing Press, 1977).

150. The distinction between "caste" and "tribe" was muddled. The terms were often applied interchangeably by colonial officials to groups like the Vaghris, who—economically, socially, and spatially—inhabited the fringes of Gujarati rural society. For an illuminating discussion on the caste/tribe divide in Gujarat, see Ajay Skaria, "Shades of Wildness: Tribe, Caste, and Gender in Western India," *Journal of Asian Studies* 56, no. 3 (1997): 726–45.

151. David Hardiman, *Peasant Nationalists of Gujarat* (Delhi: Oxford University Press, 1981), 47.

152. Interview with Sabarbhai Tadbda, May 2, 1995, and fieldnotes May 14, 1995.

153. In 1995, the going per vigha rate was Rs. 700–800 for melon *(teti)* cultivation and Rs. 1500–2000 for tomato: steep sums for short-term leases.

154. Fieldnotes, Limbasi, March 31, 1995.

155. The name Vankar is a synthesis of the Gujarati noun *van* (meaning "unginned cotton") and the verb *kar* (to do); hence a Vankar is someone who transforms cotton—in short, a weaver.

156. Highest educational attainment in years averaged 9.11 in Vankar households, as contrasted to 6.50 in Rajput and 10.88 in Patel households.

157. The common English names for *Prosopis juliflora* are mesquite and honey mesquite.

158. Gilles Deleuze, *Foucault,* trans. Séan Hand (Minneapolis: University of Minnesota Press), 71–72.

159. Deleuze, *Foucault,* 73.

160. Michel Foucault, *Discipline and Punish: The Birth of the Prison* (New York: Vintage, 1979).

161. Foucault, *History of Sexuality,* 1:139.

162. The term "state effect," taking cue from Althusser's notions of "aesthetic effect," "ideology effect," and "knowledge effect," nicely summarizes antijuridical theories of the state. On the subject of "effects," see Louis Althusser and Etienne Balibar, *Reading Capital,* trans. Ben Brewster (London: Verso, 1997 [1968]) and Althusser, "A Letter on Art in Reply to André Daspre," *Lenin and Philosophy,* trans. Ben Brewster (London: NLB, 1970), 221–28. The argument of antijuridi-cal state theorists is *not* that the state apparatus is illusory; rather, their modest

(if unsettling) claim is that there is no self-adequate entity, which merits the appellation, "the State." What exist are diffuse institutionalized knowledges and practices that enable "actions upon actions" and recuperatively produce the State as immanent cause of its effects. Two superb articles spell out the implications of an antijuridical approach particularly well; they are: Moira Gatens, "Through a Spinozist Lens: Ethology, Difference, Power," in *Deleuze: A Critical Reader*, ed. Paul Patton (Oxford: Blackwell Publishers, 1996), 162–87 (but esp. 164–67); and Timothy Mitchell, "Society, Economy, and the State Effect," in *State/Culture: State Formation After the Cultural Turn*, ed. George Steinmetz (Ithaca, N.Y.: Cornell University Press, 1999), 76–97. Mitchell points out that "the State" is produced as a concrete abstraction, real in its effects like "capital" and, like it, lacking presence outside of its effects.

163. Further discussions of this can be found in Michel Foucault, "Truth and Power," *Essential Works of Foucault, 1954–1984*, 3:123; and in the same volume, James Faubion's editorial "Introduction," esp. xiv–xv.

164. Deleuze, *Foucault*, 74 (italics mine). Scholars like Peter Hallward allege that Deleuze has characteristically *mis*appropriated a theorist, in this case Foucault, for his own normative ends—*his* ethological project; cf. Peter Hallward, "The Limits of Individuation, or How to Distinguish Deleuze and Foucault," *Angelaki* 5, no. 2 (August 2000): 93–111. According to Hallward, "Deleuze's own much-vaunted reading of *Foucault* is seriously flawed, especially his determination to read Foucault's ethics in terms that anticipate the terminology of *The Fold*" (101). Hallward builds this critique of Deleuze in an extremely erudite article, and summons an array of objections to support his claim that Deleuze tendentiously misreads Foucault. His argument that Foucault wants to "purge the subject, to eliminate everything that specifies or objectifies the subject" (101) and write "a philosophy of the limit as such (at the limits of classification, at the edge of the void that lies beyond every order of recognition or normalization)" (93), in contrast to Deleuze who "would like to get rid of the relational subject altogether, to clear some space for a creative coherence beyond the creatural altogether" (101) and thereby produce "a philosophy without limits" is, both, illuminating and compelling. But the same article can also be charged with a questionable rendering of Deleuze (for example, contrast Hallward's cavalier treatment of the category "thought" in Deleuze to Daniel W. Smith's careful examination of the same category in "Deleuze's Theory of Sensation: Overcoming the Kantian Duality," in Patton, ed., *Deleuze: A Critical Reader*, 29–56). Ultimately, given the figures we are concerned with (Deleuze and Foucault) distance from error or the veracity of a reading is a decidedly odd criterion for judging the power (that is, capacity for affect and effect) of either Deleuze's reading of Foucault or Hallward's reading of Deleuze. In my view it is pointless ask whether Deleuze has forced a "nomadic" reading of "microphysics" on Foucault because Deleuze would no doubt respond that his reading is merely an effect, one among many, of Foucault's text. Its capacity to provoke, incite, elicit, or generate unexpected connections—to mobilize "thought," understood in the Heideggerian manner as departure from habit, cliché or convention—is precisely the microphysics of power of Foucault's writing. Given this, the question that Deleuze would prefer to be asked is, how *affective* is his reading of Foucault? Does it open ways of thinking that aid us in our analysis?

165. See my article, "The Unbearable Modernity of 'Development'?: An Essay on Canal Irrigation and Development Planning in Western India," *Progress in Planning*

58, no. 1 (2002): 1–80, for a review of postdevelopment theories. It will be apparent to the reader who has read that article and this chapter that my formulation of the critique of postdevelopment, while retaining some of the same complaints (particularly the monolithic rendering of development and its workings by postdevelopment scholars), now takes a rather different—and, alas, more persistently thought through—line of attack.

166. We are not too far here from Amartya Sen's figuring of "freedoms" as "capabilities to function," although we are distant from his individualism and voluntarism and his formula of prescriptions for achieving development's freedoms.

167. I should point to *at least* two (there are probably many more) excellent attempts to bring Gramsci and Foucault into engagement. The first is an article by Barry Smart, "The Politics of Truth and the Problem of Hegemony," in *Foucault: A Critical Reader,* ed. David Hoy (New York: Basil Blackwell, 1986), 157–74; the second, a book by Mark Olssen, *Michel Foucault: Materialism and Education* (Westport, Conn.: Greenwood Publishing, 1999). My basis for arguing that Gramsci and Foucault are compatible is, however, somewhat different from both Smart and Olssen.

168. See, in particular, Foucault's essay, "The Subject and Power." On the perforations within discourse and the resonance with my reading of hegemony, see Foucault, *The History of Sexuality,* trans. Robert Hurley (New York: Vintage Books), 1:100.

169. Fieldnotes, Govindpura, June 23, 1994.

170. CBI: Central Bureau of Investigation, a federal agency that is the equivalent of the U.S. FBI.

171. Pravin Sheth, *Political Development in Gujarat* (51), writes that "the manifesto of the Lok Paksha . . . clearly shows how a rightist ideology, similar to the ideology of the later . . . Swatantra Party had taken shape in Gujarat even as early as in 1952."

172. Mukta, "On the Political Culture of Authoritanism," discusses this topic.

173. See, for example, David Hardiman, "Class Base of Swaminarayan Sect," *Economic and Political Weekly* 23, no. 37 (September 10, 1988): 1907–12; Ghanshyam Shah, "The BJP and Backward Castes in Gujarat," *South Asia Bulletin* 14, no. 1 (1994): 57–65; Raymond Brady Williams, *An Introduction to Swaminarayan Hinduism* (Cambridge: Cambridge University Press, 2001); and David Hardiman, "Purifying the Nation: The Arya Samaj in Gujarat 1895–1930," *Indian Economic and Social History Review* 44, no. 1 (2007): 41–65.

174. Sudhir Chandra, "From Gujarati Asmita to Gujaratni Rashtriya Asmita: A Comparative Note on Regional and Pan-Indian Nationalisms During the Later Nineteenth Century," in *Regional Roots of Indian Nationalism,* ed. Makrand Mehta (Delhi: Vishwa Kala Prakashan, 1990), 39–64 (but esp. 41–42).

175. Shani, *Communalism, Caste, and Hindu Nationalism,* makes a compatible argument using evidence from communal violence in Ahmedabad. Contrary to received wisdom, she argues that the growth of communalism and unitary Hindu nationalism does not follow straightforwardly from a history of Hindu-Muslim antagonism. Instead, she underscores how upper-caste anger against state reservation policies advantaging lower and backward castes and classes combined in volatile ways with the insecurities of mill workers displaced from previously secure jobs by the closure of Ahmedabad's large textile mills in the 1980s. Thanks in part to the political acumen of Hindutva strategists, dalits—who bore the brunt of upper-caste

violence in the 1981 antireservation riots—were enrolled to a Hindutva historic bloc by the latter part of the 1985 riots. The 1985 events began as antireservation protests targeting backward castes but "transmogrified into communal violence even though there was no prior religious tension between Hindus and Muslims, and local Muslims had no part in the reservation dispute between forward- and backward-caste Hindus."(13) Bizarrely, Dalits participated in violence against Muslims in the 1985 riots—and again, in the 2002 riots. The Sangh Parivar's success is mobilizing lower castes (and subsequently, tribal groups) owed to a conscious strategy of embracing them within Hindu society and holding out open channels for social mobility and respect within it. On the Parivar's recruitment of dalit and tribal communities see, in addition to Shani's study, Yagnik and Sheth, *The Shaping of Modern Gujarat;* Nikita Sud, "Secularism and the Gujarati State: 1960–2005," paper prepared for the 50th Anniversary Conference of Queen Elizabeth House, University of Oxford; and Concerned Citizens' Tribunal, *Crime Against Humanity,* vol. 1. On the spatiality of hegemonizing, see Satish Despande, "Hindutva and Its Spatial Strategies," in his *Contemporary India: A Sociological View* (New Delhi: Viking, 2003).

176. Deleuze and Guattari, *A Thousand Plateaus,* 215.

177. Deleuze and Guattari, *A Thousand Plateaus,* 215.

178. Gilles Deleuze, from whom I have adapted this formulation, asks: "What do we mean here by immanent cause? It is a cause that is realized, integrated and distinguished *in its effect.* Or rather the immanent cause is realized, integrated and distinguished *by its effect*" (italics mine). See Deleuze, *Foucault,* trans. Seán Hand (Minneapolis: University of Minnesota Press, 1988), 37.

179. Whitehead, *Process and Reality,* 53.

180. Deleuze and Guattari, *A Thousand Plateaus,* 230.

4. Distinction

1. Fieldnotes, Ambodi, October 31, 2004.

2. 1 *vigha* = 0.5875 acres.

3. Fieldnotes, Astha, December 8, 1994.

4. In formal analysis this change would correspond to an easing of the agent's budget constraint.

5. See, for example, B. Fleisher and T. Kneisner, *Labor Economics: Theory, Evidence, and Policy* (Englewood Cliffs, N.J.: Prentice-Hall, 1984); M. Gunderson and C. Riddell, *Labor Market Economics,* 2nd ed. (Toronto: McGraw-Hill Ryerson, 1987); and E. N. Wolff, *Economics of Poverty, Inequality and Discrimination* (Cincinnati: South-Western College Publishing, 1997).

6. The caste hierarchy in Kheda begins with various subcastes of Brahmins, after which, in descending order of ritual status, follow Rajput Garasias, Vanias, Patels, Panchals, Kolis and Baraiyas, and Bharwads. Vankars, Rohits, Vaghris, and Bhangis—in that order of ranking—constitute the so-called Scheduled Castes, who were previously labeled (and are still treated in villages as) "Untouchables."

7. Fieldnotes, Ashapuri, December 19, 1994.

8. Louis Althusser, "Marxism and Humanism," in his *For Marx,* trans. Ben Brewster (London: NLB, 1977), 233 (italics in original). Later on that same page, Althusser writes: "So ideology is a matter of the *lived* relation between men and

their world. This relation, that only appears as *'conscious'* on the condition that it is *unconscious*, in the same way only seems to be simple on condition that it is complex, that it is not a simple relation but a relation between relations, a second degree relations."

9. See, in particular, Pierre Bourdieu, *Outline of a Theory of Practice*, trans. Richard Nice (Cambridge: Cambridge University Press, 1977); and Michel Foucault, *The Order of Things: An Archaeology of Human Sciences* (New York: Vintage, 1994).

10. The Mahi Right Bank Canal (MRBC) project incorporated into its command area fifty-seven villages from the Limbasi and Matar subdivisions of the Taluka. The remaining twenty-five villages in the Taluka, which fall in Navagam subdivision, were bypassed by the project. Cultivation in the Navagam area is mostly rainfed, with conjunctive river, pond, and groundwater irrigation available to some farmers.

11. Vimal Shah and C. H. Shah, *Re-Survey of Matar Taluka* (Bombay: Vora Publishers, 1974). The Shah and Shah study was sponsored by the Planning Commission of India.

12. Vimal Shah, C. H. Shah, and S. Iyengar, *Agricultural Growth With Equity* (Delhi: Concept Publishers, 1990). This re-survey was conducted under the auspices of the Gujarat Institute of Area Planning (now the Gujarat Institute of Development Research).

13. Shah and Shah, *Re-Survey of Matar Taluka*, chap. 11.

14. See, among others, V. K. Ramachandran, *Wage Labor and Unfreedom in Agriculture: An Indian Case Study* (Delhi: Oxford University Press. 1990); John Harriss, "Population, Employment and Wages: A Comparative Study of North Arcot Villages, 1973–1983," in *The Green Revolution Re-Considered: The Impact of High-Yielding Rice Varieties in South India*, P. B. R. Hazell and C. Ramasamy, eds. (Baltimore: Johns Hopkins University Press, 1991); Karin Kapadia, *Siva and Her Sisters: Gender, Class and Caste in Rural South India* (Boulder, Colo.: Westview Press, 1995); Jan Breman, *Of Peasants, Migrants, and Paupers* (Delhi: Oxford University Press, 1985), Jan Breman, *Footloose Proletariat: Working in India's Informal Economy* (Cambridge: Cambridge University Press, 1996); and Jean Dreze and N. Sharma, "Palanpur: Population, Society, Economy," in *Economic Development in Palanpur Over Five Decades*, ed. P. Lanjouw and N. Stern (Oxford: Clarendon Press, 1998).

15. Ramachandran, *Wage Labor and Unfreedom in Agriculture*, chap. 9.

16. Breman, *Of Peasants, Migrants, and Paupers*, 279.

17. Harriss, "Population, Employment and Wages," 115.

18. See, for instance, Louis Althusser and Étienne Balibar, *Reading Capital*, trans. Ben Brewster (London: Verso, 1997 [1968]); and Gilles Deleuze, *Foucault*, trans. Séan Hand (Minneapolis: University of Minnesota Press, 1988).

19. August Comte, "Positive Method in Its Application to Social Phenomena," in *Auguste Comte and Positivism: The Essential Writings*, ed. Gertrud Lenzer (New Brunswick, N.J.: Transactions Publishers), 218–52. Cf. Benedictus de Spinoza, *Spinoza: Complete Works*, ed. Michael L. Morgan, trans. Samuel Shirley (Indianapolis: Hackett Publishing Company, 2002).

20. To invoke the anthropologist Donald Donham's felicitous phrase from a book by (nearly) the same title.

21. See Jacques Derrida, "That Dangerous Supplement," in his *Of Grammatology*, corrected ed., trans. Gayatri Chakravorty Spivak (Baltimore: Johns Hopkins University Press, 1997), 141–64; and Derrida, *Limited, Inc.*, ed. Gerald Graff,

trans. Jeffrey Mehlman and Samuel Weber (Evanston, Ill.: Northwestern University Press, 1988).

22. Ian Hacking, *The Social Construction of What?* new ed. (Cambridge, Mass.: Harvard University Press, 2000).

23. Andrew Sayer, *Radical Political Economy: A Critique* (Oxford: Blackwell, 1995), 128.

24. Some of the similarities and differences between marginalist and Marxist approaches are summarized, from a rational choice perspective, in John Roemer, *Free to Lose* (Cambridge, Mass.: Harvard University Press, 1988); Pranab Bardhan, ed., *The Economic Theory of Agrarian Institutions* (Oxford: Clarendon Press, 1989); and Joseph Stiglitz, "Post Walrasian and Post Marxian Economics," *Journal of Economic Perspectives* 7, no. 1 (1992): 109–14. For Marxist critiques of Walrasian NIE, see Ellen Meiksins Wood, "Rational Choice Marxism: Is the Game Worth the Candle?" *New Left Review* 177 (September–October 1989): 41–88, and Tom Brass, *Towards a Comparative Political Economy of Unfree Labor: Case Studies and Debates* (London: Frank Cass Publishers, 1999). For broadly Marxist appraisals of post-Walrasian NIE, see Gillian Hart, "Interlocking Transactions: Obstacles, Precursors or Instruments of Agrarian Capitalism?" *Journal of Development Economics* 23, no. 1 (1986): 173–203; Samuel Bowles and Herbert Gintis, "The Revenge of Homo Economicus: Contested Exchange and the Revival of Political Economy," *Journal of Economic Perspectives* 7, no. 1 (1993): 83–102; and Ben Rogaly, "Explaining Diverse Labor Arrangements in Rural South Asia," in *The Institutional Approach to Labor and Development*, G. Rodgers, K. Fóti, and L. Lauridsen, eds. (London: Frank Cass, 1996).

25. Hence, my position is the relatively noncontroversial one, bordering on truism, that all awareness of the world and of the self is mediated by interpretation, rather than the radical one that reality itself is brought into being by acts of interpretation.

26. Quoted in Donald Donham, *History, Power, Ideology* (Cambridge: Cambridge University Press, 1990), 55.

27. Notable exceptions include those Hegelian Marxists and contemporary left sociologists of labor who have pondered deeply on the phenomenological aspects of work, as evident from their investigations of phenomena such as "alienation," "drudgery," and the pernicious distinction between "mental" and "manual" labor. On alienation, see Georg Lukács, *History and Class Consciousness*, trans. R. Livingstone (Cambridge, Mass.: MIT Press, 1971 [1922]); Istvan Meszaros, *Marx's Theory of Alienation* (London: Merlin Press, 1970); Bertell Ollman, *Alienation: Marx's Conception of Man in Capitalist Society*, 2nd ed. (Cambridge: Cambridge University Press, 1976); and Moishe Postone, *Time, Labor, and Social Domination: A Reinterpretation of Marx's Critical Theory* (Chicago: University of Chicago Press, 1996). On drudgery, see Harry Braverman, *Labor and Monopoly Capital* (London: Monthly Review Press, 1974) and Michael Burawoy, *The Politics of Production* (London: Verso, 1985). On mental versus manual labor, see Raymond Williams, "Marx and Culture," in his *What I Came to Say* (London: Hutchinson Radius, 1989).

28. One exception is the Nobel-prize winning economist George Akerlof, who has tried to model labor contracts and worker effort as functions of geographically variable "fair-wage" norms. See, for instance, his "Labor Contracts as Partial Gift

Exchange," in his *An Economic Theorist's Book of Tales* (Cambridge: Cambridge University Press, 1984), as well as George Akerlof and Janet Yellen, "The Fair Wage-Effort Hypothesis and Unemployment," *Quarterly Journal of Economics* 105, no. 2 (1990): 255–83.

29. Michael Storper and Richard Walker, *The Capitalist Imperative: Territory, Technology and Industrial Growth* (Oxford: Blackwell, 1989).

30. Hence, post-Walrasian economists such as Shapiro and Stiglitz, Akerlof and Yellen, and Solow have questioned the Walrasian orthodoxy of market-clearing wages by pointing to persistent *in*voluntary unemployment in labor markets. Each has derived a different explanation for the existence of an unemployment equilibrium. Whereas Shapiro and Stiglitz view wage premiums above the market-clearing wage as a "worker disciplining device" (a pool of unemployed workers keeps the employed in line), Akerlof and Yellen see the wage premium as an unwitting social artifact, where employers saddled with imperfect and costly surveillance of worker effort are forced to meet the "fair-wage expectations" of workers (because workers who are paid subpar wages can shirk on the job and inflict productivity losses on employers). Solow, meanwhile, attributes the failure of wages to adjust to market-clearing levels to their "downward stickiness"—itself a historical byproduct of social norms that prohibit and inhibit "outsiders" (unemployed workers) from under-bidding "insiders" (employed workers). A noteworthy aspect of each of these narratives is their recognition of the importance of social structures, values, and coalition bargaining in shaping economic outcomes. This marks a fundamental break from the abstracted, parametric models of conventional neoclassical theory. See Carl Shapiro and Joseph Stiglitz, "Equilibrium Unemployment as a Worker-Disciplining Device," *American Economic Review* 74, no. 3 (1984): 433–44; Akerlof and Yellen, "The Fair Wage-Effort Hypothesis and Unemployment"; and Robert Solow, *The Labor Market as a Social Institution* (Oxford: Blackwell, 1990).

31. Modern varieties (MVs) include "improved varieties"—crop hybrids that have either been bred in situ from local "traditional varieties" by cultivators, or by professional plant breeders at agricultural research stations; and "high-yielding varieties" (HYVs)—genetically altered strains produced in laboratories. MVs are typically more yield-responsive to water and fertilizer inputs than are traditional varieties.

32. For instance, Keith Griffin, *The Political Economy of Agriculture* (New York: Macmillan, 1974); Terry Byres, "The New Technology, Class Formation, and Class Action in the Indian Countryside," *Journal of Peasant Studies* 8, no. 4 (1981); and John Harriss, *Capitalism and Peasant Farming* (Delhi: Oxford University Press, 1982).

33. See Michael Lipton and Richard Longhurst, *New Seeds and Poor People* (Baltimore: Johns Hopkins University Press, 1989), and Hazell and Ramasamy, eds., *The Green Revolution Re-Considered*.

34. The pioneering work on the marginalist approach to institutional change is Lance Davis and Douglass North, *Institutional Change and American Economic Growth* (Cambridge: Cambridge University Press, 1970), in which they identified two subcategories of institutions: the "basic institutional environment," which consists of decision rules and property rights and may be specified as formal laws or custom, and the "secondary institutional environment," which consists of specific agreements/contracts governing the way in which agents share in the use of resources. The tenets of this strand of NIE are summarized in Y. Hayami and

M. Kikuchi, *Asian Village Economy at the Crossroads* (Baltimore: Johns Hopkins University Press, 1982), chap. 2.

35. Some key references are S. Ahmad, "On the Theory of Induced Innovations," *Economic Journal* 76 (1966): 344–57; Y. Hayami and V. Ruttan, *Agricultural Development: An International Perspective* (Baltimore: Johns Hopkins University Press, 1971); and Y. Hayami, *Understanding Village Community and the Direction of Agrarian Change in Asia* (Delhi: Hindustan Publishing Corp., 1981). The "induced innovation" hypothesis has little to say on the *speed* of institutional change. The speed depends, among other factors, on the efficiency with which price signals are transmitted to agents. When information flows are imperfect, agents can suffer from cognitive dissonance in registering price signals or may interpret them in vastly different ways; see Douglass North, *Institutions, Institutional Change and Economic Performance* (Cambridge: Cambridge University Press, 1990). Complementarities (a type of externality where particular actions by one set of actors induces other actors to pursue similar actions) and the social coordination problems associated with them can result in institutional inertia and path-dependence, and slow or skew the process of change; see Brian Arthur, *Increasing Returns and Path Dependence in the Economy* (Ann Arbor: University of Michigan Press, 1994) and Debraj Ray, *Development Economics* (Princeton, N.J.: Princeton University Press, 1998).

36. The collective production benefits of irrigation and MVs have two components: a "seasonal yield effect" from the cultivation of MVs and an "annual yield effect" linked to the potential increase in cropping intensity. An "area effect" that permits expansion of net sown area is also possible, but rare, since the land frontier has been long exhausted in most green revolution tracts.

37. A. Booth and R. M. Sundrum, *Labor Absorption in Agriculture* (Delhi: Oxford University Press, 1984).

38. Specifically, growth in workforce should not exceed growth in labor absorption.

39. Lipton and Longhurst, *New Seeds and Poor People,* 179.

40. Three excellent monographs that address this topic are Francesca Bray, *The Rice Economies: Technology and Development in Asian Societies* (Oxford: Basil Blackwell, 1986); Susan Mann, *Agrarian Capitalism in Theory and Practice* (Chapel Hill: University of North Carolina Press, 1990); and Miriam Wells, *Strawberry Fields: Politics, Class and Work in California Agriculture* (Ithaca, N.Y.: Cornell University Press, 1996).

41. See Pranab Bardhan, *Land, Labor, and Rural Poverty* (Delhi: Oxford University Press, 1984), chap. 4, and C. Ramasamy, P. B. R. Hazell, and P. K. Aiyasamy, "North Arcot and the Green Revolution," in *The Green Revolution Re-Considered,* ed. Hartzell and Ramasamy.

42. A. Mukherjee, "Labor," in *Economic Development in Palanpur Over Five Decades,* ed. Lanjouw and Stern.

43. This is the well-known "dual labor market" theory first sketched out by Peter Doeringer and Michael Piore, *Internal Labor Markets and Manpower Analysis* (Lexington, Mass.: D.C. Heath and Company, 1971). Shapiro and Stiglitz ("Equilibrium Unemployment") adapted the general idea into a formal model, where higher-than-equilibrium wages to a group of primary workers came to serve as a "worker disciplining device." Empirical studies of tiered and segmented rural

labor markets can be found in Jan Breman, *Of Peasants, Migrants, and Paupers* (Delhi: Oxford University Press, 1985); Hart, "Interlocking Transactions"; J. Mohan Rao, "Fragmented Rural Labor Markets," *Journal of Peasant Studies* 15, no. 2 (1988): 238–57; and Ramachandran, *Wage Labor and Unfreedom in Agriculture.*

44. For contending explanations of contractual diversity, see the useful survey by Rogaly, "Explaining Diverse Labor Arrangements in Rural South Asia."

45. Hence, the Marxist historian Robert Brenner writes that "different class structures, specifically property relations or surplus-extraction relations, once established, tend to impose rather strict limits and possibilities, indeed rather specific long-term patterns, on a society's economic development"; Brenner, "The Social Basis of Economic Development," in *Analytical Marxism,* ed. John Roemer (Cambridge: Cambridge University Press, 1987), 12.

46. Jonathan Pincus, *Class, Power and Agrarian Change: Land and Labor in Rural West Java* (London: Macmillan, 1996), 93 (italics in original).

47. The various concepts of "power" within mainstream economic theory are, without exception, positivist. See, for example, R. Bartlett, *Economics and Power: An Inquiry into Human Relations and Markets* (Cambridge: Cambridge University Press, 1989), or Pranab Bardhan, "On the Concept of Power in Economics," *Economics and Politics* 3, no. 3 (1991): 265–77. After reviewing various formulations of power, Bartlett, for instance, opts to characterize power as "a force that alters the quality of human life" (*Economics and Power,* 31–32); and formalizes it as the ability of one agent to alter the lifetime utility of another agent. And Bardhan suggests that the ability to exert power in social relations "essentially depends on the capacity to bear risks," and concludes that capitalists are ordinarily more powerful than workers because their greater wealth, which is explained *in part* by the fact that their capital assets are scarce relative to labor-power, thus rendering capital more valuable—conferring upon them an "obviously ... larger risk-bearing capacity" ("On the Concept of Power in Economics," 272).

48. Since slavery, feudal patron–client ties, and nominally unconstrained labor market transactions are all modeled as contractual relations between rational, choice-exerting actors, with ideology occasionally smuggled in as truncated preference sets or miscognited prices, it seems necessary to ask how NIE can possibly claim a substantive notion of "freedom." See the critique by Brass, *Towards a Comparative Political Economy of Unfree Labor,* chap. 5.

49. Lukács, *History and Class Consciousness,* 83. In the same book, Lukács describes the reification of commodities as follows: "A commodity is a mysterious thing because in it the social character of men's labor appears as an objective character stamped upon the product of that labor; because the relation of the producers to the sum total of their own labor is presented to them as a social relation, existing not between themselves, but between the products of their labor" (86).

50. Karl Marx, *Capital,* vol. 1: *A Critique of Political Economy,* trans. Ben Fowkes (London: Penguin, 1976 [1867]), 280.

51. Marx, *Capital,* 292.

52. Tom Brass, "Unfree Labor and Capitalist Restructuring in the Agrarian Sector: Peru and India," *Journal of Peasant Studies* 14, no. 1 (1986): 51.

53. In fact, Walrasian economics rests on a *set* of assumptions: perfection competition among workers and employees, perfect information, and perfect rationality (which, in turn, presupposes reflexivity, transitivity, and continuity in agents'

preferences). The cognitive and psychological untenability of the rationality axiom is now increasingly accepted by mainstream economists, largely due to the growing weight of evidence generated by scholars in the field of "experimental economics." See the collection of essays edited by T. Connolly, H. Arkes, and K. Hammond, *Judgment and Decision Making: An Interdisciplinary Reader* (Cambridge: Cambridge University Press, 2000).

54. Hence, the bargaining game contains the element of conflict *and* an incentive for cooperation. The classic treatments are John Nash, "The Bargaining Problem," *Econometrica* 18 (1950): 155–62; Thomas Schelling, *The Strategy of Conflict* (Cambridge, Mass.: Harvard University Press, 1960); D. R. Luce and H. Raiffa, *Games and Decisions* (New York: Dover, 1985 [1957]); and Clive Bell, "A Comparison of Principal-Agent and Bargaining Solutions: The Case of Tenancy Contracts," in Bardhan, ed., *The Economic Theory of Agrarian Institutions*.

55. Ray, *Development Economics,* 465.

56. Bell, "A Comparison of Principal-Agent and Bargaining Solutions."

57. In fact, Bell probably overstates the omnipotence of the principal. Even in standard principal–agent models, the principal's choice set is somewhat constrained. He or she cannot offer the agent any contract, only those which satisfy the agent's participation and incentive constraints; cf. Oliver Hart and Bengt Holmstrom, "The Theory of Contracts," in *Advances in Economic Theory,* ed. T. Bewley (Cambridge: Cambridge University Press, 1987); Yujiro Hayami and Keijiro Otsuka, *The Economics of Contract Choice* (Oxford: Clarendon Press, 1993), esp. chap. 2; and Debraj Ray, *Development Economics* (Princeton, N.J.: Princeton University Press, 1998), chap. 12. There is another large problem with bargaining games that theorists rarely confront: how real actors (as opposed to the fictive, asocial agents who inhabit bargaining models) interpret the meanings of various possible "moves" in situations of strategic interaction, and how their interpretations affect equilibrium outcomes; see Judith Mehta, "Meaning in the Context of Bargaining Games—Narratives in Opposition," in *Economics and Language,* ed. W. Henderson, T. Dudley-Evans and R. Backhouse (London: Routledge, 1993).

58. Peyton Young, "The Economics of Convention," *Journal of Economic Perspectives* 10, no. 7 (1996): 116.

59. Although it has been proposed that a very poor person, with little or nothing to lose, may actually be a "gambler" (in other words, risk-loving), it has been shown, in fact, that when potential gains and losses in a lottery situation are low, people are liable to gamble. But when stakes go up, these gambling instincts disappear and conservatism takes over. Since the consequences of a "subsistence failure" from unemployment are likely to be quite injurious to a laborer with low savings and a poorly diversified income portfolio, it seems more plausible to assume that they will be risk-averse. This is the implicit logic in James C. Scott's book, *The Moral Economy of the Peasant* (New Haven: Yale University Press, 1976), where he develops the powerful notion of a peasant "subsistence ethic."

60. The phrase "to favor the employer" can be interpreted in several ways. From the perspective of neoclassical economics it could either be a case where the worker (1) is paid less than his or her marginal value product ("exploitation" in the neoclassical sense); (2) is driven down to his or her "reservation utility level"; or (3) from the standpoint of factor shares, is party to a division of output where the employer's

share of total output exceeds the worker's share. From the Marxist perspective, the phrase "to favor the employer" would simply mean "exploitation" associated with various forms and degrees of absolute and/or relative surplus extraction.

61. This point is forcefully advanced by Postone, *Time, Labor, and Social Domination.*

62. Karl Marx, *Economic and Philosophical Manuscripts of 1844* (Buffalo, N.Y.: Prometheus Books, 1988 [1844]), 33 (italics in original).

63. See, for instance, Norman Geras, "The Controversy about Marx and Justice," *New Left Review* 150 (1985): 47–85.

64. Marx, *Capital*, 1:361.

65. Roemer, *Free to Lose* (chap. 9) claims there are serious problems with the surplus value model of exploitation. He argues instead for a property-relations approach to exploitation that makes explicit ethical judgments about the initial distribution of the means of production. If that distribution were regarded as unjust (say, because the means of production were obtained in an unjust manner) then the unequal income flowing from the control of those assets would be regarded as "exploitative." Wood, "Rational Choice Marxism: Is the Game Worth the Candle?" has sharply criticized Roemer's formulation.

66. See T. Brenkert, "Freedom and Private Property in Marx," in *Marx, Justice and History,* ed. M. Cohen, T. Nagel, and T. Scanlon (Princeton, N.J.: Princeton University Press, 1980), as well as the papers by G. A. Cohen, "The Labor Theory of Value and the Concept of Exploitation," and Z. I. Husami, "Marx on Distributive Justice," in the same collection.

67. Hayami and Kikuchi, *Asian Village Economy at the Crossroads.*

68. M. Kikuchi, H. Anwar, H. and Y. Hayami, "Changes in Rice Harvesting Contracts and Wages in Java," in *Contractual Arrangements, Employment, and Wages in Rural Labor Markets in Asia,* ed. H. Binswanger and M. Rosenzweig (New Haven: Yale University Press, 1984).

69. Kikuchi, Anwar, and Hayami, "Changes in Rice Harvesting Contracts," 118.

70. Pincus, *Class, Power, and Agrarian Change,* chap. 4.

71. Pincus, *Class, Power, and Agrarian Change,* 96.

72. Pincus, *Class, Power, and Agrarian Change,* 119.

73. See, for instance, the linguistic critique of the "bargaining game" in Judith Mehta, "Meaning in the Context of Bargaining Games—Narratives in Opposition."

74. Nancy Folbre expresses a popular MPE viewpoint when she writes: "Individuals are born into social structures that shape their sense of identity and ability to pursue their interests. Choice, in other words, is limited. A theory of social structures is key to any conceptualization of the context in which choice takes place." Folbre, *Who Pays for the Kids? Gender and the Structures of Constraint* (London: Routledge, 1994), 29.

75. Karl Marx was well aware of the disciplinary aspect of piecework. In his chapter on piece-wages in *Capital,* he writes: "Given the system of piece-wages, it is naturally in the personal interest of the worker that he should strain his labor-power as intensely as possible; this in turn enables the capitalist to raise the normal degree of intensity of labor more easily" (1:695).

76. Ramachandran, *Wage Labor and Unfreedom in Agriculture,* 194.

77. It is worth noting that while NIE and MPE do try to take into account the cultural realities of actors, they do so in largely unsatisfactory ways. NIE trucks in the concept of "culture" and reduces it to a set of enumerable normative injunctions that either truncate the preference set internally or, in what is the operational equivalent, function as constraints on maximizing behavior, in the form of behavioral inertia modeled as the cost of departing from custom or as a miscognition of relative prices. The first approach is represented by George Akerlof, "A Theory of Social Custom, of which Unemployment May Be One Consequence," *Quarterly Journal of Economics* 94 (1980); the second, by Avner Greif, "On the Interrelations and Economic Implications of Economic, Social, Political, and Normative Factors: Reflections from Two Late Medieval Societies," in *The Frontiers of the New Institutional Economics,* ed. J. A. Drobak and J. V. C. Nye (San Diego: Academic Press, 1997). A third strategy is to introduce culture as an argument in the utility function—hence, "altruism" or other-regarding behavior, viewed as an artifact of culture, is modeled via interdependent utility functions. Meanwhile, the common MPE approach is to reduce culture to "false consciousness": a set of controlling ideas and institutional forms that are imposed from above and create a world of "appearances" in service of class domination; see, for instance, Karl Marx, *The German Ideology* (New York: International Publishers, 1970 [1846]), or G. A. Cohen, *Karl Marx's Theory of History: A Defence* (Princeton, N.J.: Princeton University Press, 1978). A far more compelling approach, more in line with my Althusserian reading of the cultural, is to be found in Paul Willis, *Learning to Labor: Why Working Class Kids Get Working Class Jobs* (New York: Columbia University Press, 1977).

78. Louis Althusser, "Marxism and Humanism," 233.

79. On process and institutional change, see the excellent book by Dubash in which he discusses the evolution of groundwater markets and contracts in north Gujarat. He adopts a similarly agnostic approach to NIE and MPE, although, like me, his position is markedly closer to MPE; cf. Navroz Dubash, *Tubewell Capitalism: Groundwater Development and Agrarian Change in Gujarat* (New Delhi: Oxford University Press, 2002).

80. I deliberately use the word "conjunctural" rather than "stochastic" in order to indicate that system tendencies *do* exist and *can* exert causal force, but that actual outcomes depend on a particular concatenation of tendencies with the cultural praxis of actors.

81. Mehta, "Meaning in the Context of Bargaining Games—Narratives in Opposition," 94.

82. Ernesto Laclau, *On Populist Reason* (London: Verso, 2004), ix.

83. Being is the attempt to fix. Or as Brian Massumi puts it: "*A thing is when it isn't doing.* . . . *Concrete is as concrete doesn't.*" In Massumi, *A User's Guide Capitalism and Schizophrenia: Deviations from Deleuze and Guattari* (Cambridge, Mass.: MIT Press, 1992), 6 (italics in original).

84. Gayatri Chakravorty Spivak, *A Critique of Postcolonial Reason: Toward a History of the Vanishing Present* (Cambridge, Mass.: Harvard University Press, 1999), 120.

85. Willis, *Learning to Labor,* 2.

86. Richard Biernacki, *The Fabrication of Labor: Germany and Britain, 1640–1914* (Berkeley: University of California Press, 1995).

87. One only has to recall the acrimonious exchanges between Marx and his contemporaries (the "bourgeois political economists," as he termed them) over the "true" nature of the labor process and the source of "surplus value" to give substance to this claim. I take for granted the mutual contaminations of the "economic," "political," and "cultural."

88. David Pocock, *Kanbi and Patidar* (Oxford: Clarendon Press, 1972), 11.

89. See Georges Canguilhem, "Normality and Normativity," in *A Vital Rationalist: Selected Writings from Georges Canguilhem,* ed. Francois Delaporte (New York: Zone Books, 2000), 351–84.

90. Massumi, *A User's Guide to Capitalism and Schizophrenia,* 9.

91. Norbert Elias, *The Civilizing Process: The History of Manners* (London: Basil Blackwell, 1978 [1939]), 53–204.

92. Willis, *Learning to Labor,* 2.

93. The canonical essay is Michel Foucault, "Governmentality," in *The Foucault Effect: Studies in Governmentality,* ed. G. Burchell, C. Gordon, and P. Miller (Chicago: University of Chicago Press, 1991). But there are numerous other venues where Foucault elaborates on the varied operations of this mode of power.

94. By "economy" Foucault intends its modern meaning, following Rousseau, as "wise superintendence" of wealth *and* individual behavior so as to produce "the common welfare of all" (that is, not just the family, as implied in the Greek concept of *oeconomy,* but rather all members of a given population or collectivity); Foucault, "Governmentality," 92.

95. The specific elements of "governmentality" that matter to me here are (a) the emphasis on governance or management of practices *at different scales* (self, family, caste, population, and higher-order groupings such as "society"); (b) the notion that power as *biopower* achieves its *productive* and *normalizing* effects by suffusing bodies and the body politic; and (c) the underlying rationale of regulation in the service of a public notion of *collective welfare.* On caste groupings in India as effects of colonial and postcolonial governmentality, see, for instance (among many others), Nicholas Dirks, "The Invention of Caste: Civil Society in Colonial India," *Social Analysis* 25 (1989): 42–52; Partha Chatterjee, *The Nation and Its Fragments* (Princeton, N.J.: Princeton University Press, 1993); Arjun Appadurai, "Patriotism and Its Futures," in his *Modernity at Large: Cultural Dimensions of Globalization* (Minneapolis: University of Minnesota Press, 1996); and Susan Bayly, *Caste, Society and Politics in India from the Eighteenth Century to the Modern Age* (Cambridge: Cambridge University Press, 1999).

96. Peter Hallward, *Badiou: A Subject to Truth* (Minneapolis: University of Minnesota Press, 2003); and also, Alain Badiou, "A Speculative Disquisition on the Concept of Democracy," in his *Metapolitics,* trans. Jason Barker (London: Verso, 2005), 78–95.

97. Thorstein Veblen, *The Theory of the Leisure Class* (New York: Dover Books, 1994 [1899]), 24.

98. Pierre Bourdieu, *Distinction: A Social Critique of the Judgement of Taste,* trans. Richard Nice (Cambridge, Mass.: Harvard University Press, 1984), 55 (italics in original).

99. I borrow the term "general economy" in a strict sense from Georges Bataille, *The Accursed Share: An Essay on General Economy,* vol. 1: *Consumption,* trans. Robert Hurley (New York: Zone Books, 1991), see esp. part 1.

100. Hardiman, *Peasant Nationalists of Gujarat,* 35.

101. Again, Hardiman observes that Lewa Kanbis "who owned a small amount of land either sought alternative employment of a respectable nature (such as shop-keeping or schoolmastering), or rented in a sufficient amount of land to be able to maintain the life-style of a middle peasant. . . . [Lewa Kanbis] were . . . expected to maintain certain standards, and in practice the majority did so" (*Peasant Nationalists of Gujarat,* 35). These work preferences are manifest even today. I did not encounter a single Patel household (from the ones I formally interviewed and the numerous others I informally canvassed) that engaged in agricultural wage work. Poorer Patel households eke out a living either by leasing land from wealthier caste members and/or by sending younger male members to work in factories or urban retail and vocational occupations.

102. M. Keith and S. Pile, "Introduction Part 1: The Politics of Place," in *Place and the Politics of Identity,* ed. M. Keith and S. Pile (London: Routledge, 1993), 5–6.

103. K. R. Unni, based on his research in Kerala, furnishes a vivid illustration of the geographic character of work-linked stigma. He found members of impoverished high-caste Nair families migrating to towns to become factory workers, cooks, and waiters in restaurants. When left with no alternative except agricultural labor, they preferred to migrate to a distant village where they were unknown rather than disgrace themselves in their own village. See Unni, "Sources of Agricultural Labor in Kerala: Some Social Perspectives," in *Culture and Society,* ed. B. N. Nair, (Delhi: Thomson Press, 1975).

104. Breman, *Of Peasants, Migrants, and Paupers,* 85.

105. J. Tharamangalam, *Agrarian Class Conflict: The Political Mobilization of Agricultural Laborers in Kuttanad, South India* (Vancouver: University of British Columbia Press, 1981), 40.

106. Williams, "Marx and Culture," 208.

107. Williams, "Marx and Culture," 208–9.

108. Elias, *The Civilizing Process,* chap. 1.

109. Max Weber, *The Protestant Ethic and the Spirit of Capitalism* (New York: Charles Scribners' Sons, 1958 [1903–5]).

110. Fieldnotes, Sandhana, November 20, 1994.

111. Mario Rutten, *Farms and Factories* (Delhi: Oxford University Press, 1995), 277.

112. Thus, in 1995 the average ownership landholding of Patels in Shamli was 14.79 acres, in contrast to average holdings of 4.91, 11.01, 5.51, and 2.53 acres among Baraiya Kolis, Bharwads, Vankars, and Rohits, respectively.

113. Hence, it is neither clear that labor, unlike leisure, is always a source of disutility—as neoclassical theory typically assumes; nor is aversion to manual and/or agricultural labor inevitable. Paul Willis, whose ethnographic study of working-class youth in the United Kingdom I briefly discuss, has shown how *manual* as opposed to mental labor can acquire a positive connotation for certain groups. Similarly, in the rural Indian context, Sharad Chari shows in a superb work of ethnography how the cultivating caste of Gounders in Tamil Nadu valorize "toil"; cf. Chari, *Fraternal Capital: Peasant-Workers, Self-Made Men and Globalization in Provincial India* (Stanford: Stanford University Press, 2004). And, of course, who can forget Max Weber's famous thesis on the Protestant work ethic?

114. The mortgagee or *giro rakhnaar* is held in high esteem within the village community because the ability to keep mortgaged land is regarded as a sign of

accumulated surpluses. A comparable view from South India is found in Venkatesh Athreya, Goran Djurfeldt and Stefan Lindberg, *Barriers Broken: Production Relations and Agrarian Change in Tamil Nadu* (New Delhi: Sage Publications, 1990).

115. See S. J. M. Epstein, *The Earthy Soil* (Delhi: Oxford University Press, 1988), 5, on the importance of educational capital. Similarly, A. H. Somjee asserts that Patel *agevans* (leading men of the community) came to recognize the economic and cultural payoffs of formal education early, as evidenced by the establishment of the Charotar Education Society in Anand at the beginning of the twentieth century; see Somjee, "Social Mobility Among the Patidars of Kaira," *Contributions to Asian Studies* 12 (1982): 111.

116. L. V. M. Robertson to the Collector of Kaira (No. 268 of 1.7.1916), 7, in Selections from the Records of the Bombay Government, New Series, *Papers Relating to the Second Revision Survey Settlement of Matar Taluka of the Kaira District* (Bombay: Govt. Central Press, 1920).

117. Breman, *Of Peasants, Paupers and Migrants*, has documented similar strategies of labor control in south Gujarat.

118. John Harriss argues in a comparable vein that differences in wage rates between his North Arcot study villages depended significantly on whether or not the dominant caste was Agamudaiyan Mudaliar. The Agamudaiyan Mudaliar, he notes, are given to a "seigneurial lifestyle," which prompts them to shun cultivation work when possible, and instead rely on hired and semipermanent labor. Hence, villages such as Randam and Vegamangalam, where the Agamudaiyan Mudaliar are the dominant caste, exhibit higher wage rates for agricultural work than non-Mudaliar villages. See Harriss, "Population, Employment and Wages," 119–20.

119. Conversation with K. D. Patel, Astha, July 24, 1995.

120. Change in paddy acreage computed from data obtained from Shah, Shah, and Iyengar, *Agricultural Growth with Equity*, Table 2.15, p. 42; and Kheda Jilla Panchayat, *Jilla ni Ankdakiya Rooprekha*, 1989–90 (Nadiad: Kheda Jilla Panchayat, nd), Table 4.5, p. 41.

121. Panchayat, *Jilla ni Ankdakiya Rooprekha*, Table 5, p. 77.

122. A trend of rising real wages for agricultural operations is illustrative. Thus, in Matar Taluka the daily real wage for weeding, an operation that is common to all cereal crops, increased from 2.22 kilograms of paddy in 1965, to 2.39 in 1974, and 6.41 in 1994. There have been other shifts in labor contracting as well, which collectively point to an increase in labor's bargaining power. For instance, in peak agricultural periods employers often have to recruit laborers for work the night before and by paying the daily wage in advance.

123. Breman, *Footloose Proletariat*, 238–39.

124. "Use value" of labor is simply the ability of individuals to produce innately useful products by the act of laboring. "Exchange value" is the wage individuals command for selling their labor power as a commodity. Exchange value presupposes the ability of labor to produce use value.

125. Georg Lukács observes that the fate of the worker, who must present himself or herself as the "owner" of his or her labor power, as if it were a commodity, is "typical of society as a whole in that this self-objectification, this transformation of a human function into a commodity reveals in all its starkness the dehumanised and dehumanising function of the commodity relation" (*History and Class*

Consciousness, 92). Complete or partial devalorization of labor tries to ease precisely this sense of alienation, and in the process, communicate freedom from compulsion. I want to dispel the notion that (agrarian or industrial) capitalism is somehow reversible via devalorizing strategies. Given that capitalism is a social-structural formation, this is clearly an inadmissible prospect.

5. Interruption

1. Here is how GIDC advertises itself on its Web page, http://www.gidc.gov.in/ about.asp (last accessed 15 April 2007): "GIDC the most customer-oriented corporation, came into existence in 1962, under the Gujarat Industrial Development Act, 1962, with a vision of accelerate the pace of industrialization in the State of Gujarat. Since then there was no looking back. . . . An entrepreneur, wishing to start an industry, would always look for availability of ready infrastructure, not only for speedy implementation but also to reduce pre-project implementation cost/time. To enable an entrepreneur to set up the project envisaged within available resources, GIDC identifies locations suitable for industrial development and arranges for infrastructure facilities that one would normally look for. GIDC industrial estates are equipped with essential infrastructure facilities like roads, drainage, power, water supply, and streetlights. Then there are the supportive amenities and commercial facilities like banking, telecommunication, shopping complex, canteens, schools, dispensaries, police chowky, community hall, etc. In many estates, there are housing facilities for workers and executives. These low cost ready to occupy houses prove to be a major boon, doing away with the need for commuting from great distances. This helps the entrepreneurs in attracting better talent and also results in enhanced productivity. . . . Gujarat Industrial Development Corporation (GIDC) truly believes in a win-win business philosophy. With this in mind, GIDC has created 171 functional industrial estates spread all over Gujarat providing the entrepreneurs with industrial infrastructure which serves as a solid base for the natural outcome of growth and prosperity."

2. Directorate of Economics and Statistics (Government of Gujarat), *Socio-Economic Review, Gujarat State, 2003–4,* mimeo.

3. See http://www.gujaratindia.com/. Under the tab "Business" and subheading "Investment Opportunities," the Web site (last accessed 15 April 2007) states: "Ever since its inception, Gujarat has been showing a new direction to the nation during the last 43 years. It is conquering new grounds and is ill at ease with the Number One position among different states in the country. In the 21st Century, its goal is to be compared with the economic growth rate of developed nations. . . . With just 5 percent of the India's total population and 6 percent of geographical area, Gujarat contributes to 16 percent of the country's total investment, 10 percent of expenditure, 16 percent of exports and 30 percent of stock market capitalization. The state's annual growth rate has been 10 to 12 percent for the last five years. As per the latest data of Centre for Monitoring Indian Economy (CMIE) of January 2003, Gujarat stands first in industrialization in India. Projects worth Rs. 33,958 crore [US$7.54 billion at the current exchange rate] are under implementation."

It is notable that Gujarat was one of the few states in India that lacked—and continues to lack—an active communist presence. The Communist Party of India

(CPI) and the Communist Party of India–Marxist (CPI–M), the two largest communist political parties in India, are nonfactors in the state. The closest Gujarat has come to socialism is Gandhian socialism and even its visible proponents, such as Morarji Desai (ex-Chief Minister of Gujarat and ex-Prime Minister of India), were openly and ardently anticommunist. As a result, organized labor movements in Gujarat—whether in the industrial sector or the agricultural—have been mostly absent; or have taken other identitarian forms. See, for example, Sujata Patel, *The Making of Industrial Relations: The Ahmedabad Textile Industry 1918–1939* (Delhi: Oxford University Press, 1987), and Jan Breman, "An Informalised Labor System: End of Labor Market Dualism," Review of Labor, *Economic and Political Weekly* 36, no. 52: 4804–21.

4. Development also functions as a supplement to capitalism. For a trenchant analysis, see Joel Wainwright, *Decolonizing Development: Colonial Power and the Maya*, 1st ed. (Malden, Mass.: Blackwell, 2007).

5. T. K. Jayaraman, "Farmer's Organisations in Surface Irrigation Projects," *Economic and Political Weekly* 16, no. 39 (Review of Agriculture, September 26, 1981), A-91.

6. Personal communication, Motabhai Chhanabhai Dabhi, dairy secretary of Pehlagam village, April 20, 1995 (name of individual and village have been altered). According to Dabhi, Ishwarbhai Chawda—then *pramukh* (head) of the Kheda Jilla Panchayat (the elected district-level administrative body)—was so appalled by the drinking water quality on a visit to Pehlagam in 1987 that he personally instructed district officials to convey water samples to M.S. University for chemical analysis. Motabhai says that scientists described the water unfit for livestock, let alone humans. Ishwarbhai Chawda arranged for funds to the Pehlagam village panchayat to sink a tube well. The tube well was installed only after protracted wrangling with the *sarpanch* (village head) and *talati* (village accountant) of Pehlagam, who, according to Motabhai, were corrupt and in the business of misappropriating panchayat funds.

7. Partial evidence for this claim is available. In comparison to Limbasi, where per-acre rice production is in the range of fourteen to twenty-one quintals, average production in Navagam is in the range of ten to eighteen quintals—cultivators at the higher end being those with access to good-quality groundwater. Water pollution in the Khari has produced three direct consequences for agriculture:

(1) Recurrently, cultivators are either unable to prepare seedlings *(dharu)* in time for sowing unless they have access to well water or an arrangement with someone who does. This is especially true in years when rainfall in June—the month in which seedbeds are planted—is sparse in the catchments of the Khari and Meshwo rivers. Between 1983 and 1993, there were six such years. In other years, excessive contamination from dyestuff effluents impairs germination and growth, with the result that seedling development is either stunted or their density so winnowed by mortality that only a portion of the cultivator's lands could be transplanted. By the time this becomes apparent—in late July or early August—it is too late as per the agricultural calendar to prepare new seedbeds. Some cultivators are able to purchase surplus seedlings from large farmers, but the quality of these seedlings is uncertain; and the possibility of purchase itself is often a matter of chance.

(2) Use of polluted water in rice-beds affects grain quality. Cultivators in Navagam villages told me that the size of grains from the Masuri and Gujarat-17

varieties are smaller in size *(zeena)* than those from the same varieties grown in Limbasi villages. Since marketable (husked) rice is typically 50 to 60 percent by weight of unhusked paddy, and since traders and milling agents attach a price on grain based—among other factors—upon its size and texture, small grain size and blotchiness can impose severe pecuniary losses on cultivators. Some cultivators also insisted that paddy grown with contaminated water is more susceptible to pest attacks (I was not able to confirm these assertions independently).

(3) Soil alkalis have reacted with acidic water from the Khari to form salts, thereby aggravating the existing problem of salinity in the Navagam area, and causing permanent diminution in land productivity in certain tracts.

8. An assay of water samples collected daily by hydrologists from Gujarat Agricultural University between March 13 and March 18, 1995, revealed that the samples had an average pH of 2.5 as a result of contamination by chemical effluents dumped into the Khari-Cut Canal by small-scale dyestuff industries situated upstream in the Vatva, Narol, and Odhav industrial zones of Ahmedabad City (*Gujarat Samachar,* March 23, 1995, Ahmedabad edition). The scientists noted that the water in the Khari-Cut Canal in its present, highly acidic condition was "absolutely unfit for agriculture." In May 1995, a repeat assay revealed an average pH of 3.0. The Khari is in low ebb from November through May; hence, the pH of any contaminated flow is likely to be high. However, water assays by an agronomist from the Sardar Patel University in Ahmedabad, done in the *monsoon* months of 1994, when flow in the Khari River is brisk, revealed that the pH tended to fluctuate between 5.0 and 6.0—rendering the water at best *marginally* fit for agriculture (personal communication, Shri Gordhanbhai Shambhubhai Patel, Navagam, May 13, 1995).

9. See my article, "The Unbearable Modernity of 'Development'? Canal Irrigation and Development Planning in Western India," *Progress in Planning* 58, no. 1 (July–August 2002): 1–80, for details on state-sponsored groundwater development in Matar Taluka, and charges of pervasive corruption among contractors and state officials. On the issue of salinity: the subdistrict was submerged under the Indian Ocean in geological time, as a result of which the lower soil profiles are infested with salt. Its proximity to the sea (specifically, to the Gulf of Khambhat) also causes problems of salinity ingress into freshwater aquifers.

10. Interest rates border on the usurious, ranging from 10 to 12 percent per month (simple interest) for those unable to offer fungible collateral (such as jewelry, utensils, or livestock). Those able to offer collateral, usually family jewelry or utensils, can get loans at 5 to 6 percent per month—still high by the standards of villages in the Limbasi tract, where interest rates on informal loans average around 3 percent. With the decline in irrigation, land is no longer a sure form of collateral—except in instances where the lender has access to substitute irrigation from unsalinated groundwater, which can be taken to the borrower's field(s) without undue costs or complications.

11. In contrast to Navagam, the Limbasi tract receives assured irrigation to most villages in the kharif season from the MRBC project and conjunctive irrigation in the rabi season. One indication of Limbasi's current prosperity relative to villages in Navagam is the price that agricultural land fetches on the market: 15,000 to 20,000 rupees (US$333–444) per vigha for unirrigated land, and 40,000 to 60,000 rupees ($889–1333) per vigha for irrigated land.

12. Only since 2003 has the water scarcity eased somewhat as a result of irrigation flows being funneled into the Khari system, via the Shedhi River, from the recently operational Narmada canal project.

13. Jacques Derrida, "Différance," in his *Margins of Philosophy*, trans. Alan Bass (Chicago: University of Chicago Press, 1982 [1972]), 15.

14. Jacques Derrida and Maurizio Ferraris, "I Have a Taste for the Secret," in *A Taste for the Secret* (Cambridge: Polity, 2001), 33.

15. Michael Hardt and Antonio Negri, *Multitude* (New York: Penguin Press, 2004), 351.

16. Cf. Benedictus de Spinoza, *Spinoza: Complete Works*, ed. Michael L. Morgan, trans. Samuel Shirley (Indianapolis: Hackett Publishing Company, 2002).

17. G. W. F. Hegel, *Hegel's Preface to the Phenomenology of Spirit* (hereafter, *Preface*), trans. Yirmiyahu Yovel (Princeton: Princeton University Press, 2005), 110. The standard translation is *Hegel's Phenomenology of Spirit* by A. V. Miller (Oxford: Oxford University Press, 1977) (hereafter, *Phenomenology*). Here, I have opted for Yovel's more recent translation of the Preface because it is stylistically clearer, although both Miller and Yovel rely on Hegel's original German text *Phänomenologie des Geistes*, edited by J. Hoffmeister (Hamburg: Félix Meiner Verlag, 1952).

18. Hegel never names "Europe" as such in the 1807 *Phenomenology*, but does later in the 1830 *Lectures;* see G. W. F. Hegel, *Lectures on the Philosophy of World History: Introduction*, trans. H. B. Nisbet (Cambridge: Cambridge University Press, 1975) (hereafter, *Lectures*). I have borrowed the formulation, S/subject of Europe, from Gayatri Chakravarty Spivak's essay, "Can the subaltern speak?" in Cory Nelson and Lawrence Grossberg (eds.) *Marxism and the Interpretation of Culture* (Urbana and Chicago: University of Illinois Press, 1988), 271–313.

19. Hegel writes: " '*To sublate*' has a twofold meaning in language: on the one hand it means to preserve, to maintain, and equally it also means to cease, to put an end to. Even 'to preserve' includes a negative element, namely, that something is removed from its immediacy and so from an existence that is open to external influences, in order to preserve it. Thus what is sublated is at the same time preserved; it has only lost its immediacy but is not on that account annihilated." G. W. F. Hegel, *Hegel's Science of Logic* [hereafter, *Logic*] trans. A. V. Miller (Amherst, N.Y.: Humanity Books, 1969), 107 (italics in original). Also see Jacques Derrida's fascinating essay on Bataille's critique of Hegel's philosophy; Derrida, "From Restricted to General Economy," in his *Writing and Difference*, trans. Alan Bass (Chicago: University of Chicago Press, 1978), 251–77.

20. Gilles Deleuze, *Difference and Repetition*, trans. Paul Patton (New York: Columbia University Press, 1994), 51.

21. On the forms of and traffic between Buddhist/Hindu and Greek dialectics, see Thomas McEvilley, *The Shape of Ancient Thought* (New York: Allworth Press, 2002).

22. Hegel, *Lectures*, trans. H. B. Nisbet (Cambridge: Cambridge University Press, 1975), 126–27. In the original text, this entire passage appeared in italics.

23. Immanuel Kant, "What Is Enlightenment?" in his *On History*, trans. Lewis White Beck (Indianapolis: Bobbs-Merrill, 1963).

24. See Karl Marx, *Grundrisse*, trans. Martin Nicolaus (London: Penguin Books, 1973 [1858]).

25. Hegel, *Lectures*, 127.

26. Wilhelm Halbfass, *India and Europe: An Essay in Understanding* (Albany: State University of New York Press, 1988), 87; originally published in German (Basel: A. G. Schwabe & Co., 1981).

27. Louis Althusser, "The Errors of Classical Economics," in Althusser and Etienne Balibar, *Reading Capital*, trans. Ben Brewster (London: Verso: 1997 [1970]), 96.

28. There are more open-ended ways of reading Hegel than Althusser. For writings that seem to bear out Althusser's allegations, see Hegel's chapters "The Realisation of Spirit in History" and "The Course of World History" in G. W. F. Hegel, *Lectures on the Philosophy of World History: Introduction*, 44–123 and 124–51; also chap. 3 on "Being-for-Self" in Hegel, *Logic*, 157–84. For those who argue that Hegel has been unjustly branded a theorist of closure and identity rather than one of perpetual tension and never-ending dialogue between freedom and order, see, for example, the "Introduction" by Duncan Forbes in Hegel, *Lectures*. Also see the interventions by Judith Butler in Butler, Ernesto Laclau, and Slavoj Žižek, *Contingency, Hegemony, Universality: Contemporary Dialogues on the Left* (London: Verso, 2000); Jean-Luc Nancy, *Hegel: The Restlessness of the Negative*, trans. Jason Smith and Steven Miller (Minneapolis: University of Minnesota Press); Catherine Malabou, *The Future of Hegel: Plasticity, Temporality and Dialectic*, trans. Lisabeth During (London: Routledge, 2005); and John W. Burbidge, *Hegel's Systematic Contingency* (New York: Palgrave Macmillan, 2007).

29. For an instructive, if ultimately problematic, account of the principles of "dialectics" (particularly as applicable to Marxist theorizing), see David Harvey, "Dialectics," in *Justice, Nature and the Geography of Difference* (Cambridge, Mass.: Blackwell Publishers, 1996), chap. 2. For a more sustained meditation on the topic, see Roy Bhaskar, *Dialectic: The Pulse of Freedom* (London: Verso, 1993).

30. The clearest and bleakest statement of this can be found in Max Horkheimer and Theodor Adorno, "The Concept of Enlightenment," in *Dialectic of Enlightenment* (New York: Continuum, 1976), 3–42.

31. Such a normative vision draws inspiration from Marx's propositions in the *Grundrisse*, but also from some of his prominent twentieth-century interlocutors—specifically (if in unlikely combination) Antonio Gramsci, Theodor Adorno, Walter Benjamin, Georges Canguilhem, Louis Althusser, Michel Foucault, Raymond Williams, Enrique Dussel, and Gilles Deleuze.

32. Marx, *Grundrisse*, 296.

33. Ibid., 297.

34. Louis Althusser, "The Errors of Classical Economics," in Althusser and Balibar, *Reading Capital*, 98.

35. The literature is rife with critiques of the labor theory of value by both opponents and sympathizers of Marx, and this is clearly not the place to visit these debates. The formulation of "value" I offer here builds on a reading of Diane Elson's rewarding article, "A Value Theory of Labor," *Value*, ed. Diane Elson (London: CSE, 1979). Elson circumvents critiques that attribute to Marx a theory of value that stands—and falls—on labor being the physical substance of value. By contrast, Elson argues that Marx intended to draw attention to *the rationalizing practices whereby labor is continuously enrolled in abstracted form through the wage/money relation*. This not only involves a disciplining of labor through surveillance, monitoring, punishment, and incentive contracts; but, more pointedly, these mechanisms are to be themselves

viewed as symptomatic of a system of generalized commodity exchange—that is to say, a dominant and more or less competitive market system—where wealth and worth are measured in an impersonal, abstract money form. Thus, a value theory of labor as Elson presents it is a condensed expression of the imperative for capitalists to constantly cut labor costs and raise labor productivity in order to survive, and for workers to become continuously more productive at their tasks in order to not become dispensable. In Elson's words: "My argument is that the *object* of Marx's theory of value was labor. It is not a matter of seeking an explanation of why prices are what they are and finding that it is labor [thus, Elson sidesteps the nettlesome "transformation problem"]. But rather of seeking an understanding why labor takes the form it does, and what the political consequences are" (123). The accumulating trend toward outsourcing and threat of outsourcing that employers constantly wield over workers (actively dissuading workers, for instance, from organizing into unions) is a vivid illustration of a value theory of labor in operation. For provocative discussions of capitalism as a social formation ruled by abstractions that have become *lived* reality, see Moishe Postone, *Time, Labor, and Social Domination: A Reinterpretation of Marx's Critical Theory* (Cambridge: Cambridge University Press, 1996) and Jason Read, *The Micro-Politics of Capital: Marx and the Prehistory of the Present* (Albany: State University of New York Press, 2003). Echoing Elson's thesis, Read writes: "The effectivity of the social average of all labors is that which imposes itself on this or that particular labor as a norm: failure to produce according to the speed and productivity of this norm is a failure to produce value or profit. This norm makes necessary the [attempted] equalization of the diverse and heterogeneous labors of diverse and distinct individuals into an average capable of being measured" (69). Postone's and Read's arguments can be read in a rewarding way next to Elson's. But neither of these theorists considers the possibility that what counts as "labor," or value-creating practice, has a historical *and* geographical dimension such that capitalism itself could be then posited as a social formation where the abstracted money form of value continuously struggles to sublate other existing regimes of value. One excellent book that only approximates the sort of intervention I am proposing, however, is David Graeber's, *Toward an Anthropological Theory of Value* (New York: Palgrave, 2001).

36. Althusser, "The Errors of Classical Economics," 98–99.

37. Althusser, "The Errors of Classical Economics," 99.

38. Derrida, "I Have a Taste for the Secret," 33.

39. Gilles Deleuze and Félix Guattari, *A Thousand Plateaus: Capitalism and Schizophrenia*, trans. Brian Massumi (Minneapolis: University of Minnesota Press, 1987), 11 (italics in original).

40. Names of persons and villages have been altered. The ethnographic accounts that follow are re-presentations in a very literal sense. After some early bad experiences with trying to tape record conversations and interviews, I decided to give that up altogether and to simply rely on field notes—scribbled and composed as we were talking, or soon after a conversation was completed. What I reproduce here are not, therefore, verbatim accounts. But they are faithful to the notes I took at the time.

41. The Gujarati word is *jan-pehchaan*, which I have translated as "connections" (in the sense of someone being widely networked or well connected).

42. NSCs and KVPs are treasury bonds issued by the Central Government, and sold through local post offices, that double their value in five-and-a-half to six years. Until the equity market (share bazaar) craze swept India—and particularly Gujarat—in 1994–95, they used to be a very popular form of savings with middle classes in rural and urban areas. During that particular stay in Gujarat, when share-bazaar mania was at its peak, I was constantly asked for and offered investment tips on obscure companies that were going to be the next big thing. Many, as it was apparent by late 1996—when the stock market bubble finally collapsed—had been nothing more than shell operations. Their stocks were floated, then driven up through strategic buys by a small network of powerful stockbrokers, who simultaneously flooded the market with "tips" on these unknown companies (if this seems eerily familiar, that's because almost identical practices were responsible for the late 1990s stock market boom in the United States). The strategy, which was duplicated at smaller scales by small-time, often provincial brokers (like Hasmukhbhai), was spectacularly successful in drawing the savings of ordinary citizens—virtually anyone with little to invest—into the financial markets. (There were variants of the scam too: for example, promises of huge returns from nonexistent "sal" (*Shorea robusta*) and "teak" (*Tectona grandis*) plantations, promoted via glossy brochures). Many ended up losing their life savings when the bubble burst. One of the figures who became iconic for his misdeeds—but simultaneously admired for his ingenuity and salesmanship (much like Michael Milken in the United States)—was a Bombay-based stockbroker, originally from Gujarat, called Harshad Mehta: popularly known as "The Bull."

43. Virtually all government positions can be "purchased"—in fact, *have* to be. In 1994, the going rate for a primary schoolteacher appointment, with an inflation-adjusted monthly salary of approximately 4,500 rupees (US$100) was Rs. 1.2 lacs ($2,667); and for higher-level appointments, such as Hasmukhbhai's, anywhere between 2.5 to 3 lacs rupees ($5,556 to $6,667)—for an inflation-adjusted monthly salary of 7,000 rupees ($156). In short, it would take a person about three years to break-even on the bribe ignoring the opportunity cost of their cash payout. Small wonder that there is an incentive to misappropriate funds, where possible, in a government job—and this is precisely what Hasmukhbhai seems to have done. On a recent visit to Astha in October 2004, I was told that Hasmukhbhai has been accused of pocketing 60,000 rupees in government funds targeted for repairs and upkeep of Astha's school building. Many, as I indicated, view such diversion of public funds as legitimate returns on their "investments" in government jobs. The language of the market permeates everyday life, but the attitude that informs is not of productive accumulation but rather of exchange, speculation, and rent seeking.

44. Once, when he had agreed in the company of three of his Patel allies and one of their wives, he had quickly turned our discussion into a soliloquy on sex: first regaling us with stories of his sexual drive—how he liked to do "it" after lunch every afternoon, especially in these slow summer months when it was so easy to get bored, the positions he had experimented with, and his trysts with other women ("Everyone does it, Vinaybhai"); later, the questions had been turned on me—did I know the word "fock," how many "girlfriends" did I have in America, were they white, did I "fock" a lot, which times of the day did I most like to do it, which positions, and so on.

45. The responses are paraphrased, not direct quotes, based on what I scribbled down in a notebook during and after the encounter. As previously mentioned, after some initial attempts to use a tape recorder, which inevitably skewed or killed conversations, I gave up trying.

46. *Abroo* is a Gujarati term that combines at least three different shades of meaning: personal reputation, family status, and history of creditworthiness.

47. As discussed in chapter 2, lending rates in the informal credit market vary sharply: from a low of 2 percent per month (simple interest) to a high of 6 to 7 percent per month. In addition, there are several lending arrangements— increasingly less frequent, but still prevalent—that border on the usurious (such as *ardho-man athva man dangar*—ten or twenty kilograms of paddy—per hundred rupees loaned, which at the then-prevailing average price of ninety-five rupees for twenty kilograms of paddy translated into an interest rate of 50 to 100 percent over six months, or between 8 to 16 percent per month!

48. This question was prompted by an earlier remark of Kashibhai's, complaining about all the government officials who came looking for bribes: the *gram sevak* (village-level agricultural extension agent, of whose utility Kashibhai—who is widely feted for his farming acumen—was utterly dismissive); the officer from the *sichain khata* (irrigation department) wanted an *inam* (reward) because he was going to make sure there was enough water flowing in the subminor that ran past Kashibhai's fields; and the labor department officer who never talked to the *khet majoor* (farm laborers) but came straight to the house of one the big farmers and expected to be offered refreshments—and (this was Kashibhai's biggest grouse) asked to take a look at a register, which employers are expected to maintain, of who was hired on a given day and paid what, which both Kashibhai and the labor officer knew was entirely fictitious. The statutory minimum wage for agricultural workers in Gujarat at the time—until 1996—was fifteen rupees (the lowest in India), after which it was revised up to thirty-two rupees.

49. The sums Dasarath stated seemed large to me and I wondered where the profits had disappeared.

50. In the jargon of institutional economics, an undivided family would be an institutional arrangement that provides partial risk pooling.

51. Dasarath was talking about the village credit cooperative in Astha, which at the time was authorized to lend approximately 2,200 rupees per vigha to cultivators who were in good standing. Almost all villages in Matar Taluka, with the exception of the smallest, have a credit cooperative that receives government funds through a district cooperative bank. Cultivators are given loans in April and May and loans are repayable with statutory interest (13 percent per annum in 1994) the following March. Default is often high, particularly around election years, because there is an expectation that an incumbent government will wipe outstanding debts off the books in order to consolidate electoral support (opposition parties often promise debt waivers too as an electoral strategy). In the case of Dasarath's family, their default made them ineligible for a loan in the next season and, furthermore, eligible for a penalty—because the outstanding loan had to be serviced at an annual rate of 18 percent, instead of the standard 13 percent.

52. Shamabhai was responsible for getting money from the Gujarat Government and AMUL Dairy to put up a new dairy building in Astha. In my time in Astha I never heard anyone speak ill of him. The adjectives used to describe him, when

I asked, were *dahyo* (good), *samjhan valo* (perspicacious), *buddhishaali* (intelligent), and *mehnatu* (hard-working).

53. The account presented in the text is constructed from field notes dated March 12, 2005. It is not a verbatim account.

54. *Tuver* (pigeonpea) is a legume that is popular in Gujarat, and grown in rain-fed *goradu* (sandy silt) soils. The long-duration tuver grown in Gujarat takes approximately eight to eight and a half months (>220 days) to mature from planting, but requires almost no inputs. The fruit is a pod that contains tan-colored peas, usually sold skinned and split, which reveals their yellow interiors. But the unsplit peas are also cooked in the form of a vegetable *(tuver nu shak)*. The term *ponkh* refers to just ripening pods, freshly plucked, and fired over charcoal. The same is done with wheat (hence, *gehun na ponkh*). It's a time-consuming process from start to finish. A common agrarian custom in the near past, it is now less widespread—possibly because the dietary and time preferences of many villagers have shifted. The practice of firing pods has, however, seen a recent revival in urban areas as "rural chic" at expensive outdoors restaurants that offer "authentic rural cuisine."

55. This account is drawn from field notes dated March 21, 1994. A longer version of this excerpt, with one very minor difference, has previously appeared in my article, "The Quest for Distinction: A Re-Appraisal of the Rural Labor Process in Kheda District (Gujarat), India," *Economic Geography* 76, no. 2 (2000): 145–68.

56. For one of the more astute recent critiques of anthropology, from a literary critic within the field of postcolonial studies, see Qadri Ismail, *Abiding by Sri Lanka: On Peace, Place, and Postcoloniality* (Minneapolis: University of Minnesota Press, 2005).

57. Paolo Virno, *A Grammar of the Multitude* (Los Angeles: Semiotext(e), 2004), 78 (italics in original).

58. Brian Massumi, *A User's Guide to Capitalism and Schizophrenia: Deviations from Deleuze and Guattari* (Cambridge, Mass.: MIT Press, 1992), 10–11 (italics mine).

59. Michel Foucault, "What Is Enlightenment?" in *Michel Foucault: Ethics: Subjectivity and Truth, Essential Works of Foucault 1954–1984,* vol. I, ed. Paul Rabinow (New York: The New Press, 1997), 315.

60. Here, I would include the devalorizing practices of labor deployment that Patels use as tactics of self-governance and identity management (see chapter 4). On a different front, it warrants mention that Hannah Arendt, in *The Human Condition,* also draws a distinction between "labor" and "work." My use of these categories is not related. Cf. Arendt, *The Human Condition,* 2nd ed. (Chicago: University of Chicago Press, 1998).

61. Theodor Adorno, Negative Dialectics, trans. E. B. Ashton (New York: Continuum, 1973), 5.

62. Marx, *Grundrisse,* 295–96.

63. Derrida, "I Have a Taste for the Secret," 33.

64. One *must,* of course, gender these assertions. Ajibhai may arrange his use of labor, but does he let his wife and children also arrange their use of labor at their pleasure? I suspect not. In addition, the liquor he is alleged to brew is sold as a commodity—and what should we make of *that?*

65. Antonio Gramsci, "Americanism and Fordism," in *The Antonio Gramsci Reader: Selected Writings, 1916–1935,* ed. David Forgacs (New York: New York University Press, 2000), 291.

66. Marx, *Grundrisse*, 286–87.

67. V. K. Ramachandran, *Wage Labor and Unfreedom in Agriculture: An Indian Case Study* (Delhi: Oxford University Press, 199), 194.

68. Georg Lukács, *History and Class Consciousness*, trans. Rodney Livingstone (Cambridge: MIT Press, 1971 [1922]), 90.

69. See David Harvey, *Limits to Capital*, new ed. (London: Verso, 1999 [1982]) and Dipesh Chakrabarty, *Provincializing Europe: Postcolonial Thought and Historical Difference* (Princeton, N.J.: Princeton University Press, 2000). Unless otherwise noted, the page citations in the text refer to these works. The staging of this encounter is a considerably elaborated version of my article, "Limits to Capital: Questions of Politics and Provenance," *Antipode* 36, no. 3 (2004): 527–42.

70. Chakrabarty, *Provincializing Europe*, 63.

71. Chakrabarty, *Provincializing Europe*, 64.

72. Chakrabarty, *Provincializing Europe*, 66.

73. Hence, this assertion: "Peoples possessed of the utmost diversity of historical experience, living in an incredible variety of physical circumstances, have been welded, sometimes greatly and cajolingly but more often through the exercise of ruthless brute force, into a complex *unity* under the international division of labor" (*Limits to Capital*, 373; italics mine).

74. *Limits* treats as marginal those struggles centered around caste, ethnicity, patriarchy, race, and religion. And even opposition to capital is, ostensibly, one of doomed negativity because "[c]onceived of as an object essentially dominated by capital ... the laborer is nothing but *variable capital*, an aspect of capital itself"; Harvey, *Limits to Capital*, 380–81 (italics in original).

75. This Marxist lineage (to offer a severely truncated list) includes: Karl Kautsky, Vladimir Lenin, E. P. Thompson, Raymond Williams, Maurice Godelier, Eric Wolf, Claude Meillassoux, Sidney Mintz, Henry Bernstein, Jairus Banaji, Terry Byres, Goran Hyden, Tom Brass, John Harriss, Michael Taussig, James C. Scott, Susan Mann, Sara Berry, David Goodman, Gillian Hart, and Michael Watts.

76. Such functionalism is a recurrent feature of *Limits to Capital;* hence: "Capitalists can and do seize upon ... differentiations and actively use them to divide and rule the working class—hence, the importance of racism, sexism, nationalism, religious, and ethnic prejudice to the circulation of capital.... Capitalists can ... move back and forth between support and opposition for social policies that eliminate racial, sexual, religious, etc., discrimination in labor markets, depending upon the circumstance" (383).

77. David Scott, *Refashioning Futures* (Princeton, N.J.: Princeton University Press, 1999), 13.

78. See Gayatri Chakravarty Spivak, *A Critique of Postcolonial Reason: Toward a History of the Vanishing Present* (Cambridge, Mass.: Harvard University Press, 1999), esp. chap. 4, for a postcolonial literary critic's take on "culture"; also Raymond Williams, "Ideas of Nature," in *Culture and Materialism* (London: Verso, 2005 [1985]), for a critique of "nature." Gramsci's prescient observations on the ideology of Nature in his "Some Aspects of the Southern Question" in *The Antonio Gramsci Reader*, 173, are also noteworthy. Although past agrarian studies scholars have tended to treat "culture" and "nature" as self-evident domains, recent scholarship denaturalizes these categories by revealing them as contested terrains.

79. These terms derive from Hegel's *Logic* and are taken up by Marx in *Grundrisse*, 275, to organize his arguments about capital. Very simply, the "particular" is a concrete or actual instance of the (abstract) "universal," whereas the "singular"—by definition—is that which cannot be reduced to a particular example of the general or universal. It marks the irreducible or the inassimilable. Gilles Deleuze puts it in a slightly different way. He characterizes the "unique or singular" as that which has "no equal or equivalent"—and belongs, as such, to the realm of "repetition" rather than "difference." Cf. Deleuze, *Difference and Repetition*.

80. See Judith Butler's remarks in *Contingency, Hegemony, Universality*, 33.

81. Gramsci, from whom the word "subaltern" is taken, used it to describe a dominated group, "which has not yet gained consciousness of its strength, its possibilities, of how it is to develop"; (Gramsci, "Some Theoretical and Practical Aspects of 'Economism,'" *The Antonio Gramsci Reader*, 210). In its usage within South Asian history the word came to designate all those "persons and groups cut off from upward—and, in that sense, "outward"—social mobility. This also meant that these persons and groups were cut off from the "cultural lines that produced the colonial subject"; Spivak, *A Critique of Postcolonial Reason*, 325. Moreover, while early Subaltern Studies scholarship invoked subaltern consciousness in an essentialist manner, Spivak elsewhere has helpfully suggested that it could be seen "as a strategic use of positivist essentialism in a scrupulously visible political interest [namely, undoing hegemonic master narratives of colonialism, nationalism, and capitalism]"; Spivak, "Subaltern Studies: Deconstructing Historiography," *In Other Worlds: Essays in Cultural Politics* (London: Routledge, 1986), 205. Later subaltern historians have increasingly come to employ "subaltern" as a signifier that marks "the place of a difference rather than an identity" (204).

82. Harvey, *Limits*, 83.

83. E. P. Thompson, "Time, Work-Discipline, and Industrial Capitalism," 352–403.

84. Harvey, *Limits*, 15.

85. Harvey, *Limits*, 14.

86. Harvey, *Limits*, 17.

87. I am grateful to Eric Sheppard for this observation.

88. Chakrabarty, *Provincializing Europe*, 7.

89. Marx, *Grundrisse*, 105.

90. Pranav Jani, "Karl Marx, Eurocentrism, and the 1857 Revolt in British India," in *Marxism, Modernity, and Postcolonial Studies*, ed. Crystal Bartolovich and Neil Lazarus (Cambridge: Cambridge University Press), 81–100.

91. August Nimtz, "The Eurocentric Marx and Engels and Other Related Myths," in *Marxism, Modernity, and Postcolonial Studies*, ed. Bartolovich and Lazarus, 65.

92. Dipesh Chakrabarty, *Re-thinking Working Class History: Bengal 1890 to 1940* (Princeton, N.J.: Princeton University Press, 1989), 229.

93. Chakrabarty, *Re-Thinking Working Class History*, 64.

94. Chakrabarty, *Re-Thinking Working Class History*, 92–93.

95. Chakrabarty, *Re-Thinking Working Class History*, 50.

96. Chakrabarty, *Re-Thinking Working Class History*, 50.

97. Karl Marx, *Capital*, vol. 1: *A Critique of Political Economy*, trans. Ben Fowkes (London: Penguin Books/NLR, 1976 [1867]), 128.

98. Marx's account of this in *Capital* is well known: "Equality in the full sense between different kinds of labor can be arrived at only if we abstract from their real inequality, if we reduce them to the characteristic they have in common, that of being the expenditure of human labor-power, of human labor in the abstract. . . . [But] [m]en do not . . . bring the products of their labor into relation with each other because they see these objects merely as the material integuments of homogenous human labor. The reverse is true: by equating their different products to each other in exchange as values [through money], they equate their different kinds of labor as human labor. They do so without being aware of it. Value, therefore, does not have it description branded on its forehead; it rather transforms every product of labor into a social hieroglyphic" (1:166–67).

99. Jacques Derrida, *Specters of Marx*, trans. Peggy Kamuf (New York: Routledge, 1994), 157.

100. Chakrabarty, *Provincializing Europe*, 64.

101. Marx, *Grundrisse*, 105 (italics mine).

102. Gilles Deleuze, *Difference and Repetition*, 49–50. As I have previously indicated in this chapter, there are unresolved issues about whether Hegel deserves these criticisms or whether he can be read in another, more open, way.

103. Hence, Derrida's comment that Hegel "determined ontology as absolute logic"; see *Of Grammatology*, trans. Gayatri Chakravorty Spivak (Baltimore: The Johns Hopkins University Press, 1976), 24. In this regard, also see Michael Hardt's essay, "Introduction: Hegel and the Foundations of Poststructuralism," in *Gilles Deleuze: An Apprenticeship in Philosophy* (Minneapolis: University of Minnesota Press, 1993).

104. The terms are substitutable but not identical; see Derrida, *Of Grammatology*, 93.

105. Gayatri Chakravorty Spivak, "Translator's Preface," in Jacques Derrida, *Of Grammatology*, xvii.

106. Chakrabarty, *Provincializing Europe*, 93.

107. Chakrabarty, *Provincializing Europe*, 270–71, notes 31 and 32.

108. Harvey, *Limits*, 113.

109. Marx, *Grundrisse*, 297–98 (italics in original).

110. Marx, *Grundrisse*, 298.

111. Harvey, *Limits*, 447.

112. Harvey, *Limits*, 116.

113. On textuality, see Noel Castree's excellent essay, "Invisible Leviathan: Marx, Spivak, and the Question of Value," *Rethinking Marxism* 9, no. 2 (1996): 45–78. He explains that for postcolonial critics like Spivak, "textuality" underscores not only the bringing into presence of worlds through the active labor of writing—hence, in *Limits*, Harvey brings into view the world of capital; but also to the fact that (a) texts "are open and harbor *discontinuities* within them . . . [because] it is the very nature of writing to make impossible the absolute fixation of meaning" (68) and (b) that textuality denies "transparent access to an 'extratextual' realm of the 'real world'" (69).

114. Postone, *Time, Labor, and Social Domination*.

115. On this point, see Jacques Derrida, "From Restricted to General Economy: A Hegelianism without Reserve," in his *Writing and Difference*, trans. Alan Bass (Chicago: University of Chicago Press, 1978), 251–77.

116. Harvey, *Limits*, 193 n. 2 (italics mine).

117. Ranajit Guha, "On Some Aspects of the Historiography of Colonial India," in *Mapping Subaltern Studies and the Postcolonial*, ed. Vinayak Chaturvedi (London: Verso, 2000), 5; first published in *Subaltern Studies I: Writings on South Asian History and Society* (Delhi: Oxford University Press, 1982), 1–8.

118. Unless, as Marx points out in *Grundrisse* (549), the travel is underwritten by a creditor: "A pseudo-buyer B—i.e., someone who really *pays* but does not really buy—mediates the transformation of capitalist A's product into money. But B himself is paid only after capitalist C has bought A's product." However, Marx is quite clear that "the *costs of circulation* as such, do not add anything to the value of the product, are not value-positing costs, regardless of how much labor they may involve. They are merely *deductions from the created* value" (624; italics in original). Not all Marxist geographers agree with Marx on this point.

119. Gayatri Chakravarty Spivak, "Scattered Speculations on the Question of Value," in her *In Other Worlds: Essays in Cultural Politics* (New York: Routledge, 1986), 161.

120. Karl Marx and Frederick Engels, *The Communist Manifesto* (New York: Prometheus Books, 1988), 224.

121. While Moishe Postone endorses a politics of use-value, he is precise in situating it so that it does not become an apology for consumerism; cf. Postone, *Time, Labor and Social Domination* (Chicago: University of Chicago Press, 1996). In a difficult but rewarding exegesis he argues for a critical theory that can reveal the possibility of "a secular form of life" that has "more substantive meaning for people than the form of life structured by [the instrumental logic of] capital" (354). He rejects the postulate of "the proletariat as the true Subject of history" (357). Instead, he argues that it is only when the proletariat stops being the primary identification of the masses will "capital" be truly abolished. This, in turn, requires that the structural basis of alienation, namely, private property—that which permits "value" to operate as a category—be abolished.

122. Antonio Negri, *Marx Beyond Marx: Lessons on the Grundrisse*, trans. H. Cleaver, M. Ryan, M. Viano (Brooklyn, N.Y.: Autonomedia, Inc, 1991), 71–72 (italics in original).

123. Spivak, "Scattered Speculations on the Question of Value," 162 (italics in original).

124. Marx's acknowledgment of these can be found in *The German Ideology* (New York: Prometheus Books, 1998), 47–51.

125. Georges Canguilhem, "Normality and Normativity," in *A Vital Rationalist*, ed. Francois Delaporte (New York: Zone Books, 2000), 351–84.

Afterword

1. J. C. Kumarappa, *A Survey of Matar Taluka in Kheda District* (Ahmedabad: Gujarat Vidyapeeth, 1931). This publication was reissued by Gujarat Vidyapeeth in 1952 with the slightly amended title, *An Economic Survey of Matar Taluka.*

2. The full references are Karl Kautsky, *The Agrarian Question*, 2 vols., trans. Peter Burgess (Winchester, Mass.: Zwan Publications, 1988 [1899]); V. I. Lenin, *The Development of Capitalism in Russia* (Moscow: Progress Publishers, 1956 [1899]); and A. V. Chayanov, *The Theory of Peasant Economy*, ed. D. Thorner, B. Kerblay, and

R. E. F. Smith (Madison: University of Wisconsin Press, 1986 [1924–28]). Kritsman was the leading member of the School of Agrarian Marxists in the Communist Academy of the USSR in the 1920s. Their views on agrarian class differentiation in the Soviet Union were strongly opposed to those of the Organization and Production School led by A. V. Chayanov. The English translation of Kritsman's essay, "Class Stratification and the Soviet Countryside," first appeared in a special issue of the *Journal of Peasant Studies*, 11, no. 2 (1984), devoted to a critical assessment of his work; republished as Terry Cox and Gary Littlejohn, eds., *Kritsman and the Agrarian Marxists* (London: Frank Cass Publishers, 1984).

3. Specifically, Eric Wolf, *Peasants* (Englewood Cliffs, N.J.: Prentice-Hall, 1966), and Teodor Shanin, *The Awkward Class: Political Sociology of the Peasantry in a Developing Society: Russia, 1910–1925* (Oxford: Clarendon Press, 1972).

4. Tom Kessinger, *Vilyatpur, 1848–1968: Social and Economic Change in a North Indian Village* (Berkeley: University of California Press, 1974).

5. Arvind Das, "Changel: Three Centuries of an Indian Village," *Journal of Peasant Studies* 15, no. 1 (1987): 3–59.

6. Hugh Raffles, *In Amazonia: A Natural History* (Princeton, N.J.: Princeton University Press, 2002), 11.

7. Gayatri Chakravorty Spivak, "Scattered Speculations on the Question of Value," in her *In Other Worlds: Essays in Cultural Politics* (New York: Routledge, 1986), 154–78.

8. Thus Bruno Latour, citing postcolonial critiques of anthropology and academic production, observes that ethnographers have had to "come *back*" to the metropole in order to secure validation for their information gathering enterprises; see Latour, "Visualization and Cognition: Thinking with Eyes and Hands," *Knowledge and Society* 6 (1986): 1–40.

9. *Aporia* comes from ancient Greek *a* (without) and *poros* (way or passage). In Jacques Derrida's work, from where I adapt the term, aporia entails an undecidable decision or, more precisely, a decision *and* a responsibility in the course of negotiating some border crossing. I want to foreground *this entanglement of decision and responsibility* (what I call the "ethicopolitical") here.

10. We could say, paraphrasing Kierkegaard, that it is that moment of decision which is the moment of madness; in other words, a dislocation when *and* where the structures that putatively ground us (furnish cause, purpose, or intent) are singularly unable to prescribe the right course of action. See the related notion of aporia in the previous note. See Søren Kierkegaard, *Concluding Unscientific Postscript to Philosophical Fragments*, vol. 1, new ed.: *Kierkegaard's Writings*, 12 vols., trans. and ed. Howard V. Hong and Edna H. Hong (Princeton: Princeton University Press, 1992). Also Julie E. Maybee, "Kierkegaard on the Madness of Reason," *Man and World* 29, no. 4 (October 1996): 387–406.

11. Ernesto Laclau, *New Reflections on the Revolution of Our Time* (London: Verso, 1997).

12. Given the disproportionate profit that has accrued to male researchers, it only seems fitting to use the masculine pronoun in this critique of academic production.

13. Any such counterhegemonic research and writing strategies will be aporetic, marked by impossibility even as they seek to repudiate the protocols of the academy. What forms might these take? One tactic might be to give "voice" to those in positions

of subalternity in academic work, while acknowledging the aporias of representing subalterns. Another might be to undertake collaborative scholarship and shared authorship with those in the global South whose labors enable academic production. Neither redresses the global political economy of academic production, namely, that the researcher in the metropole has a disproportionate *structural* advantage when it comes to activating the machinery of research. Given their privileged access to the means of knowledge production (time, funding, library resources, infrastructure, etc.) northern researchers can influence research agendas in ways that collaborators in the South cannot. A third—and also aporetic—strategy that strives for a radical dispossession of the metropolitan author *qua* producer may be necessary in order to destabilize the gradient that connects scholars in the North to collaborators and research destinations in the South. Provisionally, this would involve displacing the "author" as producer by a figure that more closely approximates a "witness." There is etymological precedent here. As Giorgio Agamben points out, the Latin word *auctor* from which the modern meaning of "author" derives is linked to another meaning: "witness." Specifically, "*auctor* signifies the witness insofar as his testimony always presupposes something—a fact, a thing, or a word—that preexists him and whose reality and force must be validated or certified"; Agamben, *Remnants of Auschwitz: The Witness and the Archive* (New York: Zone Books, 2002), esp. 148–50. In short, the witness is the always insufficient author of a testimony, whose existence—and consequently "speech"—is *enabled* and *necessitated* by the labors and suffering of subaltern others. Such a witnessing, of course, presupposes a very different sort of engagement and writing than that conventionally associated with academic research. To what extent this is possible within the current structure of the academy is moot. I am indebted to Arjun Chowdhury for reminding me of Agamben's figure of witness as author, and its generative possibilities.

14. In February–March 2002, Gujarat was the scene of an anti-Muslim pogrom that, conservatively, resulted in the brutal deaths of at least fifteen hundred men, women, and children, the destruction of a large number of Muslim-owned business establishments (particularly in the city of Ahmedabad), and the displacement from their homes of approximately 150,000 Muslims, who now live in squalid conditions in urban refugee camps.

15. All names of persons and villages have been altered.

16. V. I. Lenin, *The Development of Capitalism in Russia,* 11.

17. Pierre Bourdieu, *Outline of a Theory of Practice,* trans. Richard Nice (Cambridge: Cambridge University Press, 1977).

Index

Vinay Gidwani is associate professor in the Department of Geography and at the Institute for Global Studies at the University of Minnesota.